Critical Thinking Handbook:

6th-9th-Grades

**A Guide for Remodelling Lesson Plans
in
Language Arts, Social Studies, & Science**

by
**Richard Paul, A.J.A. Binker, Douglas Martin,
Chris Vetrano, & Heidi Kreklau**

Center for Critical Thinking and Moral Critique
Sonoma State University
Rohnert Park, CA 94928
707-664-2940
© 1989

Acknowledgements
We wish to acknowledge the many helpful suggestions
and criticisms of Penny Caudle, Jennifer Adrian, Lynne
Mitchell, and Jane Kelsberg. They are, of course, not
responsible for any errors, mistakes, or misconceptions.

Price: $18.00
ISBN # 0-944583-02-4
Library of Congress Catalog Card Number: 88-64125

Contents

Appendices

Introduction

The Design of the Book

This Handbook has a two-fold goal, and everything it contains can be seen as aiming at one or both of these objectives: 1) to clarify the concept of critical thinking and the principles that underlie it, and 2) to help teachers learn how to teach it. The second goal has two forms: *a)* presenting general strategies which can be used at any time to foster critical thinking, and *b)* demonstrating how lesson remodelling can help bring critical thinking into the heart of everyday classroom activities. Most sections of the book combine goals 1 and 2.

This introduction, besides explaining the structure of the Handbook as a whole, introduces the reader to the concepts of critical thinking and education for critical thinking and makes recommendations for using this handbook. In the second chapter, "Remodelling: a Foundation for Staff Development," we explain and justify the lesson plan remodelling approach and describe its use in staff development. This method of infusing instruction for critical thinking is the main concern of this book. Chapter 3, "Global Critical Thinking Strategies," combines the objectives of clarifying critical thinking and suggesting general teaching strategies. It does not directly address remodelling. The first section explains the necessity for *strong sense* critical thinking across the curriculum. The second section introduces the technique of Socratic discussion, first in general terms, then by illustration in a transcript of a Socratic discussion. The next section briefly introduces another general technique: role playing and reconstructing opposing views. The last two sections address the importance of having students analyze their experiences, and emphasize the role of reasoned judgment.

Chapter four, "Thinking Critically About Teaching: From Didactic to Critical Teaching" contrasts standard approaches to education with a critical theory of education and describes some of the most common problems we found in 6th-9th grade texts. Chapter five, "Strategies," clarifies the idea of critical thinking further and suggests how it can be taught by introducing and explaining the thirty-five specific teaching strategies at the heart of our remodelling process. The next sections contain examples of our use of the remodelling process on standard lessons, lesson fragments, and units. We introduce each subject area with a general discussion of a critical approach to the subject and brief criticisms of texts.

Following the sample remodels in language arts, social studies, and science is a sampling of remodels that we are beginning to collect and which, for the most part, represent teachers' early efforts in remodelling their lessons. These sample remodels are not divided into subject areas.

Since lesson remodelling is most effective when it is integrated into a long-term, multi-faceted, critical thinking staff development plan, we include next a copy of one such project, "The Greensboro Plan." Perusal of it will suggest a variety of problems one should recognize as intrinsic to district-wide efforts at moving from didactic to critical modes of teaching. Following the Greensboro Plan is a compilation of teacher statements of "What Critical Thinking Means to Me." These statements demonstrate the room there is in critical thinking for a variety of individual articulations, all consistent with developing the "critical spirit" in instruction and learning. Next is a list of basic critical thinking vocabulary which should help teachers to synthesize some of the various dimensions of critical thinking into a more coherent picture. Not all of the concepts briefly explained there will be immediately intelligible. The recognition of the usefulness of these distinctions will emerge progressively over time as teachers become more and more familiar with critical thinking and critical teaching.

The final major section of the handbook describes some additional resources for critical thinking staff development. Once again, we need to remember that a long-term evolution is necessary to bring critical thinking successfully into the mainstream of school life. As time goes by, teachers will need a variety of resources to facilitate this evolutionary process.

Our Concept of Critical Thinking

The term 'critical,' as we use it, does not mean thinking which is negative or finds fault, but rather thinking which evaluates reasons and brings thought and action in line with our evaluations, our best sense of what is true. The ideal of the critical thinker could be roughly expressed in the phrase 'reasonable person.' Our use of the term 'critical' is intended to highlight the intellectual autonomy of the critical thinker. That is, as a critical thinker, I do not simply accept conclusions (uncritically). I evaluate or critique reasons. My critique enables me to distinguish poor from strong reasoning. To do so to the greatest extent possible, I make use of a number of identifiable and learnable skills. I analyze and evaluate reasons and evidence; make assumptions explicit and evaluate them; reject unwarranted inferences or "leaps of logic"; use the best and most complete evidence available to me; make relevant distinctions; clarify; avoid inconsistency and contradiction; reconcile apparent contradictions; and distinguish what I know from what I merely suspect to be true.

The uncritical thinker, on the other hand, doesn't reflect on or evaluate reasons for a particular set of beliefs. By simply agreeing or disagreeing, the uncritical thinker accepts or rejects conclusions, often without understanding them, and often on the basis of egocentric attachment or unassessed desire. Lacking skills to analyze and evaluate, this person allows irrelevant reasons to influence conclusions; doesn't notice assumptions, and therefore fails to evaluate them; accepts any inference that "sounds good"; is unconcerned with the strength and completeness of evidence; can't sort out ideas, confuses different concepts, is an unclear thinker; is oblivious to contradictions; feels certain, even when not in a position to know. The classic uncritical thinker says, "I've made up my mind! Don't confuse me with facts." Yet, critical thinking is more than evaluation of simple lines of thought.

As I evaluate beliefs by evaluating the evidence or reasoning that supports them (that is, the "arguments" for them), I notice certain things. I learn that sometimes I must go beyond evaluating small lines of reasoning. To understand an issue, I may have to think about it for a long time, weigh many reasons, and clarify basic ideas. I see that evaluating a particular line of thought often forces me to re-evaluate another. A conclusion about one case forces me to come to a certain conclusion about another. I find that often my evaluation of someone's thinking turns on the meaning of a concept, which I must clarify. Such clarification affects my understanding of other issues. I notice previously hidden relationships between beliefs about different issues. I see that some beliefs and ideas are more fundamental than others. In short, I must orchestrate the skills I have learned into a longer series of moves. As I strive for consistency and understanding, I discover opposing sets of basic assumptions which underlie those conclusions. I find that, to make my beliefs reasonable, I must evaluate, not individual beliefs but, rather, large sets of beliefs. Analysis of an issue requires more work, a more extended process, than that required for a short line of reasoning. I must learn to use my skills, not in separate little moves but together, coordinated into a long sequence of thought.

Sometimes, two apparently equally strong arguments or lines of reasoning about the same issue come to contradictory conclusions. That is, when I listen to one side, the case seems strong. Yet when I listen to the other side, that case seems equally strong. Since they contradict each other, they cannot both be right. Sometimes it seems that the two sides are talking about different situations or speaking different languages, even living in different "worlds." I find that the skills which enable me to evaluate a short bit of reasoning do not offer much help here.

Suppose I decide to question two people who hold contradictory conclusions on an issue. They may use concepts or terms differently, disagree about what terms apply to what situations and what inferences can then be made, or state the issue differently. I may find that the differences in their conclusions rest, not so much on a particular piece of evidence or on one inference, as much as on vastly different perspectives, different ways of seeing the world, or different conceptions of such basic ideas as, say, human nature. As their conclusions arise from different perspectives, each, to the other, seems deluded, prejudiced, or naive. How am I to decide who is right? My evaluations of their inferences, uses of terms, evidence, etc., also depend on perspective. In a sense, I discover that I have a perspective.

I could simply agree with the one whose overall perspective is most like my own. But how do I know I'm right? If I'm sincerely interested in evaluating beliefs, should I not also consider things from other perspectives?

As I reflect on this discovery, I may also realize that my perspective has changed. Perhaps I recall learning a new idea or even a system of thought that changed the way I see myself and the world around me in fundamental ways, which even changed my life. I remember how pervasive this change was — I began to interpret a whole range of situations differently, continually used a new idea, concept or phrase, paid attention to previously ignored facts. I realize that I now have a new choice regarding the issue under scrutiny.

I could simply accept the view that most closely resembles my own. But, thinking further, I realize that I cannot reasonably reject the other perspective unless I understand it. To do so would be to say, "I don't know what you think, but, whatever it is, it's false." The other perspective, however strange it seems to me now, may have something both important and true, which I have overlooked and without which my understanding is incomplete. Thinking along these lines, I open my mind to the possibility of change of perspective. I make sure that I don't subtly ignore or dismiss these new ideas; I realize I can make my point of view richer, so it encompasses more. As I think within another perspective, I begin to see ways in which it is right. It points out complicating factors I had previously ignored; makes useful distinctions I had missed; offers plausible interpretations of events I had never considered; and so on. I become able to move between various perspectives, hence freed from the limitations of my own thought.

One of the most important stages in my development as a thinker, then, is a clear recognition that I have a perspective, one that I must work on and change as I learn and grow. To do this, I can't be inflexibly attached to any particular beliefs. I strive for a consistent "big picture." I approach other perspectives differently. I ask how I can reconcile the points of view. I see variations between similar but different perspectives. I use principles and insights flexibly and do not approach analysis as a mechanical, "step one, step two" process. I pursue new ideas in depth, trying to understand the perspectives from which they come. I am willing to say, "This view sounds new and different; I don't yet understand it. There's more to this idea than I realized; I can't just dismiss it."

Or, looked at another way, suppose I'm rethinking my stand on an issue. I re-examine my evidence. Yet, I cannot evaluate my evidence for its completeness, unless I consider evidence cited by those who disagree with me. I find I can discover my basic assumptions by considering alternative assumptions, alternative perspectives. I use fairmindedness to clarify, enhance, and improve my perspective.

A narrowminded critical thinker, lacking this insight, says, not, "This is how *I* see it," but, "This is how *it is.*" While working on pieces of reasoning, separate arguments, and individual beliefs, this person tends to overlook the development of perspective as such. Such thinking consists of separate or fragmented ideas and the examination of beliefs one at a time without appreciation for connections between them. While conscious and reflective about particular conclusions, this type of thinker is unreflective about his or her own point of view, how it affects his or her evaluations of reasoning, and how it is limited. When confronted with alternative perspectives or points of view, this person assesses them by their degree of agreement with his or her own view and lumps together similar, though different, perspectives. Such an individual is given to sweeping acceptance or sweeping rejection of points of view and is tyrannized by the words he or she uses. Rather than trying to understand why others think as they do, he or she dismisses new ideas, assuming the objectivity and correctness of his or her own beliefs and responses.

As I strive to think fairmindedly, I discover resistance to questioning my beliefs and considering those of others. I find a conflict between my desire to be fairminded and my desire to be right. I realize that without directly addressing the obstacles to critical thought, I tend to seek its appearance rather than its reality, that I tend to accept rhetoric rather than fact, that without noticing it, I hide my own hypocrisy, even from myself.

By contrast, the critical thinker who lacks this insight, though a good arguer, is not a truly reasonable person. Giving good-sounding reasons, this person can find and explain flaws in opposing views and has well-thought-out ideas but never subjects his or her own ideas to scrutiny. Though giving lip service to fairmindedness and describing views opposed to his or her own, this thinker doesn't truly understand or seriously consider them. One who often uses reasoning to get his or her way, cover up hidden motives, or make others look stupid or deluded is merely using skills to reinforce his or her own views and desires, without subjecting them to scrutiny.

To sum up, the kind of critical thinker we want to foster contrasts with at least two other kinds of thinkers. The first kind has few intellectual skills of any kind and tends to be naive, easily manipulated and controlled, and so easily defeated or taken in. The second has skills, but only of a restricted type, which enable pursuit of narrow, selfish interests and effective manipulation of the naive and unsuspecting. The first we call 'uncritical thinkers' and the second 'weak sense,' or selfish, critical thinkers. What we aim at, therefore, are "strong sense" critical thinkers, those who use their skills in the service of sincere, fairminded understanding and evaluation of their beliefs.

Critical Thinking and Education

The foundation for fairminded, as against self-serving, critical thinking is laid in the early years of one's life. The same is true of uncritical thought. We can raise children from the earliest years to passively accept authority figures and symbols. We can systematically manipulate and inculcate children so they are apt to become adults highly susceptible to manipulation.

Or we can foster the development of intellectual skills while ignoring the ultimate use to which the learner puts them. We can ignore the problems of egocentrism, the natural tendencies of the mind toward self-deception and ego-justification. We can assume that students will use those skills fairmindedly. In this case we ignore the problem of integrating cognitive and affective life. And so we make it likely that our more successful students will become intelligent manipulators rather than fairminded thinkers. They will gain intellectual empowerment at the expense of a selfish use of that power to further egocentric ends.

But there is a legitimate third option on which we should focus our efforts: fostering the development of intellectual skills in the context of rational dispositions and higher critical thinking values. We can emphasize the intimate interplay of thought and feeling, not set them off as separate or oppositional. We can recognize the existence of both rational and irrational passions and cognitions. We can accentuate the insight that only through the development of rational passions or intellectual virtues can we prevent our intelligence from becoming the tool of egocentric emotions.

The earlier we lay the foundation for intellectual fairness, the better our chance for success. If we want children to develop into adults with a passion for clarity, accuracy, and fairmindedness, a fervor for exploring the deepest issues, a propensity for listening sympathetically to opposition points of view; if we want children to develop into adults with a drive to seek out evidence, with an aversion to contradiction, sloppy thinking, and inconsistent applications of standards; then we had better pay close attention to the affective dimension of their lives from the beginning. We had better recognize the need to unite cognitive and affective goals.

The highest development of intelligence and conscience creates a natural marriage between the two. Each is distinctly limited without the other. Each requires special attention in the light of the other.

In this workbook, we provide something more than a set of remodelled lessons which accentuate needed intellectual skills. We have tried to keep in mind our vision of the conscientious, fairminded, critical person. Many of the strategies for remodel that we use explicitly call for a blending of the skills of critical thinking with the dispositions or intellectual virtues that foster critical thinking values. All of the strategies have been used with this overall end in mind.

The remodel strategies should be viewed, therefore, not as isolated intellectual activities, but as insight builders that mutually support each other and work toward a unified end. Wherever possible there is a cognitive/affective integration.

How To Use This Book

You may choose to read this book as you would any other book, but if you do, you will probably miss a good deal of the benefit that can be derived from it. There are no algorithms or recipes for understanding or teaching critical thinking. Although we separate aspects of critical thinking, the global concept is behind each aspect, and each aspect relates to it and the others. Thus, to develop critical thought, one must continually move back and forth between the global ideal of the rational and fairminded thinker and the details describing what such a thinker does. Similarly, although we separate the aspects of staff development for integrating critical thinking into the curriculum (understanding the concept, critiquing present practice, formulating remodels), teachers must continually move back and forth between these activities.

If you are a 6ᵗʰ-9ᵗʰ grade teacher and you want to improve your ability to teach for critical thinking, this book can help you develop the ability to remodel your own lesson plans. Your own teaching strategies will progressively increase as your repertoire of critical thinking strategies grows. As you begin, try to develop a baseline sense of your present understanding of critical thinking and of your ability to critique and redesign lesson plans. The critiques and remodels that follow, and the principles and strategies that precede them, may provide an immediate catalyst for you to take your lesson plans and redesign them. But the longer critiques and remodels here might seem intimidating. Some of the strategies may seem unclear or confusing, and you may bog down as soon as you attempt to redesign your own lessons keep in mind that in some of our remodels, we put as many ideas as we could, in order to provide as many examples and varieties of applications as possible. Thus, some of the remodelled plans are longer and more elaborate than you might initially be willing to produce or teach.

We therefore suggest alternative approaches and ways of conceiving the process:

• Read through the strategies and a couple of remodels, then write critiques and remodels of your own. After you have attempted a critique and remodel, read our critique and remodel of a similar lesson. By using this procedure, you will soon get a sense of the difficulties in the critique-remodel process. You will also have initiated the process of developing your own skills in this important activity.

• Another way of testing your understanding of the critical insights is to read the principle section of a strategy, and write your own application section.

• You could review a remodel of ours and find places where strategies were used but not cited and places where particular moves could be characterized by more than one strategy.

• You may want to take several strategies and write a passage about their interrelationships.

• Or you might take a subject or topic and list significant questions about it. Share and discuss your lists with colleagues.

• If, when reviewing a remodel, you find a particular strategy confusing, review the principle and application in the strategy chapter. If, when reading the strategy chapter, you feel confused, review the critiques and remodels of the lessons listed below it. If you are still confused, do not use the strategy. Review it periodically until it becomes clear.

• When remodelling your own lessons, you will probably find that sometimes you can make more drastic changes, or even completely rewrite a lesson, while at others you may make only minor adjustments. Some of your remodels may make use of many strategies, say, two or more affective strategies, and a macro-ability requiring coordinated use of several micro- skills. For other remodels, you may use only one strategy. It is better to use one clearly understood strategy than to attempt to use more than you clearly understand.

• You may want to begin remodelling by using only one or two strategies clearest to you. After remodelling some lessons, you will likely find ourself spontaneously using those strategies. You could then reread the strategy chapter and begin infusing a couple of additional strategies with which you feel comfortable. Thus, as the number of strategies you regularly use grows, your teaching can evolve at the pace most comfortable to you.

• If students don't grasp a critical idea or skill when you introduce it, don't give up. Critical insight must be developed over time. For instance, suppose the first attempt to get students to fairmindedly consider each others' views fails. It is likely that students are not in the habit of seriously considering each other's positions, and hence may not listen carefully to each other. If you make restating opposing views a routine part of discussion, students will eventually learn to prepare themselves by listening more carefully.

• Although the main function of this book is to help you remodel your lesson plans, we have not restricted our suggestions to the remodelling process. We strongly urge you to apply the insights embedded in the strategies to all aspects of classroom experience (including discussions, conflicts, and untraditional lessons — for instance, movies.) You may also use our remodels, or sections of them. Though many of our lessons are too long for one class period, we did not suggest where to break them up. Nor did we provide follow-up questions. If you decide to experiment with any of our remodels, you will probably have to remodel them somewhat to take your own students and text into account.

• We urge you to apply your growing critical insight to the task of analyzing and clarifying your concept of education and the educated person. Of each subject you teach, ask yourself what is most basic and crucial for an educated person to know or to be able to do. Highlight those aspects and teach them in a way that most fosters in-depth and useful understanding.

• Texts often have the same features — whether problems or opportunities for critical thought — occurring over and over again. Hence, remodelling a couple of lessons from a text can give you a basic structure to use many times over the course of the year.

• When comparing your work to ours, keep in mind that this is a flexible process; our remodel is not the only right one. Any changes which promote fairminded critical thought are improvements.

However you use what follows in this book, your understanding of the insights behind the strategies will determine the effectiveness of the remodels. Despite the detail with which we have delineated the strategies, they should not be translated into mechanistic, step-by-step procedures. Keep the goal of the well-educated, fairminded critical thinker continually in mind. Thinking critically involves insightful critical judgments at each step along the way. It is never done by recipe.

Diagram 1

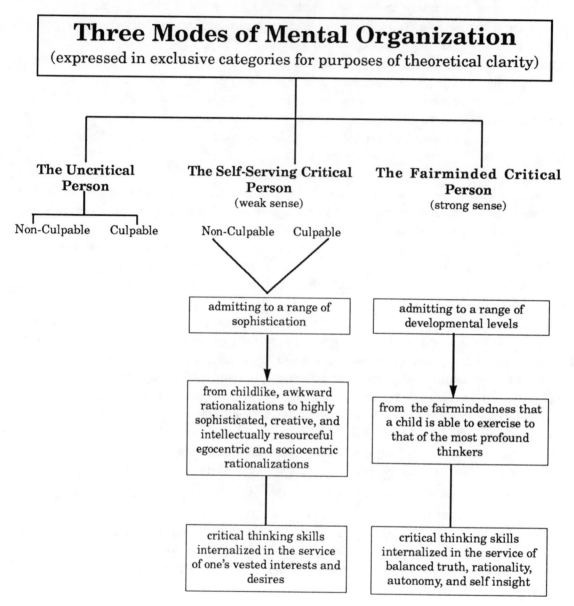

Three Modes of Mental Organization
(expressed in exclusive categories for purposes of theoretical clarity)

The Uncritical Person

Non-Culpable   Culpable

The Self-Serving Critical Person
(weak sense)

Non-Culpable   Culpable

admitting to a range of sophistication

from childlike, awkward rationalizations to highly sophisticated, creative, and intellectually resourceful egocentric and sociocentric rationalizations

critical thinking skills internalized in the service of one's vested interests and desires

The Fairminded Critical Person
(strong sense)

admitting to a range of developmental levels

from the fairmindedness that a child is able to exercise to that of the most profound thinkers

critical thinking skills internalized in the service of balanced truth, rationality, autonomy, and self insight

---

Note

Children enter school as fundamentally non-culpable, uncritical and self-serving thinkers. The educational task is to help them to become, as soon as possible and as fully as possible, responsible, fairminded, critical thinkers, empowered by intellectual skills and rational passions. Most people are some combination of the above three types; the proportions are the significant determinant of which of the three characterizations is most appropriate. For example, it is a common pattern for people to be capable of fairminded critical thought only when their vested interests or ego-attachments are not involved, hence the legal practice of excluding judges or jury members who can be shown to have such interests.

Diagram 2

Critical Thinking Lesson Plan Remodelling

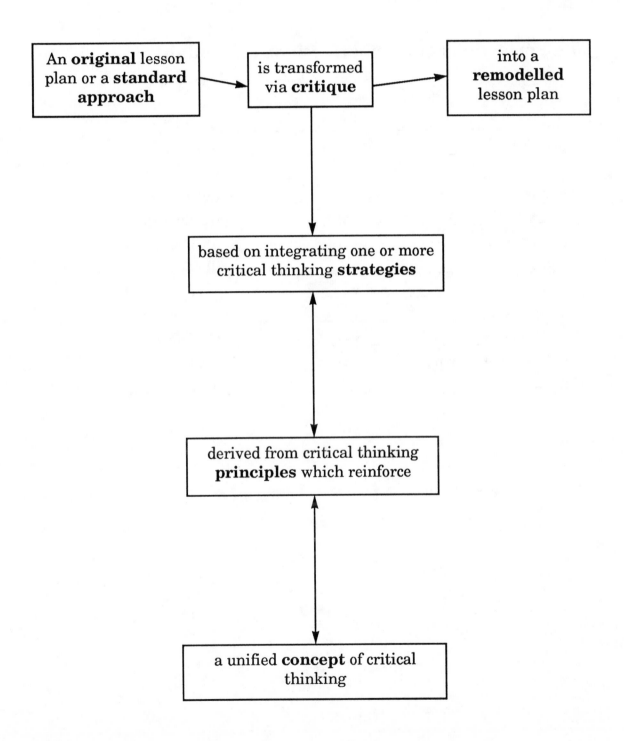

Diagram 3

The Perfections and Imperfections of Thought

clarity_____vs _____unclarity

precision _____vs _____imprecision

specificity _____vs _____vagueness

accuracy_____vs _____inaccuracy

relevance _____vs _____irrelevance

consistency _____vs _____inconsistency

logical_____vs _____illogical

depth _____vs _____superficiality

completeness _____vs _____incompleteness

significance_____vs _____triviality

adequacy (for purpose)_____vs _____inadequacy

fairness _____vs _____bias or one-sidedness

Remodelling: A Foundation For Staff Development

The basic idea behind lesson plan remodelling as a strategy for staff development in critical thinking is simple. Every practicing teacher works daily with lesson plans of one kind or another. To remodel lesson plans is to critique one or more lesson plans and formulate one or more new lesson plans based on that critical process. It is well done when the remodeller understands the strategies and principles used in producing the critique and remodel, when the strategies are well-thought-out, when the remodel clearly follows from the critique, and when the remodel teaches critical thought better than the original. The idea behind our particular approach to staff development of lesson plan remodelling is also simple. A group of teachers or a staff development leader who has a reasonable number of exemplary remodels with accompanying explanatory principles can design practice sessions that enable teachers to begin to develop new teaching skills as a result of experience in lesson remodelling.

When teachers are provided with clearly contrasting "befores" and "afters," lucid and specific critiques, a set of principles clearly explained and illustrated, and a coherent unifying concept, they can increase their own skills in this process. One learns how to remodel lesson plans to incorporate critical thinking only through practice. The more one does it the better one gets, especially when one has examples of the process to serve as models.

Of course, a lesson remodelling strategy for critical thinking in-service is not tied to any particular handbook of examples, but it is easy to indicate the advantages of having such a handbook, assuming it is well-executed. Some teachers do not have a clear concept of critical thinking. Some think of it as negative, judgmental thinking, which is a stereotype. Some have only vague notions, such as "good thinking," or "logical thinking," with little sense of how such ideals are achieved. Others think of it simply in terms of a laundry list of atomistic skills and so lack a clear sense of how these skills need to be orchestrated or integrated, or of how they can be misused. Rarely do teachers have a clear sense of the relationship between the component micro-skills, the basic, general concept of critical thinking, and the obstacles to using it fully.

11

It is theoretically possible but, practically speaking, unlikely that teachers will sort this out for themselves as a task in abstract theorizing. In the first place, most teachers have very little patience with abstract theory and little experience in developing it. In the second place, few school districts could give them the time to take on this task, even if they were qualified and motivated enough themselves. But getting the basic concept sorted out is not the only problem. There is also the problem of translating that concept into "principles," linking the "principles" to applications, and implementing them in specific lessons.

On the other hand, if we simply present teachers with prepackaged finished lesson plans designed by the critical thinking of someone else, by a process unclear to them, then we have lost a major opportunity for the teachers to develop their own critical thinking skills, insights, and motivations. Furthermore, teachers who cannot use basic critical thinking principles to critique and remodel some of their own lesson plans probably won't be able to implement someone else's effectively. Providing teachers with the scaffolding for carrying out the process for themselves and examples of its use opens the door for continuing development of critical thinking skills and insights. It begins a process which gives the teacher more and more expertise and more and more success in critiquing and remodelling the day-to-day practice of teaching.

Lesson plan remodelling can become a powerful tool in critical thinking staff development for other reasons as well. It is action-oriented and puts an immediate emphasis on close examination and critical assessment of what is taught on a day-to-day basis. It makes the problem of critical thinking infusion more manageable by paring it down to the critique of particular lesson plans and the progressive infusion of particular principles. It is developmental in that, over time, more and more lesson plans are remodelled, and what has been remodelled can be remodelled again; more strategies can be systematically infused as they become clear to the teacher. It provides a means of cooperative learning for teachers. Its results can be collected and shared, both at the site and district levels, so that teachers can learn from and be encouraged by what other teachers do. The dissemination of plausible remodels provides recognition for motivated teachers. It forges a unity between staff development, curriculum development, and student development. It avoids recipe solutions to critical thinking instruction. And, finally, properly conceptualized and implemented, it unites cognitive and affective goals and integrates the curriculum.

Of course, it is no panacea. It will not work for those who are deeply complacent or cynical or for those who do not put a high value on students' learning to think for themselves. It will not work for those who have a low command of critical thinking skills coupled with low self-esteem. It will not work for those who are "burned out" or have given up on change. Finally, it will not work for those who want a quick and easy solution based on recipes and formulas. It is a long-term solution that transforms teaching by degrees as the critical thinking insights and skills of the teachers develop and mature. If teachers can develop the art of critiquing the lesson plans they use and learn how to use that critique to remodel those lesson plans more and more effectively, they will progressively 1) refine and develop their own critical thinking skills and insights, 2) reshape the actual or "living" curriculum (what is in fact taught), and 3) develop their teaching skills. (See diagram #2.)

The approach to lesson remodelling developed by the Center for Critical Thinking and Moral Critique is based on the publication of handbooks, such as this one, which illustrate the remodelling process, unifying well-thought-out critical thinking theory with practical application. The goal is to explain critical thinking by translating general theory into specific teaching strategies. The strategies are multiple, allowing teachers to infuse more strategies as they clarify more dimensions of critical thought. This is especially important since the skill at and insight into critical thought vary.

This approach, it should be noted, respects the autonomy and professionality of teachers. They choose which strategies to use in a particular situation, and control the rate and style of integration. It is a flexible approach, maximizing the creativity and insight of the teacher. The teacher can apply the strategies to any kind of material: text lesson, lessons or units the teacher has created, discussion outside of formal lessons, discussion of movies, etc.

In teaching for critical thinking in the strong sense, we are committed to teaching in such a way that children, as soon and as completely as possible, learn to become responsible for their own thinking. This requires that they learn how to take command of their thinking, which in turn requires that they learn how to notice and think about their own thinking, as well as the thinking of others. Consequently, we teach so as to help children to talk about their thinking in order to be mindful and directive in it. We want them to study their own minds and how they operate. We want them to gain tools by which they can probe deeply into and take command of their own mental processes. Finally, we want them to gain this mentally skilled self-control with a view to becoming more honest with themselves and more fair to others, not only to "do better" in school. We want them to develop mental skills and processes in an ethically responsible context. This is not a "good-boy/bad-boy" approach to thinking, for people must think their own way to the ethical insights that underlie becoming fairminded. We are careful not to judge the content of the student's thinking. Rather, we facilitate a process whereby the student's own insights can be developed.

The global objectives of critical thinking-based instruction are intimately linked to specific objectives. It is precisely because we want students to learn how to think for themselves in an ethically responsible way that we use the strategies we do; why we help them to gain insight into their tendency to think in narrowly self-serving ways (egocentricity); why we stimulate them to empathize with the perspectives of others; to suspend or withhold judgment when they do not have the evidence to justify making a judgment; to clarify issues and concepts, to evaluate sources, solutions, and actions; to notice when they make assumptions, how they make inferences and where they use, or ought to use, evidence; to consider the implications of their ideas; to identify the possible contradictions or inconsistencies in their thinking; to consider the qualifications or lack of qualifications in their generalizations; and why we do all of these things in encouraging, supportive, non-judgmental ways. The same principles of education hold for staff development.

To help teachers generalize from specific remodelling moves, and so facilitate their grasp of strong sense critical thinking and how it can be taught, we have devised a list of teaching strategies. Each strategy highlights an aspect of critical thought. Each use illustrates how that aspect can be encouraged in students. In the chapter, "Strategies," we explain the thirty-five strategies illustrated in the remodels. Each is linked to the idea of strong sense critical thinking, in the "principle." And for each we explain some ways the aspect of critical thought can be encouraged, in the "application." When a strategy is used in a remodel, we have drawn attention to it by putting its strategy symbol in the remodel, e.g., "*S-13.*"

To make the list more manageable, we have divided the strategies into three types: those which emphasize the affective side of critical thought, Affective Strategies, promoting intellectual virtues, empathy, and understanding of obstacles to critical thought; those which generally require extended use of cognitive skills, Cognitive-Macro-abilities, emphasizing extended exploration of ideas, perspectives, and basic issues; and those which highlight a specific, usually brief,

13

critical move, Cognitive-Micro-skills. These divisions are not absolute, however. Critical thought requires integration of the affective and cognitive dimensions of thinking. Macro-abilities usually require use of micro-skills. And micro-skills are pointless unless used to some end.

Strategies for Infusing Critical Thinking

Let us now consider how we can incorporate these general understandings into in-service design. There are five basic goals or tasks teachers need to aim for to learn the art of lesson remodelling. Each can be the focus of some stage of in-service activity:

1) Clarifying the global concept — How is the fairminded critical thinker unlike the self-serving critical thinker and the uncritical thinker? What is it to think critically?

2) Understanding component teacher strategies that parallel the component critical thinking values, processes, and skills — What are the basic values that (strong sense) critical thinking presupposes? What are the micro-skills of critical thinking? What are the macro-processes? What do critical thinkers do? Why? What do they avoid doing? Why?

3) Seeing a variety of ways in which the various component strategies can be used in classroom settings — When can each aspect of critical thought be fostered? When are they most needed? What contexts most require each dimension? What questions or activities foster it?

4) Getting experience in lesson plan critique — What are the strengths and weaknesses of this lesson? What critical principles, concepts, or strategies apply to it? What important concepts, insights, and issues underlie this lesson? Are they adequately emphasized and explained? Of what use will the well-educated person make of this material? Will that usefulness be apparent to the students?

5) Getting experience in lesson plan remodelling — How can I take full advantage of the strengths of this lesson? How can this material best be used to foster critical insights? Which questions or activities should I drop, use, alter or expand upon? What should I add to it? How can I best promote genuine and deep understanding of this material?

Let us emphasize at the outset that these goals or understandings are interrelated and that the achievement of any or all of them is a matter of degree. We therefore warn against trying to achieve "complete" understanding of any one of these in some absolute sense, before proceeding to the others. Furthermore, we emphasize that understanding in each case should be viewed practically or pragmatically. One does not learn about what critical thinking is by memorizing a definition or a set of distinctions. The teacher's mind must be actively engaged at each point in the process — concepts, principles, applications, critiques, and remodels. At all of these levels, "hands-on" activities should immediately follow any introduction of explanatory or illustrative material. If, for example, teachers are shown a handbook formulation of one of the principles, they should then have an opportunity to brainstorm applications of the principle, or an opportunity to try out their own formulations of another principle. When they are shown the critique of one lesson plan, they should be given an opportunity to remodel it or critique another. If they are shown a complete remodel — original lesson plan, critique, and remodel — they should be given an opportunity to do a full critique of their own, individually or in groups. This back-and-forth movement between example and practice should characterize the staff development process overall. These practice sessions should not be rushed, and the products of that practice should be collected and shared in some form with the group as a whole. Teachers need to see that they are fruitfully engaged in this process; dissemination of the products of the process demonstrates this fruitfulness. Of course, it ought to be a common understanding of staff development participants that initial practice is not the same as final product, that what is remodelled today by critical thought can be re-remodelled tomorrow and improved progressively thereafter as experience, skills, and insights grow.

Teachers should be asked early on to formulate what critical thinking means to them. You can examine some teacher formulations in the section "What Critical Thinking Means to Me." However, be careful not to spend too much time on the general formulations of what critical thinking is before moving to the level of particular principles and strategies. The reason for this is simple. People tend to have trouble assimilating general concepts unless they are clarified through concrete examples. Furthermore, we want teachers to develop an *operational* view of critical thinking, to understand it as particular intellectual behaviors derivative of basic insights, commitments, and principles. Critical thinking is not a set of high-sounding platitudes, but a very real and practical way to think things out and to act upon that thought. Therefore, we want teachers to make realistic translations from the general to the specific as soon as possible, and periodically revise their formulations of the global concept in light of their work on the details. Aim at a process whereby teachers move back and forth from general formulations of what critical thinking means to them to specific strategies in specific lessons. We want teachers to see how acceptance of the general concept of critical thinking translates into clear and practical critical thinking teaching and learning strategies, and use those strategies to help students develop into rational and fair thinkers.

For this reason, all the various strategies explained in the handbook are couched in terms of behaviors. The principles express and describe a variety of behaviors of the "ideal" critical thinker; they become applications to lessons when teachers canvass their lesson plans to find appropriate places where those behaviors can be fostered. The practice we recommend helps guard against teachers using these strategies as recipes or formulas, since in each case good judgment is required in the application process.

Some Staff Development Design Possibilities

1) Clarifying the global concept

After a brief exposition or explanation of the global concept of critical thinking, teachers might be asked to reflect individually (for, say, 10 minutes) on people they have known who are basically uncritical thinkers, those who are basically selfish critical thinkers, and those who are basically fairminded critical thinkers. After they have had time to think up meaningful personal examples, divide them up into groups of twos to share and discuss their reflections with another teacher.

An alternative focus might be to have them think of dimensions of their own lives in which they are most uncritical, selfishly critical, and fairminded.

2) Understanding component teaching strategies that parallel the component critical thinking values, processes, and skills

Each teacher could be asked to choose one of the strategies to read and think about for approximately 10 minutes. Their task following this period is to explain the strategy to another teacher, without reading from the handbook. The role of the other teacher is to ask questions about the strategy. Once one has finished explaining his or her strategy, they trade roles. Following this, pairs could link up with other pairs and explain their strategies to each other. At the end, each teacher should have a basic understanding of four strategies.

3) Seeing a variety of ways in which the various component strategies can be used in classroom settings

Teachers could be asked to reflect for about 10 minutes on how the strategies that they choose might be used in a number of classroom activities or assignments. Following this, they could share their examples with other teachers.

4) Getting experience in lesson plan critique

Teachers can be asked to bring one lesson, activity, or assignment to the inservice session. This lesson, or one provided by the inservice leader, can be used to practice critique. Critiques can then be shared, evaluated, and improved.

5) Getting experience in lesson plan remodelling

Teachers can then remodel the lessons which they have critiqued and share, evaluate, and improve the results.

• Copy a remodel, eliminating strategy references. Groups of teachers could mark strategies on it, share, discuss, and defend their versions, etc. Remember, ours is not "the right answer." In cases where participants disagree with, or don't understand why we cited the strategies we did, they could try to figure out why we cited those strategies.

• Over the course of a year, the whole group can work on at least one remodel for each participant.

• Participants could each choose several strategies and explain their interrelationships, mention cases in which they are equivalent, or when one could be used as part of another, etc.

The processes we have described thus far presupposes motivation on the part of the teacher to implement changes. Unfortunately, we cannot presuppose this motivation. We must address it directly. This can be done by focusing attention on the insights that underlie the strategies in each case. We need to foster discussion of them so that it becomes clear to teachers not only *that* critical thinking requires this or that kind of activity but *why*, that is, what desirable consequences it brings about. If, for example, teachers do not see why thinking for themselves is of high importance for the well-being and success of their students, they will not take the trouble to implement activities that foster it, even if they know what these activities are.

To meet this motivational need, we have formulated "principles" so as to suggest important insights. For example, consider the brief introduction which is provided in the strategy chapter for the strategy "exercising fairmindedness":

Principle: To think critically about issues, we must be able to consider the strengths and weaknesses of opposing points of view; to imaginatively put ourselves in the place of others in order to genuinely understand them; to overcome our egocentric tendency to identify truth with our immediate perceptions or long-standing thought or belief. This trait correlates with the ability to reconstruct accurately the viewpoints and reasoning of others and to reason from premises, assumptions, and ideas other than our own. This trait also correlates with the willingness to remember occasions when we were wrong in the past despite an intense conviction that we were right, as well as the ability to imagine our being similarly deceived in a case at hand. Critical thinkers realize the unfairness of judging unfamiliar ideas until they fully understand them.

The world consists of many societies and peoples with many different points of view and ways of thinking. In order to develop as reasonable persons we need to enter into and think within the frameworks and ideas of different peoples and societies. We cannot truly understand the world if we think about it only from *one* viewpoint, as Americans, as Italians, or as Russians.

Furthermore, critical thinkers recognize that their behavior affects others, and so consider their behavior from the perspective of those others.

If teachers reflect on this principle in the light of their own experience, they should be able to come up with their own reasons why fairmindedness is important. They might reflect upon the personal problems and frustrations they faced when others — spouses or friends, for example — did not or would not empathically enter their point of view. Or they might reflect on their frustration as children when their parents, siblings, or schoolmates did not take their point of view seriously. Through examples of this sort, constructed by the teachers themselves, insight into the need for an intellectual sense of justice can be developed.

Once the insight is in place, we are ready to put the emphasis on discussing the variety of ways that students can practice thinking fairmindedly. As always, we want to be quite specific here, so that teachers understand the kinds of behaviors they are fostering. The handbook, in each case, provides a start in the application section following the principle. For more of our examples, one can look up one or more remodelled lesson plans in which the strategy was used, referenced under each. Remember, it is more important for teachers to think up their own examples and applications than to rely on the handbook examples, which are intended as illustrative only.

Lesson plan remodelling as a strategy for staff and curriculum development is not a simple, one-shot approach. It requires patience and commitment. But it genuinely develops the critical thinking of teachers and puts them in a position to understand and help structure the inner workings of the curriculum. While doing so, it builds confidence, self-respect, and professionality. With such an approach, enthusiasm for critical thinking strategies will grow over time. It is an approach worth serious consideration as the fundamental thrust of a staff development program. If a staff becomes proficient at critiquing and remodelling lesson plans, it can, by redirecting the focus of its energy, critique and "remodel" any other aspect of school life and activity. In this way, the staff can become increasingly less dependent on direction or supervision from above and increasingly more activated by self-direction from within. Responsible, constructive critical thinking, developed through lesson plan remodelling, is a vehicle for this transformation.

In addition to devising in-service days that facilitate teachers developing skills in remodelling their lessons, it is important to orchestrate a process that facilitates critical thinking infusion on a long-term, evolutionary basis. As you consider the "big picture," remember the following principles:

✔ **Involve the widest possible spectrum of people** in discussing, articulating, and implementing the effort to infuse critical thinking. This includes teachers, administrators, board members, and parents.

✔ **Provide incentives to those who move forward in the implementation process.** Focus attention on those who do make special efforts. Do not embarrass or draw attention to those who do not.

✔ **Recognize that many small changes are often necessary before larger changes can take place.**

✔ **Do not rush implementation.** A slow but steady progress with continual monitoring and adjusting of efforts is best. Provide for refocusing on the long-term goal and ways of making the progress visible and explicit.

✔ **Work continually to institutionalize the changes made** as the understanding of critical thinking grows, making sure that the goals and strategies being used are deeply embedded in school-wide and district-wide statements and articulations. Foster discussion on the question of how progress in critical thinking instruction can be made permanent and continuous.

✔ **Honor individual differences among teachers.** Maximize the opportunities for teachers to pursue critical thinking strategies in keeping with their own educational philosophy. Enforcing conformity is incompatible with the spirit of critical thinking.

For an outstanding model of long-term critical thinking development, review "The Greensboro Plan."

> *Teachers who don't learn how to use basic critical thinking principles to critique and remodel their own lesson plans probably won't be able to implement someone else's effectively. Providing teachers with the scaffolding for carrying out the process for themselves, and examples of its application, opens the door for continuing development of critical thinking skills and insights.*

Global Critical Thinking Strategies: Beyond Compartmentalized Subject-Matter Teaching

I. The Role of the Teacher

Ateacher committed to teaching for critical thinking must think beyond subject matter, teaching to ends and objectives that transcend subject matter classification. To teach for critical thinking is, first of all, to create an environment in the class and in the school that is conducive to critical thinking. It is to help make the classroom and school environment a mini-critical society, a place where the values of critical thinking (truth, open-mindedness, empathy, autonomy, rationality, and self-criticism) are encouraged and rewarded. In such an environment, students learn to believe in the power of their own minds to identify and solve problems. They learn to believe in the efficacy of their own thinking. Thinking for themselves is not something they fear. Authorities are not those who tell them the "right" answers, but those who encourage and help them to figure out answers for themselves, who encourage them to discover the powerful resources of their own minds.

The teacher is much more a questioner than a preacher on this model. The teacher learns how to ask questions that probe meanings, that request reasons and evidence, that facilitate elaboration, that keep discussions from becoming confusing, that provide incentive for listening to what others have to say, that lead to fruitful comparisons and contrasts, that highlight contradictions and inconsistencies, and that elicit implications and consequences. Teachers committed to critical thinking realize that the primary purpose of all education is to teach students how to learn. Since there are more details than can be taught and no way to predict which the student will use, teachers emphasize thinking about basic issues and problems. Thus, details are learned as a necessary part of the process of settling such questions, and so are functional and relevant.

The teacher who teaches students how to learn and think about many basic issues gives them knowledge they can use the rest of their lives. This teacher realizes that subject matter divisions are arbitrary and a matter of convenience; that the most important problems of everyday life rarely fall neatly into subject matter divisions; that understanding a situation fully usually requires a synthesis of knowledge and insight from several subjects. An in-depth understanding of one subject requires an understanding of others. (One cannot answer questions in history, for example, without asking and answering related questions in psychology, sociology, etc.) Students must discover the value of "knowledge" "evidence," and "reasoning" by finding significant payoffs in dealing with their everyday life problems outside of school. Recognizing the universal problems we all face, the teacher should encourage each student to find personal solutions through self-reflective experiences and thought processes:

> Who am I? What is the world really like? What are my parents, my friends, and other people like? How have I become the way I am? What should I believe in? Why should I believe in it? What real options do I have? Who are my real friends? Whom should I trust? Who are my enemies? Need they be my enemies? How did the world become the way it is? How do people become the way they are? Are there any really bad people in the world? Are there any really good people in the world? What is good and bad? What is right and wrong? How should I decide? How can I decide what is fair and what is unfair? How can I be fair to others? Do I have to be fair to my enemies? How should I live my life? What rights do I have? What responsibilities?

The teacher who believes in personal freedom and thinking for oneself does not spoon- feed students with predigested answers to those questions. Nor should students be encouraged to believe that the answers to them are arbitrary and a matter of sheer opinion. Raising probing questions whenever they are natural to a subject under discussion, the teacher realizes that, in finding the way to answers, the student forges an overall perspective into which subject matter discoveries will be fit. Neither the discussion nor the student should be forced to conclusions that do not seem reasonable to the student.

Thus, such teachers reflect upon the subjects they teach, asking themselves,"What ideas and skills are the most basic and crucial in this subject? What do practitioners in this field do? How do they think? Why should students be familiar with this subject? What use does a well-educated person and citizen of a republic make of this subject? How can these uses be made apparent to and real for my students? Where do the various subject areas overlap? How should the tools and insights of each subject inform one's understanding of the others? Of one's place in the world?"

The teacher committed to teaching for critical thinking realizes that the child has two sources of "belief": beliefs that the child forms as a result of personal experience, inward thinking, and interaction with peers and environment, and beliefs that the child learns through instruction by adults. The first could be called "real" or "operational" beliefs. They are what define the child's real world, the foundation for action, the source of acted-upon values. They are a result of the child making sense of or figuring out the world. They are heavily influenced by what has been called "pleasure-principle thinking." They are in large measure egocentric, unreflective, and unarticulated.

The child (and most adults too for that matter) believes in many things for egocentric, irrational reasons: because others hold the belief, because certain desires may be justified by the belief, because of feeling more comfortable with the belief, because of being rewarded for the belief, because of ego-identification with the belief, because of not being accepted by peers without acting on the belief, because the belief helps to justify feelings of like or dislike toward people.

The child, of course, also has spontaneously formed reasonable beliefs. Some of those are inconsistent with the expressed beliefs of parents and teachers. As a result of this contradiction with authority, the child rarely raises these beliefs to what Piaget calls "conscious realization." Children have also developed their own theories about psychology, sociology, science, language, and so on, covering most subjects. The totality of these real beliefs is unsynthesized and contains many contradictions which the child will discover only if encouraged to freely express them in an atmosphere that is mutually supportive and child-centered.

The other source of belief, didactic instruction from adult authority figures, is an adult's interpretation of reality, not the child's. The child learns to verbalize it but does not synthesize it with operational belief. Therefore, the child typically does not recognize contradictions between these two belief systems. The child's own theories and beliefs are not necessarily replaced with the knowledge offered in school.

The teacher concerned with this problem, then, provides an environment wherein students can discover and explore their beliefs. Such teachers refrain from rushing students who are struggling to express their beliefs, allow time for thoughtful discussion, refuse to allow anyone to attack students for their beliefs, reward students for questioning their own beliefs, and support students when they consider many points of view.

Unless the teacher provides conditions in which students can discover operational beliefs through reflective thinking, these two systems of beliefs will exist in separate dimensions of their lives. The first will control their deeds, especially private deeds; the second will control their words, especially public words. The first will be used when acting for themselves; the second when performing for others. Neither, in a sense, will be taken seriously. Neither will be subjected to rational scrutiny: the first because it isn't openly expressed and challenged verbally; the second because it is not tested in the crucible of action and practical decision-making. This dichotomy, when embedded in an individual's life, creates a barrier to living an "examined life." Students lack the wherewithal to explore contradictions, double standards, and hypocrisies. They will use critical thinking skills, if at all, as weapons in a struggle to protect themselves from exposure, and to lay bare the contradictions of the "other," the "enemy." When they integrate critical thinking skills into this dichotomous thinking, they become self-serving, not fairminded, critical thinkers.

The role of the teacher could be summarized as follows:
- help break big questions or tasks into smaller, more manageable parts
- create meaningful contexts in which learning is valued by the students
- help students clarify their thoughts by rephrasing or asking questions
- pose thought-provoking questions
- encourage students to explain things to each other
- help students find what they need to know by suggesting and showing students how to use resources

II. Socratic Questioning: Wondering Aloud About Meaning and Truth

Introduction

Socratic discussion, wherein students' thought is elicited and probed, allows students to develop and evaluate their thinking by making it explicit. By encouraging students to slow their thinking down and elaborate on it, Socratic discussion gives students the opportunity to develop and test their ideas — the beliefs they have spontaneously formed and those they learn in school. Thus, students can synthesize their beliefs into a coherent and well-developed perspective.

Socratic questioning requires teachers to take seriously and wonder about what students say and think: what they mean, its significance to them, its relationship to other beliefs, how it can be tested, to what extent and in what way it is true or makes sense. Teachers who wonder about the meaning and truth of students' statements can translate that curiosity into probing questions. By wondering aloud, teachers simultaneously convey interest in and respect for student thought, and model analytical moves for students. Fruitful Socratic discussion infects students with the same curiosity about the meaning of and truth of what they think, hear, and read and gives students the clear message that they are expected to think and to take everyone else's beliefs seriously.

Socratic questioning is based on the idea that all thinking has a logic or structure, that any one statement only partially reveals the thinking underlying it, expressing no more than a tiny piece of the system of interconnected beliefs of which it is a part. Its purpose is to expose the logic of someone's thought. Use of Socratic questioning presupposes the following points: All thinking has assumptions; makes claims or creates meaning; has implications and consequences; focuses on some things and throws others into the background; uses some concepts or ideas and not others; is defined by purposes, issues, or problems; uses or explains some facts and not others; is relatively clear or unclear; is relatively deep or superficial; is relatively critical or uncritical; is relatively elaborated or undeveloped; is relatively monological or multi-logical. Critical thinking is thinking done with an effective, self-monitoring awareness of these points.

Socratic instruction can take many forms. Socratic questions can come from the teacher or from students. They can be used in a large group discussion, in small groups, one-to-one, or even with oneself. They can have different purposes. What each form has in common is that someone's thought is developed as a result of the probing, stimulating questions asked. It requires questioners to try on others' beliefs, to imagine what it would be to accept them and wonder what it would be to believe otherwise. If a student says that people are selfish, the teacher may wonder aloud as to what it means to say that, how the student explains acts others call altruistic, what sort of example that student would accept as an unselfish act, or what the student thinks it means to say that an act or person was unselfish. The discussion which follows should help clarify the concepts of selfish and unselfish behavior, as well as the kind of evidence required to determine whether or not someone is or is not acting selfishly, and the consequences of accepting or rejecting the original generalization. Such a discussion enables students to examine their own views on such concepts as generosity, motivation, obligation, human nature, right and wrong.

Some people erroneously believe that holding a Socratic discussion is like conducting a chaotic free-for-all. In fact, Socratic discussion has distinctive goals and distinctive ways to achieve them. Indeed, any discussion — any thinking — guided by Socratic questioning is structured. The discussion, the thinking, is structured to take student thought from the unclear to the clear, from the unreasoned to the reasoned, from the implicit to the explicit, from the unexamined to the examined, from the inconsistent to the consistent, from the unarticulated to the articulated. To learn how to participate in it, one has to learn how to listen carefully to what others say, to look for reasons and evidence, to recognize and reflect upon assumptions, to discover implications and consequences, to seek examples, analogies, and objections, to seek to discover, in short, what is really known and to distinguish it from what is merely believed.

Socratic Questioning

- raises basic issues
- probes beneath the surface of things
- pursues problematic areas of thought
- helps students to discover the *structure* of their own thought
- helps students develop sensitivity to clarify, accuracy, and relevance
- helps students note claims, evidence, conclusions, questions-at-issue, assumptions, implications, consequences, concepts, interpretations, points of view

---

Three Kinds of Socratic Discussion

We can loosely categorize three general forms of Socratic questioning: the spontaneous, the exploratory, and the issue-specific. There are therefore three basic kinds of preparation for each.

Spontaneous or unplanned

Every teacher's teaching should be imbued with the Socratic spirit. We should always keep our curiosity and wondering alive. If we do, there will be many occasions in which we will spontaneously ask students questions about what they mean and explore with them how we might find out if something is true. If one student says that a given angle will be the same as another angle in a geometrical figure, we may spontaneously wonder how we might go about proving or disproving that. If one student says Americans love freedom, we may spontaneously wonder about exactly what that means (Does that mean, for example, that we love freedom more than other people do? How could we find out?). If in a science class a student says that most space is empty, we may be spontaneously moved to raise some question on the spot as to what that might mean and how we might find out.

Such spontaneous discussions provide models of listening critically as well as exploring the beliefs expressed. If something said seems questionable, misleading, or false, Socratic questioning provides a way of helping students to become self-correcting, rather than relying on correction by the teacher. Spontaneous Socratic discussion can prove especially useful when students become interested in a topic, when they raise an important issue, when they are on the brink of grasping or integrating something, when discussion becomes bogged down or confused or hostile. Socratic questioning provides specific moves which can fruitfully take advantage of the interest, effectively approach the issue, aid integration and expansion of the insight, move a troubled discussion forward, clarify or sort through what appears confusing, and diffuse frustration or anger.

Although by definition there can be no pre-planning for a particular spontaneous discussion, teachers can prepare themselves by becoming familiar and comfortable with generic Socratic questions, and developing the art of raising probing follow-up questions and giving encouraging and helpful responses. Ask for examples, evidence, or reasons, propose counter-examples, ask the rest of class if they agree with a point made, suggest parallel or analogous cases, ask for a paraphrase of opposing views, rephrase student responses clearly and succinctly. These are among the most common moves.

• If you see little or no relevance in a student comment, you may think, "I wonder why this student mentioned that now?" and ask, "What connection do you see between our discussion and your point that ...?" or "I'm not sure why you mentioned that now. Could you explain how it's related to this discussion?" or "What made you think of that?"Either the point is germane so you can clarify the connection, or only marginally related, so you can rephrase it and say "A new issue has been raised." That new issue can be pursued then, or tactfully postponed, or can generate an assignment.

• If a student says something vague or general, you may think, "I wonder about the role of that belief in this student's life, the consequences of that belief, or how the student perceives the consequences, or if there are any practical consequences at all" and so may ask, "How does that belief affect how you act? What, for example, do you do or refrain from doing because you believe that?" You might have several students respond and compare their understandings, or suggest an alternative view and have students compare its consequences.

To summarize: Because we begin to wonder more and more about meaning and truth, and so think aloud in front of our students by means of questions, Socratic exchanges will occur at many unplanned moments in our instruction. However, in addition to these unplanned wonderings we can also design or plan out at least two distinct kinds of Socratic discussion: one that explores a wide range of issues and one that focuses on one particular issue.

Exploratory

What we here call *exploratory* Socratic questioning enables teachers to find out what students know or think and to use it to probe into student thinking on a variety of issues. Hence you may use it to learn students' impressions of a subject in order to assess their thought and ability to articulate it, you may use it to see what students value, or to uncover problematic areas or potential biases, or find out where students are clearest and fuzziest in their thinking. You may use it to discover areas or issues of interest or controversy, or to find out where and how students have integrated school material into their belief systems. Such discussions can serve as preparation in a general way for later study or analysis of a topic, as an introduction, as review or to see what students understood from their study of a unit or topic preparatory to taking a test, or to suggest where they should focus study for test, or as a basis for or guide to future assignments, or to prepare for an assignment. Or, again, you might have students take (or pick) an issue raised in discussion and give their own views, or have students form groups to discuss the issue or topic.

This type of Socratic questioning raises and explores a broad range of interrelated issues and concepts. It requires minimal pre-planning or pre-thinking. It has a relatively loose order or structure. You can prepare by having some general questions ready to raise when appropriate by considering the topic or issue, related issues and key concepts. You can also prepare by predicting students' likeliest responses and preparing some follow-up questions. Remember, however, that once students' thought is stimulated there is no predicting exactly where discussion will go.

What follows are some suggestions and possible topics for Socratic discussions:

• "What is social studies?" If students have difficulty, ask, "When you've studied social studies, what have you studied/talked about?" If students list topics, put them on the board. Then have students discuss the items and try to group them. "Do these topics have something in common? Are there differences between these topics?" Encourage students to discuss details they know about the topics. If, instead of listing topics, they give a general answer or definition, or if they are able to give a statement about what the topics listed have in common, suggest examples that fit the definition but are not social studies. For example, if a student says, "It's about people," mention medicine. Have them modify or improve their definition. "How is social studies like and unlike other subjects? What basic questions does the subject address? How does it address them? Why study social studies? Is it important? Why or why not? How can we use what we learn in social studies? What are the most important ideas you've learned from this subject?"

• When, if ever, is violence justified? Why are people as violent as they are? What effects does violence have? Can violence be lessened or stopped?

• What is a friend?

• What is education? Why learn?

• What is most important?

• What is right and wrong? Why be good? What is a good person?

• What is the difference between living and non-living things?

• Of what sorts of things is the universe made?

• What is language?

• What are the similarities and differences between humans and animals?

There may be occasions when you are unsure whether to call a discussion exploratory or issue-specific. Which you call it is not important. What is important is what happens in the discussion. For example, consider this group of questions:

• What does 'vote' mean?

　　How do people decide whom to elect? How should they decide? How could people predict how a potential leader is likely to act? If you don't know about an issue or the candidates for an office, should you vote on it?

　　Is voting important? Why or why not? What are elections supposed to produce? How? What does that require? What does that tell us about voting?

　　Why are elections considered a good idea? Why is democracy considered good? What does belief in democracy assume about human nature?

　　How do people become candidates?

　　Why does the press emphasize how much money candidates have? How does having lots of money help candidates win?

　　Why do people give money to candidates? Why do companies?

These questions could be the list generated as possible questions for an exploratory discussion. Which of them are actually used would depend on how students respond. For an issue-specific discussion, these questions and more could be used in an order which takes students from ideas with which they are most familiar, to those with which they are least familiar.

Issue-Specific

Much of the time you will approach your instruction with specific areas and issues to cover. This is the time for issue-specific Socratic questioning. To really probe an issue or concept in depth, to have students clarify, sort, analyze and evaluate thoughts and perspectives, distinguish the known from the unknown, synthesize relevant factors and knowledge, students can engage in an extended and focused discussion. This type of discussion offers students the chance to pursue perspectives to their most basic assumptions and through their furthest implications and consequences. These discussions give students experience in engaging in an extended, ordered, and integrated discussion in which they discover, develop, and share ideas and insights. It requires pre-planning or thinking through possible perspectives on the issue, grounds for conclusions, problematic concepts, implications, and consequences. You can further prepare by reflecting on those subjects relevant to the issue: their methods, standards, basic distinctions and concepts, and interrelationships — points of overlap or possible conflict. It is also helpful to be prepared by considering likeliest student answers. This is the type of Socratic questioning most often used in the lesson remodels themselves. Though we can't provide the crucial follow-up questions, we illustrate pre-planning for issue-specific Socratic questioning in numerous remodels.

All three types of Socratic discussion require development of the art of questioning. They require the teacher to develop familiarity with a wide variety of intellectual moves and sensitivity to when to ask which kinds of questions, though there is rarely one best question at any particular time.

Some Suggestions for Using Socratic Discussion

• Have an initial exploratory discussion about a complex issue in which students break it down into simpler parts. Students can then choose the aspects they want to explore or research. Then have an issue-specific discussion where students share, analyze, evaluate, and synthesize their work.

• The class could have a "fishbowl" discussion. One third of the class, sitting in a circle, discusses a topic. The rest of the class, in a circle around the others, listens, takes notes, then discusses the discussion.

• Assign an essay asking students to respond to a point of interest made in a discussion.

A Taxonomy of Socratic Questions

It is helpful to recognize, in light of the universal features in the logic of human thought, that there are identifiable categories of questions for the adept Socratic questioner to dip into: questions of clarification, questions that probe assumptions, questions that probe reasons and evidence, questions about viewpoints or perspectives, questions that probe implications and consequences, and questions about the question. Here are some examples of generic questions in each of these categories:

Questions of Clarification

- What do you mean by _____?
- What is your main point?
- How does _____ relate to ___?
- Could you put that another way?
- What do you think is the main issue here?
- Is your basic point _____ or _____?
- Let me see if I understand you; do you mean _____ or _____?
- How does this relate to our discussion/ problem/ issue?
- What do you think John meant by his remark? What did you take John to mean?
- Jane, would you summarize in your own words what Richard has said? ... Richard, is that what you meant?

- Could you give me an example?
- Would this be an example: _____?
- Could you explain that further?
- Would you say more about that?
- Why do you say that?

Questions that Probe Assumptions

- What are you assuming?
- What is Karen assuming?
- What could we assume instead?
- You seem to be assuming _____. Do I understand you correctly?
- All of your reasoning is dependent on the idea that ___. Why have you based your reasoning on _____ rather than _____?
- You seem to be assuming ___. How would you justify taking this for granted?
- Is it always the case? Why do you think the assumption holds here?

Questions that Probe Reasons and Evidence

- What would be an example?
- What are your reasons for saying that?
- What other information do we need to know?
- Could you explain your reasons to us?
- But is that good evidence to believe that?
- Are those reasons adequate?
- Is there reason to doubt that evidence?
- Who is in a position to know if that is the case?
- What would you say to someone who said ___?
- Can someone else give evidence to support that response?
- By what reasoning did you come to that conclusion?
- How could we go about finding out whether that is true?

- How do you know?
- Why did you say that?
- Why do you think that is true?
- What led you to that belief?
- Do you have any evidence for that?
- How does that apply to this case?
- What difference does that make?
- What would convince you otherwise?

Questions About Viewpoints or Perspectives

- You seem to be approaching this issue from _____ perspective. Why have you chosen this rather than that perspective?
- How would other groups/types of people respond? Why? What would influence them?
- How could you answer the objection that _____ would make?
- Can/did anyone see this another way?
- What would someone who disagrees say?
- What is an alternative?
- How are Ken's and Roxanne's ideas alike? Different?

Questions that Probe Implications and Consequences
- What are you implying by that?
- When you say _____, are you implying _____?
- But if that happened, what else would also happen as a result? Why?
- What effect would that have?
- Would that necessarily happen or only probably happen?
- What is an alternative?
- If this and this are the case, then what else must also be true?

Questions About the Question
- How can we find out?
- How could someone settle this question?
- Is the question clear? Do we understand it?
- Is this question easy or hard to answer? Why?
- Would _____ put the question differently?
- Does this question ask us to evaluate something?
- Do we all agree that this is the question?
- To answer this question, what questions would we have to answer first?
- I'm not sure I understand how you are interpreting the main question at issue.
- Is this the same issue as _____?
- Can we break this question down at all?
- How would _____ put the issue?
- What does this question assume?
- Why is this question important?

Wondering (And Wondering About Your Wonderings)

As a blossoming critical thinker, you will find yourself wondering in many directions. You will often, however, be unsure about how many of these wonderings to share with your students. You certainly don't want to overwhelm them. Neither do you want to confuse them or lead them in too many directions at once. So when do you make the wonderings explicit in the form of a question and when do you keep them in the privacy of your mind?

There is no pat formula or procedure for answering these questions, though there are some principles:

- "Test and find out." There is nothing wrong with some of your questions misfiring. You won't always be able to predict what questions will stimulate students thought. So you must engage in some trial-and-error questioning.

- "Tie into student experience and perceived needs." You may think of numerous examples of ways students can apply what they learn, and formulate questions relating academic material to students' lives.

- "Don't give up too soon." If students don't respond to a question, wait. If they still don't respond, you could rephrase the question or break it down into simpler questions.

The teacher must use care and caution in introducing students to Socratic questioning. The level of the questions should match the level of the students' thought. It should not be assumed that students will be fully successful with it, except over a considerable length of time. Nevertheless, properly used, it can be introduced in some form or other at virtually any grade level.

Transcript of a 4th Grade Socratic Discussion

The following is a transcript of a 4th-grade exploratory Socratic discussion. The discussion leader was with these particular students for the first time. The purpose was to determine the status of the children's thinking on some of the abstract questions whose answers tend to define our broadest thinking. The students were eager to respond and often seemed to articulate responses that reflected potential insights into the character of the human mind, its relation to the body, the forces that shape us, the influence of parents and peer group, the nature of morality and of ethnocentric bias. The insights are disjointed, of course, but the questions that elicited them and the responses that articulated them could be used as the basis of future discussions or simple assignments with these students.

While reading the transcript which follows, you may want to formulate questions that could have been asked but weren't: student responses that could have been followed up, or other directions the discussion could have taken. Other ways to approach the manuscript would include explaining the function of each question or categorizing the questions.

Transcript

→ *How does your mind work?*
Where's your mind?

Student: "In your head." (numerous students point to their heads)

→ *Does your mind do anything?*

Student: "It helps you remember and think."

Student: "It helps, like, if you want to move your legs. It sends a message down to them."

Student: "This side of your mind controls this side of your body and that side controls this other side."

Student: "When you touch a hot oven it tells you whether to cry or say ouch!"

→ *Does it tell you when to be sad and when to be happy?*
How does your mind know when to be happy and when to be sad?

Student: "When you're hurt it tells you to be sad."

Student: "If something is happening around you is sad."

Student: "If there is lightning and you are scared."

Student: "If you get something you want."

Student: "It makes your body operate. It's like a machine that operates your body."

→ *Does it ever happen that two people are in the same circumstance but one is happy and the other is sad? Even though they are in exactly the same circumstance?*

Student: "You get the same toy. One person might like it. The other gets the same toy and he doesn't like the toy."

➤ *Why do you think that- some people come to like some things and some people seem to like different things?*

Student: "Cause everybody is not the same. Everybody has different minds and is built different, made different."

Student: "They have different personalities?"

➤ *Where does personality come from?*

Student: "When you start doing stuff and you find that you like some stuff best."

➤ *Are you born with a personality or do you develop it as you grow up?*

Student: "You develop it as you grow up."

➤ *What makes you develop one rather than another?*

Student: "Like, your parents or something."

➤ *How can your parent's personality get into you?*

Student: "Because you're always around them and then the way they act if they think they are good and they want you to act the same way then they'll sort of teach you and you'll do it."

Student: Like, if you are in a tradition. They want you to carry on something that their parents started."

➤ *Does your mind come to think at all the way the children around you think? Can you think of any examples where the way you think is like the way children around you think? Do you think you behave like other American kids?*

Student: "Yes."

➤ *What would make you behave more like American kids than like Eskimo kids?*

Student: "Because you're around them."

Student: "Like, Eskimo kids probably don't even know what the word 'jump-rope' is. American kids know what it is."

➤ *And are there things that the Eskimo kids know that you don't know about?*

Student: "Yes."

Student: "And also we don't have to dress like them or act like them and they have to know when a storm is coming so they won't get trapped outside."

➤ *O.K., so if I understand you then, parents have some influence on how you behave and the kids around you have some influence on how you behave... Do you have some influence on how you behave? Do you choose the kind of person you're going to be at all?*

Student: "Yes."

➤ *How do you do that do you think?*

Student: "Well if someone says to jump off a five-story building, you won't say O.K. You wouldn't want to do that..."

➤ *Do you ever sit around and say, "Let's see shall I be a smart person or a dumb one?"*

Student: "Yes."

➤ *But how do you decide?*

Student: "Your grades."

➤ *But I thought your teacher decided your grades. How do you decide?*

Student: "If you don't do your homework you get bad grades and become a dumb person but if you study real hard you'll get good grades."

➤ *So you decide that, right?*

Student: "And if you like something at school like computers you work hard and you can get a good job when you grow up. But if you don't like anything at school you don't work hard.

Student: "You can't just decide you want to be smart, you have to work for it."

Student: "You got to work to be smart just like you got to work to get your allowance."

➤ *What about being good and being bad, do you decide whether you're good or you're bad? How many people have decided to be bad? (3 students raise their hands) To first student: Why have you decided to be bad?*

Student: "Well, I don't know. Sometimes I think I've been bad too long and I want to go to school and have a better reputation but sometimes I feel like just making trouble and who cares."

➤ *Let's see, is there a difference between who you are and your reputation? What's your reputation? That's a pretty big word. What's your reputation?*

Student: "The way you act. If you had a bad reputation people wouldn't like to be around you and if you had a good reputation people would like to be around you and be your friend."

➤ *Well, but I'm not sure of the difference between who you are and who people think you are. Could you be a good person and people think you bad? Is that possible?*

Student: "Yeah, because you could try to be good. I mean, a lot of people think this one person's really smart but this other person doesn't have nice clothes but she tries really hard and people don't want to be around her."

➤ *So sometimes people think somebody is real good and they're not and sometimes people think that somebody is real bad and they're not. Like if you were a crook, would you let everyone know you're a crook?*

Students: Chorus of "NO!"

➤ *So some people are really good at hiding what they are really like. Some people might have a good reputation and be bad; some people might have a bad reputation and be good.*

Student: "Like, everyone might think you were good but you might be going on dope or something."

Student: "Does reputation mean that if you have a good reputation you want to keep it just like that? Do you always want to be good for the rest of your life?"

➤ *I'm not sure...*

Student: "So if you have a good reputation you try to be good all the time and don't mess up and don't do nothing?"

➤ *Suppose somebody is trying to be good just to get a good reputation -- why are they trying to be good?*

Student: "So they can get something they want and they don't want other people to have?"

Student: "They might be shy and just want to be left alone."

Student: "You can't tell a book by how it's covered."

➤ *Yes, some people are concerned more with their cover than their book. Now let me ask you another question. So if its true that we all have a mind and our mind helps us to figure out the world and we are influenced by our parents and the people around us, and sometimes we choose to do good things and sometimes we choose to do bad things, sometimes people say things about us and so forth and so on... Let me ask you: Are there some bad people in this world?*

Student: "Yeah."

Student: "Terrorists and stuff."

Student: "Nightstalker."

Student: "The TWA hijackers."

Student: "Robbers."

Student: "Rapers."

Student: "Bums."

➤ *Bums, are they bad?*

Student: "Well, sometimes."

Student: "The Klu Klux Klan"

Student: "The Bums... not really cause they might not look good but you can't judge them by how they look. They might be really nice and everything."

➤ *O.K., so they might have a bad reputation but be good, after you care to know them. There might be good bums and bad bums.*

Student: "Libyan guys and Machine gun Kelly"

➤ *Let me ask you, do the bad people think they're bad?*

Student: "A lot of them don't think they're bad but they are. They might be sick in the head."

➤ *Yes, some people are sick in their heads.*

Student: "A lot of them (bad guys) don't think they're bad."

➤ *Why did you say Libyan people?*

Student: "Cause they have o' lot a terrorists and hate us and bomb us..."

➤ *If they hate us do they think we are bad or good?*

Student: They think we are bad."

➤ *And we think they are bad? And who is right?*

Student: "Usually both of them."

Student: "None of us are really bad!"

Student: "Really, I don't know why our people and their people are fighting. Two wrongs don't make a right."

Student: "It's like if there was a line between two countries, and they were both against each other, if a person from the first country crosses over the line, they'd be considered the bad guy. And if a person from the second country crossed over the line he'd be considered the bad guy."

➤ *So it can depend on which country you're from who you consider right or wrong, is that right?*

Student: "Like a robber might steal things to support his family. He's doing good to his family but actually bad to another person."

➤ *And in his mind do you think he is doing something good or bad?*

Student: "It depends what his mind is like. He might think he is doing good for his family or he might think he is doing bad for the other person."

Student: "It's like the underground railroad a long time ago. Some people thought it was bad and some people thought it was good."

➤ *But if lots of people think something is right and lots of people think something is wrong, how are you supposed to figure out the difference between right and wrong?*

Student: "Go by what you think!"

➤ *But how do you figure out what to think?*

Student: "Lots of people go by other people."

➤ *But somebody has to decide for themselves, don't they?*

Student: "Use your mind?"

➤ *Yes, let's see, suppose I told you: "You are going to have a new classmate. Her name is Sally and she's bad." Now, you could either believe me or what could you do?*

Student: "You could try to meet her and decide whether she was bad or good."

➤ *Suppose she came and said to you: "I'm going to give you a toy so you'll like me." And she gave you things so you would like her, but she also beat up on some other people, would you like her because she gave you things?*

Student: "No, because she said I'll give you this so you'll like me. She wouldn't be very nice."

➤ *So why should you like people?*

Student: "Because they act nice to you."

➤ *Only to you?*

Student: "To everybody!"

Student: "I wouldn't care what they gave me. I'd see what they're like inside."

➤ *But how do you find out what's on the inside of a person?*

Student: "You could ask but I would try to judge myself."

Socratic questioning is flexible. The questions asked at any given point will depend on what the students say, what ideas the teacher wants to pursue, and what questions occur to the teacher. Generally, Socratic questions raise basic issues, probe beneath the surface of things, and pursue problematic areas of thought.

The above discussion could have gone in a number of different directions. For instance, rather than focussing on the mind's relationship to emotions, the teacher could have pursued the idea 'mind' by asking for more examples of its functions, and having students group them. The teacher could have followed up the response of the student who asked, "Does reputation mean that if you have a good reputation you want to keep it just like that?" He might, for instance, have asked the student why he asked that, and asked the other students what they thought of the idea. Such a discussion may have developed into a dialogical exchange about reputation, different degrees of goodness, or reasons for being bad. Or the idea 'bad people' could have been pursued and clarified by asking students why the examples they gave were examples of bad people. Students may then have been able to suggest tentative generalizations which could have been tested and probed through further questioning. Rather than exploring the influence of perspective on evaluation, the teacher might have probed the idea, expressed by one student, that no one is 'really bad.' The student could have been asked to explain the remark, and other students could have been asked for their responses to the idea. In these cases and others, the teacher has a choice between any number of equally thought provoking questions. No one question is the 'right' question.

To participate effectively in Socratic questioning, one must:
• listen carefully to what others say
• take what they say seriously
• look for reasons and evidence
• recognize and reflect upon assumptions
• discover implications and consequences
• seek examples, analogies, and objections
• seek to distinguish what one *knows* from what one merely *believes*
• seek to enter empathetically into the perspectives or points of view of others
• be on the alert for inconsistencies, vagueness, and other possible problems in thought
• look beneath the surface of things
• maintain a healthy sense of skepticism
• be willing to helpfully play the role of devil's advocate

III. Role Playing and Reconstructing Opposing Views

A fundamental danger for human thought is narrowness. We do not naturally and spontaneously open our minds to the insights of those who think differently from us. We have a natural tendency to use our native intelligence and our cognitive skills to protect and maintain our system of beliefs rather than to modify and expand it, especially when ideas are suggested that have their origin in a very different way of thinking. We can never become fairminded unless we learn how to enter sympathetically into the thinking of others, to reason from their perspectives and eventually to try seeing things as they see them.

Learning how to accurately reconstruct the thinking of others and how to role play their thinking (once reconstructed) are fundamental goals of critical thinking instruction. Very little work has yet been done in giving students opportunities to role play the reasoning of others. So it is not now clear to what extent or in what forms role playing to enhance critical reciprocity is possible.

But imagine some possible experiments. Students could brainstorm two lists, one list of their reasons for being allowed to stay out late and one for the reasons their parents might give forbidding it. A role play might be devised in which two students would pretend that they were parents and were asked, in that role, to give their reasons why their children should not be allowed to stay out late. It would be interesting to see how accurately the students could reconstruct the reasoning of their parents. They will probably find this challenging and should be encouraged to be as clear as possible in their reasons. Socratically questioning them would reveal more about their thinking. If a student gives the reason that "kids can't be trusted," the teacher might ask, "What does trust mean to you?" Or ,"What kinds of things can kids not be trusted to do? Do you think that all kids are untrustworthy? What circumstances have caused you not to trust one of your kids?" Then one might experiment with a discussion between a student playing "parent" and another student playing "daughter" or "son." The class might subsequently discuss what the best reasons were on each side of the dispute and who seemed to have the stronger argument.

History lessons might also provide opportunities for initial role playing experiences. For instance, students could role play discussions between Northerners and Southerners on disputed questions of the Civil War period or between a member of the British royalty and a colonist concerning the events that led up to the Boston Tea Party.

An interesting follow-up exercise might be to have the students either in pairs or singly compose a dialogue on a given issue or on a chosen one. Remind them to brainstorm lists of reasons for both sides of the issue, being sure to focus on the side they don't hold. Then have them write a dialogue expressing the opposing viewpoints. Some of the pairs of students could present their dialogues to the class.

IV. Analyzing Experiences

The necessary role of insights and intellectual virtues — such traits as intellectual empathy, intellectual courage, intellectual integrity, and confidence in reason — in significant learning has been largely ignored in schooling. This deficiency is intimately connected with another one, the failure of schools to help students recognize the need, not only to test what they "learn" in school against their own experience, but also to test what they experience by what they "learn" in school.

We subject little of our experience to critical analysis. We seldom take our experiences apart, to get some sense of their true worth. We seldom separate experiences into their parts of *raw data*, and interpretations of the data. Students need to recognize that the same event or situation is often interpreted differently and therefore experienced differently. Failing to recognize the difference between aspects of our experiences, we ignore how the interests, goals, and desires we bring to those data shape and structure our interpretations. Similarly, we rarely seriously entertain the possibility that our interpretation (and hence the total experience) might be selective, biased, or misleading.

The process of developing intellectual virtues and insights is part of developing an interest in taking our experiences apart, in order to recognize when biased subjectivity is distorting our experience. What is more, we need to continually keep in mind the fact that the world is complex and that there are often a variety of legitimate ways to experience the same event or situation. Meta-experiences become important benchmarks and guides for future thought. They make possible modes of thinking and maneuvers in thinking of which the irrational mind is incapable.

To teach for the intellectual virtues, therefore, one must recognize the significant differences between the higher order critical thinking of a fairminded person and the lower order critical thinking of a self-serving person. Though both kinds of thinkers share a certain command of the micro-skills of critical thinking and hence would, for example, score well on tests such as the Watson-Glaser Critical Thinking Appraisal or the Cornell Critical Thinking Tests, they would be unequal at tasks which presuppose the intellectual virtues. The self-serving (weak sense) critical thinker would lack the insights that underlie and support these virtues.

To reason well in domains in which I am prejudiced — hence, eventually to reason my way out of prejudices — I must develop a set of analyzed examples of such reasoning. Of course, to do so, I must see that when I am prejudiced, it seems to me that I am not, and conversely, that those who are not prejudiced as I am will nevertheless seem to me to be prejudiced — to a prejudiced person an unprejudiced person seems prejudiced. I will realize this only to the degree that I have analyzed experiences in which I have first been intensely convinced that I was correct on an issue, judgment, or point of view, only to find after a series of challenges, reconsiderations, and new reasonings that my previous conviction was, in fact, prejudiced. I must take this experience apart in my mind, clearly understand its elements and how these elements fit together (how I became prejudiced; how I inwardly experienced that prejudice; how intensely that prejudice appeared as insight to me; how I progressively began to break it down by seriously considering opposing lines of reasoning; how I slowly came to new assumptions, new information, and ultimately new conceptualizations).

Only by this special kind of inner experience of reasoning one's way out of prejudices does one gain the sort of higher order abilities a fairminded critical thinker requires. The somewhat abstract articulation of the intellectual virtues will take on concrete meaning in the light of these *analyzed experiences*. We grasp their true meaning only when we take apart our own experience in this way. For example, suppose you had developed a habit of getting angry when other people were late but typically felt justified when you were late. In fact, suppose you felt hostility toward others when they expressed exasperation at your being late. You would probably have a great deal of difficulty in separating your anger and the thinking that fostered that anger from the objective events: you or someone else is late. But if you came to do so, to see inconsistency in your responses to lateness, you could begin to reshape your own responses and be fairer to others. Once we begin to analyze experiences in this way, we begin to develop the insights upon which the intellectual virtues depend.

To generalize, in order to develop intellectual virtues, we must develop a variety of analyzed experiences that represent to us personal models, not only of the pitfalls of our own previous thoughts and experiences, but also of processes we used to reason our way out of or around them. These model experiences must be charged with meaning for us. We cannot be *indifferent* to them. We must sustain them in our minds by our sense of their importance, that they may sustain and guide us in our thought.

What does this imply for teaching? For one thing, it implies a somewhat different content or material focus. Our own minds and experiences must become the subject of our study and learning. Indeed, only to the extent that the content of our own experiences becomes an essential part of what is studied will the "usual" subject matter be truly learned. By the same token, the experiences of others must also become part of our studies. But experiences of any kind should always be critically analyzed, and all students must do their own analysis of the experience to be assessed and recognize what indeed they are doing.

This entails that students grasp the logic of experience and come to see that, for example, every experience has three elements, each of which may require some special scrutiny in the analytic process: 1) something to be experienced (some actual situation or other); 2) an experiencing subject (with a point of view, framework of beliefs, attitudes, desires, and values); and 3) some interpretation or conceptualization of the situation. To take apart any experience, I must ponder three distinctive questions (as well as their interrelation):

1) What are the raw facts, the most neutral description, of the situation?
2) What interests, attitudes, desires, or concerns am I bringing to the situation?
3) How am I conceptualizing or interpreting the situation in light of my point of view?

If students are given a wide range of assignments requiring them to analyze their experiences and the experiences of others along these lines and ample opportunity to argue among themselves about which interpretations make the most sense and why, then they will begin to amass a collection of critically analyzed experiences. As these experiences illuminate the pitfalls of thought, their identification with the analyses will lay the foundation for their intellectual traits and moral character. They will have intellectual virtues, because they thought their own way to them and internalized them as concrete understandings and insights. Their basic values and their thinking processes now feed each other. Their intellectual and affective life becomes more integrated. Critical standards for thinking become part of their own thinking rather than external to them in texts, teachers, or the authority of a peer group.

There will be many opportunities in the day-to-day life of school activities to help students develop their intellectual courage, empathy, integrity, perseverance, confidence in reason, and fairmindedness. We need not pressure students to develop these traits, but merely provide conditions which support their growth. The same can be said for fostering essential insights, such as insight into the difference between objective situations and our own special interpretations of them. If we provide situations that call upon students to express their own interpretations while distinguishing basic facts from those interpretations, they will develop crucial insights over time. We must take care, however, not to encourage students to believe either that every interpretation of an event is equally "correct" or that only one interpretation contains *the* truth. Students should learn over time that some interpretations of events are more justified than others (more accurate, relevant, or insightful), while no one interpretation of an event contains *all the truth.*

V. Teaching the Distinction Between Fact, Opinion, and Reasoned Judgment

Many texts claim to foster critical thinking by teaching students to divide all statements into facts and opinions. When they do so, students fail to grasp the significance of dialogical thinking and reasoned judgment. When an issue is fundamentally a matter of fact (e.g., "What is the weight of this block of wood?" or "What are the dimensions of this figure?"), there is no reason to argue about the answer; one should carry out the process that gets us the correct answer. Sometimes this might require following complex procedures. In any case, weighing and measuring, the processes needed for the questions above, are not typically matters of debate.

On the other hand, questions that raise matters of mere opinion, such as, "What sweater do you like better?" "What is your favorite color?" or "Where would you like to spend your vacation?" do not have any one correct answer since they ask us merely to express our personal *preferences.*

But most of the important issues we face in our lives are not exclusively matters of fact or matters of preference. Many require a new element: that we reason our way to conclusions while we take the reasoned perspectives of others into account. As teachers, we should be clear in encouraging students to distinguish these three different situations: the ones that call for facts alone, the ones that call for preference alone, and the ones that call for reasoned judgment. When, as members of a jury, we are called upon to come to a judgment of innocence or guilt, we do not settle questions of pure fact, and we are certainly not expected to express our subjective preferences.

Students certainly need to learn procedures for gathering facts, and they doubtless need to have opportunities to express their preferences, but their most important need is to learn how to develop their capacities for reasoned judgment, how to come to conclusions of their own based on evidence (facts) and reasoning of their own within the framework of their own perspectives. Their values and preferences will, of course, play a role in their perspectives and reasoning, but their perspectives should not be a matter of pure opinion or sheer preference. I should not believe in things or people just because *I want to.* I should have good reasons for my beliefs, except, of course, where it makes sense to have pure preferences. It does make sense to prefer butterscotch to chocolate pudding, but it does not make sense to prefer taking advantage of someone rather than respecting his rights. Over time, students need to distinguish fact, opinion, and reasoned judgment, since they will never be good thinkers if they commonly confuse them, as most students now do. (See the section on Text Treatment of Critical Thinking in "Thinking Critically about Teaching: From Didactic to Critical Teaching.")

In passing, be sure not to confuse this distinction with that of convergent and divergent questions. Questions of opinion and questions of reasoned judgment are both divergent, but the first does not involve the question of truth or accuracy (because it calls for expression of preference), while the second does (since reasoned judgment can be more or less reasonable, more or less prejudiced, more or less justified).

We have put this distinction into the Global Strategies section of this handbook to underscore its importance as a pervasive emphasis in all instruction. In any event, we should always keep in mind global, as well as more specific, strategies in fostering critical thinking. When we habitually play the role of Socratic questioner, habitually seek opportunities to have students reconstruct and role play the thinking of others, habitually encourage students to develop intellectual virtues, and habitually encourage students to distinguish preference from reasoned judgment, we will discover new possibilities for critical thinking instruction and will develop global insights that help guide us in understanding and applying the strategies illustrated more specifically in the lesson remodels that follow.

> *This is not a "good-boy/bad-boy" approach to thinking, for everyone must think his own way to the ethical insights that underlie becoming a fairminded thinker. We are careful not to judge the content of the student's thinking. Rather, we facilitate a process whereby the student's own insights can be developed.*

All the various strategies explained in the handbook are couched in terms of behaviors. The principles express and describe a variety of behaviors of the 'ideal' critical thinker; they become applications to lessons when teachers canvass their lesson plans to find appropriate places where those behaviors can be fostered. The practice we recommend helps guard against teachers using these strategies as recipes or formulas, since in each case good judgment is required in the application process.

4 Thinking Critically About Teaching: From Didactic to Critical Teaching

John Dewey once asked a class he visited, "What would you find if you dug a hole in the earth?" Getting no response, he repeated the question: again he obtained nothing but silence. The teacher chided Dr. Dewey, "You're asking the wrong question." Turning to the class, she asked, "What is the state of the center of the earth?" The class replied in unison, "Igneous fusion."

To begin to teach critical thinking one must critique present educational practices and the beliefs underlying them and develop a new conception of knowledge and learning. Educators must ask themselves crucial questions about the nature of knowledge, learning, and the human mind. Educators should reflect on their own thought processes, their own experiences of learning, misunderstanding, confusion, and insight. They should recall and analyze their successes and failures when attempting to teach. They should examine the conceptions and assumptions implicit in their educational practices and self-consciously develop their own theories of education through analysis, evaluation, and reconstruction of their understanding of education and what it means to learn.

Most instructional practice in most academic institutions around the world presupposes a didactic theory of knowledge, learning, and literacy, ill-suited to the development of critical minds and persons. After a superficial exposure to reading, writing, and arithmetic, schooling is typically fragmented thereafter into more or less technical domains, each with a large technical vocabulary and an extensive content or propositional base. Students memorize and reiterate domain-specific details. Teachers lecture and drill. Active integration of the students' daily non-academic experiences is rare. Little time is spent stimulating student questions. Students are expected to "receive" the knowledge "given" them. Students are not typically encouraged to doubt what they are told in the classroom or what is written in their texts. Students' personal points of view or philosophies of life are considered largely irrelevant to education. Classrooms with teachers talking and students listening are the rule. Ninety percent of teacher questions require no more thought than recall. Dense and typically speedy coverage of content is typically followed by content-specific testing. Interdisciplinary synthesis is ordinarily viewed as a personal responsibility of the student and is not routinely tested. Technical specialization is considered the natural

41

goal of schooling and is correlated with getting a job. Few multi-logical issues or problems are discussed or assigned and even fewer teachers know how to conduct such discussions or assess student participation in them. Students are rarely expected to engage in dialogical or dialectical reasoning and few teachers are proficient analysts of such reasoning. Knowledge is viewed as verified intra-disciplinary propositions and well-supported intra-disciplinary theories. There is little or no discussion of the nature of prejudice or bias, little or no discussion of metacognition, and little or no discussion of what a disciplined, self-directed mind or self-directed thought requires. The student is expected to develop into a literate, educated person through years of what is essentially content memorization and ritual performance.

The above dominant pattern of academic instruction and learning is based on an uncritical theory of knowledge, learning, and literacy that is coming under increasing critique by theorists and researchers. Those who operate on the didactic theory in their instruction rarely formulate it explicitly. Some would deny that they hold it, even though their practice implies it. In any case, it is with the theory implicit in practice that we are concerned.

To illustrate, consider this letter from a teacher with a Master's degree in physics and mathematics, with 20 years of high school teaching experience in physics:

> After I started teaching, I realized that I had learned physics by rote and that I really did not understand all I knew about physics. My thinking students asked me questions for which I always had the standard textbook answers, but for the first time it made me start thinking for myself, and I realized that these canned answers were not justified by my own thinking and only confused my students who were showing some ability to think for themselves. To achieve my academic goals I had to memorize the thoughts of others, but I had never learned or been encouraged to learn to think for myself.

The extent and nature of "coverage" for most grade levels and subjects implies that bits and pieces of knowledge are easily attained, without any significant consideration of the basis for that knowledge. Speed coverage of content contradicts the notion that it is essential for the student to seriously consider content before accepting it. Most of us have experienced the difference between 'intellectual' or merely verbal 'knowledge' and true understanding — "Aha! So that's what that means!" Most teaching and most texts, designed to achieve the former kind of knowledge rather than the latter, are, in this sense, intellectually unrealistic, and hence foster intellectual arrogance in students, particularly in those who have a retentive memory and can repeat back what they have heard or read. Pretending to know is encouraged. Students rarely grapple with content. Much standardized testing, which frames problems isolated from their real-life contexts and provides directions and hints regarding their correct solution, validates this pretense.

This has led Alan Schoenfeld, for example, to conclude that "most instruction in mathematics is, in a very real sense, deceptive and possibly fraudulent." In "Some Thoughts on Problem-Solving Research and Mathematics Education," (Mathematical Problem Solving: Issues in Research, Frank K. Lester and Joe Garofalo, editors, " 1982 Franklin Institute Press), he cites a number of examples, including the following:

> Much instruction on how to solve worked problems is based on the "key word" algorithm, where the student makes his choice of the appropriate arithmetic operation by looking for syntactic cues in the problem statement. For example, the word 'left' in the problem "John had eight apples. He gave three to Mary. How many does John have left?"...serves to tell the students that subtraction is the appropriate operation to perform. (p.27)

In a widely used elementary text book series, 97 percent of the problems "solved" by the key-word method would yield (serendipitously?) the correct answer.

Students are drilled in the key-word algorithm so well that they will use subtraction, for example, in almost any problem containing the word "left." In the study from which this conclusion was drawn, problems were constructed in which the appropriate operations were addition, multiplication, and division. Each used the word 'left' conspicuously in its statement and a large percentage of the students subtracted. In fact, the situation was so extreme that many students chose to subtract in a problem that began "Mr. Left..." (p. 27)

I taught a problem-solving course for junior and senior mathematics majors at Berkeley in 1976. These students had already seen some remarkably sophisticated mathematics. Linear algebra and differential equations were old hat. Topology, Fourier transforms, and measure theory were familiar to some. I gave them a straightforward theorem from plane geometry (required when I was in the tenth grade). Only two of eight students made any progress on it, some of them by using arc length integrals to measure the circumference of a circle. (Schoenfeld, 1979). Out of the context of normal course work these students could not do elementary mathematics. (pp. 28-29)

In sum, all too often we focus on a narrow collection of well-defined tasks and train students to execute those tasks in a routine, if not algorithmic fashion. Then we test the students on tasks that are very close to the ones they have been taught. If they succeed on those problems we and they congratulate each other on the fact that they have learned some powerful mathematical techniques. In fact, they may be able to use such techniques mechanically while lacking some rudimentary thinking skills. To allow them and ourselves, to believe that they "understand" the mathematics is deceptive and fraudulent. (p. 29)

This approach to learning in math is too often paralleled in the other subject areas. Grammar texts, for example, present skills and distinctions, then drill students in their use. Thus, students, not genuinely understanding the material, do not spontaneously recognize situations calling for the skills and distinctions covered. Such "knowledge" is generally useless to them. They fail to grasp the uses of and reasoning behind the knowledge presented to them.

Most teachers made it through their college classes mainly by "learning the standard textbook answers" and were neither given an opportunity nor encouraged to determine whether what the text or the professor said was "justified by their own thinking."

Predictable results follow. Students, on the whole, do not learn how to work by, or think for, themselves. They do not learn how to gather, analyze, synthesize, and assess information. They do not learn how to recognize and define problems for themselves. They do not learn how to analyze the diverse logic of the questions and problems they face and hence how to adjust their thinking to those problems. They do not learn how to enter sympathetically into the thinking of others, nor how to deal rationally with conflicting points of view. They do not learn to become critical readers, writers, speakers, and listeners. They do not learn to use their native languages clearly, precisely, or persuasively. They do not, therefore, become "literate" in the proper sense of the word. Neither do they gain much in the way of genuine knowledge, since, for the most part, they could not explain the basis for what they believe. They would be hard pressed to explain, for example, which of their beliefs were based on rational assent and which on simple conformity to what they have been told. They have little sense as to how they might critically analyze their own experience or identify national or group bias in their own thinking. They are much more apt to learn on the basis of irrational than rational modes of thought. They lack the traits of mind of a genuinely educated person: intellectual humility, courage, integrity, perseverance, and confidence in reason.

If this is a reasonable characterization of a broad scholastic effect, instruction based on a didactic theory of knowledge, learning, and literacy is the fundamental determining cause. Administrators and teachers need to explicitly grasp the differences that exist between instruction based on two very different sets of assumptions, the first deeply buried in the hearts and minds of most educators, parents, and administrators; the second emerging only now as the research base for a critical theory progressively expands. We express the basic difference as follows: "Knowledge can be 'given' to one who, upon receiving it, knows;" rather than "Knowledge must be created, in a sense, and rediscovered by each knower."

Only if we see the contrast clearly, will we be empowered to move from the former conception to the latter. Now let us set out the two opposing theories systematically in terms of specific contrasting assumptions and practices.

Two Conflicting Theories of Knowledge, Learning, and Literacy: The Didactic and the Critical

The Scholastically Dominant Theory of Knowledge, Learning and Literacy assumes:

1 That the fundamental need of students is to be taught more or less directly *what to think, not *how* to think. (That students will learn *how* to think if only they know *what* to think.) • Thus, students are *given* or told details, definitions, explanation, rules, guidelines, reasons to learn.

2 That knowledge is independent of the thinking that generates, organizes, and applies it. • Thus, students are said to know when they can repeat what has been covered. Students are given the finished products of others' thoughts.

3 That educated, literate people are fundamentally repositories of content analogous to an encyclopedia or a data bank, directly comparing situations in the world with "facts" that they carry about fully formed as a result of an absorptive process. That an educated, literate person is fundamentally a true believer, that is, a possessor of truth, and therefore

The Emerging Critical Theory of Knowledge, Learning, and Literacy assumes:

1 That the fundamental need of students is to be taught *how* not *what* to think. • Thus, significant content would be taught by raising live issues that stimulate students to gather, analyze and assess that content.

2 That all knowledge or "content" is generated, organized, applied, analyzed, synthesized, and assessed by thinking; that gaining knowledge is unintelligible without engagement in such thinking. (It is *not* assumed that one can think without something, some content, to think about.) • Thus, students should be given opportunities to puzzle their way through to knowledge and explore its justification, as part of the process of learning.

3 That an educated, literate person is fundamentally a repository of strategies, principles, concepts, and insights embedded in processes of thought rather than in atomic facts. Experiences analyzed and organized by critical thought, rather than facts picked up one-by-one, characterize the educated person. Much of what is "known" is con-

44

claims much knowledge. • Thus, texts, assignments, lectures, discussions, and tests are detail-oriented, and content-dense.

structed by the thinker *as needed* from context to context, not *prefabricated* in sets of true statements about the world. That an educated literate person is fundamentally a seeker and questioner rather than a true believer, therefore cautious in claiming knowledge. • Thus, classroom activities should consist of questions and problems for students to discuss and discover how to solve. Teachers should model insightful consideration of questions and problems, and facilitate fruitful discussions.

4 That knowledge, truth, and understanding can be transmitted from one person to another by verbal statements in the form of lectures or didactic writing. • Thus, for example, social studies texts present principles of geography and historical explanations. Questions at the end of the chapter are framed in identical language and can be answered by repeating the texts. "The correct answer" is in bold type or otherwise emphasized.

4 That knowledge and truth can rarely, and insight never, be transmitted from one person to another by the transmitter's verbal statements alone. That one person cannot directly give another what he has learned; one can only facilitate the conditions under which people learn for themselves by figuring out or thinking things through. • Thus, students offer their own ideas, and explore ideas given in the texts, providing their own examples and reasons. Students come to conclusions by practicing reasoning historically, geographically, scientifically, etc.

5 That students do not need to be taught skills of listening in order to learn from others; they only need to learn to pay attention, which requires self-discipline or will power. Students should therefore be able to do so on command by the teacher. • Thus, students are told to listen carefully and are tested on their abilities to remember and to follow directions.

5 That students need to be taught how to listen critically, an active and skilled process that can be learned by degrees with various levels of proficiency. Learning what others mean by what they say requires questioning, trying on, testing; hence, engaging in public or private debates with them. • Thus, teachers would continually model active critical listening, asking probing and insightful questions of the speaker.

6 That the basic skills of reading and writing can be taught without emphasis on higher-order critical thinking skills. • Thus, reading texts provide comprehension questions requiring recall of random details. Occasionally, "main point," "plot," and "theme" lessons cover these concepts. Literal comprehension is distinguished from "extras" such as inferring, evaluating, thinking beyond. Only after basic literal comprehension has been established is the deeper meaning probed.

6 That the basic skills of reading and writing are inferential skills that require critical thinking, that students who cannot read and write critically are defective readers and writers, and that critical reading and writing involve dialogical processes in which probing critical questions are raised and answered. (What is the fundamental issue? What reasons, what evidence, is relevant? Is this authority credible? Are these reasons adequate? Is this evidence accurate and sufficient? Does this contradict that? Does this conclusion follow? Should another point of view be considered?) • Thus, teachers should routinely require students to *explain* what they have read, reconstruct the ideas, and evaluate written material. Students should construct and compare interpretations, reasoning their way to the most plausible interpretations.

Discussion moves back and forth between what was said and what it means.

7 That students who have no questions typically are learning well, while students with many questions are experiencing difficulty in learning; that doubt and questioning weaken belief.

7 That students who have no questions typically are not learning, while those who have pointed and specific questions are. Doubt and questioning, by deepening understanding, strengthen belief by putting it on more solid ground. • Thus, teachers can evaluate their teaching by asking themselves: Are my students asking better questions — insightful questions, question which extend and apply what they have learned? ("Is that why...?" Does this mean that ...?" "Then what if ...?)

8 That quiet classes with little student talk are typically reflective of students learning, while classes with much student talk are typically disadvantaged in learning.

8 That quiet classes with little student talk are typically classes with little learning, while student talk, focused on live issues, is a sign of learning (provided students learn dialogical and dialectical skills).

9 That knowledge and truth can typically be learned best by being broken down into elements and the elements into sub-elements, each taught sequentially and atomistically. Knowledge is additive. • Thus, texts provide basic definitions and masses of details, but have little back-and-forth movement between them. They break knowledge into pieces, each of which is is to be mastered one by one: subjects are taught separately. Each aspect is further broken down: each part of speech is covered separately; social studies texts are organized chronologically, geographically, etc.

9 That knowledge and truth are heavily systemic and holistic and can be learned only by continual synthesis, movement back and forth between wholes and parts, tentative graspings of a whole guiding us in understanding its parts, periodic focus on the parts (in relation to each other) shedding light upon the whole, and that the *wholes* that we learn have important relations to other wholes as well as to their own parts and hence need to be frequently canvassed in learning any whole. (This assumption implies that we cannot achieve in-depth learning in any given domain of knowledge unless we grasp its relation to *other* domains of knowledge.) • Thus, education should be organized around issues, problems, and basic concepts which are pursued and explored through all relevant subjects. Teachers should routinely require students to relate knowledge from various fields. Students should compare analogous events or situation, propose examples, apply new concepts to other situations.

10 That people can gain significant knowledge without seeking or valuing it, and hence that education can take place without a significant transformation of values for the learner. • Thus, for example, texts tend to inform students of the importance of studying the subject or topic covered, rather than proving it by showing its immediate usefulness.

10 That people gain only the knowledge that they seek and value. All other learning is superficial and transitory. All genuine education transforms the basic values of the person educated, resulting in persons becoming life long learners and rational persons. • Thus, instruction poses problems meaningful to students, requiring them to use the tools of each academic domain.

11 That understanding the mind and how it functions, its epistemological health and pathology, are not important or necessary parts of learning. To learn the basic subject matter of the schools, one need no focus on such matters, except perhaps with certain disadvantaged learners.

12 That ignorance is a vacuum or simple lack, and that student prejudices, biases, misconceptions, and ignorance are automatically replaced by the knowledge given them. • Thus, little if any attention is given to students' beliefs. Material is presented from the point of view of the authority, the one who knows.

13 That students need not understand the rational ground or deeper logic of what they learn in order to absorb knowledge. Extensive but superficial learning can later be deepened. • Thus, for example historical and scientific explanations are presented to students as givens, not as having been reasoned to. In language arts, skills and distinctions are rarely explicitly linked to such basic ideas of 'good writing' or 'clear expression.'

14 That it is more important to cover a great deal of knowledge or information superficially than a small amount in depth. That only after the facts are understood, can students discuss their meaning; that higher order thinking can and should only be practiced by students who have mastered the material. That thought-provoking discussions are for the gifted and advanced, only.

15 That the roles of teacher and learner are distinct and should not be blurred.

11 That understanding the mind and how it functions, its health and pathology, are important, are necessary parts of learning. To learn the basic subject matter of the schools in depth requires that we see how we as thinkers and learners process that subject matter.

12 That prejudices, biases, and misconceptions are built up through actively constructed inferences embedded in experience and must be broken down through a similar process; hence, that students must reason their way out of them. • Thus, students need many opportunities to express their views, however biased and prejudiced, in a non-threatening environment to argue their way out of their internalized misconceptions. Teachers should cultivate in themselves a genuine curiosity about how students look at things, why they think as they do, and the structure of students' thought. The educational process starts where the students are, and walks them through to insight.

13 That rational assent is essential for all genuine learning; that an in-depth understanding of basic concepts and principles is essential for rational assent to non-foundational concepts and facts. That in-depth understanding of root concepts and principles should organize learning within and across subject matter domains. • Thus, students are encouraged to discover how the details relate to basic concepts. Details are traced back to the foundational purposes, concepts, and insights.

14 That it is more important to cover a small amount of knowledge or information in-depth (deeply probing its foundation, meaning, and worth) than a great deal of knowledge superficially. That the "slowest," as well as the brighter, students can and must probe the significance and justification of what they learn.

15 That we learn best by teaching or explaining to others what we know; likewise students need many opportunities to teach what they know and formulate their understandings in different ways, and to respond to diverse questions from other learners.

16 That the teacher should correct the learners' ignorance by telling them what they don't know and correcting their mistakes.

16 That students need to learn to distinguish for themselves what they know from what they don't know. Students should recognize that they do not genuinely know or comprehend what they have merely memorized. Self-directed learning requires recognition of ignorance. • Thus, teachers respond to mistakes and confusion by probing with questions, allowing students to correct themselves and each other. Teachers routinely allow students the opportunity to supply their own ideas on a subject before reading their texts.

17 That the teacher has the fundamental responsibility for student learning. • Thus, teachers and texts provide knowledge, questions, and practice.

17 That students should have increasing responsibility for their own learning. Students should see that only they can learn for themselves and actively and willingly engage themselves in the process. • Thus, the teacher provides opportunities for students to decide what they need to know and helps them develop strategies for finding and figuring out.

18 That students will automatically transfer what they learn in didactically taught courses to relevant real-life situations. • Thus, for example, students are told to perform a given skill on a given group of items. The text will *tell* students when, how, and why to use that skill.

18 That most of what students memorize in didactically taught courses is either forgotten or inert, and that the most significant transfer requires in-depth learning which focuses on experiences meaningful to the student.

19 That the personal experience of the student has no essential role to play in education.

19 That the personal experience of the student is essential to all schooling at all levels and in all subjects, that it is a crucial part of the content to be processed (applied, analyzed, synthesized, and assessed) by the students.

20 That students who can correctly answer questions, provide definitions, and apply formulae while taking tests have proven their knowledge or understanding of those details. Since the didactic approach tends to assume, for example, that knowing a word is knowing its definition (and an example), didactic instruction tends to overemphasize definitions. By merely supplementing definitions with assignments that say "Which of these twelve items are X?", students do not come to see the usefulness of the concept and fail to use it spontaneously when appropriate.

20 That students can often provide correct answers, repeat definitions, and apply formulae while yet not understanding those questions, definitions, or formulae. That proof of knowledge and understanding are found in the students' ability to explain in their own words, with examples, the meaning and significance of the knowledge, why it is so, to *spontaneously* use it when appropriate.

21 That learning is essentially a private monological process in which learners can proceed more or less directly to established truth, under the guidance of an

21 That learning is essentially a public, communal dialogical and dialectical process in which learners can only proceed indirectly to truth, with much zigging and zagging, back-in such truth. The authoritative answers that teachers have are the fundamental standards for assessing students' learning.

tracking, misconception, self-contradiction, and frustration along the way. Not authoritative answers, but authoritative standards are the criteria for engagement in the communal, dialogical process of enquiry.

Common Problems with Texts

One crucial aspect of remodelling remains to be discussed: that of choosing which lessons to remodel. It is our view, after examining hundreds of Middle School and Junior High School lesson plans, that many of them ought to be abandoned rather than remodelled. Many of them are exercises in what might be called "trivial pursuit," wherein the student is presented with or led to discover random facts and esoteric vocabulary. The object behind many 6th-9th-grade lesson plans seems to be to expose students to a wide variety of unassessed "facts," on the assumption that, since this constitutes new information for them, it is good in itself.

We, however, feel that school time is too precious to spend any sizeable portion of it on random facts. The world, after all, is filled with an infinite number of facts. No one can learn more than an infinitesimal portion of them. Random fact-collecting is therefore pointless. True, we need facts and information, but there is no reason why we cannot gain facts as part of the process of learning how to think, as part of broader cognitive-affective objectives. Problem-solving or exploring basic ideas or issues are effective ways to find and use facts and to discover why facts interest us in the first place. We ought not to overburden students' minds with facts that they cannot put to use in their thinking. If we don't apprehend the relevance and significance of facts, we tend to forget them rather quickly. We encourage the reader therefore to develop a skeptical eye for lesson plans that fall into the category of trivial pursuit or "fact-for fact's sake." Keep a wastebasket handy.

Often, though the lesson as a whole covers significant material, parts of it are trivial. The student's text provides insignificant details, the teacher's edition suggests trivial activities, which interrupts discussion of significant ideas. As a rule, texts fail to properly distinguish the trivial from the significant. Useless details receive equal time to basic concepts. End-of-chapter review questions especially confuse major with minor points. Structuring instruction around basic ideas and issues highlights crucial details.

Beyond the lessons and activities that need to be abandoned for their triviality, there are also lesson plans and activities that drill students — reading or filling out graphs, timelines, and charts, generalizing, categorizing, researching, experimenting, problem-solving. Such lessons turn skills of thought and crucial insights into mechanical procedures. Students practice the skills for practice itself, seldom in a context in which the skill aids understanding; thus, students fail to learn when to apply this or that procedure and so need to be told when to use it. The application of the skill is often merely memorized (and so easily forgotten), rather than understood. Students look for "indicator words," or verbal cues, rather than recognizing the logic of situations requiring use of the skill. Thus they can use the skill *on request*, that is, when given directions to do so, rather than learning to recognize contexts in which the skill is needed. Students read maps, charts, graphs, etc., at the most basic level, rattling off facts, but they do not discuss the meaning, significance, or implications of what they find. They copy charts and graphs, or formats for them, fill in graphs and timelines, but do not then use them as helpful displays. The purposes, contexts within which skills are needed and reasons for applying them certain ways, should be discussed or discovered by students. Students should interpret the details they find, and explore their implications or significance.

This integration should be viewed, not as slowing down, but as deepening the understanding of the material. We should view the critical thinking that students practice as providing them with powerful concepts which they can use in a host of circumstances thereafter, and laying the foundation for the "I-can-figure-things-out-for-myself" attitude essential for education. Standard practice and testing methods, whenever possible, should be replaced with tasks and problems which require skills, insights, and information, presented to students with minimal direction given beforehand and minimal guidance given only when students are hopelessly bogged down.

Standard Treatment of Critical Thinking, Reasoning, and Argumentation

Finally, we recommend that the teacher keep an eye out for texts, questions, and activities that claim to emphasize or teach critical thinking, logic, reasoning, or argumentation. Often what is taught, or the way it is taught discourages clear and fairminded thought.

Texts generally lack an integrated theory of critical thinking or the critical person. Lessons fail to clarify the relationship of specific critical skills and insights to the idea of the critical thinker. Critical thinking should not be conceived merely as a set of discrete skills and ideas, but should be unified and grounded in a consistent, complete, and accurate theory of thought and reason, to the practical problem of deciding what to believe, question, or reject, the distinction between the reasonable and the unreasonable person. Particular distinctions and insights should be connected to that theory, specific skills placed within it. A unified conception of reasoning includes a unified conception of poor reasoning. Thus, each flaw in reasoning should be understood in terms of the underlying principles of good reasoning such as consistency, completeness, clarity, relevance, as well as being tied into a well developed conception of why we reason poorly and are influenced by poor reasoning.

The following problems are among the most common:

• Instruction in critical thinking should be integrated into the rest of the subjects whenever useful, rather than appear occasionally in separate lessons. Instead of consistently using such terms as conclusion, inference, interpretation, reasons whenever they apply, texts often restrict their use to too narrow contexts. Aspects of critical thinking are generally tacked on — taught in separate lessons and taught as drill, rather than brought in whenever relevant or taught in context. Lacking a complete and explicit theory of reasoning and the rational person, text writers limit the use of critical skills and insights, failing to bring them in when interpretation, exploration, organization, analysis, synthesis, or evaluation are discussed or most needed.

• Some texts give checklists for evaluating reasoning. They rarely mention looking at the argument as a whole and evaluating it as a whole. Students are asked to spot strengths and weaknesses in arguments but are given little guidance in figuring out how the points add up. Critical thinking lessons in texts have an overall lack of context when discussing arguments or conclusions. They use snippets rather than complete arguments, and ignore the larger context of the issue itself. Texts often seem to assume that students' final conclusions can be based solely on the analysis and evaluation of one piece of writing. Critical insight should lead to clearer and richer understanding, more rationally informed beliefs about the issue — not merely a critique of a particular argument.

• A common misconception found in texts is the problem of vagueness. Texts typically misunderstand the nature of the problem. Usually texts mistakenly claim that some words are "vague" because "people have their own definitions." The cure is to provide your definition. We, on the other hand, claim that words themselves are not vague. Claims are vague (in some contexts). A particular word or phrase within a vague claim may be the culprit requiring clarification *in the context of that issue* — the word itself is not vague in and of itself (nor are the words making up the phrase) but only in some contexts. Definitions, since worded abstractly, rarely usefully clarify a word used vaguely. We recommend discussions like those mentioned in the strategy "clarifying and analyzing the meanings of words or phrases."

• Many texts emphasize micro-skills. Yet they seldom attempt to teach critical vocabulary to students. Perhaps this is fortunate, since they often misuse the vocabulary of critical thinking or logic. Many texts use the words 'infer' or 'conclude' when requiring students to recall, describe, or guess. Micro-skills (like many other skills) are treated as things in themselves, rather than as tools which assist understanding. Many texts drill micro-skills but fail to mention or have students apply them when they are most useful. Instead, "analysis of arguments" too often consists of "separating fact from opinion," rather than clarifying or evaluating arguments.

• Teachers' notes often suggest debates. Yet traditional debate, with its emphasis on winning and lack of emphasis on rationality or fairminded understanding of the opposition, with its formal structure and artificial limits, rarely provides for the serious, honest, fairminded analysis and evaluation of ideas and arguments we want to foster. If afterward students merely vote on the issue, they need not rationally evaluate the views or justify their evaluations. Ultimately, such activities may encourage treatment of questions calling for reasoned judgment as questions of preference. Of course, the form of debate can be useful if students are required to sympathetically consider both sides of an issue and not just defend their side, and assess arguments for their rational persuasiveness rather than mere cleverness.

• Many texts tend to simply ask students to agree or disagree with conclusions. They fail to require that students show they understand or have rationally evaluated what they agree or disagree with. Discussion is limited. Micro-skills are rarely practiced or orchestrated in these contexts which most require them. Argument evaluation is further oversimplified, since only two choices are presented: agreement or disagreement. Students are not asked "To what extent do you agree with this claim, or with what aspect of it?"

"Fact/Opinion," "Emotive Language," Value, and Bias

By far, the most all-pervasive, confused, and distorted ideas about critical thinking are found in the manner in which students are encouraged to "distinguish fact from opinion," and in the treatment of "emotive language," values, and bias. Texts generally set up or presuppose a false dichotomy with facts, rationality, and critical thinking on one side and values, emotions, opinions, bias, and irrationality on the other.

Texts give one or more of the following explanations of the "fact/opinion distinction": Facts are true; can be proven; are the most reliable source of information. Opinions are what someone thinks is true; are not necessarily true for everyone; are disputed; are judgments. Opinions are not necessarily either right or wrong. Often opinion is treated as equivalent to bias; *any* writing which expresses opinion, feeling, or judgment is biased.

Among our criticisms of the uses of the fact/opinion distinction are the following: 1) Students are often asked to judge the truth of claims they are not in a position to know; 2) the way the distinction is drawn in examples and exercises promotes uncritical thought, for example, the distinction often unhelpfully lumps together significantly different types of claims; 3) often neither category is presented so as to allow for rational assessment. (Facts are presented as true, and therefore need no debate; opinions are just opinions, so there is no "truth of the matter." Texts generally speak of exchanging opinions, but rarely of assessing them.)

When asked to make this distinction, students are typically given two or more statements. They are asked to read them and determine into which of the two categories each fits. Since the statements lack context, their truth or *reasonableness* typically cannot be rationally judged. Hence, as a rule, students are forced to make their judgments on superficial bases. In place of some reasoned assessment, students are given "indicators of fact." For example, statements judged to be facts are those which contain numbers or statements about observations or statements in "neutral" language. Statements judged to be opinions are those which contain such expressions as: 'I think,' 'good,' 'worst,' 'should,' 'I like,' or any evaluative term.

Since facts are defined as true, in effect, texts typically teach students to accept any statement with numbers, descriptions, etc., in it. Fact/opinion exercises typically teach students that every statement that "sounds like a fact" is *true* and *should be accepted.* Claims which seem factual are not open to question. Students are often not in a position to know whether or not the claim is true, but, since they need only look at the form of the statement and not its content, they can "get the right answers" to the exercises.

Students are often told that history is fact. (The evaluations and interpretations that appear in students' history books are forgotten.) Thus, if they read that a certain condition caused an historical event, they are in effect encouraged to believe it is fact and therefore true. But causes of historical events must be reasoned to. They are not written on the events for all to see. The interpretation inextricably part of any historical account is ignored.

This "distinction" has no single, clear purpose. Sometimes text writers seem to intend to teach students to distinguish acceptable from questionable claims, and at other times, statements which are empirically verifiable from those which are not (that is, whether evidence or observation alone verify the claim). In effect, many texts confuse these two distinctions by shifting from one to the other. Given the way texts usually teach the distinction, the claim, "I think there are four chairs in that room," would be categorized as opinion, since it begins with 'I think,' (an opinion indicator) and, since the speaker is unsure, the claim cannot be counted as true. Yet, by the second sense of the distinction, the claim is factual in a sense — that is, we need only look in the room to verify it. It requires no interpretation, analysis, evaluation, judgment; it expresses no preference.

Texts virtually never address claims that are certainly true, but are not empirical, for example: "Murder is wrong." or "A diet of potato chips and ice cream is bad for you." Students following the "indicator word" method of drawing the distinction, are forced to call these claims opinion. They are then forced to say that, although they agree with them, they may not be true for everybody; the opposite opinion is just as valid; no objective support can be marshalled for them or objective criteria or standards used to evaluate them. Students who look at the contents of the claims would call them "facts," because they are unquestionably true. These students would miss the distinction between these claims and claims that can be tested by experiment or observation.

The distinction is often drawn in such other guises as the distinction between accurate and biased or slanted accounts, news and editorials, history and historical fiction, knowledge or information and belief or value. Thus, on the criterion above, a passage, selection, article or book which contains nothing but "facts" could not possibly be biased or untrustworthy. Yet a "purely factual" account could well be biased. What the writer claims as facts could simply be false, or without basis — that is, I could simply say it, without verifying it. (When I claim that there are four chairs in that room, I may have pulled that number out of the sky.) Crucial facts which could influence one's interpretation of the facts could have been left out. Interpretations or inferences can be implied.

The distinction as typically covered lumps together too many completely different kinds of statements. Among the opinions we found were the following: "I detest that TV show." "Youth is not just a time, it is an age." "Jon is my best student." "Most children in Gail's class do not like her." Thus, expressions of preference, evocative statements, evaluations, and descriptions of people's attitudes are put in the same category, given the same status.

Many of the distinctions covered in a confused way might be covered so as to foster critical thinking. Unfortunately, as texts are presently written, this end is seldom achieved. We recommend that students distinguish acceptable from questionable claims and evidence from interpretation, and that the teacher use the applications such as those given in the strategy "clarifying issues, conclusions, or beliefs."

Texts often seem to assume that evaluation and emotion are antithetical to reason, always irrational or arational; that all beliefs, except belief in facts, are irrational, arational or mere whim. Values (like emotions) are "just there." They cannot be analyzed, clarified, assessed, or restructured. Judging another's opinions amounts to checking them against your own, rather than open-mindedly considering their support. Evaluative terms are often described as "emotive language" and are linked to the concepts of opinion and bias. Students are cautioned to look out for such terms and not allow their beliefs to be influenced by them. We recommend these points be replaced with the more pertinent distinction of rationally justified use of evaluative terms from unjustified, or supported from unsupported use of evaluative language, and that students analyze and assess values and discuss standards or criteria. Students can then share their views regarding the status of such claims and the significance of their disagreements. Students should be encouraged, not to abandon evaluative language, but to use it appropriately, when its use is justified; not to discount it, but to evaluate it. They should learn to analyze terms and determine what kinds of facts are required to back them up; set reasonable standards and apply them fairmindedly.

Texts are right about distinguishing when someone tries to influence belief from other kinds of writing and speech (as a basic distinction of critical thinking), but then they fall. They lump together what we would next separate: attempts to persuade, convince, or influence *by reason*, from other attempts to influence (such as by force, repetition, or obviously irrelevant association). Not all appeals to emotion are equivalent; they can be relevant or irrelevant, well-supported or unsupported.

According to texts, bias consists in a writer or speaker expressing a feeling on a topic. However developed the explanations of bias, however, students practice invariably consists of examining single sentences and underlining words that show bias, that is, "emotive" or evaluative words. Students do not evaluate passages for bias. Students do not distinguish contexts in which writers' conclusions and evaluations are appropriately expressed from when they are not, or when the feelings or opinions have rational grounds from when they reflect mere whim, impression, or prejudice, or when evaluations are supported from when they are merely asserted. Nor do students discuss *how* they should take bias into consideration — for example, by considering other views. The practical effect of the standard approach is to teach students to notice when someone uses evaluative terms, and then measure that use against their own beliefs. We suggest that instead, students consider questions like the following: What is wrong with bias? Why? How can I detect it? How does that fit in with the ideal of the fairminded critical thinker? What should I do when I realize the author is biased? What does the text mean by warning me against being "unduly influenced" by bias?

> *Everyone learning to deepen her critical thinking skills and dispositions comes to insights over time. We certainly can enrich and enhance this process, even help it to move at a faster pace, but only in a qualified way. Time to assimilate and grow is essential.*

Strategies

Introduction

Each strategy section has three parts. The "principle" provides the theory of critical thinking on which the strategy is based and links the strategy to the ideal of the fairminded critical thinker. The "application" provides examples of when and how the strategy can be used. Our lists of possible questions are often larger and more detailed here than in the remodels. Each strategy description concludes with a list of lesson plans in which we use the strategy.

The reader should keep in mind the connection between the principles and applications, on the one hand, and the character traits of a fairminded critical thinker, on the other. Our aim, once again, is not a set of disjointed skills, but an integrated, committed, thinking person. The strategies and remodels should be used to illuminate each other. If puzzled by a remodel (ours or your own), see the strategies. If puzzled by a strategy, see the originals and our critiques and remodels for clarification.

The strategies listed below are divided into three categories — one for the affective and two for the cognitive. This of course is not to imply that the cognitive dimension of critical thinking should be given twice as much emphasis. Indeed, the affective dimension is every bit as important to critical thinking. No one learns to think critically who is not motivated to do so. In any case, whatever dimension is emphasized, the other dimension should be integrated. We want students to continually use their emerging critical thinking skills and abilities in keeping with the critical spirit, and the critical spirit can be nurtured only when actually practicing critical thinking in some (cognitive) way. One cannot develop one's fairmindedness, for example, without actually thinking fairmindedly. One cannot develop one's intellectual independence without actually thinking independently. This is true of all the essential critical thinking traits, values, or dispositions. They are developmentally embedded in thinking itself. In teaching for critical thinking in a strong sense, the affective dimension of thinking is fully as important as the cognitive.

Furthermore, just as the cognitive and affective dimensions are interdependent and intertwined, so also are the various individual strategies. For purposes of learning, we articulate separate principles and applications. In the beginning, the connections between them may be obscure.

Nevertheless, eventually we begin to discover how progress with any one principle leads inevitably to other principles. To see this let us look first at the individual strategies in the affective dimension.

The Interdependence of Traits of Mind

Affective strategies are interdependent because the intellectual traits they imply develop best in concert with each other. Consider intellectual humility. To become aware of the limits of our knowledge, we need the courage to face our own prejudices and ignorance. To discover our own prejudices in turn, we often must empathize with and reason within points of view toward which we are hostile. To achieve this end, we must typically persevere over a period of time, for learning to empathically enter a point of view against which we are biased takes time and significant effort. That effort will not seem justified unless we have the confidence in reason to believe we will not be "tainted" or "taken in" by whatever is false or misleading in the opposing viewpoint. Furthermore, merely believing we can survive serious consideration of an "alien" point of view is not enough to motivate most of us to consider them seriously. We must also be motivated by an intellectual sense of justice. We must recognize an intellectual responsibility to be fair to views we oppose. We must feel obliged to hear them in their strongest form to ensure that we are not condemning them out of ignorance or bias on our part. At this point, we come full circle back to where we began: the need for intellectual humility.

Or, to begin at another point, consider intellectual good faith or integrity. Intellectual integrity is clearly a difficult trait to develop. We are often motivated, generally, of course without admitting to or being aware of this motivation, to set up inconsistent intellectual standards. Our egocentric or sociocentric tendencies make us ready to believe positive information about those we like, and negative information about those we dislike. We are likewise strongly inclined to believe what serves to justify our vested interest or validate our strongest desires. Hence, all humans have some innate mental tendencies to operate with double standards, which of course is paradigmatic of intellectual bad faith. Such modes of thinking often correlate quite well with getting ahead in the world, maximizing our power or advantage, and getting more of what we want.

Nevertheless, it is difficult to operate explicitly or overtly with a double standard. We therefore need to avoid looking at the evidence too closely. We need to avoid scrutinizing our own inferences and interpretations too carefully. At this point, a certain amount of intellectual arrogance is quite useful. I may assume, for example, that I know just what you're going to say (before you say it), precisely what you are really after (before the evidence demonstrates it), and what actually is going on (before I have studied the situation quite carefully). My intellectual arrogance may make it easier for me to avoid noticing the unjustifiable discrepancy between the standards I apply to you and the standards I apply to myself. Of course, if I don't have to empathize with you, that too makes it easier to avoid seeing my duplicity. I am also better positioned if I lack a keen need to be fair to your point of view. A little background fear of what I might discover if I seriously considered the consistency of my own judgments can be quite useful as well. In this case, my lack of intellectual integrity is supported by my lack of intellectual humility, empathy, and fairmindedness.

Going in the other direction, it will be difficult to use a double standard if I feel a responsibility to be fair to your point of view, see that this responsibility requires me to view things from your perspective empathically, and do so with some humility, recognizing I could be wrong, and you right. The more I dislike you personally, or feel wronged in the past by you or by others who share your way of thinking, the more pronounced in my character the trait of intellectual integrity and good faith must be to compel me to be fair.

Distinguishing Macro-Abilities From Micro-Skills

Our reason for dividing cognitive strategies into macro-abilities and micro-skills is not to create a hard and fast line between the most elementary skills of critical thinking (the micro-skills) and the process of orchestrating those elementary skills, but rather to provide teachers with a way of thinking about two levels of learning. We use these two levels in most complex abilities. For intuitive examples, consider what is involved in learning to play the piano, learning to play good tennis, mastering ballet, or becoming a surgeon. In each of these areas, there is a level of skill learning which focuses on the most elementary of moves. For example, learning to practice the most elementary ballet positions at the bar, learning to play scales on the piano, or learning to hit various tennis strokes on the backboard. One must often return to this micro-level to ensure that one keeps the fundamentals well in hand. Nevertheless, dancing ballet is not practicing at the bar. Playing the piano is not simply playing scales. And hitting tennis balls against a backboard is not playing tennis. One must move to the macro level for the real thing. So, too, in critical thinking. Students have to learn the fundamentals: What an assumption is, what an implication is, what an inference and conclusion are, what it is to isolate an issue, what it is to offer reasons or evidence in support of what one says, how to identify a contradiction or a vague sentence.

But thinking critically in any actual situation is typically doing something more complex and holistic than this. Rarely in thinking critically do we do just one elementary thing. Usually we have to integrate or make use of a variety of elementary critical thinking skills. For example, when we are reading (a macro-ability) we have to make use of a variety of critical thinking micro-skills, and we have to use them in concert with each other. We might begin by reflecting on the implications of a story or book title. We might then begin to read the preface or introduction and start to identify some of the basic issues or objectives the book or story is focused on. As we proceed along, we might begin to identify particular sentences that seem vague to us. We might consider various interpretations of them. As we move along, we would doubtless dip into our own experience for possible examples of what the author is saying. Or we might begin to notice assumptions the author is making. We would be making all of these individual moves as part of one integrated activity: the attempt to make sense of, to follow, what we are reading. As always, the whole is greater than and more important than the parts. We read not to practice our critical thinking micro-skills. We use our critical thinking micro-skills in order to read, or better, in order to read clearly, precisely, and accurately. Keep this principle of interdependence in mind as you read through the various strategies.

35 Dimensions of Critical Thought

A.   Affective Strategies

S-1   thinking independently

S-2   developing insight into egocentricity or sociocentricity

-3   exercising fairmindedness

S 4   exploring thoughts underlying feelings and feelings underlying thoughts

S-5   developing intellectual humility and suspending judgment

S-6   developing intellectual courage

S-7   developing intellectual good faith or integrity

S-8   developing intellectual perseverance

S-9   developing confidence in reason

B.   Cognitive Strategies — Macro-Abilities

S-10   refining generalizations and avoiding oversimplifications

S-11   comparing analogous situations: transferring insights to new contexts

S-12   developing one's perspective: creating or exploring beliefs, arguments, or theories

S-13   clarifying issues, conclusions, or beliefs

S-14   clarifying and analyzing the meanings of words or phrases

S-15   developing criteria for evaluation: clarifying values and standards

S-16   evaluating the credibility of sources of information

S-17   questioning deeply: raising and pursuing root or significant questions

S-18   analyzing or evaluating arguments, interpretations, beliefs, or theories

S-19   generating or assessing solutions

S-20   analyzing or evaluating actions or policies

S-21   reading critically: clarifying or critiquing texts

S-22   listening critically: the art of silent dialogue

S-23   making interdisciplinary connections

S-24   practicing Socratic discussion: clarifying and questioning beliefs, theories, or perspectives

S-25   reasoning dialogically: comparing perspectives, interpretations, or theories

S-26   reasoning dialectically: evaluating perspectives, interpretations, or theories

C.   Cognitive Strategies — Micro-Skills

S-27   comparing and contrasting ideals with actual practice

S-28   thinking precisely about thinking: using critical vocabulary

S-29   noting significant similarities and differences

S-30   examining or evaluating assumptions

S-31   distinguishing relevant from irrelevant facts

S-32   making plausible inferences, predictions, or interpretations

S-33   evaluating evidence and alleged facts

S-34   recognizing contradictions

S-35   exploring implications and consequences

S-1 Thinking Independently

Principle: Critical thinking is autonomous thinking, thinking for oneself. Many of our beliefs are acquired at an early age, when we have a strong tendency to form beliefs for irrational reasons (because we want to believe, because we are rewarded for believing). Critical thinkers use critical skills and insights to reveal and eradicate beliefs to which they cannot rationally assent. In formulating new beliefs, critical thinkers do not passively accept the beliefs of others; rather, they analyze issues themselves reject unjustified authorities, and recognize the contributions of justified authorities. They thoughtfully form principles of thought and action; they do not mindlessly accept those presented to them. They do not accept as true, or reject as false, beliefs they do not understand. They are not easily manipulated.

Independent thinkers strive to incorporate all known relevant knowledge and insight into their thought and behavior. They strive to determine for themselves when information is relevant, when to apply a concept, or when to make use of a skill.

Application: A critical education respects the autonomy of the student. It appeals to rationality. Students should be encouraged to discover information and use their knowledge, skills and insights to think for themselves. Merely giving students "facts" or telling them the "right way" to solve a problem hinders the process of critiquing and modifying pre-existing beliefs with new knowledge.

Rather than simply having students discuss ideas in their texts, the teacher can have them brainstorm ideas and argue among themselves, for instance, about problems and solutions to problems. Before reading a section of text that refers to a map, chart, time-line, or graph, students could read and discuss what the map, or the rest, shows. Students could develop their own categories instead of being provided with them. "Types of Literature" lessons could be remodelled so that students group and discuss writings they have read, entertaining different ways to classify them.

When giving written assignments, those assignments should provide many opportunities for the student to exercise independent judgment: in gathering and assembling information, in analyzing and synthesizing it, and in formulating and evaluating conclusions. Have students discuss how to organize their points in essays.

In science, students could put their own headings on charts or graphs they make, or decide what kind of graph would be most illuminating.

Students could review material themselves, rather than relying on their texts for summaries and review questions. The teacher could routinely ask students, *"What are the most important points covered in the passage (chapter, story, etc.)?* "as a discussion beginner. The class could brainstorm about what they learned when studying a lesson or unit. Only after they have exhausted their memories should the teacher try to elicit any crucial points neglected.

When discussing specific countries and periods of history, have students look at and discuss political, population distribution, physical, historical, linguistic, and land use maps before reading their texts. They could also discuss trade routes and difficulty or ease of travel, note what other groups or countries are nearby, predict potential areas of conflict, etc. Whenever they are about to use a map, first ask them what kind of map they need, and how and where to find it.

Lesson plans in which the strategy is used

S-2 Developing Insight Into Egocentricity or Sociocentricity

Principle: Egocentricity is the confusion of immediate perception with reality. It manifests itself as an inability or unwillingness to consider others' points of view, to accept ideas or facts which would conflict with gratification of desire. In the extreme, it is characterized by a need to be right about everything, a lack of interest in consistency and clarity, an all or nothing attitude ("I am 100% right; you are 100% wrong."), and a lack of self-consciousness of one's own thought processes. The egocentric individual is more concerned with the appearance of truth, fairness, and fairmindedness, than with actually being correct, fair, or fairminded. Egocentricity is the opposite of critical thought.

As people are socialized, egocentricity tends to produce sociocentricity. Egocentric identification extends to groups. The individual goes from *"I* am right!" to *"We* are right!" To put this another way, people find that they can often best satisfy their egocentric desires through a group. 'Group think' results when people egocentrically attach themselves to a group. One can see this in both children and adults: My daddy is better than your daddy! My school (religion, country, race, etc.) is better than yours.

If egocentricity and sociocentricity are the disease, self-awareness is the cure. In cases in which their own egocentric commitments are not supported, few people accept another's egocentric reasoning. Most can identify the sociocentricity of members of opposing groups. Yet when we are thinking egocentrically or sociocentrically, it seems right to us (at least at the time). Our belief in our own rightness is easier to maintain because we suppress the faults in our thinking. We automatically hide our egocentricity from ourselves. We fail to notice when our behavior contradicts our self-image. We base our reasoning on false assumptions we are unaware of making. We fail to make relevant distinctions, though we are otherwise aware of, and able to make them (when making such distinctions does not prevent us from getting what we want). We deny or conveniently 'forget' facts inconsistent with our conclusions. We often misunderstand or distort what others say.

The solution, then, is to reflect on our reasoning and behavior; to make our assumptions explicit, critique them, and, when they are false, stop making them; to apply the same concepts in the same ways to ourselves and others; to consider every relevant fact, and to make our conclusions consistent with the evidence; and to listen carefully and open-mindedly to those with whom we disagree. We can change egocentric tendencies when we see them for what they are: irrational and unjust. Therefore, the development of students' awareness of their egocentric and sociocentric patterns of thought is a crucial part of education in critical thinking.

Application: Although everyone has egocentric, sociocentric, and critical (or fairminded) tendencies to some extent, the purpose of education in critical thinking is to help students move away from egocentricity and sociocentricity, toward increasingly critical thought. Texts usually neglect obstacles to rationality, content to point out or have students point out irrationality and injustice. We recommend that students repeatedly discuss *why* people think irrationally and act unfairly.

The teacher can facilitate discussions of egocentric or sociocentric thought and behavior whenever such discussions seem relevant. Such discussions can be used as a basis for having students think about their own egocentric or sociocentric tendencies. The class can discuss conditions under which people are most likely to be egocentric and how egocentricity interferes with our ability to think and listen. Students should be encouraged to recognize common patterns of egocentric thought. The class can discuss some of the common false assumptions we all make at times (e.g., "Anyone who disapproves of anything I do is wrong or unfair. I have a right to have everything I want. Truth is what I want it to be.") Teachers can also have students point out the contradictions of egocentric attitudes. ("When I use something of yours without permission, it is 'borrowing'; when you use something of mine, it is 'stealing.' Taking something without asking is O.K. Taking something without asking is wrong.") Sometimes story characters illustrate egocentricity.

The most real and immediate form of sociocentricity students experience is in the mini-society of their peers. Student attitudes present a microcosm of the patterns which exist on a larger scale in societies. All of your students share some attitudes which are sociocentric. Furthermore, students divide themselves into "subcultures" or cliques, each of which is narrower than the school-wide "culture." Honest and realistic exploration of these phenomena allows students to clarify and evaluate the ways in which "group think" limits them.

Often texts attempt to discourage sociocentricity by encouraging tolerance — asking students to agree that people whose ways are different are not necessarily wrong. Yet, by keeping discussion general and not introducing specific advantages of different ways, students are left with a vague sense that they should be tolerant, rather than a clear sense that others have ways worth knowing about and learning from.

Some texts inadvertently foster sociocentricity by presenting only the American side of issues or presenting some groups in a distinctly negative light. The teacher could encourage students to recognize sociocentric bias, reconstruct and consider other views of current and historical issues, and discuss how to avoid thinking sociocentrically.

Texts include many subtle forms of sociocentricity, displaying a narrowly European or American perspective in word choice. For example, societies are described as "isolated" rather than "isolated from contact with Europeans."

Before beginning study of another culture, the teacher could elicit students' ideas of that group, including stereotypes and misconceptions. Ask, *"What are these people like? What do you think of when you think of them? How have you seen them portrayed in movies and on T.V.?"* After study, students could evaluate these ideas in light of what they have learned.

Lesson plans in which the strategy is used

S-3 Exercising Fairmindedness

Principle: To think critically about issues, we must be able to consider the strengths and weaknesses of opposing points of view; to imaginatively put ourselves in the place of others in order to genuinely understand them; to overcome our egocentric tendency to identify truth with our immediate perceptions or long-standing thought or belief. This trait correlates with the ability to reconstruct accurately the viewpoints and reasoning of others and to reason from premises, assumptions, and ideas other than our own. This trait also correlates with the willingness to remember occasions when we were wrong in the past despite an intense conviction that we were right, as well as the ability to imagine our being similarly deceived in a case at hand. Critical thinkers realize the unfairness of judging unfamiliar ideas until they fully understand them.

The world consists of many societies and peoples with many different points of view and ways of thinking. In order to develop as reasonable persons we need to enter into and think within the frameworks and ideas of different peoples and societies. We cannot truly understand the world if we think about it only from one viewpoint, as Americans, as Italians, or as Russians.

Furthermore, critical thinkers recognize that their behavior affects others, and so consider their behavior from the perspective of those others.

Application: The teacher can encourage students to show reciprocity when disputes arise or when the class is discussing issues, evaluating the reasoning of story characters, or discussing people from other cultures.

When disputes naturally arise in the course of the day, the teacher can ask students to state one another's positions. Students should be given an opportunity to correct any misunderstanding of their positions. The teacher can then ask students to explain why their fellow student might see the issue differently than they do. *"What is Sue angry about? Why does that make her mad? Sue, is that right?"*

Students can be encouraged to consider evidence and reasons for positions they disagree with, as well as those with which they agree. For example, have students *consider positions from their parents' or siblings' points of view. "Why doesn't your mother want you to ...? Why does she think it's bad for you (wrong, etc.)? What does she think will happen?"*

Although texts often have students consider a subject or issue from a second point of view, discussion is brief, rather than extended, and no attempt is made to have students integrate insights gained by considering multiple perspectives. If students write a dialogue about an issue from opposing points of view, or contrast a story character's reasoning with an opposing point of view, or role play discussions, the teacher can have them directly compare and evaluate different perspectives.

When the class is discussing different cultures the teacher can encourage students to consider *why* people choose to do things differently or why other people think their ways are best. For example, ask, *"What would be some advantages to arranged marriages? Why might some people prefer that system to ours? What problems would it solve or lessen?"*

Lesson plans in which the strategy is used

S-4 Exploring Thoughts Underlying Feelings and Feelings Underlying Thoughts

Principle: Although it is common to separate thought and feeling as if they were independent opposing forces in the human mind, the truth is that virtually all human feelings are based on some level of thought and virtually all thought generative of some level of feeling. To think with self-understanding and insight, we must come to terms with the intimate connections between thought and feeling, reason and emotion. Critical thinkers realize that their feelings are their response (but not the only possible, or even necessarily the most reasonable response) to a situation. They know that their feelings would be different if they had a different understanding or interpretation of that situation. They recognize that thoughts and feelings, far from being different kinds of "things," are two aspects of their responses. Uncritical thinkers see little or no relationship between their feelings and their thoughts.

When we feel sad or depressed, it is often because we are interpreting our situation in an overly negative or pessimistic light. We may be forgetting to consider positive aspects of our life. We can better understand our feelings by asking ourselves "How have I come to feel this way? How am I looking at the situation? To what conclusion have I come? What is my evidence? What assumptions am I making? What inferences am I making? Are they sound inferences? Are there other possible ways to interpret this situation?" We can learn to seek patterns in our assumptions, and so begin to see the unity behind our separate emotions. Understanding oneself is the first step toward self-control and self-improvement. This self-understanding requires that we understand our feelings and emotions in relation to our thoughts, ideas, and interpretations of the world.

Application: Whenever a class discusses someone's feelings (e.g., that of a character in a story), the teacher can ask students to consider what the person might be thinking to have that feeling in that situation. *Why does he feel this way? How is he interpreting his situation? What led him to that conclusion? Would you have felt the same if you had been in his circumstances? Why or why not? What accounts for the difference? What could he have thought instead? Then what would he have felt?*

This strategy can be used in the service of developing an intellectual sense of justice and courage. Students can discuss the thoughts underlying passionate commitment to personal or social change. Students can discuss reasons for resistance to change: greed, fear, self-interest, and other negative or hampering feelings.

When discussing a case of mixed feelings, the teacher could ask, *"What was she feeling? What else? (Encourage multiple responses.) What led to this feeling? That one? Are these beliefs consistent or contradictory? How could someone have contradictory responses to one situation?"*

Students can also generalize about thoughts behind various emotions: behind fear, thoughts like — "This is dangerous. I may be harmed;" behind anger, thoughts like — "This is not right, not fair;" behind indifference, thoughts like — "This does not matter;" behind relief, thoughts like — "Things are better now. This problem is gone."

Lesson plans in which the strategy is used

S-5 Developing Intellectual Humility and Suspending Judgment

Principle: Critical thinkers recognize the limits of their knowledge. They are sensitive to circumstances in which their native egocentrism is likely to function self-deceptively; they are sensitive to bias, prejudice, and limitations of their views. Intellectual humility is based on the recognition that one ought not claim more than one actually knows. It does not imply spinelessness or submissiveness. It implies the lack of intellectual pretentiousness, arrogance, or conceit. It implies insight into the foundations of one's beliefs: knowing what evidence one has, how one has come to believe, what further evidence one might examine or seek out.

Thus, critical thinkers distinguish what they know from what they don't know. They are not afraid of saying "I don't know" when they are not in a position to be sure. They can make this distinction because they habitually ask themselves, "How could one know whether or not this is true?" To say "In this case I must suspend judgment until I find out x and y," does not make them anxious or uncomfortable. They are willing to rethink conclusions in the light of new knowledge. They qualify their claims appropriately.

Application: Texts and testing methods inadvertently foster intellectual arrogance. Most text writing says, "Here's the way it is. Here's what we know. Remember this, and you'll know it, too." Behind student learning, there is often little more thought than "It's true because my textbook said it's true." This often generalizes to, "It's true because I read it somewhere."

Teachers can take advantage of any situation in which students are not in a position to know, to encourage the habit of exploring the basis for their beliefs. When materials call on students to make claims for which they have insufficient evidence, we suggest the teacher encourage students to remember what is said in the materials but also to suspend judgment as to its truth. The teacher might first ask for the evidence or reasons for the claim and have students probe its strength. Students can be encouraged to explain what they would need to learn in order to be more certain. You might have students consider how reasonable persons respond to gossip or the news on T.V. They hear what is said, remember what they have heard, but do not automatically believe it.

In exposing students to concepts within a field, we can help students to see how all concepts depend on other, more basic concepts and how each field of knowledge is based on fundamental assumptions which need to be examined, understood, and justified. We can help students to discover experiences in their own lives which help support or justify what a text may be saying. We should always be willing to entertain student doubts about what a text is saying.

We can model intellectual humility by demonstrating a willingness to admit limits in our own knowledge and in human knowledge generally. Routinely qualify statements: "I believe," "I'm pretty sure that," "I doubt," "I suspect," "Perhaps," "I'm told," "It seems," etc. This trait can be encouraged by frequent discussion in which ideas new to the students are explored for evidence and support.

The teacher can have students brainstorm questions they have *after* study. Students could keep question logs during the course of research projects, periodically recording their unanswered questions. Thus, they can come to see that even when they have learned what is expected of them, they do not know all.

Lesson plans in which the strategy is used

S-6 Developing Intellectual Courage

Principle: To think independently and fairly, one must feel the need to face and fairly deal with unpopular ideas, beliefs, or viewpoints. The courage to do so arises from the recognition that ideas considered dangerous or absurd are sometimes rationally justified (in whole or in part) and that conclusions or beliefs inculcated in us are sometimes false or misleading. If we are to determine for ourselves which is which, we must not passively and uncritically accept what we have "learned." We need courage to admit the truth in some ideas considered dangerous and absurd, and the distortion or falsity in some ideas strongly held in our social group. It will take courage to be true to our own thinking, for honestly questioning our deeply held beliefs can be difficult and sometimes frightening, and the penalties for non-conformity are often severe.

Application: Intellectual courage is fostered through a consistently openminded atmosphere. Students should be encouraged to honestly consider or doubt any belief.

Students who disagree with or doubt their peers or text should be given support. The teacher should raise probing questions regarding unpopular ideas which students have hitherto been discouraged from considering. The teacher should model intellectual courage by playing devil's advocate.

Texts often seem to suggest that standing up for one's beliefs is fairly easy; they ignore the difficulty of "doing the right thing." Students could discuss questions like the following: *Why is it hard to go against the crowd? If everyone around you is sure of something, why is it hard to question it or disagree? When is it good to do so? When might you hesitate? When should you hesitate? Is it hard to question your own beliefs? Why? Why does this idea bother you?*

Students who have been habitually praised for uncritically accepting others' claims may feel the rug pulled out from under them for a while when expected to think for themselves. Students should be emotionally supported in these circumstances and encouraged to express the natural hesitancy, discomfort, or anxiety they may experience so they may work their way through their fears. A willingness to consider unpopular beliefs develops by degrees. Teachers should exercise discretion beginning first with mildly unpopular rather than with extremely unpopular beliefs.

Lesson plans in which the strategy is used

S-7 Developing Intellectual Good Faith or Integrity

Principle: Critical thinkers recognize the need to be true to their own thought, to be consistent in the intellectual standards they apply, to hold themselves to the same rigorous standards of evidence and proof to which they hold others, to practice what they advocate for others, and to honestly admit discrepancies and inconsistencies in their own thought and action. They believe most strongly what has been justified by their own thought and analyzed experience. They have a commitment to bringing the self they are and the self they want to be together. People in general are often inconsistent in their application of standards once their ego is involved positively or negatively. When people like us, we tend to over-estimate their positive characteristics; when they dislike us, we tend to underrate them.

Application: Texts often inadvertently encourage the natural split between "school belief" and "real life" belief and between verbal or public belief and belief that guides action. There is an old saying to the effect that "They are good prophets who follow their own teachings." And sometimes parents say, "Do as I say, not as I do." There is often a lack of integrity in human life. Hypocrisy and inconsistency are common. As educators, we need to highlight the difficulties of being consistent in an often inconsistent world.

As teachers, we need to be sensitive to our own inconsistencies in the application of rules and standards, and we need to help students to explore their own. Peer groups often pressure students to judge in-group members less critically than out-group members.

When evaluating or developing criteria for evaluation, have students assess both themselves and others, noting their tendency to favor themselves.

Texts often preach. They unrealistically present goodness and change as easy when it is often not. They ask general and loaded questions ("Do you listen to other views? Is it important to treat others fairly?") to which students are likely to simply respond with a "Yes!" Such questions should be remodelled. For example, ask "When have you found it difficult to listen to others?" or "Why are people often unfair?"

Language Arts texts sometimes have students roundly criticize characters without taking into account the difficulties of living up to worthy ideals. Students should be encouraged to give more realistic assessments: *Would you have done otherwise? Would it have been easy? Why or why not? Why do so few people do this?*

Social studies texts are harsher judges of other societies than of ours. Students should evaluate their texts' consistency in evaluation. The teacher may have to help students to recognize this problem.

Lesson plans in which the strategy is used

S-8 Developing Intellectual Perseverance

Principle: Becoming a more critical thinker is not easy. It takes time and effort. Critical thinkers are willing to pursue intellectual insights and truths in spite of difficulties, obstacles, and frustrations. They recognize the need to struggle with confusion and unsettled questions over an extended period of time in order to achieve deeper understanding and insight. They recognize that significant change requires patience and hard work. Important issues often require extended thought, research, struggle. Considering a new view takes time. Yet people are often impatient to "get on with it" when they most need to slow down and think carefully. People rarely define issues or problems clearly; concepts are often left vague; related issues are not sorted out, etc. Students need to gain insight into the need for intellectual perseverance.

Application: Critical thinking is reflective and recursive; that is, we often go back in our thoughts to previous problems to re-consider or re-analyze them. Intellectual perseverance can be developed by reviewing and discussing the kinds of difficulties that were inherent in previous problems worked on, exploring why it is necessary to struggle with them over an extended period. Studying the work of great inventors or thinkers through biography can also be of use, with students discussing why long-range commitment was necessary. In time, students will see the value in pursuing important ideas at length.

Raise difficult problems again and again over the course of the year. Design long-term projects for which students must persevere. Of course, it is important to work with students on skills of breaking down complex problems into simpler components, so that they will see how to attack problems systematically.

Texts will sometimes say of a problem that it is hard to solve. Divide the class into groups and have them discuss various ways in which the problem could be approached, seeing if they can break the problem down into simple components. It is important to devote considerable time to problem analysis, in order to develop student confidence in their ability to distinguish hard from easy problems and to recognize when a longer term commitment will be necessary. Students will not develop intellectual perseverance unless they develop confidence in their ability to analyze and approach problems with success. You should not overwhelm students with problems so difficult that they have little hope of making progress.

Take a basic idea within a subject ("well-written," "justice," "culture," "life," "matter," etc.). Have students write their ideas on it and discuss them. Every month or so, have them add to, revise, or write another paper. At the end of the year, they can assess the changes in their understanding from repeated consideration over the course of the year, graphically illustrating progress and development achieved through perseverance.

For students to recognize the need for further study of an idea, they need to have some sense of how their present knowledge is limited. Presenting some problems that are beyond their knowledge can be useful if the class can come to see what they would have to learn about to solve them. In this context, students can successfully uncover what they don't know, thereby fostering intellectual humility as well as laying the foundation for intellectual perseverance.

Illustrate how getting answers is not the only form of progress, show them how having better, clearer questions is also progress. Point out progress made. Sympathize with students' natural frustration and discouragement.

Have students discuss the importance of sufficient thought regarding significant decisions and beliefs, and the difficulty of becoming rational and well-educated, fairminded people.

When study and research fail to settle key question, from the inadequacy of available resources, the class could write letters to appropriate faculty of one or two colleges. Have students describe their research and results and pose their unanswered questions.

Lesson plans in which the strategy is used

S-9 Developing Confidence in Reason

Principle: The rational person recognizes the power of reason, the value of disciplining thinking in accordance with rational standards. Virtually all the progress that has been made in science and human knowledge testifies to this power, and so to the reasonability of having *confidence* in reason. To develop this faith is to come to see that ultimately one's own higher interests and those of humankind at large will be served best by giving the freest play to reason, by encouraging people to come to their own conclusions through a process of developing their own rational faculties. It is to believe that, with proper encouragement and cultivation, people can develop the ability to think for themselves, to form reasonable points of view, draw reasonable conclusions, think coherently and logically, persuade each other by reason and, ultimately, become reasonable persons, despite the deep-seated obstacles in the native character of the human mind and in society as we know it. It is to reject force and trickery as standard ways of changing another's mind. This confidence is essential to building a democracy in which people come to genuine rule, rather than being manipulated by the mass media, special interests, or by the inner prejudices, fears, and irrationalities that so easily and commonly tend to dominate human minds.

You should note that the act of faith we are recommending is not to be blind but should be tested in everyday experiences and academic work. In other words, we should have confidence in reason, because reason works. Confidence in reason does not deny the reality of intuition; rather, it provides a way of distinguishing intuition from prejudice.

Application: As a teacher, you can model confidence in reason in many ways. Every time you show your students that you can make rules, assignments, and classroom activities intelligible to them so that they can see that you are doing things for well-thought-out reasons, you help them to understand why confidence in reason is justified. Every time you help them solve a problem with the use of their own thinking or "think aloud" in front of them, you encourage them to develop confidence in reason. Every time you encourage them to *question* the reasons behind rules, activities, and procedures, you help them to recognize that we should expect *reasonability* to be at the foundation of our lives. Every time you display a patient willingness to hear their reasons for their beliefs and actions you encourage confidence in reason. Every time you clarify a standard of good reasoning, helping them to grasp *why* this standard makes sense, you help them to develop confidence in reason.

One reason students have little faith in reason is that they don't see reason being used in their everyday lives. Power, authority, prestige, strength, intimidation, and pressure are often used instead of reason. Students develop a natural cynicism about reason which educators should help them to overcome.

Give students multiple opportunities to try to persuade each other and you. Insist that students who disagree *reason* with each other, rather than using ridicule, intimidation, peer pressure, etc.

Texts often make knowledge acquisition seem mysterious, as though scientists, for example, have some mystical mental powers. Make the reasoning behind what they study clear, and students will feel that knowledge and reason are within their grasp.

Have students compare and contrast the following concepts: intimidate, convince, persuade, trick, brainwash.

Lesson plans in which the strategy is used

S-10 Refining Generalizations and Avoiding Oversimplifications

Principle: It is natural to seek to simplify problems and experiences to make them easier to deal with. Everyone does this. However, the uncritical thinker often oversimplifies, and as a result misrepresents problems and experiences. What should be recognized as complex, intricate, or subtle is viewed as simple, elementary, and obvious. For example, it is typically an oversimplification to view people or groups as *all good* or *all bad*, actions as *always right* or *always wrong*, one contributing factor as *the cause*, etc., and yet such beliefs are common. Critical thinkers try to find simplifying patterns and solutions but not by misrepresentation or distortion. Making a distinction between useful simplifications and misleading oversimplifications is important to critical thinking.

One of the strongest tendencies of the egocentric, uncritical mind is to see things in terms of black and white, "all right" and "all wrong." Hence, beliefs which should be held with varying degrees of certainty are held as certain. Critical thinkers are sensitive to this problem. They understand the relationship of evidence to belief and so qualify their statements accordingly. The tentativeness of many of their beliefs is characterized by the appropriate use of such qualifiers as 'highly likely,' 'probably,' 'not very likely,' 'highly unlikely,' 'often,' 'usually,' 'seldom,' 'I doubt,' 'I suspect,' 'most,' 'many,' and 'some.'

Critical thinkers scrutinize generalizations, probe for possible exceptions, and then use appropriate qualifications. Critical thinkers are not only clear, but also *exact* or *precise*.

Application: Whenever students or texts oversimplify, the teacher can ask questions which raise the problem of complexity. For instance, if a student or text over- generalizes, the teacher can ask for counter-examples. If a text overlooks factors by stating one cause for a problem, situation, or event, the teacher can raise questions about other possible contributing factors. If different things are lumped together, the teacher can call attention to differences. If interconnected or overlapping phenomena are too casually separated, the teacher can probe overlaps or connections. If only one point of view is expressed, though others are relevant, the teacher can play devil's advocate, bringing in other points of view. Texts often state such vague generalities as "People must work together to solve this problem." Such a statement ignores complications which could be raised by the teacher. *Why don't they? Why wouldn't this seemingly obvious solution work? So, what else must be done? How could these needs and interests be reconciled?*

Among the most common forms of oversimplification found in social studies texts is that of vaguely expressed explanations. Students can better understand explanations and descriptions of historical events, and peoples' reactions to them, by considering offered explanations in depth. For example, texts often say that citizens of a former colony resented the rule they lived under. Students could discuss questions like the following: *Why do many people resent being ruled by others? What, exactly made them unhappy with their situation? How would present day Americans feel about being conquered and ruled? What consequences might arise from our being taken over? Why? How might Americans respond? Why? Why would a country want to rule another group? What would it get out of it? Why wouldn't they want to give it up? What do they say are their reasons for not giving it up? Why don't the people they rule accept those reasons? Was this group's treatment of that group consistent with those reasons?*

Another common form of oversimplification in history texts occurs when texts describe the reason or cause of present or historical situations. This treatment serves texts' sociocentric bias when discussing the causes of wars in which the U.S. has been involved. Thus, the enemy bears total responsibility.

When generalizations are made or discussed, the teacher could ask students for counter-examples. The class can then suggest and evaluate more accurate formulations of the claim: *Is this always the case? Can you think of a time when an x wasn't a y? Given that example, how could we make the claim more accurate?* ("Sometimes ...." "When this is the case, that happens ...." "It seems that....")

The teacher can encourage students to qualify their statements when they have insufficient evidence to be certain. By asking for the evidence on which student claims are based and encouraging students to recognize the possibility that alternative claims may be true, the teacher can help students develop the habits of saying "I'm not sure," and of using appropriate probability qualifiers.

Scientific models simplify the phenomena they represent. The class can examine ways such models break down.

Lesson plans in which the strategy is used

S-11 Comparing Analogous Situations: Transferring Insights to New Contexts

Principle: An idea's power is limited by our capacity to see its application. Critical thinkers' ability to use ideas mindfully enhances their ability to transfer ideas critically. They practice using ideas and insights by appropriately applying them to new situations. This allows them to organize materials and experiences in different ways, to compare and contrast alternative labels, to integrate their understanding of different situations, and to find fruitful ways to conceptualize novel situations. Each new application of an idea enriches understanding of both the idea applied and the situation to which it is applied.

Application: Critical teaching, focussing more on basic concepts than on artificial organization of material, encourages students to apply what they have just learned to different but analogous contexts. It provides for more than one way to organize material. Using similar information from different situations makes explanations clearer, less vague.

When students master a new skill, or discover an insight, they can be encouraged to use it to analyze other situations. Combine the strategy with independent thought by asking students to name or find analogous situations.

Students can find analogies between historical events or beliefs and present day actions and claims. Such parallel situations can be compared, and insights into each applied to the other.

When students have learned a scientific law, concept, or principle, they can enrich their grasp of it by applying it to situations not mentioned in the text. By exploring student understanding of such situations, teachers can discover misunderstandings.

Lesson plans in which the strategy is used

S-12 Developing One's Perspective: Creating or Exploring Beliefs, Arguments, or Theories

Principle: The world is not given to us sliced up into categories with pre-assigned labels on them. There is always a large number of ways that we can "divide up" and so experience the world. How we do so is essential to our thinking and behavior. Uncritical thinkers assume that their perspective on things is the only correct one. Selfish critical thinkers manipulate the perspectives of others to gain advantage for themselves. Fairminded critical thinkers learn to recognize that their own way of thinking and that of all other perspectives are subject to error. They learn to develop their point of view through a critical analysis of their experience. They learn to question commonly accepted ways of understanding things and avoid uncritically accepting the viewpoints of their peer groups or society. They know what their perspectives are and can talk insightfully about them. To do this, they must create and explore their own beliefs, their own reasoning, and their own theories.

Application: Perspective is developed through extended thought, discussion, and writing. Students who are unsure what to think can be given time to reflect and come to tentative conclusions. Students who have definite conclusions about the subject at hand can consider ideas from other perspectives, answer questions about what they think, or reflect on new situations or problems. Students can compare what they say they believe with how they act.

One-to-one Socratic questioning may facilitate development of perspective, especially for students who think they've exhausted their ideas. This strategy will often coincide with evaluating actions and policies, arguments, or assumptions.

Students could explain how what they have learned has changed their thinking in some way. A written assignment could be used as an opportunity for a student to explore an idea in depth, and either come to conclusions, or clarify issues and concepts.

In general, we should look for opportunities to ask students what *they* believe, how *they* see things, what reasons seem most persuasive to *them*, what theory

72

they think best explains what we are trying to explain, and so forth. We should look for occasions in which they can name and describe their own perspectives, philosophies, and ways of thinking.

Lesson plans in which the strategy is used

S-13 Clarifying Issues, Conclusions, or Beliefs

Principle: The more completely, clearly, and accurately an issue or statement is formulated, the easier and more helpful the discussion of its settlement or verification. Given a clear statement of an issue, and prior to evaluating conclusions or solutions, it is important to recognize what is required to settle it. And before we can agree or disagree with a claim, we must understand it clearly. It makes no sense to say "I don't know what you are claiming, but I deny it, whatever it is." Critical thinkers recognize problematic claims, concepts, and standards of evaluation, making sure that understanding precedes judgment. They routinely distinguish facts from interpretations, opinions, judgments, or theories. They can then raise those questions most appropriate to understanding and evaluating each.

Application: Teachers should encourage students to slow down and reflect before coming to conclusions. When discussing an issue, the teacher can ask students first, *"Is the issue clear? What do you need to know to settle it? What would someone who disagreed with you say?"* Students should be encouraged to continually reformulate the issue in light of new information. They should be encouraged to see how the first statement of the issue or problem is rarely best (i.e., most accurate, clear, complete) and that they are in the best position to settle questions only after they have developed as clear a formulation as possible.

When discussing an issue, teachers can have students ask themselves such questions as: Do I understand the issue? Do I know how to settle it? Have I stated it fairly? (Does my formulation assume one answer is correct? Would everyone involved accept this as a fair and accurate statement of the issue?) Are the words clear? Do I have to analyze any concepts? Do I know when the key terms apply and don't apply? Does this question ask something about facts, or about the meanings of words? Am I evaluating anything? What? Why? What criteria should I use in the evaluation? What facts are relevant? How can I get the evidence I need? How would the facts be gathered? What would researchers have to do to conduct such a study? What problems would they face? How could those obstacles be surmounted?

When a claim is unclear, the class can discuss such questions as: *How can we know whether or not this is true? What would it be like for this claim to be true? False? Do we clearly understand the difference? What evidence would count for it?*

Against it? Are any concepts (words or phrases) unclear? What does this claim assume? What does this claim imply? What does its opposite imply? Is there a clearer way to word this claim? Is there a more accurate way to word it? Can it be rephrased? Do the different ways of putting it say the same thing? Why would someone agree with this claim? Disagree?

This strategy provides a way of remodelling lessons that focus on "Fact/Opinion," or which have vague passages of text.

To encourage students to distinguish fact from interpretation, for example, the teacher could use questions like the following: *Does this description stick to the facts, or is reasoning or response included? Is this something that can be directly seen, or would you have to interpret what you saw to arrive at this statement? Is this how anyone would tell about the situation, or would someone else see it differently? What alternative descriptions or explanations are there?* Students could then examine the assumptions, inferences, and theories underlying the alternatives.

Lesson plans in which the strategy is used

S-14 Clarifying and Analyzing the Meanings of Words or Phrases

Principle: Critical, independent thinking requires clarity of thought. A clear thinker understands concepts and knows what kind of evidence is required to justify applying a word or phrase to a situation. The ability to supply a definition is not proof of understanding. One must be able to supply clear, obvious examples and use the idea appropriately. In contrast, for an unclear thinker, words float through the mind unattached to clear, specific, concrete cases. Distinct concepts are confused. Often the only criterion for the application of a term is that the case in question "seems like" an example. Irrelevant associations are confused with what are necessary parts of the idea (e.g., "Love involves flowers and candlelight.") Unclear thinkers lack independence of thought because they lack the ability to analyze a concept, and so critique the way it is used.

Application: There are a number of techniques the teacher can use for analyzing concepts. Rather than simply asking students what a word or phrase means, or asking them for a definition, the teacher can use one of the techniques mentioned below.

When introducing concepts, paraphrasing is often helpful for relating the new term (word or phrase) to ideas students already understand. The teacher can also supply a range of examples, allowing students to add to the list.

When introducing or discussing a concept that is not within students' experience, the teacher can use analogies which relate the idea to one with which students are familiar. Students could then compare the ideas.

When discussing words or phrases with which students are familiar, we suggest that teachers have students discuss clear examples of the concept, examples of its opposite (or examples which are clearly not instances of the concept), and examples for which neither the word or its opposite are completely accurate (borderline cases). Have students compare the facts relevant to deciding when the term and its opposite apply. Students could also discuss the implications of the concept and why people make a distinction between it and its opposite. *"Give me examples of X and the opposite of X. Why is this an X? What is it about this that makes you call it an X? What are you saying about it when you call it that? Why would someone use this expression? Why would someone want to bring it to people's attention? What are the practical consequences of calling it that? How do we feel about or treat X's? Why?"* *(Do the same for the opposite.)* When discussing examples, always start with the clearest, most obvious, indisputable cases and opposite cases. Only when those have been examined at length move to the more problematic, controversial, difficult, or borderline examples. *"Why is this case different from the others? Why do you kind of want to call it X? Why do you hesitate to call it X? What can we call this case?"*

When clarifying a concept expressed by a phrase rather than a single word, discuss cases in which the phrase applies, instead of merely discussing the individual words. For example, if clarifying the idea of a 'just law,' though a general discussion of 'justice' may be helpful, the more specific idea 'just *law*' should be discussed and contrasted with its opposite.

For ideas that commonly have a lot of irrelevant associations, the teacher can have students distinguish those associations which are logically related to the concept, from those which are not. Have the class brainstorm ideas associated with the term under discussion. Then ask the students if they can imagine using the term for situations lacking this or that listed idea. Students may see that many of their associations are not part of the concept. They are left with a clearer understanding of what is relevant to the concept and will be less tempted to confuse mere association with it.

Lesson plans in which the strategy is used

S-15 Developing Criteria for Evaluation: Clarifying Values and Standards

Principle: Critical thinkers realize that expressing mere preference does not substitute for evaluating something. Awareness of the process or components of evaluating facilitates thoughtful and fairminded evaluation. This process requires the development and use of criteria or standards of evaluation, or making standards or criteria explicit. Critical thinkers are aware of the values on which they base their judgments. They have clarified them and understand *why* they are values.

When developing criteria, critical thinkers should understand the object and purpose of the evaluation, and what function the thing being evaluated is supposed to serve. Critical thinkers take into consideration different points of view when attempting to evaluate something.

Application: Whenever students are evaluating something, — an object, action, policy, solution, belief — the teacher can ask students what they are evaluating, the purpose of the evaluation, and the criteria they used. Criteria for evaluating an object usually presuppose a purpose of the object. With practice, students can see the importance of developing clear criteria and applying them consistently. When developing criteria, rational discussion and fairmindedness are usually more important than reaching consensus.

The class could discuss questions like the following: *What are we evaluating? Why? Why do we need an X? Name or describe some good X's vs. bad X's. Why? What are the differences? Given these reasons or differences, can we generalize and list criteria? Can we describe what to look for when judging an X? What feature s does an X need to have? Why?*

Much of Language Arts instruction can be viewed as developing and clarifying criteria for evaluating writing. Students should continually evaluate written material and discuss their criteria. Specific grammatical points should be explained in terms of the values they support (such as clarity or vividness).

Students could relate the evaluation of governments to their perspectives on the purposes and functions of governments. During discussions in which they evaluate specific actions or policies of some government, they could relate their evaluations to this discussion of criteria and underlying values.

Lesson plans in which the strategy is used

S-16 Evaluating the Credibility of Sources of Information

Principle: Critical thinkers recognize the importance of using reliable sources of information when formulating conclusions. They give less weight to sources which either lack a track record of honesty, contradict each other on key questions, are not in a position to know, or have a vested interest in influencing belief. Critical thinkers recognize when there is more than one reasonable position to be taken on an issue; they compare alternative sources of information, noting areas of agreement; they analyze questions to determine whether or not the source is in a position to know; and they gather further information where sources disagree. They recognize obstacles to gathering accurate and pertinent information. They realize that preconception, for example, influences observation — that we often see only what we expect to see and fail to notice things we aren't looking for.

Application: When the class is discussing an issue about which people disagree, the teacher can encourage students to check a variety of sources supporting different points of view. This strategy can be used in history and news lessons.

The class can discuss the relevance of a source's past dependability, how to determine whether a source is in a position to know, and how the motives should be taken into account when determining whether a source of information is credible. The teacher can ask the following questions: *Is this person in a position to know? What would someone need, to be in a position to know? Was this person there? Could he have directly seen or heard, or would he have to have reasoned to what he claims to know? What do we know about this person's expertise and experience? What experience would you need to have to be an expert? What must you have studied? What does he claim about this issue? Where did he get his information? Is there reason to doubt him? Has he been reliable in the past? Does he have anything to gain by convincing others? Who commissioned this report? Why?*

To more fully explore the idea of expertise with respect to a particular topic, the teacher could ask, "*What subjects, perspectives, theories, what kinds of details, what sorts of analyses would someone need knowledge of, in order to develop a complete and fairminded view of this subject?*" (For example, if the subject is a political conflict, an expert would need to know the historical background of the groups, their cultures, religions and world views — including, for example, how each group sees itself and the others, how much diversity is within each group — the geography of the area, the economic system or systems under which the groups live, etc.)

Finally, the teacher can use examples from the students' personal experience (e.g., trying to determine who started an argument) and encourage students to recognize the ways in which their own motivations can affect their interpretations and descriptions of events.

Lesson plans in which the strategy is used

S-17 Questioning Deeply: Raising and Pursuing Root or Significant Questions

Principle: Critical thinkers can pursue an issue in depth, covering germane aspects in an extended process of thought or discussion. When reading a passage, they look for issues and concepts underlying the claims expressed. They come to their own understanding of the details they learn, placing them in the larger framework of the subject and their overall perspective. They contemplate the significant issues and questions underlying subjects or problems studied. They can move between basic underlying ideas and specific details. When pursuing a line of thought, they are not continually dragged off subject. They use important issues to organize their thought and are not bound by the organization given by another. Nor are they unduly influenced by the language of another. If they find that a set of categories or distinctions is more appropriate than that suggested by another, they will use it. Recognizing that categories serve human purposes, they use those categories which best serve their purpose at the time. They are not limited by accepted ways of doing things. They evaluate both goals and how to achieve them.

Application: Each of the various subject areas has been developed to clarify and settle questions peculiar to itself. The teacher can use such questions to organize and unify details covered in the subject. Perhaps more important are basic questions everyone faces about what people are like, the nature of right and wrong, how we know things, and so on. Both general and subject-specific basic questions should be repeatedly raised and discussed at length.

Texts fail to develop this trait of pursuing root questions by presenting preformulated conclusions, categories, solutions, and ideals, by failing to raise crucial or thought-provoking issues (and so avoiding them), by suggesting a too-limited discussion of them, by mixing questions relevant to different issues or by pursuing their objectives in a confusing way. To rectify these problems, teachers need to provide opportunities for students to come to their own conclusions, construct their own categories, devise their own solutions, and formulate their own ideals. They need to raise thought-provoking issues, allow extended discussion of them and keep the discussion focussed, so that different issues are identified and appropriately dealt with. The students, in turn, need to be clear about the objectives and to see themselves as accomplishing them in a fruitful way.

Rather than asking students to place objects into pre-existing categories, for instance, the teacher can encourage students to form their own categories. Students can then discuss the reasons they had for forming each category. *When different students have used different sets of categories to form groups, the teacher can ask such questions as: When would this set of categories be most useful? When would that set be best? Why would someone else make different groupings?*

When a class discusses rules, institutions, activities, or ideals, the teacher can facilitate a discussion of their purposes, importance, or value. Students should be encouraged to see institutions, for example, as a creation of people, designed to fulfill certain functions, not as something that is "just there." They will be in a better position, when they are adults, to see that it fulfills its goals. Or, for another example, ideals will be better understood as requiring specific kinds of actions, instead of being left as mere vague slogans, if the class examines their value.

When the text avoids important issues related to or underlying the object of study, the teacher or students could raise them and discuss them at length. Students can go through the assigned material, and possibly other resources, using the chosen issue or issues to organize the details, for example, making a chart or issue map. Socratic questioning, it should be noted, typically raises root issues. (See the section on Socratic discussion in chapter 3 "Global Strategies.")

When a lesson does raise root questions but has too few and scattered questions, the teacher can pull out, rearrange, and add to the relevant questions, integrating them into an extended and focussed, rather than fragmented, discussion. Students can begin study with one or more significant questions and list relevant details as they read.

Lesson plans in which the strategy is used

S-18 Analyzing or Evaluating Arguments, Interpretations, Beliefs, or Theories

Principle: Rather than carelessly agreeing or disagreeing with a line of reasoning based on their preconceptions of what is true, critical thinkers use analytic tools to understand them and determine their relative strengths and weaknesses. When analyzing arguments, critical thinkers recognize the importance of asking for reasons and considering alternative views. They are especially sensitive to possible strengths of arguments that they disagree with, recognizing the tendency of humans to ignore, oversimplify, distort, or otherwise dismiss them. Critical thinkers analyze questions and place conflicting arguments, interpretations and theories in opposition to one another, as a means of highlighting key concepts, assumptions, implications, etc.

When giving or being given an interpretation, critical thinkers, recognizing the difference between evidence and interpretation, explore the assumptions on which it is based, and propose and evaluate alternative interpretations for their relative strength. Autonomous thinkers consider competing theories and develop their own theories.

Application: Often texts claim to have students analyze and evaluate arguments, when all they have them do is state preferences and locate factual claims, with very limited discussion. They fail to teach most techniques for analyzing and evaluating arguments. Texts that do address aspects of argument critique tend to teach such skills and insights in isolation, and fail to mention them when appropriate and useful. (See "Text Treatment of Critical Thinking and Argumentation," in chapter 4.)

Instead of simply asking students why they agree or disagree with a line of reasoning, students should be encouraged to place competing arguments, interpretations, or theories in opposition to one another. Ask, *"What reasons are given? What would someone who disagreed with this argument say?"* Students should be encouraged to argue back and forth, and modify their positions in light of the strengths of others' positions. Students can become better able to evaluate reasoning by familiarizing themselves with, and practicing, specific analytic techniques, such as making assumptions explicit and evaluating them; clarifying issues, conclusions, values, and words, developing criteria for evaluation; recognizing contradictions; distinguishing relevant from irrelevant facts; evaluating evidence; and exploring implications. (See strategies addressing these skills.) After extended discussion, have students state their final positions. Encourage them to qualify their claims appropriately.

When learning scientific theories, students should be encouraged to describe or develop their own theories and compare them with those presented in their texts. Students can compare the relative explanatory and predictive powers of various theories, whenever possible testing the predictions with experiments.

Lesson plans in which the strategy is used

S-19 Generating or Assessing Solutions

Principle: Critical problem-solvers use everything available to them to find the best solution they can. They evaluate solutions, not independently of, but in relation to one another (since 'best' implies a comparison). They take the time to formulate problems clearly, accurately, and fairly, rather than offering a sloppy, half-baked description and then immediately leaping to a solution. They examine the causes of the problem at length. They have reflected on such questions as, "What makes some solutions better than others? What does the solution to this problem require? What solutions have been tried for this and similar problems? With what results?" But alternative solutions are often not given, they must be generated or thought-up. Critical thinkers must be creative thinkers as well, generating possible solutions in order to find the best one. Very often a problem persists, not because we can't tell which available solution is best but because the best solution has not yet been made available — no one has thought it up yet. Therefore, although critical thinkers use all available information relevant to their problems, including the results of solutions others have used in similar situations, they are flexible and imaginative, willing to try any good idea whether it has been done before or not.

Fairminded thinkers take into account the interests of everyone affected by the problem and proposed solutions. They are more committed to finding the best solution than to getting their way. They approach problems realistically.

Application: The best way to develop insight into problem-solving is to solve problems. If problems arise in the class — for example, if discussions degenerate into shouting matches — students should be assisted in developing and instituting their own solutions. If the first attempt fails or causes other problems, students should consider why and try again. Thus, they can learn the practical difficulties involved in discovering and implementing a workable solution.

We recommend first that the teacher have students state the problem, if that has not been done. Students should explore the causes at length, exploring and evaluating multiple perspectives. Encourage them to integrate the strong points within each view. As the process of exploring solutions proceeds, students may find it useful to reformulate the description of the problem.

Rather than simply asking students if a given solution is good, the teacher could encourage an extended discussion of such questions as: *Does this solve the problem? How? What other solutions can you think of? What are their advantages and disadvantages? Are we missing any relevant facts? (Is there anything we need to find out before we can decide which solution is best?) What are the criteria for judging solutions in this case? (How will we know if a solution is a good one?) Why do people/have people behaved in the ways that cause the problem? How do the solutions compare with each other? Why? What are some bad ways of trying to solve the problem? What is wrong with them? Do any of these solutions ignore some-one's legitimate concerns or needs? How could the various needs be incorporated? If this fact about the situation were different, would it change our choice of solutions? Why or why not?*

Fiction often provides opportunities for analysis of problems and evaluation of solutions. Texts' treatments are often too brief, superficial, and unrealistic.

History texts often provide opportunities for use of this strategy when they describe problems people or government attempted to solve, for instance, by passing new laws. Students can evaluate the text's statement of the problem and its causes, evaluate the solution tried, and propose and evaluate alternatives. Students should be encouraged to explore the beliefs underlying various choices of solutions. (For instance, ask, *"Why do conservatives favor this solution and liberals that one? What does each claim causes the problem? What does each perspective assume? What sort of evidence would support each perspective? What other per-spectives can there be? Can the perspectives be reconciled? What is your perspective on this problem? Why?"*)

When presenting problem-solving lessons or activities, texts tend to provide lists of problem-solving steps which unnecessarily limit the process. For example, texts rarely encourage students to consider how others solved or tried to solve the same or a similar problem. They generally make "describing the problem" step one, without having students reformulate their descriptions after further examination.

Social studies texts provide innumerable opportunities for exploring crucial problems. *What problems do we have in our country or part of the country? Why? Who is involved in this? Who contributes? How? Why? Who's affected? How? Why? What should be done? Why? Why not do it? What could go wrong? What do other people think should be done? Why? How can we find out more about the causes of this? How can we find out what different people want? Can the wants be recon-ciled? How? Why not? What compromises are in order?*

What does this passage say was the problem? The cause? Explain the cause. What other explanations are there? Evaluate the explanations. What else was part of the cause? What was the solution tried? (Action, law, set of laws, policy, amendment, etc.) What were the effects? Who was affected? Did it have the desired effects? Undesirable effects? What should have been done differently, or what should we do now to rectify the problems that solution caused? Do we need the law now?

Lesson plans in which the strategy is used

S-20 Analyzing or Evaluating Actions and Policies

Principle: Critical thinking involves more than an analysis of clearly formulated instances of reasoning; it includes analysis of behavior or policy and a recognition of the reasoning that behavior or policy presupposes. When evaluating the behavior of themselves and others, critical thinkers are conscious of the standards they use, so that these, too, can become objects of evaluation. Critical thinkers are especially concerned with the consequences of actions and recognize these as fundamental to the standards for assessing both behavior and policy.

Critical thinkers base their evaluations of behavior on assumptions to which they have rationally assented. They have reflected on such root questions as: What makes some actions right, others wrong? What rights do people have? How can I know when someone's rights are being violated? Why respect people's rights? Why be good? Should I live according to rules? If so, what rules? If not, how should I decide what to do? What policies should be established and why? What are governments supposed to do? What shouldn't they do?

Application: The teacher can encourage students to raise ethical questions about actions and policies of themselves and others. Students can become more comfortable with the process of evaluating if they are given a number of opportunities to consider the following kinds of questions: *Why did x do this? What reasons were given? Were they the real reasons? Why do you think so? What are the probable consequences of these actions? How would you feel if someone acted this way toward you? Why? What reasons were your evaluations based on? Might someone else use a different standard to evaluate? Why? Do you think the action was fair, smart, etc.? Why or why not?*

Too often history texts fail to have students evaluate the behavior and policies about which they read. Texts often assume that people's stated reasons were their real reasons. Sometimes texts describe behavior inconsistent with the stated intentions, yet fail to have students discuss these inconsistencies. *Why did that group or government say they took this action? What did they do? What result did they say they wanted? What results did it actually have? Who was helped? Hurt? Why? Is the stated reason consistent with that behavior? Was the reason they gave their real reason? Why do you think so?*

Students should evaluate the behavior of important people of the past. Such evaluation can be enhanced by having interested students report on the long-term consequences of past actions and policies. Future citizens of a democracy need to develop their own sense of how leaders and countries should and shouldn't behave.

Lesson plans in which the strategy is used

S-21 Reading Critically: Clarifying or Critiquing Texts

Principle: Critical thinkers read with a healthy skepticism. But they do not doubt or deny until they understand. They clarify before they judge. They realize that everyone is capable of making mistakes and being wrong, including authors of textbooks. They also realize that, since everyone has a point of view, everyone sometimes leaves out some relevant information. No two authors would write the same book or write from exactly the same perspective. Therefore, critical readers recognize that reading a book is reading one limited perspective on a subject and that more can be learned by considering other perspectives. Critical readers ask themselves questions as they read, wonder about the implications of, reasons for, examples of, and meaning and truth of the material. They do not approach written material as a collection of sentences, but as a whole, trying out various interpretations until one fits all of the work, rather than ignoring or distorting statements that don't fit their interpretation.

Application: Students should feel free to raise questions about materials they read. When a text is ambiguous, vague, or misleading, teachers can raise such questions as: *What does this passage say? What does it imply? Assume? Is it clear? Does it contradict anything you know or suspect to be true? How do you know? How could you find out? What might someone who disagreed with it say? Does the text leave out relevant information? Does it favor one perspective? Which? Why do you suppose it was written this way? How could we rewrite this passage to make it clearer, fairer, or more accurate?*

In Language Arts, rather than simply using recall questions at the end of fictional selections, have students describe the plot. Furthermore, don't forget that students should continually evaluate what they read.

Students can evaluate unit, chapter, section titles and headings in their texts. *What is the main point in this passage? What details does it give? What ideas do those details support, elaborate on, justify? Is the heading accurate? Misleading? Could you suggest a better heading?*

Often passages which attempt to instill belief in important American ideals are too vague to mean more than the idea that our ideals are important. Such passages could be reread slowly with much discussion. Such passages typically say that the ideals are important or precious, that people from other countries wish they had them or come here to enjoy them, that we all have a responsibility to preserve them, and so on.

The class could discuss questions like the following: *Why is this right important? How is this supposed to help people? Does not having this right hurt people? How? Why? Why would someone try to prevent people from voting or speaking out? How could they? Have you ever denied someone the right to speak or be heard? Why? Were you justified? Why or why not? What should you have done? Why would someone want to find out how people voted? Why is this right precious? Why are these rights emphasized? Do you have other rights? Why doesn't the text (or Constitution) say that you have the right to eat pickles? What are the differences between that right and those mentioned? Does everyone believe in this or want this?*

How do you know? Have you ever heard anyone say that tyranny is the best kind of government, or free speech is bad? Why? Is there a basic idea behind all of these rights? Why does the text say people have this responsibility? How, exactly, does this help our country? Why do some people not do this? What does it require of you? And how do you do that? Is it easy or hard? What else does it mean you should do?

The teacher could make copies of passages from several sample texts which cover the same material and have students compare and critique them.

Students can discuss their interpretations of what they read. Have them compare their paraphrases and interpretations.

Lesson plans in which the strategy is used

S-22 Listening Critically: The Art of Silent Dialogue

Principle: Critical thinkers realize that listening can be done passively and uncritically or actively and critically. They know that it is easy to misunderstand what is said by another and difficult to integrate another's thinking into our own. Compare speaking and listening. When we speak, we need only keep track of our own ideas, arranging them in some order, expressing thoughts with which we are intimately familiar: our own. But listening is more complex. We must take the words of another and translate them into ideas that make sense to us. We have not had the experiences of the speakers. We are not on the inside of their point of view. We can't anticipate, as they can themselves, where their thoughts are leading them. We must continually interpret what others say within the confines of our experiences. We must find a way to enter into their points of view, shift our minds to follow their trains of thought.

What all of this means is that we need to learn how to listen actively and critically. We need to recognize that listening is an art involving skills that we can develop only with time and practice. We need to learn, for example, that to listen and learn from what we are hearing, we need to learn to ask key questions that enable us to locate ourselves in the thought of another. We must practice asking questions like the following: "I'm not sure I understand you when you say ..., could you explain that further?" "Could you give me an example or illustration of this?" "Would you also say ...?" "Let me see if I understand you. What you are saying is .... Is that right?" "How do you respond to this objection?" Critical readers ask questions as they read and use those questions to orient themselves to what an author is saying. Critical listeners ask questions as they listen to orient themselves to what a speaker is saying: Why does she say that? What examples could I give to illustrate that point? What is the main point? How does this detail relate? Is she using this word as I would, or somewhat differently? These highly skilled and activated processes are crucial to learning. We need to heighten student awareness of and practice in them as often as we can.

Application: The first and best way to teach critical listening is to model it. It is necessary that we listen to what students say actively and constructively, demonstrating the patience and skill necessary to understand them. We should not casually assume that what they say is clear. We should not pass by their expressions too quickly. Students rarely take seriously their own meanings. They rarely listen to themselves. They rarely realize the need to elaborate or exemplify their own thoughts. And we are often in a position to help them to do so with a facilitating question that results from close, enquiring listening.

Secondly, students rarely listen carefully to what other students have to say. They rarely take each other seriously. We can facilitate this process with questioning interventions. We can say things like: "Joel, did you follow what Dianne said? Could you put what she said in your own words?" Or we can say,"Richard, could you give us an example from your own experience of what Jane has said? Has anything like that ever happened to you?"

The success of Socratic questioning and class discussion depends upon close and critical listening. Many assignments are understood or misunderstood through word of mouth. We need to take the occasion of making an assignment an occasion for testing and encouraging critical listening. In this way, we will get better work from students, because in learning how to listen critically to what we are asking them to do they will gain a clearer grasp of what that is, and hence do a better job in doing it. Students often do an assignment poorly, because they never clearly understood it in the first place.

Lesson plans in which the strategy is used

S-23 Making Interdisciplinary Connections

Principle: Although in some ways it is convenient to divide knowledge up into disciplines, the divisions are not absolute. Critical thinkers don't allow the somewhat arbitrary distinctions between academic subjects to control their thinking. When considering issues which transcend subjects, they bring relevant concepts, knowledge and insights from many subjects to the analysis. They make use of insights into one subject to inform their understanding of other subjects. There are always connections between subjects (language and logic; history, geography, psychology, anthropology, physiology; politics, geography, science, ecology; math, science, economics). To understand, say, reasons for the American Revolution (historical question), insights from technology, geography, economics, philosophy, etc., can fruitfully apply.

Application: Any time another subject is relevant to the object of discussion, those insights can be used and integrated. Some teachers allot time for coverage of topics in different subjects so that the topic is examined from the perspective of several subjects. Study of the news can combine with nearly every subject — language arts, social studies, math, geography, science, health, etc.

Socratic questioning can be used to make subject connections clear. The teacher can use discussion of students' issues and problems to show the importance of bringing insights from many subjects to bear.

Students could compare how data is gathered and used in different subjects, for example, scientific studies and public opinion polls.

The class could evaluate writing in their texts from a literary or composition standpoint. *Given what you know about good writing, is this passage well written? Organized? Interesting? Why or why not? How can it be improved? Is the quote used evocative? To the point? How does it illustrate or enhance the point made?*

Students can evaluate the psychological, sociological, or historical accuracy or sophistication of fiction and biography.

Lesson plans in which the strategy is used

S-24 Practicing Socratic Discussion: Clarifying and Questioning Beliefs, Theories, or Perspectives

Principle: Critical thinkers are nothing, if not questioners. The ability to question and probe deeply, to get down to root ideas, to get beneath the mere appearance of things, is at the very heart of the activity. And, as questioners, they have many different kinds of questions and moves available and can follow up their questions appropriately. They can use questioning techniques, not to make others look stupid, but to learn what they think, helping them develop their ideas, or as a prelude to evaluating them. When confronted with a new idea, they want to understand it, to relate it to their experience, and to determine its implications, consequences, and value. They can fruitfully uncover the structure of their own and others' perspectives. Probing questions are the tools by which these goals are reached.

Furthermore, critical thinkers are comfortable being questioned. They don't become offended, confused, or intimidated. They welcome good questions as an opportunity to develop a line of thought.

Application: Students, then, should develop the ability to go beyond the basic what and why questions that are found in their native questioning impulses. To do this, they need to discover a variety of ways to put questions which probe the logic of what they are reading, hearing, writing, or thinking. They need to learn how to probe for and question assumptions, judgments, inferences, apparent contradictions, or inconsistencies. They need to learn how to question the relevance of what is presented, the evidence for and against what is said, the way concepts are used, the implications of positions taken. Not only do we need to question students, we also need to have them question each other and themselves.

Classroom instruction and activities, therefore, should stimulate the student to question and help make the students comfortable when questioned, so that the questioning process is increasingly valued and mastered. Questioning should be introduced in such a way that students come to see it as an effective way to get at the heart of matters and to understand things from different points of view. It should not be used to embarrass or negate students. It should be part of an inquiry into issues of significance in an atmosphere of mutual support and cooperation. We therefore recommend that teachers cultivate a habit of wondering about the reasoning behind students' beliefs and translating their musings into questions.

The teacher should model Socratic questioning techniques and use them often. Any thought-provoking questions can start a Socratic discussion. To follow up responses, use questions like the following: *Why? If that is so, what follows? Are you assuming that...? How do you know that? Is the point that you are making that... or, ...? For example? Is this an example of what you mean..., or this,...? Can I summarize your point as...? What is your reason for saying that? What do you mean when using this word? Is it possible that...? Are there other ways of looking at it? How else could we view this matter?* (For more questions, see the section on Socratic discussion in chapter 3, "Global Strategies: Beyond Subject Matter Teaching.")

To develop students' abilities to use Socratic questioning, the teacher could present an idea or passage to students and have them brainstorm possible questions. For instance, they could think of questions to ask story or historical characters, a famous person or personal hero, on a particular subject. Students can practice questioning in pairs, trading the roles of questioner and questioned. The teacher may provide lists of possible initial questions and perhaps some follow-up questions. Students could also be allowed to continue their discussions another day, after they've had time to think of more questions. As students practice Socratic questioning, see it modeled, and learn the language, skills, and insights of critical thinking, their mastery of questioning techniques will increase.

The direction and structure of a Socratic discussion can be made clearer by periodically summarizing and rephrasing the main points made or by distinguishing the perspectives expressed. *"We began with this question. Some of you said ____, others ____. These arguments were given .... Joan recommended that we distinguish X from Y. We've reached an impasse on X because we can't agree about two contradictory assumptions,___ and ____. We decided we would need to find out _____. So let's take up Y."*

To practice exploring the idea of illuminating and probing Socratic questioning, students could read and evaluate different kinds of interviews, categorizing the questions asked. They could then list probing follow-up questions that weren't asked, and share their lists.

Lesson plans in which the strategy is used

S-25 Reasoning Dialogically: Comparing Perspectives, Interpretations, or Theories

Principle: Dialogical thinking refers to thinking that involves a dialogue or extended exchange between different points of view, cognitive domains, or frames of reference. Whenever we consider concepts or issues deeply, we naturally explore their connections to other ideas and issues within different domains or points of view. Critical thinkers need to be able to engage in fruitful, exploratory dialogue, proposing ideas, probing their roots, considering subject matter insights and evidence, testing ideas, and moving between various points of view. When we think, we often engage in dialogue, either inwardly or aloud with others. We need to integrate critical thinking skills into that dialogue so that it is as fruitful as possible. Socratic questioning is one form of dialogical thinking.

Application: In the Socratic transcript in Chapter 3, the teacher began with the root question, "How does your mind work?" and ended up exploring, through dialogical discussion, such seemingly diverse questions as, "Why do you think that some people come to like some things and some people seem to like different things? Where does personality come from? How can your parents' personality get into you? Does your mind come to think at all the way the children around you think? Do you decide whether you're good or bad? Are there some bad people in this world? How are you supposed to figure out the difference between right and wrong? How do you find out what's inside a person?"

The thinking of the class was moving up and back between different points of view expressed in class while it crossed subject matter domains. By routinely raising root questions and root ideas in a classroom setting, multiple points of view get expressed and the thinking proceeds, not in a predictable or straightforward direction, but in a criss-crossing, back-and-forth movement. We continually encourage the students to explore how what they think about "x" relates to what they think about "y" and "z." This necessarily requires that the students' thinking moves back and forth between their own basic ideas and those being presented by the other students, between their own ideas and those expressed in a book or story, between their own thinking and their own experience, between ideas within one domain and those in another, in short, between any two perspectives. This dialogical process will sometimes become dialectical. Some ideas will clash or be inconsistent with others.

Texts come close to teaching dialogical thinking by having students discuss perspectives other than that presented by their texts. Yet such discussion is simply tacked on; it is not integrated with the rest of the material. Thus, the ideas are merely juxtaposed, not synthesized. Rather than separate activities or discussions about different perspectives, the teacher can have students move back and forth between points of view: *What do the environmentalists want? Why? Factory owners? Why? Workers? Why? Why do the environmentalists think the factory owners are wrong? How could/do the factory owners respond to that? ... What beliefs do the sides have in common? How would ecologists look at this dispute? Economists? Anthropologists?*

S-26 Reasoning Dialectically: Evaluating Perspectives, Interpretations, or Theories

Principle: Dialectical thinking refers to dialogical thinking conducted in order to test the strengths and weaknesses of opposing points of view. Court trials and debates are dialectical in form and intention. They pit idea against idea, reasoning against counter-reasoning in order to get at the truth of a matter. As soon as we begin to explore ideas, we find that some clash or are inconsistent with others. If we are to integrate our thinking, we need to assess which of the conflicting ideas we will provisionally accept and which we shall provisionally reject, or which parts of the views are strong and which weak, or how the views can be reconciled. Students need to develop dialectical reasoning skills, so that their thinking not only moves comfortably between divergent points of view or lines of thought, but also makes some assessments in light of the relative strengths and weaknesses of the evidence or reasoning presented. Hence, when thinking dialectically, critical thinkers can use critical micro-skills appropriately.

Application: Dialectical thinking can be practiced whenever two conflicting points of view, arguments, or conclusions are under discussion. Stories and history lessons provide many opportunities. Dialectical exchange between students in science classes enables students to discover and appropriately amend their preconceptions about the physical world.

The teacher could have proponents of conflicting views argue their positions and have others evaluate them. A dialogical discussion could be taped for later analysis and evaluation. Or the teacher could inject evaluative questions into dialogical discussion: *Was that reason a good one? Why or why not? Does the other view have a good objection to that reason? What? And the answer to that objection? Does each side use language appropriately and consistently? To what evidence does each side appeal? Is the evidence from both sides relevant? Questionable, or acceptable? Compare the sources each side cites for its evidence. How can we know which of these conflicting assumptions is best? Is there a way of reconciling these views? The evidence? What is this side right about? The other side? Which of these views is strongest? Why?*

S-27 Comparing and Contrasting Ideals with Actual Practice

Principle: Self-improvement and social improvement are presupposed values of critical thinking. Critical thinking, therefore, requires an effort to see ourselves and others accurately. This requires recognizing gaps between facts and ideals. The fairminded thinker values truth and consistency and, hence, works to minimize these gaps. The confusion of facts with ideals prevents us from moving closer to achieving our ideals. A critical education strives to highlight discrepancies between facts and ideals, and proposes and evaluates methods for minimizing them. This strategy is intimately connected with "developing intellectual good faith."

Application: Since, when discussing our society, many texts consistently confuse ideals with facts, the teacher can use them as objects of analysis. Ask, *"Is this a fact or an ideal? Are things always this way, or is this statement an expression of what people are trying to achieve? Are these ideals yours? Why or why not? How have people attempted to achieve this ideal? When did they not meet the ideal? Why? What problems did they have? How can we better achieve these ideals?"* Students could rewrite misleading portions of text, making them more accurate.

Sometimes this strategy could take the form of *avoiding oversimplification*. For example, when considering the idea that Americans are free to choose the work or jobs they want, the teacher could ask, *"Can Americans choose any job they want? Always? What, besides choice, might affect what job someone has or gets? Would someone who looked like a bum be hired as a salesman? Does this mean they don't have this freedom? Why or why not? What if there aren't enough openings for some kind of work? How can this claim be made more accurate?"*

The teacher can facilitate a general discussion of the value of achieving consistency of thought and action. Ask, *"Have you ever thought something was true about yourself but acted in a way that was inconsistent with your ideal? Did you see yourself differently then? Did you make efforts to change the behavior? Is it good to have accurate beliefs about yourself and your country? Why? Can anyone think of ways to be more consistent? Why is it often hard to be honest about yourself and the groups you belong to? Is it worth the pain?"*

Sometimes texts foster this confusion in students by asking questions to which most people want to answer yes, for example: Do you like to help others? Do you listen to what other people have to say? Do you share things? Since none of us always adheres to our principles (though few like to admit it) you might consider rephrasing such questions. For example, ask, *"When have you enjoyed helping someone? When not? Why? Did you have to help that person? When is it hard to listen to what someone else has to say? Why? Have you ever not wanted to share something? Should you have? Why or why not? If you didn't share, why didn't you?"*

Obviously, the more realistic are our ideals, the closer we can come to achieving them: therefore, any text's attempt to encourage unrealistic ideals should be remodelled. For example, rather than assuming that everyone should always do everything they can for everyone anytime, allow students to express a range of views on such virtues as generosity.

S-28 Thinking Precisely About Thinking: Using Critical Vocabulary:

Principle: An essential requirement of critical thinking is the ability to think about thinking, to engage in what is sometimes called 'metacognition.' One possible definition of critical thinking is the art of thinking about your thinking while you're thinking in order to make your thinking better: more clear, more accurate, more fair. It is precisely at the level of "thinking about thinking" that most critical thinking stands in contrast to uncritical thinking. The analytical vocabulary in the English language (such terms as 'assume,' 'infer,' 'conclude,' 'criteria,' 'point of view,' 'relevance,' 'issue,' 'elaborate,' 'ambiguous,' 'objection,' 'support,' 'bias,' 'justify,' 'perspective,' 'contradiction,' 'credibility,' 'evidence,' 'interpret,' 'distinguish') enables us to think more precisely about our thinking. We are in a better position to assess reasoning (our own, as well as that of others) when we can use analytic vocabulary with accuracy and ease.

Application: Since most language is acquired by hearing words used in context, teachers should try to make critical terms part of their working vocabulary.

When students are reasoning or discussing the reasoning of others, the teacher can encourage them to use critical vocabulary. New words are most easily learned and remembered when they are clearly useful.

When introducing a term, the teacher can speak in pairs of sentences: first, using the critical vocabulary, then, rephrasing the sentence without the new term, e.g., "*What facts are relevant to this issue? What facts ought we to consider in deciding this issue? What kinds of information do we need?*" The teacher can also rephrase students' statements to incorporate the vocabulary.

When conducting discussions, participating students could be encouraged to explain the role of their remarks in the discussion: supporting or raising an objection to a conclusion, distinguishing concepts or issues, questioning relevance, etc.

S-29 Noting Significant Similarities and Differences

Principle: Critical thinkers strive to treat similar things similarly and different things differently. Uncritical thinkers, on the other hand, often miss significant similarities and differences. Things superficially similar are often significantly different. Things superficially different are often essentially the same. It is only by developing our observational and reasoning skills to a high point that we become sensitized to significant similarities and differences. As we develop this sensitivity, it influences how we experience, how we describe, how we categorize, and how we reason about things. We become more careful and discriminating in our use of words and phrases, We hesitate before we accept this or that analogy or comparison.

We recognize the purposes of the comparisons we make. We recognize that purposes govern the act of comparing and determine its scope and limits. The hierarchy of categories biologists, for instance, use to classify living things reflects biological judgment regarding which kinds of similarities and differences between species are the most important biologically and which shed the most light on how each organism is structured and how it operates. To the zoologist, the similarities whales have to horses is considered more important than their similarities to fish. The differences between whales and fish are considered more significant than those between whales and horses.

Critical thinkers distinguish between different senses of the same word or phrase, recognizing the different implications of each. They understand that a writer's or speaker's purposes determine language use. Critical thinkers recognize when two or more concepts are similar or have an important relationship to one another, yet have different meanings. They know when they are using a word in its ordinary sense or in some specialized or technical sense. They make clear distinctions and do not confuse (literally, "fuse together") distinct concepts.

Application: Texts often call on students to compare and contrast two or more things — ideas, phenomena, etc. Yet these activities rarely have a serious purpose. Merely listing similarities and differences has little value in itself. Rather than encouraging students to make such lists, these activities should be proposed in a context which narrows the range of pertinent comparisons and requires some use be made of them in pursuit of some specific goal. For example, if comparing and contrasting two cultures, students should use their understanding to illuminate the relationship between them, perhaps to explain factors contributing to conflict or war. Thus, only those points which shed light on the particular problem need be mentioned, and each point has implications to be drawn out and integrated into a broader picture.

Whenever a text or discussion uses one term in more than one sense, the teacher can ask students to state how it is being used in each case or have students paraphrase sentences in which they occur. Then the teacher can ask students to generate examples in which one, both, or neither meaning of the term applies. For example, students could distinguish ordinary from scientific concepts of work and energy. The class could rephrase such seeming absurdities as "This solid table isn't solid," into "This table that I can't pass my hand through actually has lots of empty spaces in it."

When a text confuses two distinct ideas, students can clarify them. Students can distinguish ideas by discussing the different applications and implications of the concepts. Students could rewrite passages, making them clearer. For example, a social studies text explains how 'consensus' means that everyone in the group has to agree to the decisions. The teachers' notes then suggest discussion of an example wherein a group of children have to make a decision, so they vote, and the majority gets its way. The example, though intended to illustrate the idea of consensus, misses the point and confuses the concepts 'consensus' and 'majority rule.' The class could compare the two ideas, and so distinguish them. *What did the text say 'consensus' means? What example does it give? Is this an example of everyone having to agree? What is the difference? How could the example be changed to illustrate the term?*

Lesson plans in which the strategy is used

S-30 Examining or Evaluating Assumptions

Principle:
We are in a better position to evaluate any reasoning or behavior when all of the elements of that reasoning or behavior are made explicit. We base both our reasoning and our behavior on beliefs we take for granted. We are often unaware of these assumptions. It is only by recognizing them that we can evaluate them. Critical thinkers have a passion for truth and for accepting the strongest reasoning. Thus, they have the intellectual courage to seek out and reject false assumptions. They realize that everyone makes some questionable assumptions. They are willing to question, and have others question, even their own most cherished assumptions. They consider alternative assumptions. They base their acceptance or rejection of assumptions on their rational scrutiny of them. They hold questionable assumptions with an appropriate degree of tentativeness.

Independent thinkers evaluate assumptions for themselves, and do not simply accept the assumptions of others, even those assumptions made by everyone they know.

Application:
Teachers should encourage students to make assumptions explicit as often as possible — assumptions made in what they read and assumptions they make. Teachers should ask questions that elicit the implicit elements of students' claims. Although it is valuable practice to have students make good assumptions explicit, it is especially important when assumptions are questionable. The teacher might ask, *"If this was the evidence, and this the conclusion, what was assumed?"*

There are no rules for determining when to have students evaluate assumptions. Students should feel free to question and discuss any assumptions they suspect are questionable or false. Students should also evaluate good assumptions. Doing so gives them a contrast with poor assumptions.

The following are some of the probing questions teachers may use when a class discusses the worth of an assumption: *Why do people (did this person) make this assumption? Have you ever made this assumption? What could be assumed instead? Is this belief true? Sometimes true? Seldom true? Always false? (Ask for examples.) Can you think of reasons for this belief? Against it? What, if anything, can we conclude about this assumption? What would we need to find out to be able to judge it? How would someone who makes this assumption act?*

Lesson plans in which the strategy is used

S-31 Distinguishing Relevant From Irrelevant Facts

Principle: Critical thinking requires sensitivity to the distinction between those facts that are relevant to an issue and those which are not. Critical thinkers focus their attention on relevant facts and do not let irrelevant considerations affect their conclusions. Furthermore, they recognize that a fact is only relevant or irrelevant in relation to an issue. Information relevant to one problem may not be relevant to another.

Application: When discussing an issue, solution to a problem, or when giving reasons for a conclusion, students can practice limiting their remarks to facts which are germane to that issue, problem, or conclusion. Often students assume that all information given has to be used to solve a problem. Life does not sort relevant from irrelevant information for us. Teachers can encourage students to make a case for the pertinence of their remarks, and help them see when their remarks are irrelevant. *How would this fact affect our conclusion? If it were false, would we have to change our conclusion? Why or why not? What is the connection?*

Students could read a chapter of text or story with one or more issues in mind and note relevant details. Students could then share and discuss their lists. Students can then discover that sometimes they must *argue* for the relevance of a particular fact to an issue.

Another technique for developing students' sensitivity to relevance is to change an issue slightly and have students compare what was relevant to the first issue to what is relevant to the second.

Lesson plans in which the strategy is used

S-32 Making Plausible Inferences, Predictions, or Interpretations

Principle: Thinking critically involves the ability to reach sound conclusions based on observation and information. Critical thinkers distinguish their observations from their conclusions. They look beyond the facts, to see what those facts imply. They know what the concepts they use imply. They also distinguish cases in which they can only guess from cases in which they can safely conclude. Critical thinkers recognize their tendency to make inferences that support their own egocentric or sociocentric world views and are therefore especially careful to evaluate inferences they make when their interests or desires are involved. Remember, every interpretation is based on inference, and we interpret every situation we are in.

Application: Teachers can ask students to make inferences based on a wide variety of statements and actions. Students, for example, can make inferences from story titles and pictures, story characters' statements and actions, as well as their fellow students' statements and actions. They can then argue for their inferences or interpretations.

Sometimes texts will describe details yet fail to make or have students make plausible inferences from them. The class could discuss such passages. Or groups of students might suggest possible inferences which the class as a whole could then discuss and evaluate.

Students should be encouraged to distinguish their observations from inferences, and sound inferences from unsound inferences, guesses, etc.

Teachers can have students give examples, from their experience, of inferring incorrectly and encourage them to recognize situations in which they are most susceptible to uncritical thought. The class can discuss ways in which they can successfully minimize the effects of irrationality in their thought.

Science instruction all too often provides the "correct" inferences to be made from experiments or observations rather than having students propose their own. Sometimes science texts encourage poor inferences given the observation cited. Though the conclusion is correct, students should note that the experiment alone did not prove it and should discuss other evidence supporting it.

Lesson plans in which the strategy is used

S-33 Evaluating Evidence and Alleged Facts

Principle: Critical thinkers, can take their reasoning apart in order to examine and evaluate its components. They know on what evidence they base their conclusions. They realize that unstated, unknown reasons can be neither communicated nor critiqued. They can insightfully discuss evidence relevant to the issue or conclusions they consider. Not everything offered as evidence should be accepted. Evidence and factual claims should be scrutinized and evaluated. Evidence can be complete or incomplete, acceptable, questionable, or false.

Application: When asking students to come to conclusions, the teacher should ask for their reasons. *How do you know? Why do you think so? What evidence do you have?* etc. When the reasons students supply are incomplete, the teacher may want to ask a series of probing questions to elicit a fuller explanation of student reasoning. *What other evidence do you have? How do you know your information is correct? What assumptions are you making? Do you have reason to think your assumptions are true?* etc.

When discussing their interpretations of written material, students should routinely be asked to show specifically where in the book or passage they get that interpretation. The sentence or passage can then be clarified and discussed and the student's interpretation better understood and evaluated.

95

On what evidence is this conclusion based? Where did we get the evidence? Is the source reliable? How could we find out what other evidence exists? What evidence supports opposing views? Is the evidence sufficient? Does another view account for this evidence?

Lesson plans in which the strategy is used

S-34 Recognizing Contradictions

Principle: Consistency is a fundamental — some would say the *defining* — ideal of critical thinkers. They strive to remove contradictions from their beliefs, and are wary of contradictions in others. As would-be fairminded thinkers they strive to judge like cases in a like manner.

Perhaps the most difficult form of consistency to achieve is that between word and deed. Self-serving double standards are one of the most common problems in human life. Children are in some sense aware of the importance of consistency ("Why don't I get to do what they get to do?"). They are frustrated by double standards, yet are given little help in getting insight into them and dealing with them.

Critical thinkers can pinpoint specifically where opposing arguments or views contradict each other, distinguishing the contradictions from compatible beliefs, thus focussing their analyses of conflicting views.

Application: When discussing conflicting lines of reasoning, inconsistent versions of the same story, or egocentric reasoning or behavior, the teacher can encourage students to practice recognizing contradictions. *What does x say? What does y say? Could both claims be true? Why or why not? If one is true, must the other be false? Is this behavior consistent with these beliefs or values? Where, exactly, do these views contradict each other? On what do they agree?*

Sometimes fiction illustrates contradictions between what people say and what they do. The teacher could use questions like the following: *What did they say? What did they do? Are the two consistent or contradictory? Why do you say so? What behavior would have been consistent with their words? What words would have been consistent with their behavior?*

History texts often confuse stated reasons with reasons implied by behavior. They will often repeat the noble justification that, say, a particular group ruled another group for its own good, when they in fact exploited them and did irreparable harm. Students could discuss such examples.

When arguing opposing views, students should be encouraged to find points of agreement and specify points of dispute or contradiction. *What is it about that view that you think is false? Do you accept this claim? That one? On what question or claim does your disagreement turn? What, exactly, is it in this view that you doubt or disagree with?*

The class can explore possible ways to reconcile apparent contradictions. *How could someone hold both of these views? How might someone argue for their compatibility?*

Lesson plans in which the strategy is used

S-35 Exploring Implications and Consequences

Principle: Critical thinkers can take statements, recognize their implications (i.e., if x is true, then y must also be true) and develop a fuller, more complete understanding of their meaning. They realize that to accept a statement one must also accept its implications. They can explore both implications and consequences at length. When considering beliefs that relate to actions or policies, critical thinkers assess the consequences of acting on those beliefs.

Application: The teacher can ask students to state the implications of material in student texts, especially when the text materials lack clarity. The process can help students better understand the meaning of a passage. *What does this imply/mean? If this is true, what else must be true? What were, or would be, the consequences of this action, policy, solution? How do you know? Why wouldn't this happen instead? Are the consequences desirable? Why or why not?*

The teacher can suggest, or have students suggest, changes in stories, and then ask students to state the implications of these changes and comment on how they affect the meaning of the story.

Teachers can have students explore the implications and consequences of their own beliefs. During dialogical exchanges, students can compare the implications of ideas from different perspectives and the consequences of accepting each perspective. *How would someone who believes this act? What result would that have?*

Lesson plans in which the strategy is used

> *The reader should keep in mind the connection between the principles and applications, on the one hand, and the character traits of a fairminded critical thinker, on the other. Our aim, once again, is not a set of disjointed skills, but an integrated, committed, thinking person.*

6 Remodelling Language Arts Lessons

Introduction

Language arts, as a domain of learning, principally covers the study of literature and the arts of reading and writing. All three areas — literature, reading and writing — deal with the art of conceptualizing and representing *in language* how people live and might live their lives. All three are significantly concerned with gaining command of language and expression. Of course, there is no command of language separate from command of thought and no command of thought without command of language.

Very few students will ever publish novels, poems, or short stories, but presumably all should develop insight into what can be learned from literature. Students should develop a sense of the art involved in writing a story and, hence, of putting experiences into words. At bottom is the need everyone has to make sense of human life. This requires command of our own ideas, which requires command over the words in which we express them.

In words and ideas there is power — power to understand and describe, to take apart and put together, to create systems of beliefs and multiple conceptions of life. Literature displays this power, and reading apprehends it. Students lack insight into these processes. Few have command of the language they use or a sense of how to gain that command. Not having a command of their own language, they typically struggle when called upon to read literature. They often find reading and writing frustrating and unrewarding. And worse, they rarely see the value of achieving such command. Literature seems a frill, something artificial, irrelevant, and bookish, outside of the important matters of life. Reading, except in its most elementary form, seems expendable as a means of learning. Writing is often viewed as a painful bore and, when attempted, reduced to something approaching stream-of-consciousness verbalization.

The task of turning students around, stimulating them to cultivate a new and different conception of literature, of reading, and of writing, is a profound challenge. If we value students thinking for themselves, we cannot ignore, we must meet, this challenge. If a basic goal of

English classes is to instill lifelong reading, we must seriously confront why most students have little or no interest in literature. We need to think seriously about the life-world in which they live: the music they listen to, the TV programs and movies they watch, the desires they follow, the frustrations they experience, the values they live for.

Most teachers can probably enumerate the most common features and recurring themes of, say, students' favorite movies: danger, excitement, fun, sex, romance, rock music, car chases, exploding planets, hideous creatures, mayhem, stereotypes, cardboard characters, and so on. The lyrics and values of most popular music are equally accessible, expressing as they do an exciting, fast-moving, sentimentalized, superficial world of cool-looking, athletic, sultry bodies. Much student talk consists in slang. Though sometimes vivid it is more often vague, imprecise, and superficial. Most quality literature seems dull to students in comparison.

Good English instruction must respect and challenge student's attitudes. Ignoring student preferences doesn't alter those preferences. Students must assess for themselves the relative worth of popular entertainment and quality works. Students need opportunities to scrutinize and evaluate the forms of entertainment they prefer. They need to assess the messages they receive from them, the conceptions of life they presuppose, and the values they manifest. As instruction is now designed, students typically ignore what they hear, read, and reiterate in school work and activity. They may follow the teacher's request to explain why a particular classic has lasted many generations, but this ritual performance has little influence on students' real attitudes. Critical thinking can help encourage students to refine their tastes, and we should encourage it with this end in mind. Nevertheless, under no conditions should we try to force or order students to say what they don't believe. A well-reasoned, if wrong-headed, rejection of Shakespeare is better than mindless praise of him.

The Ideal English Student

In addition to the need to enter sympathetically into the life-world of our students, appreciating how and why they think and act as they do, we must also have a clear conception of what changes we are hoping to cultivate in them. We must have a clear sense of the ideals we are striving for as teachers. Consider language itself and the way in which an ideal student might approach it. We want students to be sensitive to their language, striving to understand it and use it thoughtfully, accurately, and clearly. We want them to become autonomous thinkers and so command rather than be commanded by language.

As Critical Reader

Critical readers of literature approach literature as an opportunity to live within anothers' world or experience, to consider someone else's view of human nature, relationships, and problems. Critical readers familiarize themselves with different uses of language to enhance their understanding of and appreciation of literature. They choose to read literature because they recognize its worth. They can intelligently discuss it with others, considering the interpretations of others as they support their own.

Critical readers approach a piece of nonfiction with a view to entering a silent dialogue with the author. They realize they must actively reconstruct the author's meaning. They read because there is much that they know they do not know, much to experience that they have not experienced. Thus, critical readers do not simply pass their eyes over the words with the intention of filling their memories. They question, they organize, they interpret, they synthesize, they digest what they read. They question, not only what was said, but also what was implied or presupposed. They organize the details, not only around key ideas in the work, but also around their own key ideas. They not only interpret, they recognize their interpretations *as interpretation*, and consider alternative interpretations. Recognizing their interpretations as such, they revise and refine their interpretations. They do not simply accept or reject; they work to make ideas their own, accepting what makes most sense, rejecting what is ill-thought-out, distorted, and false, fitting their new understanding into their existing frameworks of thought.

As Critical Writer

Command of reading and command of writing go hand-in-hand. All of the understanding, attitudes, and skills we have just explored have parallels in writing. When writing, critical writers recognize the challenge of putting their ideas and experiences into words. They recognize that inwardly many of our ideas are a jumble, some supporting and some contradicting other ideas, some vague, some clear, some true, some false, some expressing insights, some reflecting prejudices and mindless conformity. Because critical writers recognize that they only partially understand and only partially command their own ideas and experiences, they recognize a double difficulty in making those ideas and experiences accessible to others.

As readers they recognize they must *actively* reconstruct an author's meaning; as writers they recognize the parallel need to *actively* construct their own as well as the probable meanings of their readers. In short, critical writers engage in parallel tasks in writing to the ones in reading. Both are challenging. Both organize, engage, and develop the mind. Both require the full and heightened involvement of critical and creative thought.

As Critical Listener

The most difficult condition in which to learn is in that of a listener. It is normal and natural for people to become passive when listening, to leave to the speaker the responsibility to express and clarify, to organize and exemplify, to develop and conclude. The art of becoming a critical listener is therefore the hardest and the last art that students develop. Of course, most students never develop this art. Most students remain passive and impressionistic in their listening throughout their lives.

Yet this need not be the case. If students can come to grasp the nature of critical reading and writing, they can also grasp the nature of critical listening. Once again, each of the understandings, attitudes, and skills of reading and writing have parallels in listening. There is the same challenge to sort out, to analyze, to consider possible interpretations, the same need to ask questions, to raise possible objections, to probe assumptions, to trace implications. As listeners we must follow the path of another person's thought. Listening is every bit as dialogical as reading and writing. Furthermore, we cannot go back over the words of the speaker as we can in reading.

What is more, our students face a special problem in listening to a teacher, for if they listen so as to take seriously what is being said, they may appear to their peers to be playing up to the teacher, or foolish, if they seem to say a wrong or dumb thing. Student peer groups expect students to listen with casual indifference, even with passive disdain. To expect students to become active classroom listeners is, therefore, to expect them to rise above the domination of the peer group. This is very difficult for most students.

The ideal English student, as you can see, is quite like the ideal learner in other areas of learning, in that critical reading, writing, and listening are required in virtually all subject areas. Yet the language arts are more central to education than perhaps any other area. Without command of one's native language, no significant learning can take place. Even other domains of learning must utilize this command. The ideal English student should therefore come close to being the ideal learner, and while helping our students to gain command of reading, writing, and listening we should see ourselves as laying the foundation for all thought and learning.

Ideal Instruction

Considering the ideal reader, writer, and listener paves the way for a brief overview of ideal instruction. In each case, we should utilize our understanding of the ideal as a model to move toward, as an organizer for our behavior, not as an empty or unrealistic dream. Reading, writing, and listening, as critical thinking activities, help to organize and develop learning. Each is based on a recognition that if we actively probe and analyze, dialogue and digest, question and synthesize, we will begin to grasp and follow alternative schemes of meaning and belief. The world of Charles Dickens is not the same world as that of George Eliot, nor are either the same world as that of Hemingway or Faulkner. Similarly, each of us lives in a somewhat different world. Each of us has somewhat different ideas, goals, values, and experiences. Each of us constructs somewhat different meanings to live by. In ideal instruction, we want students to discover and understand different worlds so that they can better understand and develop their own. We want them to struggle to understand the meanings of others so they can better understand their own meanings.

Unfortunately, most texts do not have a unified approach to this goal. They are often a patchwork, as if constructed by a checklist mentality, as if each act of learning were independent of the one that precedes or follows it. Texts typically lack a global concept of literature, language, reading, writing, and listening. Even grammar is treated as a separate, unconnected set of rules and regulations.

This is not what we want, and this is not how we should design our instruction. Rather, we should look for opportunities to tie dimensions of language arts instruction together. There is no reason for treating any dimension of language arts instruction as unconnected to the rest. Thus far, we have talked about reading, writing, listening, and literature as ways of coming to terms with the constructing and organizing of meanings. We can now use this central concept to show how one can tie grammar to the rest of language arts instruction, for clearly grammar itself can be understood as an organized system for expressing meanings. Each "subject" of each sentence, after all, represents a focus for the expression of meaning, something that we are thinking or talking about. Each "predicate" represents what is said about, the meaning we are attributing to, the subject. All adjectives and adverbs are ways of qualifying or rendering more precise the meanings we express in subjects and predicates. By the same token, each sentence we write has some sort of meaningful relationship to the sentences that precede and follow it. The same principle holds for the paragraphs we write. In each paragraph, there must be some unifying thing that we are talking about and something that we are saying about it.

To put this another way, at each level of language arts instruction, we should aim at helping the student gain insight into the idea that there is a "logic" to the language arts. This is a key insight that builds upon the idea of constructing and organizing meanings; it makes even more clear how we can tie all of the language arts together. It reminds us that there are established uses for all facets and dimensions of language, and that the reasons behind these uses can be made intelligible. Basic grammar has a logic to it, and that logic can be understood. Individual words and phrases also have a logic to them, and, therefore, they too can be understood. When we look into language use with a sense that there is intelligible structure to be understood, our efforts are rewarded. Unfortunately, we face a special obstacle in accomplishing this purpose.

Typically, students treat the meanings of words as "subjective" and "mysterious." I have my meanings of words, and you have your meanings of them. On this view, problems of meaning are settled by asking people for their personal definitions. What do *you* mean by 'love,' 'hate,' 'democracy,' 'friendship,' etc.? Each of us is then expected to come forward with a personal definition. *My* definition of love is this…. *My* definition of friendship is that….

If we are to persuade students that it is possible to use words precisely, we must demonstrate to them that all of the words in the language have established uses with established *implications* that they must learn to respect. For example, consider the words 'rise,' 'arise,' 'spring,' 'originate,' 'derive,' 'flow,' 'issue,' 'emanate,' and 'stem.' They cannot be used in any way one pleases, with a merely personal definition in mind. Each of them has different implications in use:

> 'Rise' and 'arise' both imply a coming into being, action, notice, etc., but 'rise' carries an added implication of ascent (empires *rise* and fall) and 'arise' is often used to indicate causal relationship (accidents *arise* from carelessness); 'spring' implies sudden emergence (weeds *sprang* up in the garden); 'originate' is used in indicating a definite source, beginning, or prime cause (psychoanalysis *originated* with Freud); 'derive' implies a proceeding or developing from something else that is the source (this word *derives* from the Latin) 'flow' suggests a streaming from a source like water ("Praise God, from whom all blessings *flow*"); 'issue' suggests emergence through an outlet (not a word *issued* from his lips); 'emanate' implies the flowing forth from a source of something that is non-material or intangible (rays of light *emanating* from the sun); 'stem' implies outgrowth as from a root or a main stalk (modern detective fiction *stems* from Poe).

Or consider the words 'contract,' 'shrink,' 'condense,' 'compress,' and 'deflate.' Each of them, too, has definite implications in use:

> 'Contract' implies a drawing together of surface or parts and a resultant decrease in size, bulk, or extent; to 'shrink' is to contract so as to be short of the normal or required length, amount, extent, etc. (those shirts have *shrunk*); 'condense' suggests reduction of something into a more compact or more dense form without loss of essential content (*condensed* milk); to 'compress is to press or squeeze into a more compact, orderly form (a lifetime's work *compressed* into one volume); 'deflate' implies a reduction in size or bulk by the removal of air, gas, or in extended use, anything insubstantial (to *deflate* a balloon, one's ego, etc.)

There is a parallel insight necessary for understanding how to arrange sentences in logical relationships to each other. Our language provides a wide variety of adverbial phrases that can make connecting our sentences together easier. Here, as above, students need to learn and respect this established logic:

Group I

Connectives	How they are used	Examples
besides what's more furthermore in addition	To add another thought.	Two postal cards are often more effective than one letter. *Besides*, they are cheaper.
for example for instance in other words	To add an illustration or explanation.	There is no such thing as an "unlucky number." *In other words*, this idea is pure superstition.

Group II

in fact as a matter of fact	To connect an idea with another one.	Last week I was ill, *in fact*, I had to stay in bed until Monday.
therefore consequently accordingly	To connect an idea with another one that follows from it.	The President vetoed the bill. *Consequently*, it never became a law.

Group III

of course to be sure though	To grant an exception or limitation.	He said he would study all day. I doubt it, *though*.
still however on the other hand nevertheless rather	To connect two contrasting ideas.	I like painting; *however*, I can't understand modern art.

Group IV

first next finally meanwhile later afterwards nearby eventually above beyond in front	To arrange ideas in order, time, or space.	*First*, drink some fruit juice. *Next*, have a bowl of soup. Then eat the meat. *Finally*, have some pie and coffee.
in short in brief to sum up in summary in conclusion	To sum up several ideas.	Scientists say that we should eat food that has all the proteins, fats, and vitamins we need. *In short*, they recommend a balanced diet.

Common Problems With Texts

A critical thinking approach to language arts instruction, with its emphasis on helping students understand the *logic* of what they study, can provide a strong unifying force in all of the basic dimensions of the language arts curriculum: reading, writing, language, grammar, and appreciation of literature. Unfortunately, it is rare to find this unifying stress in most language arts textbooks. As a result, the emphases in reading, writing, language, grammar, and literature do not "add-up" in the minds of students. They don't recognize common denominators between reading and writing. They don't grasp how words in language have established uses and so can be used precisely or imprecisely, clearly or vaguely. Their lack of understanding of the logic of language in turn undermines their clarity of thought when reading and writing.

By the same token, grammar seems to students to be nothing more than an arbitrary set of rules. Typically, texts take a didactic approach. They introduce principles or concepts, then provide drills. Specific skills are often torn from their proper contexts and practiced merely for the sake of practice. Yet, without context, skills have little or no meaning. An occasional simple reiteration of basic purposes or ideas is insufficient. Students need to see for themselves when, how, and why each skill is used specifically as it is.

Texts rarely even mention that most crucial distinction: well vs. poorly written. Students rarely, if ever, evaluate what they read. Students do not explore their standards for evaluating written material, or distinguish for themselves when a written work is clear or unclear, engaging or dull, profound or superficial, realistic or unrealistic, and so on.

Texts occasionally have a short lesson or activity on describing plot, identifying theme, and finding the main point. But students are rarely, if ever, called upon to describe the plots of selections, for example. Yet these basic concepts are worthy of frequent discussion.

Unfortunately, texts seldom have students examine work for themselves, discovering strengths and flaws, distinguishing main points from details, exploring the use of various techniques, formulating their conceptions of theses, plots, and themes. Texts occasionally have lessons on "identifying the main point" or on "plot." These ideas are not taught often nor integrated into reading lessons.

Some questions to raise about the logic of language and grammar

Keeping in mind the idea that language and grammar are, on the whole, logical, we should ask questions that help students discover this.

"What is a sentence? How is it different from a group of words? What is a paragraph? How is it different from a group of sentences? What are words for? What do they do? How? How are words alike? Different? How many - what different - kinds of words are there? How is each used? Why are some ways of using a word right and others wrong? What different kinds of sentences are there? When and how should each be used? Why follow the rules of grammar? How does punctuation help the reader? How does knowing about grammar help me write? Read? When do I need to know this? How should I use this? How does knowing this help me as a writer? A reader? Why and how do different types of writing differ? What do they have in common?"

Some questions to raise about the logic of literature

Stories have their own logic. Events don't just happen. They make sense within the meanings and thinking of their authors. When we ask a question, there should be method to it. The questions should lead students to discover how to come to terms with the logic of the story. In every case, we should have students support their answers by reference to passages in the story. It is not their particular answers that are of greatest importance, but rather how they support their answers with reasons and references to the story.

What happened? Why? What is the author trying to convey? Why is this important? What is the main character like? How do you know? What parts of the book gave you that idea? What has shaped the main character? How has this person shaped others? Why do the characters experience their worlds as they do? How do those experiences relate to my experience or to those of people around me? How realistic are the characters? How consistent? If they aren't (realistic, consistent) why not? Is it a flaw in the work, or does it serve some purpose? What conflicts occur in the story? What is the nature of this conflict? What is its deeper meaning? What relationship does it have to my life? What meaning does that conflict have for the character? For me? Though the world, society, lifestyle or characters are obviously different than what I know, what does this work tell me about my world, society, life, character and the characters of those around me? What needs, desires, and ideas govern these characters? Can I identify with them? Should I? How does the view presented in this work relate to my view? To what extent do I accept the conception of humanity and society present or implicit in this work? To what extent or in what way is it misleading? How does it relate to conceptions I've found in other works? How good is this work?

Some questions to raise about the logic of persuasive writing

Persuasive writing has a straightforward logic. In it, an author attempts to describe some dimension of real life and hopes to persuade us to take it seriously. We, as readers, need to grasp what is being said and judge whether it does make sense.

What parts of this work do I seem to understand? What parts don't I understand? What, exactly, is the author trying to say? Why? How does the author support what he is saying with reasons, evidence, or experiences? What examples can I think of to further illuminate these ideas? What counter-examples can be cited? What might the author say about my counter-examples? What are the basic parts of this work? How are the pieces organized? Which claims or ideas support which other claims or ideas? What beliefs does this claim presuppose? What does it imply? What are the consequences of believing or doing as the author says? What kind of writing is this? How has the writer attempted to achieve his purpose? Given that this is what I think he means, how does this claim fit in? Could he mean this instead? Which of these interpretations makes more sense? How does he know what he claims to know? Have I good reason to accept his claims? Doubt them? How could I check, or better evaluate what he says? How are such questions settled, or such claims evaluated? What deeper meaning does this work have? What criticisms can I make? What has he left out? Distorted? How does he address his opponents? Has he been fair to his opponents? Does his evidence support exactly the conclusions he draws? If not, am I sure I understand his conclusions and his evidence? Where did he get his evidence? How should I evaluate it? What has he left unexplained? What would he say about it? Of all the ideas or concepts, which does he take to be the most fundamental or basic? How does he use these concepts? To what other concepts are they related? How does his use of concepts relate to mine and to that of others? Should he have used other concepts instead? How can I reconcile what he has said with what others have said?

Some questions to ask while writing

Writing has a logic. Good substance poorly arranged loses most of its value. Whatever the principle of order chosen, thought must progress from somewhere to somewhere else. It must follow a definite direction, not ramble aimlessly. In the entire piece, as well as in in section and paragraph, ideally, each sentence should have a place of its own, and a place so plainly its own that it could not be shifted to another place without losing coherence. Remember, disorderly thinking produces disorderly writing, and, conversely, orderly thinking produces orderly writing:

What do I want to communicate? Why? What am I talking about? What do I want to say about it? What else do I want to say about it, and why? What else do I know or think about this? How is what I am saying like and unlike what others have said? What am I sure of? What questions do I have? What must I qualify? How can I divide my ideas into intelligible parts? What are the relationships between the parts? How can I show those relationships? How does this detail fit in? How does that claim illuminate my main point? What form of expression best gets this idea across? Would the reader accept this? What questions would the reader have? How can I answer those questions? If I word it this way, would the reader understand it the way I intended? How can I clarify my meaning? How could someone judge this idea or claim? How can it be supported? How would others refute it? Which of those criticisms should I take into account? How can I reconcile the criticisms with my ideas? How should I change what I've said? Will the support seem to the reader to justify the conclusion? Should I change the conclusion, or beef up the support? What counter-examples or problems would occur to the reader here? What do I want to say about them? How am I interpreting my sources? How would someone else interpret them? How can I adjust or support my interpretation?What implications do I want the reader to draw? How can I help the reader see that I mean this and not that? Which of all of the things I'm saying is the most important? How will the reader know which is most important? Why is this detail important? Have I assumed the reader knows something he may not know?

Conclusion

As a teacher of the language arts, it is essential that you develop for yourself a clear sense of the logic of language and of the unity of the language arts. If you model the insight that every dimension of language and literature makes sense, can be figured out, can be brought under our command, can be made useful to us, your students will be much more apt to make this same discovery for themselves. Remember that students are not used to unifying what they are studying. They are, rather, used to fragmented learning. They are used to forgetting, for everything to begin anew, for everything to be self-contained.

Furthermore, they are not used to clear and precise language usage. They are usually satisfied with any words that occur to them to say or write. They are unfamiliar with good writing.

Disciplined thinking is something foreign to their life and being. Therefore, don't expect the shift from a didactic approach ("The teacher tells us and we repeat it back") to a critical one ("We figure it out for ourselves and integrate it into our own thinking") to occur quickly and painlessly. Expect a slow transition. Expect the students to experience many frustrations along the way. Expect progress to come by degrees over an extended period of time. Commit yourself to the long view, to what Matthew Arnold called "the extreme slowness of things," and you will have the attitude necessary for success. Teaching in a critical manner with a critical spirit is a global transformation. Global transformations take a long time to achieve, but their effect is then often permanent. And that is what we want — students who learn to use language clearly and precisely for the rest of their lives, students who listen and read critically for the rest of their lives, students who become critical and creative persons for the rest of their lives.

> *In teaching for critical thinking in the strong sense, we are committed to teaching in such a way that children learn as soon and as completely as possible how to become responsible for their own thinking.*

Literature Logs

Objectives of the Remodelled Plan

The students will:
- explore implications of actions, events, or situations in literature
- compare perspectives or belief systems described in literature
- compare text with other readings
- think independently by analyzing text structures

Standard Approach

Literature logs are informal pieces of writing in which students explore their own experiences, ideas and feelings as related to, or stimulated by literature. The following are sample questions:

1. Which character would you choose to be? Support with specific examples.

2. Which characters change during the reading? In what ways? What caused the change?

3. What is the message or philosophy in the reading? Is there a clear-cut moral issue or dilemma?

4. In what ways was the reading similar to or different from other reading you have done?

5. Was there anything in the reading that you wished might happen to you? Support with examples.

6. What events seemed strange or interesting?

7. Comment on the author's purpose.

8. Comment on the author's style.

Critique

Literature logs provide a generous supply of questions to which students may respond in writing as they read a piece of literature. The original handout from which these questions were taken had 29 different prompts. In and of themselves they are a good way of moving away from recall type assignments. There is, however, room for improvement. The prompts need to be more challenging and less general in scope. Students, especially in middle grades, are quite literal in their responses. If you ask, "Was there one word in the reading that was particularly meaningful?", the student may simply answer, 'yes' or 'no' and go on to the next question. In some ways we have to take students by the hand and lead them down a more complicated thinking path. It is not enough to ask students what changed during the reading or even what caused the change if one does not ask students to notice the *implications* of the change as well. In the case of a personal ref-

erence, "Was there anything in the reading that you wished might happen to you?", we must ask them to go beyond the wish and ask them to predict the outcome of such a supposition. Teachers must always ask themselves if there isn't a more challenging way to present a prompt.

Strategies Used to Remodel

S-20 analyzing or evaluating actions or policies
S-35 exploring implications and consequences
S-25 reasoning dialogically: comparing perspectives, interpretations, or theories
S-1   thinking independently
S-21 reading critically: clarifying or critiquing text
S-32 making plausible inferences, predictions, or interpretations

Remodelled Lesson Plan

The revised questions have been written to present a literature log which requires more than a superficial response from students. If you have a literature log, you could to rephrase questions to utilize maximum critical skills. We have tried to keep the questions relatively short so that students may be able to refer to the log questions easily as they read through the assigned literature.

1. Choose a character you would like to exchange places with. If the exchange took place, what would you do differently in the story? Why? **S-20**

2. In what ways do characters or situations change during the reading? Why? What are the implications of those changes for the other characters? **S-35**

3. What are the belief systems of the characters presented? What can you learn from the way these people act and think? How do the belief systems compare to each other? To your own? **S-25**

4. Choose another piece of writing and analyze three ways these pieces are most alike. Then analyze three ways they are most different. **S-1**

5. Choose an action or event in the reading and assume that it happened to you. What implications would this have? Examine this from several different perspectives. (your friends', parents', teachers', etc.) **S-35**

6. Examine an event in the reading that differed from anything you would have expected. Explain why it surprised you. Is it plausible and realistic? Why or why not? **S-21** Would you change the event if you could? How?

7. What inferences can you make about the author of this reading? Why? Can you think of other authors who may have similar traits? **S-32** Compare the author to an adult you know.

8. Analyze the structure of the text. List three characteristics of style that appear consistently throughout the reading. Which is a style you would like to master? Write a few sentences in this style. **S-1**Perhaps, instead of overwhelming students with the choice of 29 prompts, the teacher could present a few at a time. Sometimes students will choose the easy way out even when they are intel-

lectually capable of handing much more, so ask students to respond to all your questions instead of giving them too wide a choice.

Literature logs which ask students to think critically will produce more interesting responses to read and share.

School time is too precious to spend any sizeable portion of it on random facts. The world, after all, is filled with an infinite number of facts. No one can learn more than an infinitesimal portion of them. Though we need facts and information, there is no reason why we cannot gain facts as part of the process of learning how to think.

Advertising

Objectives of the Remodelled Plan

The students will:

- practice listening critically by analyzing and evaluating T.V. commercials
- exercise fairmindedness by considering advertisements from a variety of perspectives
- analyze and evaluate the arguments given in ads
- practice using critical vocabulary to analyze and evaluate ads
- clarify key words
- distinguish relevant from irrelevant facts in ads
- examine assumptions in ads
- develop insight into egocentricity by exploring the ways in which ads appeal to unconscious desires

Standard Approach

> Very few texts actually address the issue of advertising. Those that do, touch upon indicators to watch for which signal the use of some sort of reasoning -- such indicators as "if...then," "because," "since," "either...or," "therefore." Students are to decide if the reasoning presented is logical or illogical. A common assignment is to have the students write their own advertisements.

Critique

We chose this lesson for its subject: advertising. Ads are a natural tie-in to critical thinking, since many are designed to persuade the audience that it needs or wants a product. Ads provide innumerable clear-cut examples of irrelevance, distortion, suppressed evidence, and vague uses of language. Analysis of ads can teach students critical thinking micro-skills and show their use in context. Practice analyzing and evaluating ads can help students develop critical listening skills. The standard approach, however, is not done in a way which best achieves these results.

Such lessons often focus more on writing ads than critiquing them. They tend to treat neutral and advertising language as basically equivalent in meaning, though different in effect, rather than pointing out how differences in effect arise from differences in meaning. They downplay the emptiness, irrelevance, repetition, questionable claims, and distortion of language in most ads. Their examples bear little resemblance to real ads. Furthermore, few of the examples given in texts are aimed at students, thus minimizing the immediate usefulness of any insights students may gain.

Since most students are exposed to more television commercials than other ads, we recommend that students discuss real commercials aimed at them. We also provide suggestions for using ads to practice use of critical vocabulary and to discuss the visual and audio aspects of commercials.

Strategies Used to Remodel

S-22 listening critically: the art of silent dialogue
S-9 developing confidence in reason
S-18 analyzing or evaluating arguments, interpretations, beliefs, or theories
S-14 clarifying and analyzing the meanings of words or phrases
S-16 evaluating the credibility of sources of information
S-3 exercising fairmindedness
S-31 distinguishing relevant from irrelevant facts
S-2 developing insight into egocentricity or sociocentricity
S-29 noting significant similarities and differences
S-28 thinking precisely about thinking: using critical vocabulary
S-35 exploring implications and consequences
S-30 examining or evaluating assumptions

Remodelled Lesson Plan S-22

Due to the number of ads to which students are exposed, and their degree of influence, we recommend that the class spend as much time as possible on the subject. As students learn to approach ads thoughtfully and analytically, and practice applying critical insight to their lives, they develop confidence in their reasoning powers. **S-9**

To focus on ads and language, begin by having students give complete descriptions of what is said in a variety of television commercials. Put the quotes on the board. For each commercial, the class can discuss the following questions: What ideas does it give you about the product (or service) and owning or using it? Does it give reasons for buying the product? If so, what reasons? Are they good reasons? **S-18** What are the key words? Do they have a clear meaning? What? **S-14** What other words could have been chosen? Who made this ad? Why? Do they have reason to distort evidence about the worth of the product? **S-16** How might someone who wasn't trying to sell the product describe it? How might a competitor describe it? **S-3** What would you need to know in order to make a wise decision about whether to buy it? Does the commercial address these points? **S-31** Why or why not? Has anyone here had experience with the product? What?

When the commercials have been discussed, have students group them by the nature of the ads (repetition, positive but empty language, etc.) or of the appeals made (to the desires to have fun, be popular, seem older, etc.) Have students fill out the groups by naming similar commercials not previously discussed. Students could discuss why these appeals are made. **S-2**

The class could also compare different ads for the same product, aimed at different audiences (e.g., fast food ads aimed at children, and at adults). **S-29** The class could compare ads for different brands of the same or similar products; compare ads to what can be read on ingredients labels; or design and conduct blind taste tests. **S-18**The teacher interested in developing students' critical vocabulary can have students practice while critiquing ads. Use questions like the following: What does the ad imply? **S-35** Does the ad make, or lead the audience to make, any assumptions? Are the assumptions true, questionable, or false? **S-30** Does the ad contain an argument? If so, what is the conclusion? Is the conclusion stated or implied? Does the ad misuse any concepts or ideas? To judge the product, what facts are relevant? Are the relevant facts presented? **S-31** Does it make any irrelevant claims? **S-28**

To gain further insight into listening critically, the class could also discuss aspects of the ads other than use of language. What does the ad show? What effect is it designed to achieve? How? Why? What is the music like? Why is it used? Do the actors and announcers use tone of voice to persuade? Facial expression? How? Are these things relevant to judging or understanding the product? **S-22**

The teacher may also have the class critique ads for any stereotyping (e.g., sexual stereotyping). The class could hypothesize about why ad campaigns and specific techniques work as well as they do, given their lack of reasonableness. **S-2**

For further practice, if a VCR is available, watch and discuss taped commercials. Students could jot notes on critical points, and share their insights.

The analytical vocabulary in the English language, with such terms as 'assume,' ' infer,' 'conclude,' 'criteria,' 'point of view,' 'relevance,' 'interpretation,' 'issue,' 'contradiction,' 'credibility,' 'evidence,' 'distinguish,' enables us to think more precisely about our thinking.

Writing, Response, and Revision

Objectives of the Remodelled Plan

The students will:
- develop criteria for evaluating writing
- respond to one another's writing, suggesting improvements
- write and revise essays, thus developing intellectual perseverance

Standard Approach

> Students write a reflective essay about their first writing experience in school. They have the class period to complete the writing and then turn it into the instructor for comments and correction.

Critique

This lesson was chosen because it best exemplifies how most writing in language arts classes is approached. The student is usually given a limited amount of time to produce a piece of writing and has only one evaluator for first draft writing, the instructor. Students need practice in generating evaluative standards and in giving their own critical commentary. Furthermore, all too often the grade the student is given is based on only one draft of writing, which is hardly representative of what the student may be capable of producing. The standard approach often does not allow students the all-important opportunity to revise. Such techniques in the teaching of writing may actually hinder the student's ability to produce a thoughtful piece, rather than help it.

Response to writing from others, especially peers, is important for students to develop a sense of a reading audience. It also exposes their writing to more people than just the teacher. Having others look at their work gives students a feeling of purpose and integrity; they realize that they write to communicate, not merely to get a grade or the teacher's approval. Evaluating student writing improves students' sense of judgment, and provides "before" and "after" examples of writing which have been improved through revision.

Strategies Used to Remodel

S-15 developing criteria for evaluation: clarifying values and standards
S-1 thinking independently
S-29 noting significant similarities and differences
S-34 recognizing contradictions
S-21 critical reading: clarifying or critiquing text
S-8 developing intellectual perseverance

Remodelled Lesson Plan *S-15*

Writing response groups in a classroom is one way to approach first- or rough-draft writing which allows students to rethink and revise their writing to a second or third draft before the instructor ever sees it. Professional writers don't turn rough drafts in for publication. We should allow our students the same revision opportunities so students can discover the worth of revision. There are many ways to respond to someone's writing. Response can be written or oral or both. Groupings can be in pairs or in small groups.

Groundwork for this lesson could be laid by having students evaluate readings from previous lessons and generalize from their evaluations. *S-1* Any such discussions could be mentioned now. Other activities can help lay the foundation for improving students' writing skills and insight into good writing.

• Have students take a sentence, and reword, re-order, paraphrase, and otherwise rewrite it. Then groups of students can share and evaluate their revisions, share the best few with the rest of the class, and explain why their choices of sentences were superior.

• Give students a problematic sentence to improve. Have groups of students share evaluate, and explain how their best sentences improve on the original. Have groups share their improved sentences and explanations with the rest of the class.

• Have a small response group critique writing in front of the whole class. This way the class sees a model for the entire evaluation process. At the end of the critique, the class can be invited to make comments about the process of evaluation.

Students should discuss how to evaluate writing, and compare good and poor writing. Ask them to mention examples of material they have read and generalize from them. Have students cite examples to clarify general points. For example, if a student says that writing should be interesting, not boring, have the student give examples of each and explain how they illustrate the point. The teacher can write contributions on the board. Next, the teacher should ask what defines a weak piece of writing contrasting that to what defines a strong piece of writing. All responses can be recorded for reference. *S-15*

The class is now ready to evaluate specific pieces of work. The teacher puts several pieces of writing on the overhead projector and reads aloud as students read silently. (The teacher may first want to have one student explain what was read, and ask others, "Is that what it says?" Then have the group mention what needs to be done to make it clearer.) *S-1* When finished, the instructor may ask, "What parts of the writing fall into the good and weak categories that we established at the start of the lesson? What makes one piece of writing stand out from the other? Why? *S-29* How can author A improve this sentence (or paragraph, or phrase)? How does author B keep your attention in this piece?"

This line of questioning allows the students to explore not only effective and dynamic prose according to their own guidelines, but also inadvertently becomes a grammar lesson. Continued modeling introduces new response approaches and reinforces those already in use.

Have students write their papers and form groups to read and discuss them. Some questions which may be useful are:

Which idea interests you the most in the essay? Why?

Can you follow the writer's ideas clearly? Are related points made together, or separated? What should be moved and to where?

Did the beginning of the essay capture your attention? Why?

How did you relate to the author's "voice" in the writing?

Did the author have a purpose? What was it?

At what point, if any, did the author go off the topic? How could you bring the author back on focus?

Are there contradictory or conflicting statements? **S-34** If so, can they be reconciled? How? **S-21**

All questions should be phrased to clarify and generate ideas, not to devalue the writing. Emphasize the need for constructive criticism and specific suggestions for improvement.

Response groups can be used for as many drafts as the class and instructor deem appropriate. **S-8** The questioning can be done orally (and it is particularly beneficial for the writers to read their work aloud) or separate question sheets can be made up ahead of time and responses to writing made on these, rather than on the actual piece of writing itself.

If working with a composition text, students could clarify key claims (definitions, rules, criteria), evaluate examples given in the text, explore their own criteria, and compare them with those given in their texts. "How can you tell if your writing follows or violates this rule?" Each specific point made in the book should be connected with central concepts of good and poor writing.

Later in the year, students can compare criteria for evaluating different kinds of writing, distinguishing universal from specific principles.

Students may revise a paper they wrote months ago. **S-8**

Short Story Analysis

Objectives of the Remodelled Plan

The students will:

* compare the short story to other genres through writing and Socratic discussion
* probe the motives for a character's actions
* evaluate a story
* discuss the effect knowing the ending has on the experience of reading a story
* explore consequences of adding another character or changing the setting

Standard Approach

> This lesson is based on "Charles," a short story by Shirley Jackson, which is frequently anthologized in literature texts at this level. The story concerns a boy named Laurie, who starts kindergarten and comes home each day to tell stories about a bad boy in class named Charles. The end of the story reveals that there is no child in the class named Charles, and implies that Laurie was describing himself. Students respond to such questions as, "Why did Laurie make up the stories about Charles?"

Critique

Short stories are commonly studied in grades 6-9, but in-depth analysis is rare. A format used in many classrooms involves reading the story, discussing the story, answering factual questions, learning new vocabulary and perhaps writing about some aspect of the story. This method is tedious for both the teacher and the students. Students know what to expect when the lesson begins, realize that not much is expected of them intellectually and become bored or lose interest. New texts do include questions beyond the factual and comprehension level, but teachers who embrace the principles of critical thinking can even go beyond this and use the short story form to clarify students' thinking and challenge them academically.

By the time students reach this level, they no doubt have been exposed to the short story form many times and often with the elements of the short story such as setting, character, plot, point of view, and theme. If these elements are presented as definitions, separate from the genre itself, they not only lose meaning, but give students the mistaken idea that literature involves formulas. As with any specialized terminology, we use these terms to discuss the subject (fiction) clearly and insightfully. The usual lackluster approach places students in a passive role and preempts discovery which involves real learning.

Standard lessons often miss the point of stories, and include little discussion of the themes or significant issues raised in them.

118

Strategies Used to Remodel

S-1 thinking independently
S-29 noting significant similarities and differences
S-35 exploring implications and consequences
S-21 critical reading: clarifying or critiquing text
S-24 practicing Socratic discussion: clarifying and questioning beliefs, theories, or perspectives
S-11 comparing analogous situations: transferring insights to new contexts

Remodelled Lesson Plan

The short story form *S-29*

Teachers who teach literature critically will invite students to generate the definition and elements of the short story. **S-1** Open a unit on the short story by having the students work in pairs and respond to questions like the following in writing:

List some characteristics of short stories besides their length.

Compare short stories to novels. Do not consider the facts of specific plots. List differences and similarities *in general.*

Compare the short story form to poetry.

Compare the short story form to plays.

After students have completed their lists, regroup them into groups of 4-6 and have them compare notes. Ask them to combine their answers into a paragraph or more describing the form of the short story and using the ideas on their lists. Then ask a representative from each group to read their answers. At this point, the teacher can clarify any points the students may be confused about or rephrase some of their terms to fit the traditional elements. For example, if students say that stories must have people in them, then the teacher could remind them that some stories involve animals and that a general term for all of them is 'characters.'

"Charles"

The next part of the lesson will involve the short story the teacher has chosen to study. The teacher should select stories carefully, since different stories provide different opportunities for analysis. Teachers should clarify in their own minds what the possible themes of the story are. Even though I will be using "Charles" as an example, the method will work for any story.

If the class needs help describing the plot, this could be done as a class facilitated by the teacher, or in small groups. Or, students who have that skill can model it (in pairs or small groups) for those who don't. Later, the other students can practice, guided by the first. **S-1**

In order to practice discussing the entire story, students could rank incidents according to their importance. What was the outcome of each incident? Identify the emotional reactions of the characters involved. **S-35**

To take advantage of the twist in this particular story, you might ask, "What did you think was going on? What was Laurie's attitude towards Charles? Now that you know the end, why do you think he had that attitude? Discuss the mother's reaction.

"Why did Laurie do those things? Make up Charles? Do you think he believed in Charles? Evaluate Laurie. Evaluate this story. Is it readable, interesting? Would you recommend it? Why or why not? Was it realistic, or did the characters seem phony?" *S-21*

Another activity that could be done after reading the story involves having students think about the concept of truth or evading responsibility. Students could participate in a large group discussion which addresses the following questions:

Do you always tell the truth?

Under what conditions would you lie? Why did Laurie lie?

In your opinion, is lying ever necessary?

Do all people receive the same message from the same statements, i.e., do some see lies where others see truth? Give examples.

Can something be totally true or totally false? Give examples. *S-24*

Stories with surprises can be fruitfully read a second time, and discussed with questions like the following: How is reading the story different this time, that is, now that you know the ending? How was the author able to keep the secret? Now that you know the ending, were there hints and clues that you missed before, that foreshadow the ending? Did you enjoy the story more the first or second time?

Divide students into triads and ask them to synthesize their knowledge. Two ways to present this are:

Change the setting of the story. Suppose, for example, the story was about a student's first day at high school. How does that change the story? *S-11*

Suggest that two more characters be added. What characters would logically fit in such a story and how would they affect what happens? *S-35*

As a writing exercise for closure, students could be asked to think about the themes of the story and then write about a minor theme that has not been discussed in class. Students would be expected to provide support from the text for their ideas.

Journals

Objectives of the Remodelled Plan

The *teacher* will:
- revise journal prompts to require critical thought
- compose thought-provoking journal prompts
- design writing assignments based on journal entries

Standard Approach

Journal writing may be approached in many ways. This lesson instructs students to make daily entries in a journal based on prompts. Example of prompts are:

If you were an animal, what kind would you be?

List all the things that are bothering you at this moment.

What you wish . . .

Keep track of your dreams and comment on them.

I would like to change . . .

Twenty such prompts were listed on a page. Journals may be evaluated by the teacher periodically or peer evaluated.

Critique

Personal journal writing is a worthwhile activity. Students improve their writing skills and explore feelings and opinions. They feel freer, and therefore less blocked by excessive worry about mechanics and fulfilling the assignment. Most journal prompts, however, are superficial and don't go far enough. They promote egocentric thinking and don't give students an opportunity to think about their present or future place in society. What could be a critical examination of assumptions and values is reduced to a lesson in vagueness and sloppy opinions.

This lesson will enable the teacher to change personal journal writing to critical journal writing. This does not mean that we stop asking students to write about their feelings or experiences. They will still write about these things, but their expression will be clear and thoughtful. In fact, one of the most common refrains of writing teachers is that students do not write in depth. They shift from one topic to another without transitions; they rarely take the time to analyze anything. This "write and flight" syndrome reflects students' thinking processes.

In order to shift to critical journal writing, teachers rewrite existing prompts to include specific questions which will enable students to respond thoughtfully, or teachers write new journal prompts which explore concepts in a critical way. When rewriting a journal prompt, it would be a good idea to adhere to the question form. Students respond more directly to this

than statement prompts such as: *Write about the part your present family life plays in selecting future goals.*

A journal entry, once written, need not be dropped. The teacher could combine the benefits of the freedom of a journal and the thoughtfulness of formal writing by having students later take an entry, expand upon it, analyze it, etc., and turn it into finished formal essay.

Strategies Used to Remodel

S-12 developing one's perspective: creating or exploring beliefs, arguments, or theories
S-35 exploring implications and consequences
S-19 generating or assessing solutions
S-29 noting significant similarities and differences
S-20 analyzing or evaluating actions or policies
S-8 developing intellectual perseverance

Remodelled Lesson Plan *S-12*

Let us use the most blatantly simple of the original prompts as an example: *"What you wish ...."* One can imagine the responses from this prompt: electronic equipment, clothes, cars, expensive houses, good grades, Mary/Mark's love, world peace and that my parents would not get a divorce or would get off my back. It would not be uncommon to find all these things in the same paragraph or the same sentence, with the student thinking that they have adequately completed a journal entry for that day. A response such as this does little to improve the students' writing or thinking skills.

To make this topic a critical journal entry, a teacher could ask the student to respond to this:

What areas in people's lives are within their control? What areas in their lives are they powerless to control? How do decisions made when people are young affect their lives later on? **S-35** When should you set future goals? What different types of goals do you have for yourself? Which are most important to you? How would you go about attaining them? Which depend on you alone, and which on others? How many of the goals that you set are material goals? Do you think young people of other countries have different goals? How do they differ? Why do they differ?

The above prompt is intentionally long, but will produce journal entries which are a significant improvement on the laundry wish list.

Next, we will use the prompt *List all the things that are bothering you at this moment* as an example for remodelling:

Daily life is full of stress but seems especially difficult when one is an adolescent. Why do some adolescents seem more emotionally distraught than people who are younger or older? What are some examples of problems in your own life that you have had recently? How did you resolve them? Could they have been resolved in a different or better way? If so, how? **S-19**

Even such prompts as *If you were an animal, what would you be?* could be improved. But prompts like this are limited and are better used at lower grade levels. If you do use these analogies, then a more critical approach would be:

What are your personal characteristics and how did you come to possess those characteristics? Which characteristics are positive and which are negative? If you chose to emphasize your positive characteristics and compare them to an animal, which animal would it be? If you chose to emphasize your negative characteristics, what animal would you compare yourself to? What are some other things, besides animals, you could compare yourself to? How would you justify these comparisons? *S-29*

Prompts which deal with favorite heroes, movies, and music could be approached in a similar manner. This will help students examine their assumptions and produce more critical responses. "What, exactly do you admire about him or her? How did he or she acquire those traits? How do you know this person is as you think? What do those who don't admire this person say? Why do they think so? How do they know? How could you find out which is right? Is there something about this person that you don't think you should emulate? What? Why?" *S-20*

Any journal prompt can be rewritten to reflect critical thinking concepts. Students should be given time to *think* about their responses before they begin to write. Beware of asking students to complete a critical response in the time it takes you to take attendance. Critical journal entries could be spread out over a period of several days, if you use the daily journal writing format.

An alternative assignment would be to have students use their journal entries as a basis for a more formal and finished essay. Students could expand on their ideas, organize their points, and rewrite rough spots. Students could discuss the ideas in small groups and then write essays. The teacher could give several prompts on related ideas, then have students put their ideas together as a longer, better developed essay. *S-8*

There is no one 'right' remodel. Many different improvements are possible.

Poetry Critically Examined

Objectives of the Remodelled Plan

The students will:

• analyze familial relationships and distinguish between those and other relationships
• clarify and discuss the meaning of Langston Hughes' "Mother to Son"
• discuss significant questions regarding the rules of standard English
• explore the use of metaphor in a poem

Standard Approach

The purpose of this lesson is to present a poem by Langston Hughes, ask several questions about it, and discuss the skills of recognizing metaphors and conversation rhythms. The poem is reproduced below.

Mother to Son

Well, son, I'll tell you:
Life for me ain't been no crystal stair.
It's had tacks in it,
And splinters,
And boards torn up
And places with no carpet on the floor —
Bare.
But all the time I'se been a climbin' on,
And reachin' landin's,
And turnin' corners,
And sometimes goin' in the dark
Where there ain't been no light.
So boy, don't you turn back.
Don't you set down on the steps
'Cause you finds it's kinder hard.
Don't you fall now —
For I'se still goin' honey,
I'se still climbin',
And life for me ain't been no crystal stair.

Critique

Poetry provides unlimited opportunity to practice critical thinking in the language arts. Few poems directly state the message the poet is trying to convey, so it becomes necessary for the reader to practice inference. Since multiple interpretations are possible, each student can develop an interpretation and defend it, citing passages in the poem that support that interpretation. Students should be encouraged to be accurate and disciplined in their thinking, dispelling the notion that all interpretations are of equal worth, while at the same time feeling confident enough to propose their interpretations.

...son was chosen because it is typical of the way that poetry is presented in literature textbooks. The poem is usually accompanied by a photograph and then students are asked several recall questions such as *"What does the mother compare her life to?"* and *"What images does the mother use to describe her difficulties?"* Such questions merely require students to either recall or skim the poem to retrieve the correct answer. The student is not asked to think about the reasons that the mother made such comparisons or why a particular image might be suitable to describe her life. It merely asks the student to repeat them. The lesson doesn't give students an opportunity to appreciate the evocative power of the extended metaphor or the simplicity of expression of the piece. One text asks, *"What advice does she give her son?"* Again, all the student has to do is recopy the passage.

Sometimes, the student is asked to distinguish between similes and metaphors (similes use the words 'like' and 'as'; metaphors don't). Students do not discuss reasons for using figurative language, or choosing particular metaphors, but simply learn to distinguish between two forms of figurative language.

Strategies Used to Remodel

S-1 thinking independently
S-32 making plausible inferences, predictions, or interpretations
S-21 critical reading: clarifying and critiquing text
S-35 exploring implications and consequences
S-17 questioning deeply: raising and pursuing root or significant questions
S-2 developing insight into egocentricity or sociocentricity
S-11 comparing analogous situations: transferring ideas to new contexts

Remodelled Lesson Plan

Even before students are asked to open their books, the teacher can provide an opportunity for making plausible inferences. Write the title of the poem on the board and ask: "What do you think such a poem might be about? **S-1** What are some common ways that mothers relate to sons, and sons to mothers? Are relationships with fathers the same or different? Why or why not? What are some things that are common to parental relationships that are not common to other types of relationships such as friendships?" **S-32** Even if the teacher does not have time for all these questions, it is important to let students know that a higher level thinking is expected of them even before they are presented with the text.

Next, read the poem aloud to the students. Then choose a student to read the poem a second time.

Have students tell what it's about, what the mother is trying to get across. "Why was mother saying this? What do we know about her? Who might want to say this to their child? What would bring her to want to say this to her son? What might the son have been saying or acting like? How does she intend to affect her son? How might he react? What do the metaphors stand for? Compare the metaphors to what they stand for. (Easy life/crystal stair. Hard life/tacks,

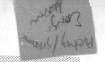

bare, dark landings. Going on vs. settin' down, etc.) Discuss at length. Why did the poet choose these metaphors?" **S-21**

Ask students what they noticed about the grammar of the poem. They will recognize that it is non-standard. Students could discuss the grammar and dialect. Have students discuss the language and syntax of the poem. "What can we tell about this woman from the way she talks? Why did the author choose to write this way? How would it have been different if it had been standard English or sounded educated?" **S-35**

Here is an excellent time to ask significant questions about linguistics: "What makes one kind of grammar or set of syntactical rules right and another wrong? How do people come to speak as they do?" If they say that they have been taught language in such a way, then ask how the people who teach language decide what form is correct. At some point, the teacher should explain that the dominant culture gets to decide correctness in language. Since they will already have noticed that the poem has a Black dialect, this becomes a segue back into the text. **S-17**

You might ask what is common to some of the adjectives or noun phrases used in the first seven lines (rough, hard, cold, bare). Now ask students to generalize about what relationship these types of words may have to a Black family's experience in America. The discussion generated by such a question may go anywhere depending on the class, but the point is that this poem gives students the opportunity to conceptualize racial issues.

At this point, the teacher could return to the poet's intent in the poem. "Why is the mother in the poem describing her life to her son and why is she using figurative language to do it? What are the implications of the mother's lifestyle? Does she assume her son will go through the same thing? Can you think of examples when life was difficult for a person because they were of a different race than the predominant race?" **S-2**

Have students evaluate the metaphor and the poem. **S-21**

For closure, ask students to focus on the image of a crystal stair and to invent another metaphor which is completely different but conveys the same meaning as the one the poet intended in the poem. **S-11**

• A writing exercise in which students are asked to relate a time when they were courageous, strong or proud would fit naturally here.

• When teaching lessons on poetry, the teacher could ask students to make copies of popular song lyrics which the class can discuss and compare with other poetry.

• Students could clarify and evaluate subjects addressed in popular entertainment and the values particular songs, shows, and movies presuppose. **S-17**

Integrated Grammar

Objectives of the Remodelled Plan

The students will:
- explore their ideas about language through Socratic discussion
- analyze a written passage and distinguish author's grammatical usage in terms of style
- evaluate a written passage

Standard Approach

The traditional pattern is based upon a format which explains the lesson, gives examples, and then provides drills for students on such topics as the following: parts of speech, verb tenses, active vs. passive verbs, dependent and independent clauses, punctuation. The simplicity or complexity of the lesson depends upon the grade level of the text.

Critique

Grammar was chosen as a lesson because it seems the least likely to be included in a discussion on critical thinking. Indeed, the traditional method utilized in grammar texts does discourage reasoning about grammar.

The facts of English are presented in a raw fashion and the student simply is expected to accept them. Some grammar texts attempt to be innovative by making grammar "fun" — using graphics and clever sentences for examples, but the message is the same: Grammar is a subject that students must learn. Soon they get the message that it is boring and worse than that, difficult and irrational. Students learn each distinction and skill in such a way that they only "know" it when specifically asked to look for it in the directions. They do not learn the details in any useful context, whether reading or writing. Students need to use grammatical analysis in order to see its importance and meaning.

Integrated Grammar is a method which was presented at a California Model Curriculum Conference. The premise is that if grammar is taught, it should be within the context of the literature that is being taught. Grammar is not a genre and it is something that we would have no use for if we didn't have something to communicate. It makes sense then to have students learn about grammar from literature and other writings. Most teachers would prefer to teach something else when given the choice. How then does a teacher who wishes to incorporate critical thinking into all areas of the curriculum teach grammar?

Strategies Used to Remodel

S-1 thinking independently
S-24 practicing Socratic discussion: clarifying and questioning beliefs, theories, or perspectives
S-21 reading critically: clarifying or critiquing texts

Remodelled Lesson Plan *s-1*

General Discussion of Language S-24

Before teachers attempt an integrated grammar lesson, the class can be divided into groups of three or four and asked some critical questions about the structure of their language. Ask one or two questions at a time, and ask one student in the group to volunteer to record the group's answers.

What are some rules a person would have to know to speak English?

How do humans acquire language? At what age? Explain exactly how it is done. What do you remember about your own language acquisition?

Are all people taught grammar and, if so, at what age do they learn it? If there are younger children at home, how are they learning (did they learn), and what mistakes did they make? Why did he say that? Why was it a mistake?

Who determines what correct English will be? What implications does this have for society?

What is the definition of syntax? (OK to use the dictionary.) Does word order matter in English? (For example, does the sentence, "Help my dog eat," and the sentence, "Help eat my dog," mean the same thing?) If someone in your group speaks another language, find out if word order is important in the construction of their language.

What are the implications for a person who can not speak at all? How do they communicate? How important is language of any kind to a person?

What are some things you would like to know about language that you were never taught?

By this time, you have involved students in thinking deeply about the importance of language. This process awakens intellectual curiosity instead of deadening it with grammar drills. The teacher may spend as much time as she likes exploring fundamental assumptions about language.

You may want to assign a writing project in which one group writes a paragraph then changes the word order in each sentence. For example, ask each group to collaborate on a short paragraph about the way children learn language. A partial response might be: *Children learn language at a very young age. Their parents are the main teachers, but sometimes children just repeat things they hear.* Then ask the group to mix up the syntax using the same words: *Very young language learn at a children age. Teachers sometimes but main parents repeat just the children are their things they hear.*

128

Groups exchange papers and try to decipher each other's paragraphs to make sense. Students could share their methods of approaching this problem. It soon dawns on students that language has a rigid structure and that although they may not be able to recite the rules governing syntax, they know them. Students that speak a non-standard variety of English could compare their syntax with standard English and generate rules for translating.

Grammar in Literature S-21

First, choose a short passage that is exceptionally descriptive, exciting or well written. Then ask students to write down the passage while you dictate it. This improves their listening and note-taking skills. Students could later compare different ways of using punctuation to write the passage.

The following passage is from John Steinbeck's *The Pearl*

> The scorpion moved delicately down the rope toward the box. Under her breath Juana repeated an ancient magic to guard against such evil, and on top of that she muttered a Hail Mary between clenched teeth. But Kino was in motion. His body glided quietly across the room, noiselessly and smoothly. His hands were in front of him, palms down, and his eyes were on the scorpion. Beneath it in the hanging box Coyotito laughed and reached up his hand toward it. It sensed danger when Kino was almost within reach of it. It stopped and its tail rose up over its back in little jerks and the curved thorn on the tail's end glistened.

Because students have written the passage, they are more prepared for the analysis you will ask them to do. Place them in groups to work on the following questions:

List some things that you notice about the writing style of this author. **S-1** Go through the passage and write down some verbs that worked especially well. Go through the passage and write down some nouns with their adjectives that made the passage more vivid. How do the adverbs contribute to the passage? List some positive and negative criticism you have of this author's writing style. **S-21**

This lesson will have students thinking about the way the grammar works in the passage. Students will develop a sense of what is powerful in writing and be able to generalize rules that will improve their own work. As a closing exercise, ask students to write a paragraph in which they imitate Steinbeck's style. They should be encouraged to invent their own fiction and not write a passage about a scorpion. These models of Steinbeck's style can be shared with the class and analyzed for points of comparison.

Thinking Skills and Testing

Objectives of the Remodelled Plan

The *teacher* will:
- recognize weak testing methods
- identify student assumptions about subject mastery
- develop new techniques for short quiz questions which require critical thinking
- restructure test questions to allow students to take and defend positions on novels read
- modify tests to include critical vocabulary

Standard Approach

Testing methods in the middle grades may take a variety of forms: true/false, objective, multiple choice, and essay. Most teachers agree that the essay form is best educationally. Close on the heels of this statement is the reality a workload of 150 students or more imposes. Teachers simply do not have the time to grade essay exams whenever they need an evaluation of a student's progress. Sometimes a teacher only wants to confirm that a student has done the reading. In these situations, the recall test is a common tool. In a five to ten question quiz, the student will be asked to supply facts from the literature, often including such questions as: Where did Mercy leave her necklace in Chapter Six? What was Harold's adopted brother-in-law's step son's name? How much did Sabella pay for her new condo?

For a model, we have used the book, *The Outsiders* by S.E. Hinton, which is frequently used in junior high.

For the first chapter, a test might include the following questions:

* What were the two gangs called? (Greasers and Socs)

* What do you know about the gangs? How?

* Who were Ponyboy's two brothers? (Soda and Darry)

* Which group did Ponyboy belong to? (Greasers)

* Where was Ponyboy coming from at the start of the chapter? (movies)

* What did the Socs do to him on the way home? (cut his hair, assaulted him)

* Who was described as the "real character" of the Greaser gang? (Dally)

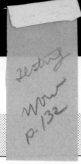

Critique

Recall quizzes do test the reader's ability to regurgitate information from the reading. But they do something more insidious as well. They give the students two messages. First, that the point of reading a novel, play, or short story is to memorize the facts presented therein. In this way, students are almost discouraged from ruminating on the *ideas* of the book. Instead they are using valuable reflection time to commit the nuts and bolts information to memory. The second questionable thing about recall exams is that they give students the notion that if they master the facts, they have mastered the book. Most teachers have experienced reading nothing but information recall in response to an essay question that specifically asked for synthesis, evaluation, or other higher level skills. At the very least, recall tests, if they must be given, should stick with the key facts, and events, and not ask for randomly selected details.

Other modes of testing present problems as well. One may construct sophisticated true/ false statements, but the test has a 50% guess factor. Multiple choice questions also have the potential for critical composition, but they take some time to compose and the potential for cheating is great if the test is reused. They also limit the responses of the students, who may have some genuine insights to convey about the book.

Strategies Used to Remodel

S-29 noting significant similarities and differences
S-32 making plausible inferences, predictions, or interpretations
S-30 examining or evaluating assumptions
S-17 questioning deeply: raising and pursuing root or significant questions
S-20 evaluating actions or policies
S-21 reading critically: clarifying or critiquing texts
S-35 exploring implications or consequences
S-4 exploring thoughts underlying feelings and feelings underlying thoughts

Remodelled Lesson Plan

For teachers interested in moving away from the recall test, we offer a variation which gives students the opportunity to use their thinking skills. If you ask students to keep the responses brief, a few words or one sentence, grading will not be difficult. Below is a sample of questions and possible answers.

• State two ways in which Ponyboy differs from his brother, Soda. (Pony reads and seems more interested in school; Pony's younger; Pony behaves like a brother, but Soda acts like a father.) **S-29**

• What can you infer about the emotional state of Pony at the opening of the book. (Happy, reflective — thinking about his brothers; he's a bit anxious about walking alone.) **S-32**

• Both of the gangs introduced in Chapter One are guilty of oversimplification. Give examples from each gang. (Socs think all Greasers are dirty, rough, stupid. Greasers think all Socs are rich snobs, aren't cool, fight without justification.) **S-30**

• Speculate on the *reasons* that these two groups exist (difference of social class; macho tendencies; makes them feel grown-up; makes them feel close). **S-17**

• Characterize the relationship between Pony and Soda in three *different* ways (parental, siblings, adoring, blind, overprotective). **S-32**

• Do you think the attitude toward women expressed by the Greasers is fair? Why/why not? (No, they call their girls broads and admire the Socs' girls. It's contradictory. No, they criticize them harshly. Yes, Greaser girls are just as misguided as the boys are.) **S-20**

• What factors led to conflict? Who bears primary responsibility for this event and why? **S-20**

This quiz requires students to use critical thinking skills to answer the questions. If the teacher uses this type of quiz frequently, students will develop the habit of reading and reflecting on the concepts presented.

If you wish, students may exchange papers and grade the quizzes. Various answers are volunteered by students. The teacher can then ask, "Does anyone have an answer that differs from those we have discussed?". The teacher may ask for the reasoning behind the answer to determine if credit will be given. Discussion may result. The process of giving and grading a quiz such as this deepens understanding for the whole class. Quizes given later in the book can have students evaluate characterization for consistency or realism.

Having students write a short description of the plot requires more than recall, since students have to select the most pertinent details to recall and describe. Requiring students to describe plots of everything they read develops the concept of plot much better than the standard method of teaching the concept in a few lessons over the course of the year.

Episode Analysis S-21

Another method of testing, which also could be used instead of the rote quiz is moving away from the question format altogether. At a Language Arts conference, Dr. Robert Calfee of Stanford University presented some critical analysis methods from Project Read. One of these, termed "Episode Analysis" is a preprinted page which could be used as a testing device. It is set up like this: **S-35**

Problem	Emotional Response	Action	Outcome

The students are expected to fill in each category. If the outcome is as yet unknown, then instruct the student to predict the outcome. For example:

Pony gets attacked by the Socs	Scared	Pony gets cut	Resentment against the Socs builds

The teacher may have students analyze more than one episode analysis. An alternative format might be: **S-4**

Event/Situation	Emotion	Assumption

If the students have had exposure to critical vocabulary, the teacher could compose a quiz which asks students to list some assumptions made by the characters. **S-30**

Any improvement on the recall test will produce a more stimulating and interesting test to grade. Because students are given the opportunity to think in ways which motivate them to be inventive, teachers may even gain insight into material they have taught many times.

> *A teacher committed to teaching for critical thinking must think beyond subject matter teaching to ends and objectives that transcend subject matter classification. To teach for critical thinking is, first of all, to create an environment that is conducive to critical thinking.*

Speeches: Clarifying 'Equality'

Objectives of the Remodelled Plan

The students will:
- clarify the abstract concept: equality
- engage in a Socratic discussion of the concept
- discuss questions raised, and organize, compose, and give speeches
- practice listening critically by evaluating and discussing the speeches
- compare the perspectives expressed in the speeches

Standard Approach————————————————————

In teaching speech, the emphasis is generally on mechanics and the attitudes necessary for successful delivery. As an introduction, students discuss the fears associated with giving a speech. The teacher asks questions like, "What don't you like about speaking in front of a group? What do you like ? Do you look forward to speaking in front of groups? Can you give some suggestions for overcoming your fears?" Various formats of speech are taught such as interviews, storytelling, oral reports, debate, parliamentary procedure, panel discussion and persuasive arguments.

To introduce the persuasive speech the students are asked to generate interesting topics. Prompts are given in the text for ideas. "_____ is a book everyone should read." "Each traveler should visit ____ ." "Nobody should miss the _____ concert." Students are asked to choose speech topics that would be of interest to particular groups: a meeting of a local sports club or a meeting of a citizen's group organized to fight pollution. They are told to begin with clear statements of what they want the listeners to do or think, including two or more reasons why they should think that way. They are then to prepare an outline for the topic they selected which they will share with the class. To prepare for actual delivery of the speech, the students brainstorm for the typical mistakes students make while giving a speech, such as, reading from a paper or forgetting to ask for questions. For practice, the students are asked to say their speeches aloud many times, pretending to speak to an audience or actually speaking to a friend.

Critique

Standard approaches to speech-making tend to overemphasize the mechanics of giving speeches at the expense of attention to content. This lesson unites speech-making and critical thinking by careful selection of topic. We present a speech lesson in which students clarify and analyze an abstract concept: equality. By first engaging in Socratic discussion of the concept, giving and hearing speeches on it, and discussing and comparing the speeches, students can begin to learn how to usefully analyze and clarify it.

134

People commonly experience great difficulty when attempting to use abstract concepts clearly, distinguishing different senses of the term — for example, numerical equality and economic equality — sorting out their relationships to related concepts, evaluating their use, applying them, exploring their implications, etc. They often incorrectly assume (or assert) that "everyone has his or her own definition" and request the speaker's definition. Definitions tend to be equally abstract and rarely useful in clarifying the concept or sense in which it is used in a particular context. We therefore suggest that the teacher help students begin to sort out the complexities of such concepts through guided discussions.

The following remodel can help students develop confidence in their ability to clarify an abstract concept.

Strategies Used to Remodel

S-14 clarifying and analyzing the meanings of words or phrases
S-27 comparing and contrasting ideals with actual practice
S-24 practicing Socratic discussion: clarifying and questioning beliefs, theories, or perspectives
S-22 listening critically: the art of silent dialogue
S-25 reasoning dialogically: comparing perspectives, interpretations, or theories
S-9 developing confidence in reason
S-8 developing intellectual perseverance

Remodelled Lesson Plan *S-14*

Before introducing the actual exercise to take place, the teacher could ask students to compare the characteristics of the prepared speech to other kinds of verbal communication. Write students' comments on the board. Among other things, students might notice that a speech is limited to a specific topic, is more formal, and has a beginning, middle, and end. Now ask what qualities an excellent speaker has. By this time, the students have begun to think about the mechanics of speech-making.

Lead students in an opening Socratic discussion which will elicit and separate aspects of and issues regarding the key concept. (The teacher should periodically relate to the concept specific points mentioned, indicating or eliciting the particular sense of 'equality' used or alluded to. The teacher can also periodically recap or have students recap the main points made in and directions taken by the discussion.) What does 'equality' mean? (Probe their responses with further questions.)

• What different senses does this word have? In what ways are all people equal? Not equal? In what ways is equality an American ideal? Why? What issues and problems does our country face that relate to some sense of equality? (List these on the board.) What, exactly, does that issue have to do with equality? Why? What sense of equality? Is one side of the dispute against equality, or does the dispute rest on how to achieve it? What does 'equality under the law' mean? What would be an example of inequality under the law? What would we have to do to determine the extent to which American citizens are given equal treatment under the law? **S-27** What does 'equal opportunity' mean? Equal opportunity to do what? What interferes with equality of opportunity? In what ways does our society try to ensure that every citizen has equal opportunities? (During the course of an extended discussion, bring in other topics, issues, related concepts, beliefs, and values, such as the following: inequality, equal rights, "We are all equally human," one man one vote, autonomy, fairness, favoritism, elitism, racism, sexism, disadvantaged, affirmative action.) **S-24**

Explain to the students that they will be working in cooperative groups of four. You may want to have them divide responsibilities and chose a student to give the speech, a student to act as recorder or note-taker, a student to keep the group on task and keep track of time, and a student to report the group's progress to the instructor.

The group will have to decide how to narrow the topic by choosing an issue, a distinction, or a specific point. Once students have narrowed the topic, they will have to develop the speech: outlining the main points, offering and organizing their views, choosing clarifying examples, etc.

Students without this instruction would probably go on to produce a vague, rhetorical speech about equality that would be weak in construction. But because students narrow the topic, they can clarify it within their chosen context and give a more focused speech. The teacher should explain that the material in the speech should reflect the thought of everyone in the group, not just one person. It is important that students consider other people's opinions and that they work together cooperatively.

Before the speeches are given, tell students that they will discuss and evaluate them. Let the students decide the standards of evaluation, which should include things such as presence, clarity of voice, clarity of thought and its expression, strength of arguments, insightfulness, etc.

After each speech, the teacher may want to have students recap the main points (allowing the speaker or group to clarify any points inadequately understood). **S-22**

After the speeches are given and evaluated, the teacher should lead a discussion about the concept of equality as expressed in the speeches. In how many different ways was the concept presented? Was it used in the same sense in each speech? Did some opinions differ? How did the different points made in the speeches relate to each other? (Irrelevant to, supported or elaborated on, contradicted or conflicted with, compatible with, etc.) What were the strengths and weaknesses of the ideas? **S-25** Is it easy or difficult for us to talk about things like equality? Why? **S-9**

Students could later have dialogical or dialectical discussions (especially if a point of controversy among students arose in the speeches), synthesize points from different speeches, or write essays responding to points made in the speeches or discussions.

If you would like to repeat this lesson, then choose another abstract concept such as patriotism, love, friendship, security, success, progress, freedom, human being, etc. Whatever the topic, you can be sure that the results will never be the same and that students will have the opportunity to express their opinions in a critical way.

Socratic questioning should be available to the teacher at all times. Questions, not answers, stimulate the mind.

Analyzing Characters

Objectives of the Remodelled Plan

The students will:
* understand the relationship between point of view and bias in the novel
* recognize personal bias
* exercise fairmindedness by writing about an incident from a reciprocal point of view
* analyze the factors that influence actions
* explore the consequences of changing a novel

Standard Approach

When the novel is taught, students are likely to spend class time studying characters. Various lessons address this: one may ask students to list the physical characteristics of people in the novel; internal and external conflicts may be discussed; or students will be instructed to write an interior monologue of a character of their choice.

One lesson used frequently is the character map. Students choose a character and work in groups to provide the following:

* Character's name
* Character's past
* Character's appearance
* Character's traits and attitudes
* Character's effect on other people
* Character's hopes and dreams
* Problems the character may face from his or her own personality and outside events

Critique

Many novels provide excellent opportunities for grasping the inner world of various characters and for comparing how they may perceive the same situations differently.

Standard lessons in and of themselves are workable, but teachers miss excellent opportunities to teach critical thinking if lessons are left at this level. The above activities are straightforward but don't require students to delve. Answers will probably be brief, and groups which work on the same character will no doubt have similar, if not identical, answers. Such lessons are unchallenging, and the students' understanding of the character remains virtually the same as before the lesson.

Many texts ask students to describe a character from a single action, rather than synthesize all of the information about the character. Students rarely, if ever, evaluate what they read. Critical thinking instruction requires that they continually do so.

138

Strategies Used to Remodel

S-1   thinking independently
S-2   developing insight into egocentricity or sociocentricity
S-35 exploring implications and consequences
S-3   exercising fairmindedness
S-16 evaluating the credibility of sources of information
S-23 making interdisciplinary connections
S-28 thinking precisely about thinking: using critical vocabulary
S-12 developing one's perspective: creating or exploring beliefs, arguments, or theories
S-20 analyzing or evaluating actions or policies
S-21 reading critically: clarifying or critiquing texts
S-33 evaluating evidence and alleged facts

Remodelled Lesson Plan

The methods outlined in this remodel may be worked into the novel unit at any time. They may be used for Socratic discussion, writing assignments, or cooperative group work as the teacher sees fit.

Introductory activities

As an introduction to discussing story characters, students could first discuss what it means to describe a real person's character or personality — how it could be done, what features or aspects should be mentioned, how examples of speech or behavior can be used. Students can compare this to developing and describing fictional characters. **S-29**

The concept of characterization in the the novel is closely connected to point of view. Most readers are unaware that the author had to make a conscious decision about which point of view to use. For students studying characterization, this is an important starting place.

• What does the term 'point of view' mean? What point of view is used in this book? From what other points of view could this book have been written? What does use of this point of view imply? Why was this point of view chosen? **S-35**

A book written from the view of a character will naturally present information as that character perceives it. Incidentally, novels written in omniscient or third person reflect the point of view of the author.

Students can gain greater insight into such points by practicing switching perspectives:

• Think of a time when you were in trouble for something. Write about this incident from your point of view. Defend yourself as best you can. Now write about the same incident from another's point of view that was opposite yours in this incident. **S-3** For example, suppose you got in trouble for inviting friends over when no one was home and it "developed" into a party. Perhaps you would write about it stating that you only meant to invite one or two friends over, but they brought some friends, and it turned into a party by accident. From your father's point of view, you used the house to party. You intentionally broke a rule about the conditions of having a party and were irresponsible. He may say that you should have put your foot down and stopped things before they got out of hand. Students might then rewrite the incident in the third person, giving an unbiased (or, at least, less biased) account.

Students could now be reminded that the same sort of thing is true in novels. We receive information through the eyes of the narrator. Students can discuss how the main character's perspective effects how information and events are conceptualized. *S-16*

Characterization

Next, students should work on understanding how characters are influenced by their past and by the present situation in the book. This is quite different from the previous character map which asks students to state the character's past.

• What time is used for the setting in this novel? Describe differences between that time and the present time. *S-23*

• What are some other major influences on the character? What made this character think or acts this way? Use supporting quotations from the text. *S-21*

• Write a personal essay in which you describe your earliest influences, your present influences, and what you think will influence you in the future. *S-12*

One of the pleasures of reading a novel is our involvement with the characters. We personally identify with some of them. Other characters remind us of people we know. Incorporating critical thinking into this personal identification will help clarify personal perspectives.

• Write about one character you enjoy or respect in the book. Do you admire the actions of this character? Why or why not? Describe that character's basic ideas and values. *S-12*

• Choose a character from the book you dislike or with whom you disagree. Outline the reasons for this, and in a small group discuss alternatives to the character's actions. Share and discuss your answers. *S-20*

Another method of deepening understanding is to assign a dialogue between characters in the book that are having a conflict and have the characters solve the conflict in the dialogue. This can be assigned before the students know the real outcome of the conflict.

Changing the story *S-35*

Yet another method of encouraging students to think about the importance of characterization is to present them with problems to solve.

• How would this book change if (a character) were not in it at all?

• What would be the effect if the age of a character was changed dramatically.

• What would change in the book if the race of the character was different?

• Suppose the book took place in a different country?

• What would change if the economic conditions were different?

Evaluating Characterization S-21

Finally, as a closure exercise at the end of the book, have students critique the book focusing on the relationships between characters and describe how the plot or action was forwarded by the characters. This could be represented in map form but could also be accompanied by a written explanation. Students will experience thinking about causal relationships in literature and how important they are to the novel as a whole.

Students could evaluate characterization. Ask, "Are the characters realistic? Are the characters consistent, or was something out of character? Did the main character change over the course of the novel? Was that change realistic? Do the characters represent anything — traits or ideas? Were the characters complex or simple?" Probe students' responses for support and analysis.

How were the characters' personalities revealed? What speeches, incidents, or thoughts seemed to you key to understanding this character?Why do you think this point of view was chosen? What would have been gained or lost by using that one, or a third person? (The order in which events were revealed, some characters' thoughts, etc.)

For a book written in the first person: Did the narrator understand what was going on? Did other characters? What clues, if any, were given the reader that the narrator was wrong?

For a book in the third person: Of which characters or actions does the author approve? Disapprove? How do you know? Do you agree? Why? **S-12**

Students can compare characters in novels to those on TV and in movies, or compare problems of characterization in books and movies. **S-29**

The goal is to explain critical thinking by translating general theory into specific teaching strategies.

Writing Less Egocentric Poetry

Objectives of the Remodelled Plan

The students will:

• evaluate a variety of poems, developing their criteria
• write poetry based on a shared experience and compare their perspectives
• write poetry from models
• incorporate concepts from outside sources in poetry writing
• use narrative information for poetry which explores a memorable event

Standard Approach

Students may be exposed to a variety of methods for learning to write poetry. The following three generalizations are commonly used:

Formula Poetry - Students are given worksheets which contain stems. The student is asked to fill in the blanks:

I love.....

Someday I want to.....

The thing I fear most is.....

The best thing about me is......

Free-write Poetry — Students are told to write a poem about anything which interests them. They are free to rhyme the lines or not.

Incorporating Poetic Devices — The teacher gives definitions and examples of figurative language such as simile and metaphor, or other poetic devices such as personification. The students are given examples and then told to practice writing their own poetry which includes the devices.

Critique

The first method above encourages students to be egocentric and not much else. While writing poetry is a highly personal endeavor, this type of lesson does not promote much thought and could only be defined as poetry writing in the weakest sense of the art. The second method gives students little direction and in most cases the poems produced with this type of prompt are also egocentric and often heavy with cliches and sing song rhyme. In both of these methods little learning is taking place. The methods may even reinforce the idea that anything is poetry and anything I write about myself is acceptable. The third method, while less egocentric, will deaden any interest in using various forms of language. While it may be useful for students to learn these terms, merely feeding students the definitions and then having them practice their use is more like rote grammar instruction than a writing lesson.

Strategies Used to Remodel

S-8 developing intellectual perseverance
S-15 developing criteria for evaluation: clarifying values and standards
S-21 reading critically: clarifying and critiquing text
S-2 developing insight into egocentricity or sociocentricity
S-11 comparing analogous situations: transferring ideas to new contexts
S-12 developing one's perspective: creating or exploring beliefs, arguments, or theories
S-1 thinking independently
S-4 exploring thoughts underlying feelings and feelings underlying thoughts

Remodelled Lesson Plan

This remodel presents several poetry writing methods which are both adaptable to any classroom and challenging to students. The methods can be used at any grade level as long as the teacher models the exercise carefully. Students that have been asked to do little more than just answer questions about themselves will perhaps complain that these approaches are "too hard." Thinking about concepts is always more difficult than writing down anything that is going through your head. The results will be well worth the extra effort and students will see this for themselves at the end of the lesson. **S-8** Egocentricity becomes less of a problem in these models because they lead students down more interesting paths.

When you plan a unit on poetry writing, incorporate some poetry reading each day. The teacher may use any source available, but it is important that students read and discuss a variety of good poetry while they are learning to write it. Have students evaluate each poem they read, discuss their reasons for their conclusions, and compare the criteria they use. **S-15**

These lessons are listed in a progression which suggests that the first is the most simple and the last is the most difficult but they do not depend upon each other for continuity. You may use them individually with success as long as you provide a clear model.

Dictation S-21

Choose a short poem (about 16 lines) and instruct the students to write it down as you dictate it. Read the poem at a slow pace all the way through and then read it once more. After you are done, ask students where they broke the lines and where they provided punctuation. This will lead to a discussion about form in poetry. Put the poem on the board or on an overhead projector and have students "correct" their breaks and punctuation. Ask students to speculate on why the poet chose these line breaks. Ask if changing the form affects the poem. If there are unconventional uses of punctuation, discuss this. If the poem has a rhyme scheme, ask students to pick it out. Does the poem have any language in it which worked especially well? Why? While this lesson does not ask students to actually write their own poems, it does provide a critical focus for poetry. How a poem is placed on the page and how poets choose to do this affects the work. Repeat this lesson with a poem that is much different in form than the one previously used. The dictation lesson also has the added bonus of having students take a very slow look at the language in the poem as they are writing it down.

Field Trip Poem

The teacher may review the idea that many poems address the fives senses. Plan a short field trip in which students must take notes on what they see, hear, smell, taste, and touch. They should record descriptions of people or pieces of conversations as well. The following day, they can incorporate as much of the acquired experience from the trip as possible. One successful version of this trip was done by taking the class to a donut shop. If you can't take them into the community, then plan a trip to another part of campus. This lesson places students in the position of the observer, outside their personal perspectives. Poetry produced in this way is rich in imagery. Students can compare their poems with each other, thus discovering differences among their experiences of the same trip. *S-2*

Model Writing

Choose a poem and ask students to use it as a model for writing their own poems. For example, if the poem is about a place, then each student's poem must also be about a place. The students should use the same form, noting the number of stanzas and rhyme scheme. They should not begin the lines with the same words but should imitate the language structure of the poet. If the poem uses vivid adjectives and adverbs, then the students should also. This lesson usually produces interesting work which breaks old habits and cliches. It enables students to analyze poetry in a non-didactic way. *S-11*

Dictionary Poems

Students are instructed to open a dictionary ten times at random and place a finger, also at random, on a word. They then use these words in a ten line poem, using one of the "found" words in each line. The student may use the word anywhere in the line and add whatever language is needed to compose the poem. This lesson encourages students to link concepts they would not ordinarily link and moves away from the typically egocentric poem. The teacher should review the words before the student starts writing, eliminating any bizarre words that would be too difficult. Any words which would be too easy, such as articles and pronouns, should also be re-chosen. *S-12*

End Word Poems

Students work in pairs. They should have a poetry book or a literature anthology at their disposal. Each student chooses a poem from the book and writes down, in order, the *last* word of each line including punctuation, if any. They should not tell their partners which poem they used. Then the partners exchange lists with the instruction that these words should appear at the *end* of each line in their poems. After the poems are completed, students are told the original source, and they may check for similarities in concept and structure. Writing "into" words in this fashion provides a structure and yet allows freedom of expression. Remind students that even though the word may be at the end of the line, that is not necessarily the end of the sentence unless punctuation so dictates. In original unstructured poetry, students often write one sentence per line. This exercise discourages limitation in form. They must often rethink lines to make them "fit" with previous lines. **S-1**

Narrative Poetry

The teacher should read some narrative poems with the students for modeling. Also, the idea of perspective should be discussed. For example, are narrative poems biased because they are told from a certain point of view? For homework, instruct students to find an adult that will relate an incident to them that is memorable. Have students take notes and hand these in with a poem based on the incident. **S-4**

With all these lessons, time should be spent on student evaluation. The notion that poetry writing is drudgery or that it must always be about one's own emotions is quickly dispelled when students are asked to think carefully about what they write.

If a staff becomes proficient at critiquing and remodelling lesson plans, it can critique and 'remodel' any other aspect of school life and activity, and so become increasingly less dependent on direction or supervision from above and increasingly more activated by self-direction from within.

Interviewing for Belief Systems

Objectives of the Remodelled Plan
The students will:
- examine aspects of the interview process
- engage in Socratic discussion regarding ethics
- identify belief systems and generate interview questions
- practice Socratic discussion by conducting interviews
- evaluate interviews

Standard Approach

Texts address the design of interview questions, i.e., what types of questions can be asked to elicit the desired information, for example, biographical. They also recommend how the interview can be written up in one of two desired formats, question and answer, or in this case, biographical essay or story format, which allows the student more creative embellishment.

Some questions considered in this lesson might be: "What were you like as a child? What was it like to grow up in such-and-such a time period? How were you similar to or different from other children?"

Critique

A lesson on interviewing can be a valuable teaching tool in that students learn a variety of questioning techniques and engage in extended discussion with people outside their peer group. A well-formulated lesson provides an opportunity for students to ask clarifying and probing questions, listen actively, and organize and synthesize what they hear.

A common lesson, the biographical interview, is an interesting choice because of its biographical concentration which is "safe" territory for interviewing, especially at this level. Most people will supply information about their past with little provocation. This type of questioning would surely elicit responses that would give students enough information to formulate a history for biographical background, but would probably give little understanding of the person being interviewed. It is too likely to elicit a simple chronology. The student would have collected a number of interesting facts or stories, but any deeper insight would be gained only by inference. Such lessons assume a didactic theory of knowledge and thought in which one needs only discover details. A critical approach would focus on the *structure* of anothers' ideas — how beliefs are linked to each other, how some beliefs are more basic, how individual beliefs form a system, how systems of belief differ.

The following remodelled lesson plan focuses on the belief systems of those being interviewed, which would not only challenge the student presenting the questions but would also allow the interviewee to give a more thoughtful and introspective interview. To illustrate, we've chosen ethics as a topic. Furthermore, the student will begin to think critically about how belief systems are formed, how they differ, and how such systems affect our daily judgment.

Strategies Used to Remodel

S-22 listening critically: the art of silent dialogue
S-29 noting significant similarities and differences
S-24 practicing Socratic discussion: clarifying and questioning beliefs, theories, or perspectives
S-12 developing ones perspective: creating or exploring beliefs, arguments, or theories
S-8 developing intellectual perseverance
S-15 developing criteria for evaluation: clarifying values and standards

Remodelled Lesson Plan S-22

Introduction

The teacher can begin this lesson by asking how an interview differs from ordinary conversation. (A conversation with an individual is unstructured; may take several turns and cover any number of topics; is two-way since usually — or, at least, ideally — both participants offer their ideas. One may have a vague objective in mind like, "Getting to know Mr. Williams." Interviews are more structured insofar as they begin with a prescribed set of questions; are one-way, insofar as *one* participant answers, the other asks; often have a narrower purpose.) **S-29**

Then, ask the students to think of different types of interviews. They may offer such responses as these: college interviews, job interviews, celebrity interviews, or interviews which probe the position of those running for elected office. Some of these interviews have specific objectives: Would this person perform well at our university? Would this person be qualified for the position? Would this person represent the people of the community on the city council?

The teacher could then assign cooperative groups the task of composing questions that would accomplish these tasks. Afterwards, one person of the group could serve as the interviewer (admissions director, employer, newspaper reporter) and another as the interviewee. The mock interviews should be conducted in front of the entire class. When the interview is over, the class should critique the process by pointing out which questions provided the best information and adding any questions that were left out.

Students could study some printed interviews, evaluate them, and formulate probing questions and follow-up questions which could have been asked. **S-21**

By now the class has begun to think about the interview process. They have witnessed a few models and have had some experience composing questions. They also will have seen how the type of questions asked depends on the objective of the interview.

Preparation for the interview

To introduce the students to their interview assignment, the teacher may ask students to consider how many different points of view on questions of right and wrong are represented in the class. Someone could take notes on the following Socratic discussion, or it could be taped.

Ask, "How do you know when something is right or wrong? When is it hard to tell what's right? Why do people do wrong? When do you blame people for doing something wrong? Not blame them? When did you first learn right from wrong? How? What do your beliefs assume about human nature? How does this assumption affect how you act? How you judge others? Should people have their own ideas of right and wrong, or should they accept the judgment of authorities? Can you think of something that would be wrong in one instance and right in another? Can you think of something that is absolutely wrong, regardless of the circumstances?" **S-12** The teacher could then ask the students to frame more specific questions about what they believe. **S-24**

Recap the main points made in the above discussion. The idea of organized belief systems can now be raised. The class could group the responses by similarities among the perspectives. Ask students to think about which views expressed by the others most resemble their own and which differ most from their own. Have them try to characterize the similarities and differences among these perspectives, distinguishing major from minor differences. **S-29**

By now the students have begun to identify their own belief systems and are now ready to begin the interview assignment. They can begin by thinking about how the questions will be framed for a "Belief System Interview." Suggest that they use some of the questions previously posed: How do you know when something is right or wrong? When did you first learn right from wrong? Did someone teach you?

The students should know that a good interviewer will ask clarifying questions like, "What exactly do you mean by that? Can you give me an example? How would you respond to this idea (give an opposing view)? What led you to that belief?" etc.

Next, the students can frame more questions. The entire class may work on this project and then choose the best of the lot. By practicing on other students first, students may better develop a sense of good follow-up questions.

Assign the interview. You may want students to tape record the interview (with permission of the interviewee). Or you may want them to develop note-taking skills and record the responses that way. The class could evaluate various ways of presenting their interviews.

Students could show their work to the interviewees for confirmation and further clarification, and then revise their reports. **S-8**

When the interviews have been shared, the class can relate points made in them to the previous discussions by comparing the perspectives expressed in them with their own, and evaluating the questions raised.

If the teacher wishes to repeat the lesson, other topics which interest students and lend themselves to analysis could be chosen:

Religion How would you define 'religion'? Do religions have anything in common? If so, what? How do religious authorities decide what is right/wrong? Can a person know right from wrong without religion? How? Are all religions equal? If not, why not? How much does religion affect what you believe? Does a person have to accept religious laws without question? Why or why not?

Prejudice How is it defined? Does it exist in our community, school, home? When were you first aware of prejudice? Why do you think prejudice exists? How could we solve some of our race problems?

Sex Education What should sex education consist of? At what age should it be taught? When did you first learn about sex? Was this a good way to get information? Should birth control be taught? Why/why not? What issues are most relevant for sex education today? Can you think of ways of discouraging teenage pregnancies?

The interview process requires careful preparation in the classroom with specific instructor intervention regarding the types of questions asked, as well as the process of clarifying information. The students not only learn to examine their own beliefs, they learn to analyze the types of questions asked, consider conflicting opinions, and evaluate the answers given. The value in this lesson is not only the interview process, but the critical evaluation of the topic. The students gain confidence in their critical thinking skills and enjoy the process as well.

Follow up brainstorming sessions with discussion of the items listed — categorizing, evaluating, analyzing, comparing, ordering, etc.

Grammar

Objectives of the Remodelled Plan

The students will:

• distinguish subject from predicate
• add modifying words and phrases to simple sentences and discuss the results
• develop insight into parts of speech by comparing the functions of words
• distinguish transitive from intransitive verbs
• apply grammatical insight to analyze and clarify the Pledge of Allegiance

Standard Approach

Texts divide sentences into subject and predicate, explaining that the subject tells who or what the sentence is about, and the predicate tells what the subject does or is. After this clarification, the class does oral and written exercises dividing sentences into subject and predicate.

To teach parts of speech, texts often use some acid test. For example, using the word to complete sentences such as, "How many _____ are there?" to test nouns. They explain the distinction or test, and drill and test students' recall and application of it. Similar explanations and drill teach such distinctions as transitive and intransitive verbs.

Critique

Grammatical points and distinctions should be taught in such a way as their usefulness is apparent to the student. For example, when reading difficult sentences, grammatical analysis gives readers a way to begin to get a handle on meaning, and to clarify vague passages. (For example, by using the principles that pronouns always refer to some noun and that transitive verbs require objects, the reader can rewrite sentences making them clearer and more explicit.)

Texts teach the parts of speech in a fragmented, mechanical way. Instead of building on the function of words within sentences, they often reduce determining parts of speech to mechanically applied tests. Each part of speech is taught in isolation from the others which tends to add to the fragmented quality of the parts-of-speech lessons.

Texts teach part of speech as a feature of the word itself, whereas words themselves are not one or another type. Many words can serve as several parts of speech, according to their role in particular sentences.

Most lessons emphasize repetition over understanding, having students repeat the given definitions or tests, and apply them again and again to given lists of words. Students need to learn to distinguish parts of speech, not memorize definitions or rules. Giving them empty practice does not

150

foster the ability to make the distinction, nor to understand the concepts in terms that make sense to the student. Furthermore, the tests themselves are often misleading; they often don't work.

Our approach to grammar encourages students to recognize the underlying logic of grammar. This logic dovetails well with the writing skills needed to construct a grammatical sentence, a paragraph, or a well-organized, logically progressive essay. These same skills also establish or reinforce the thought patterns necessary for critical thought. We believe, in other words, that well-designed grammatical instruction can reinforce critical thinking principles, and vice versa.

Dividing sentences into subject and predicate is an excellent starting point for analyzing sentence structure and parts of speech. Since the class examines whole sentences, they must observe the relationships between the subject and predicate to divide the sentences. This division also builds a foundation for later distinctions between parts of speech, because modifying words and phrases can be distinguished by whether they modify the subject, the predicate, or the whole sentence.

The following lesson plans provide specific examples of what we mean by fostering understanding of grammatical logic, rather than memorizing mechanical recognition processes. If students discover these grammatical distinctions for themselves, we increase their understanding and encourage them to think for themselves. Students can use their texts for reference.

Strategies Used to Remodel

S-1 thinking independently
S-11 comparing analogous situations: transferring insights to new contexts
S-29 noting significant similarities and differences
S-10 refining generalizations and avoiding oversimplifications
S-21 reading critically: clarifying or critiquing texts

Remodelled Lesson Plan

Subject and Predicate S-1

The teacher could begin by writing a simple sentence on the board. A good first sentence might be a simple subject and intransitive verb like, "Birds sing." To encourage analysis of the main sentence parts, the teacher could ask questions like: Which word tells you what is being talked about? Which word tells what is being done?

Have students divide a few more sentences, each one a little longer. If this process bogs down, the teacher could model the distinction for a few sentences until some students catch on. Keep questioning as you go, or have students explain their reasoning, to stimulate clarification through dialogue.

To illustrate the concept of modifiers, take the original example, "Birds sing." Ask students questions like the following: How can we make the sentence longer? What words can we add to this sentence? How can we make it give us more information? How can we make this sentence tell us more about the birds and their singing? What does each addition tell us about? What question does each answer? Which birds? What about their singing? Singing what? Singing how? Why? How does adding these words change the meaning of the sentence? If students need help, give them some examples like, "We could say, 'Blue birds sing,' or 'Blue birds sing when they are happy.'" Show them how additional words make the sentence more precise, by excluding some possibilities.

Subject	Predicate
Birds	sing.
Blue birds	sing.
Three blue birds	sing.
Three blue birds	sing together.
Three blue birds	sing together on the roof.

As each word or phrase is added, ask questions like, "What does the new word tell us about? (The birds. The subject. It tells us what color the birds are.) What does the word 'three' tell us? (More about the birds. More about the subject. How many birds there are.) What word does the word 'together' explain, something about the birds, or something about the singing? (Sing. The predicate. It tells something about how they sang, what they were doing when they sang.) What does this phrase modify? (The predicate. Sing. It tells where the birds sang.) If the class exhaustively expands a couple of the sentences in this manner, it will become clear to them that every additional word or phrase makes the sentence more precise. During the course of this activity, the teacher can introduce the names of the various parts of speech.

The teacher could strengthen student comprehension of the logic of grammar by comparing the logic of sentences to that of a well-constructed paragraph or essay. *S-11*

Parts of Speech *S-29*

The teacher could select a word that functions as more than one part of speech and write sentences using the word differently, for example, "Lock the door. Put the key in the lock." Students can characterize the differences between these uses of the same word, such as, 'bench,' 'board,' 'date,' 'bill,' 'level,' 'mob,' 'travel' 'travel agent.' Students can compare such word groups as 'think' and 'thought,' 'believe' and 'belief,' 'acquire,' 'acquisitive,' 'acquisition.'

When students have had sufficient practice, the class may compare the different parts of speech. Encourage students to test their generalizations by trying to find counter-examples, and, if necessary, revising their claims. In some cases their generalizations may be nearly always true. If so, this could be pointed out. If they make a serious mistake which they fail to correct, you may want to supply a counter-example. *S-10*

Transitive and Intransitive Verbs *S-1*

The class could also add to a sentence containing a transitive verb like, "The boy gave the girl a rose. ➔ The day he returned home, the lonely little boy sadly gave the thorny red rose that he picked from his mother's garden to the girl who broke his heart." Students can begin to see the difference between transitive and intransitive verbs when they realize that "The boy gave," isn't a complete thought — it makes us want to know "Gave what? To whom?"

The class could discuss more examples of transitive verbs and the kinds of words they require as objects. The common childhood expression "I'll tell!" can be discussed as an example of a grammatically incomplete sentence easily understood in context.

The teacher could give students sentences — some with transitive and some with intransitive verbs. Some of the sentences can lack necessary objects. Students could explain which sentences require objects.

Using Grammatical Analysis on Complex Sentences *S-21*

This section has students reducing a complex sentence to its essentials, and then adding the other pieces. Thus grammar is used to clarify statements and enhance reading ability.

Have students write and punctuate the Pledge of Allegiance. (Write variations in punctuation on the board. Compare them. Have students find a correct version.)

Using the correct version, identify or have students identify the subject, verb, and direct and indirect objects: *I pledge* (pledge what, and to whom?) *I pledge allegiance to the flag....* (and do *what* to the republic?) I pledge allegiance to the republic.... *for which it stands* (To what does 'it' refer?).... Students could find as many simple sentences in the pledge as they can, and share and discuss their rewrites.

Similar lessons can be repeated on material from texts, newspapers, or other readings. (Also, see the Social Studies lesson on the Preamble to the Constitution for another detailed description of using grammatical analysis on a long sentence.)

> *One does not learn about critical thinking by memorizing a definition or set of distinctions.*

Writing Argumentative Essays

Objectives of the Remodelled Plan

The students will:
- develop their perspectives through dialectical exchange, writing, and argument analysis and evaluation
- clarify issues and key words
- evaluate evidence
- practice critical thought by writing and revising argumentative essays

Standard Approach

> Students pick an issue or position and find reasons to support their conclusions. Sometimes students are told to state and refute opposing arguments. They research their topics, noting facts supporting their positions. Sometimes texts introduce fallacies and a bit of logic as preparation. Students write an argumentative essay, defending their positions.

Critique

Though this handbook mainly focuses on incorporating critical thinking into other lessons, lessons specifically on critical thinking can also be useful. Generally, texts' treatment of argumentation suffer from many serious flaws and misunderstandings, display fuzziness of thought, misuse terms, and lack critical insight. As a whole, texts downplay evaluation of reasoning. (Where mentioned or suggested, they give little guidance and often use confusing language). They rarely suggest evaluating the relevance of support to conclusions.

Texts mainly focus on how to defend opinions, not how to shape them more reasonably. Though they address the importance of giving reasons for beliefs, they often neglect the importance of considering opposing views, or strengthening one's reasoning by weeding out or altering unjustified beliefs. Presenting good reasons, though valuable, is only half of a discussion. The standard approach allows reactions that are too often impressionistic and based on prejudice or lack of understanding.

Rather than teaching argument analysis and evaluation, texts generally have students attempt to distinguish fact from opinion. Though the motive of having students distinguish *questionable* from *acceptable* claims is worthwhile, the usual approach does not accomplish this purpose. It produces an unquestioning attitude of acceptance for statements that *seem* factual, though factual (empirical) claims are not necessarily reliable, and students can't necessarily tell if so-called facts are true. Facts, when used in an argument, may not be complete or relevant. Since statements students are called on to judge as opinions are given without context, students cannot rationally judge whether they are mere whim or can be well defended. Rather than using the fact/opinion distinction, students can distinguish questionable from acceptable claims and fact from interpretation and judgment.

This remodel illustrates a way of orchestrating cognitive strategies to reason dialectically.

Strategies Used to Remodel

S-26 reasoning dialectically: evaluating perspectives, interpretations, or theories
S-12 developing one's perspective: creating or exploring beliefs, arguments, or theories
S-28 thinking precisely about thinking: using critical vocabulary
S-31 distinguishing relevant from irrelevant facts
S-34 recognizing contradictions
S-18 analyzing or evaluating arguments, interpretations, beliefs, or theories
S-3 exercising fairmindedness
S-13 clarifying issues, conclusions, or beliefs
S-15 developing criteria for evaluation: clarifying values and standards
S-14 clarifying and analyzing the meanings of words or phrases
S-16 evaluating the credibility of sources of information
S-33 evaluating evidence and alleged facts

Remodelled Lesson Plan S-26

Introduction

We have written these lessons as a unified unit culminating in a well-thought-out argumentative essay. Similar units, repeated over the course of the year, can greatly improve both reasoning and its expression.

Class discussions can be used to introduce and clarify aspects of critical thought through the analysis and improvement of two opposing arguments selected as models. The models should address the same issue from different perspectives, be fairly strong, but require some improvement. Small group discussions allow students to develop and clarify their positions on issues of their choice, and argue between opposing views.

For their essay and discussion groups topics, students could brainstorm issues of interest to them. Each group must share an issue about which group members disagree. The issues from which they choose should not be questions of mere preference but should call for reasoned judgment.

Each student then picks an issue and writes an essay. Students should state their positions and support them with their best reasons. This is the first draft of their argumentative essays. *S-12*

Beginning Argument Analysis S-28

The teacher might develop students' use of critical vocabulary by having them rephrase the model arguments into explicit premises, assumptions, and conclusions. To have students identify the conclusion of each model, ask, "What is the *conclusion*? What is the point of the argument? What statement is this argument trying to convince you to believe? Is the conclusion stated or implied?" Then ask, "What reasons are given? Is the reasoning complete, or is there a hidden claim, or *assumption*?"

Students could then begin to analyze and evaluate the arguments in a class discussion. You could have them give reasons for their evaluations, or guide discussion with questions like the following: "Does it present evidence? What? Are the claims clear? What do they mean? Could they mean something else? Are they *ambiguous*? Questionable? Complete? What is left out? Is this reason *relevant* — should it affect our conclusion? Why or why not? **S-31**

To help students pinpoint the conflict between the model arguments, you might ask, "Do these reasoners disagree about the facts? (Which facts?) Their interpretations of the facts? (On what theories do they base their interpretations?) Do they disagree about values? About how to realize those values? About which of two values is most important?" **S-34**

Students could suggest ways to make each argument stronger. The teacher may also model improving the arguments and their expression during this and future class discussions. **S-18**

When assigning discussion groups, emphasize the importance of listening carefully and openmindedly to other arguments. Students can take notes on, and include, opposing views in their essays. Students should argue their positions (that is, give reasons to convince the others to adopt their conclusions). The groups could note assumptions, pinpoint contradictions, and look for strengths and weaknesses in the arguments given. Each group could recap the main points of their discussion to the entire class. Encourage the groups to find some points of agreement.

You may want to have students argue each other's positions. **S-3** Students can then evaluate each other's presentations of their arguments.

Have students rewrite their papers.

Clarification

Another lesson could be used to develop students' ability to clarify issues and concepts, again using the model arguments previously mentioned. How would this arguer state the issue? The other arguer? How could we state the issue in words both sides would accept? How could this issue be settled? What concepts do we need to clarify? Is something being evaluated? (What? Why? What standards are most appropriately applied?) **S-13**

The teacher can have students identify the key terms in the model arguments. Ask students to describe examples to which the key words or phrases in the model arguments would properly apply. Then ask for examples of their opposites. Also ask what phrase could apply to both kinds of cases. Students should then discuss features common to each kind of case, and make the standards they use to judge such cases explicit. **S-15** Why is this a case of X? What does the word imply? Why does this arguer characterize the situation as X? **S-14**

Then each group can meet again to clarify the key claims and terms from their discussion groups. Have students distinguish those terms which all agree apply from disputed terms. They should then clarify the disputed terms or claims by using examples of terms, opposites, and other cases. The standards used for applying the terms or claims should be clarified, the facts required to justify evaluations made explicit.

Evaluating Claims and Evidence

You may want to focus the next section directly on distinguishing claims which need further support from those which are acceptable without further support. You may use questions like the following: Does anyone know whether or not this is true? How do you know? Is there reason to doubt this statement? Why or why not? Accept it? What would support it Undermine it? **S-13** Stress that one can't judge truth or reasonableness of a claim from its form or appearance. A statement alone doesn't tell us how much or little thought, or what quality of thought produced it.

For each model, students can evaluate the evidence cited by considering questions like the following: Where did this information come from? How could the source know this? Is this source reliable? (Do they have a good track record? Anything to lose or gain? Are they in a position to know?) **S-16** Is this evidence relevant? Is relevant evidence left out? **S-31** Would that evidence require the reasoner to change the conclusion? Why or why not? **S-33**

Students can then expand and revise their essays. They should give their new positions and arguments, supporting claims which require support. Stress that the strongest arguments take the strengths of other points of view into account. **S-12**

Students could trade their papers with other members of their groups. Students can comment on the papers requesting clarification or evidence, pointing out where the relevance of claims is unclear, or facts or assumptions are questionable, and correcting distortions of opposing points of view. Students can use the comments when revising their essays.

The teacher could have students write group papers, instead of individual papers giving all sides of the disagreement and clarifying points of disagreement.

Ten Steps for Analyzing Arguments

Objectives of the Remodelled Plan

The students will:
- extract premises and conclusions from selected text
- formulate arguments
- argue both sides of an issue
- examine and evaluate those arguments

Standard Approach

The student is introduced to a pro/con, debate, or issue-oriented format. Often the teacher would like the student to learn research techniques, and controversial topics are a likely vehicle. Among the most common topics are: abortion, gun control, capital punishment, euthanasia, nuclear energy, and animal rights. Presumably these are chosen because they are inflammatory, and because there is a wealth of information readily available. Even if a teacher suggests that students may do a paper on another topic, most will probably stay with the old standbys.

The procedure for the research project may consist of the teacher spending a great deal of time discussing the requirements of the paper — thesis, length, required number of sources, footnotes, bibliography, warnings against direct quotations without proper accreditation, etc.

Critique

Clearly, such assignments as these, properly structured, are ideal for practice and synthesis of most aspects of critical thought, from examining assumptions to exercising fairmindedness.

Probably the most fatal flaw of standard lessons is that little or no time is spent on discussing the argument itself, how one formulates an issue, what constitutes relevant evidence, the value of the counter argument or the importance of justifying a conclusion. The student goes off to the library with an opinion — pro-gun control or anti-gun control, for example — collects the requisite information, thinly disguises the plagiarism, and types up a badly connected string of other people's work. The teacher takes home great piles of these papers and reads information seen countless times before. What has the student learned? Perhaps that research papers are dull or that footnotes and bibliographies are tedious. More than likely, students have learned nothing about formulating and examining an argument. They each began with a certain position on the issue and sought only to defend it, without testing its validity.

The debate format is worse, as it usually includes only the most sensational presentation of a case, replete with graphic horrors of animals being tortured in laboratories, for example. Usually no instruction is offered in argument analysis in this instance either. When argument analysis is addressed, discussion is often uselessly vague ("Be relevant!") or confused. (See the section "Text Treatment of Critical Thinking and Argumentation," in chapter 4.) Instead, students should be taught the skills of formulating and carefully evaluating a wide range of issues.

This is presented here as a speech lesson, though a written assignment could be given at the end. This lesson outlines a method of introducing students to argument and provides a model. A ten-step plan is suggested, but if you need to alter the procedure to thirteen steps or reduce it to eight, then do so without hesitation. The lesson is offered as a "formula" only because the task of introducing argument to students at this level seems difficult at first. Many things such as identifying assumptions, and testing the credibility of sources were omitted to keep the lesson simple. For another lesson on argument analysis, see "Writing an Argumentative Essay."

Strategies Used to Remodel

S-21 critical reading: clarifying and critiquing text
S-4 exploring thoughts underlying feelings and feelings underlying thoughts
S-31 distinguishing relevant from irrelevant facts
S-25 reasoning dialogically: comparing perspectives, interpretations, or theories
S-33 evaluating evidence and alleged facts
S-13 clarifying issues, conclusions, or beliefs
S-22 listening critically: the art of silent dialogue
S-3 exercising fairmindedness
S-9 developing confidence in reason

Remodelled Lesson Plan *S-18*

This plan consists of choosing an article from the newspaper and then extracting and examining an argument. It provides an extended example of reading critically.

1. Teacher finds a suitable newspaper article.

Ideally, the article should concern a current issue of interest to students. It should be long enough to contain the major points and have quotations from the parties concerned.

The selected article concerns a woman who disrupted a beauty pageant as a form of protest. She claimed that they are demeaning to women, encouraging them to starve and otherwise unnaturally change their appearances. Interviewees affiliated with the pageant countered her arguments and claimed that she hurt contestants and organizers. In this case, two issues were addressed: Do pageants hurt all women? Was Michelle Anderson justified in disrupting the pageant? Either issue can be chosen for discussion.

The article was chosen because it is timely, interesting to adolescents, clearly controversial, and easy to formulate. At the same time, the issue allows exploration of other issues such as the right to protest, gender equity, societal values, and commercialism. It is almost a page long, an ideal length. The story was followed for several days by the media, allowing the teacher to present new material if so desired.

2. Teacher prepares an introductory exercise.

Before introducing the lesson or the article, the teacher might devise an exercise as an anticipatory set. In this case, a class discussion on beauty pageants in general is suggested. How do you feel about beauty pageants? Why? **S-4** Does anyone know someone who was in a beauty pageant? If so, what did the experience involve? Does anyone want to be in one? Why? Do you ever watch them on T.V.? At the end of the discussion you could write "Beauty Pageants" on the board with plus and minus columns. Ask students to contribute positive and negative aspects.

3. Students and teacher read the text.

Students read the text, either aloud or silently. Ask, "What is the article about? What views were expressed?" ("Should Beauty Pageants be stopped? Was Anderson's action a justifiable form of protest?") **S-21**

4. Students, with the teacher facilitating, formulate a conclusion in such a way that pro/con positions are possible.

Begin by giving a definition of "conclusion" — the statement to be proven by means of the reasons the arguer is giving. Ask students (in groups or as individuals) to try to state Michelle Anderson's conclusion. "Pageants hurt all women," or "Disrupting the contest was justified." Avoid conclusions that state a position with a negative such as, "Beauty pageants are not worthwhile." If the conclusion is stated negatively, the pro and con sides become confusing. Keep students from inserting premises into the conclusion, e.g., "Beauty pageants are wrong because they demean women."

5. Students extract reasons or premises from the text.

Next define "premise" — a reason given for believing a conclusion. Students can work in groups to find the reasons, since it saves time and encourages a cooperative atmosphere. At first, reasons should be taken from the text with as little paraphrasing as possible.

6. Students formulate the counter argument.

A counter argument, the con side of the conclusion, may be formulated by examining the pro premises and by reading the text for supporting information.

Students should reread the article, listing details relevant to the conclusions. Have the class discuss these lists and distinguish what all agree is relevant from what is of disputed relevance. To use those points of disputed relevance, relevance itself must be argued. **S-31**

Encourage students to isolate key words and phrases (e.g., demeaning, indignities, cheating the contestants, right to protest, right to compete in the pageant). Examine the issue further, having students present reasons left out of the article, and discuss why the concepts do or don't apply.

7. Students prepare to argue both sides.

Students prepare to argue in groups or pairs. It is important that you impress upon students that they are expected to argue the case — *not just repeat the premises* — by *supporting* the premise. **S-25**

Perhaps they will argue that eating disorders are rampant in the United States and that, while the contestants themselves may or may not be starving, they serve as negative or unhealthy role models for the rest of American women. They may argue that it is rare for a non-white woman to win the contest. Or they may mention that women have to spend money to be in the contests and that only one woman wins the scholarship — the others lose. They should argue, for example, why bleaching hair is demeaning. Whatever points are made should be better developed than the premises.

On the con side, they may point out that everyone is judged in life in all sorts of different situations. The beauty pageant judges also score contestants on verbal ability and talent. They may even take issue with the wording of the conclusion itself, questioning a statement that pertains to all women; even if a few women object to beauty pageants, that doesn't mean *all* women are harmed.

Students will find the notion of supporting the premises difficult at first, because usually they are expected merely to repeat information, not think about it. After the first few times, students become quite good at argument skills and look forward to exploring the issue.

8. With a two-minute warning, students present either the pro or con side.

Give time for students to present their cases. The class should take notes on the strong and weak points in preparation for the evaluation. **S-22**

9. The class evaluates the presentation.

The evaluation may take any form the teacher wishes — written or oral. Remember that it is the presentation that is to be evaluated. The task is not to decide who won, pro or con. How well did the groups defend the premises? Did they argue irrelevant points? Did they bring in convincing information to supplement the premises? Did they address opposing arguments? **S-18**

You will notice that we have avoided having the students "choose" sides. Critical thinking requires students to enter into both points of view and understand what is strong and weak on both sides.

10. The class explores the underlying or tangent issues.

After this is done, the teacher may discuss the issue with the students and come to conclusions on which side is stronger. Have students discuss their own positions and evaluations of the points raised. Students could also discuss ways their thinking changed over the course of the assignment. **S-9**

This lesson can be structured in several different ways. For example, you may want the students to practice picking out the conclusions and premises of several articles before you try the ten-step approach. You may want to model much of the whole process yourself first. Using a video camera is always a good tool in lessons such as this, because it is possible to go back and replay sections of the presentations. Later, the element of library research may be added to more advanced lessons.

One cannot develop one's fairmindedness, for example, without actually thinking fairmindedly. One cannot develop one's intellectual independence, without actually thinking independently. This is true of all the essential critical thinking traits, values, or dispositions. They are developmentally embedded in thinking itself.

News

Objectives of the Remodelled Plan

The students will:
- practice reading the news critically
- explore the consequences of working with and using different news media
- discussroot questions about the importance of following the news
- exercise independence of thought when evaluating the importance of, and emphasis on, news items
- analyze news stories by clarifying issues, claims, and criteria for evaluation, and by evaluating evidence

Standard Approach

Straight news is fact — who, what, when, where, and why. Often, however, news articles also interpret, analyze, or evaluate events, or describe an eyewitness' feelings. Texts emphasize the importance of the who, what, where, when, and why questions in news articles. Other purposes of the article are to show why an event was special, or how it was sad, funny, inspiring or unusual, and, in doing so, they make the story interesting. Texts point out that reporters sometimes tell more than the facts — they may tell how they themselves feel or how the eyewitness feels. Models of news writing are reprinted from actual articles written for different papers. The students are asked to analyze the models looking for vivid verbs, or imagining how the story would change if it were written by an eyewitness instead of the reporter.

Students are asked to bring in articles about new discoveries or to tell of a story they heard on the TV or the radio. Noting the pyramid structure of news stories, they are then to write their own stories based on one of the stories they found. They are to include the who, what, when, where and why questions as well as facts, quotes, and a catchy headline. Subsequent assignments are to write different kinds of news articles including lead paragraphs, complete news stories, and editorials. They are warned not to guess at the facts.

Some texts choose to focus on the mechanics of reading a newspaper. The use of the index and the different sections of the paper as well as the format of the stories and the kinds of information presented are emphasized. Such activities as finding particular services in the classified section or finding out about desirable vacation spots are assigned.

Critique

Critical thinking enables one to improve one's basic beliefs, and this requires having as complete information as possible. We chose this unit because of the important role that the news media have in shaping our view of the world. The earlier a person can learn to use news sources critically, the better. The critical thinker follows news, at least in part, for well-defined purposes. The critical spirit shapes one's use of news media.

163

When thinking about news, the critical thinker considers such questions as, "Why follow the news? What does 'news' mean? What situations and events are most important for me to know about? What can I believe? What should I doubt? What shapes the form and content of news I receive? What are the purposes of those who bring me news? How should I evaluate news sources?" Furthermore, the critical thinker realizes that the use of such terms as, 'news,' 'fact,' 'important,' and 'worth knowing,' all reflect one's perspective. The independent thinker makes these distinctions free of another's authority rather than blindly accepting reporters' and editors' evaluations. The critical thinker actively uses news media to develop an individual perspective, rather than passively accepting the perspective presented.

Independent thought

An enormous number of events occur everyday. No more than a small fraction can be printed or broadcast. Inclusion and placement of stories and order of details are editors' and reporters' decisions, and reflect *their* perspectives. Reporters and editors decide what to print and what to ignore, what to put on the front page and what inside. Yet texts repeatedly claim that the main or most important stories are on the front page; the most important details are in the first few paragraphs. By ignoring the effect of journalists' perspectives, texts inadvertently encourage students to unquestioningly accept others' judgments, rather than making their own.

Another factor which determines the size and placement of an article is its popularity. A popular, though unimportant, issue may receive prominent and extended coverage. Gossip, celebrity news, fads, and other trivial events often receive more prominent coverage than serious issues and events. For example, a soft drink company that changed its recipe received time and space completely out of proportion to its importance. Emphasizing that the most important news receives the most extensive and prominent coverage discourages students from examining and evaluating the importance others place on news.

Texts tend to tell students such things as why people should be well-informed, and what functions or purposes news items serve. Students should be asked to develop their own views regarding the importance and purposes of news; and define their own categories of news stories.

Fact/opinion

Texts generally use or assume the "fact/opinion distinction" throughout their treatment of news. The sections on slanted news and news vs. editorials emphasize the distinction. The use of this distinction, as usual, is highly misleading. Activities on slanted news generally have students merely distinguish factual from evaluative claims. Texts encourage students to accept claims containing precise sounding language and doubt other kinds of claims. What sounds like a fact may be more doubtful than an inference or evaluation. Students should not be led to believe that they can judge the truth of claims merely by looking at their form. Instead, they should note the sources of claims and discuss the criteria for their evaluation. Here, texts provide little guidance.

Texts promote the commonly-held misconception that the news is fact (and therefore true) and opinion (usually understood as "mere opinion") is reserved for the editorial pages. This belief ignores the following points: 1) Much of the news is quoted. Although it may well be true that this person did say that, what the person said may be false or misleading. Readers should remember whether "something they read in the paper" was quoted , and from whom and in what context. 2) Reporters make mistakes. They can get the facts wrong. 3) Facts can be reported out of context. Facts crucial to a fair understanding of an event can be left out, trivialized, or unfairly discredited. 4) When a newspaper goes on a crusade, investigating and reporting a story to champion a cause, most of that work appears in the news sections. 5) Editorial columns or letters to the editor may well contain facts (sometimes crucial facts not found elsewhere in the paper). 6) A well-reasoned, clearly present-ed "opinion" column or letter to the editor may be as well worth reading, as new, insightful, and informative, as useful for understanding an issue, as is "straight news." 7) Favored interpretations or explanations of events can be assumed or promoted, reasonable alternatives ignored. Students should learn to judge what they read on its own merit and in relation to evidence, not on the basis of the section in which it appears. (See the section on fact/opinion, in "Thinking Critically About Teaching: From Didactic to Critical Teaching.")

Superficial explanations

Texts explain that news reports serve to inform and entertain. As they stand, such explana-tions offer little help toward understanding purposes and functions of various stories. The func-tions, rather than being clarified, are left vague. What is the purpose of the distinction between entertaining and informing? How should this distinction affect how each kind of story should be read, understood, or used? Such lessons leave students with a superficial, brief answer to root questions about the function of a wide variety of news stories.

The concept of slanted news is trivialized by the text treatment. According to most texts, news is slanted by use of misleading headlines or sentences (understood in light of the fact/opinion distinction). Even when texts do not limit the definition of 'slanting' to "emotive words used in headlines," student exercises and activities generally do. Texts ignore the subtler and much more common forms, such as placement, emphasis, introduction and use of details and quotes, lack of coverage, and the time at which stories are used or ignored. A neutrally phrased headline above seemingly factual statements may be slanted. The presence of evaluative language may not show bias. Though word choice often biases readers, the bias most frequently occurs in a larger con-text than in a single sentence. Writers may have double standards regarding the use of evaluative words or phrases, or such terms may simply be asserted without support. Texts generally ignore these factors in favor of applying the fact/opinion distinction to headlines and claims and having students "find emotive words."

Trivial activities

Too much time is spent having students write headlines, leads, and stories. Introducing reflec-tive critical use of news media is more important than training reporters. Other forms of writing practice could be substituted (paraphrasing, summarizing, and writing argumentative essays).

The remodel which follows gives students the opportunity to assess and use news sources crit-ically and reflectively. This unit promotes students' confidence in reason and in their abilities to think for themselves.

Strategies Used to Remodel

S-21 reading critically: clarifying or critiquing texts
S-9   developing confidence in reason
S-29 noting significant similarities and differences
S-8   developing intellectual perseverance
S-24 practicing Socratic discussion: clarifying and questioning beliefs, theories, or perspectives
S-1   thinking independently

S-17 questioning deeply: raising and pursuing root or significant questions
S-15 developing criteria for evaluation: clarifying values and standards
S-12 developing one's perspective: creating or exploring beliefs, arguments, or theories
S-30 examining or evaluating assumptions
S-13 clarifying issues, conclusions, or beliefs
S-16 evaluating the credibility of sources of information
S-18 analyzing or evaluating arguments, interpretations, beliefs, or theories
S-34 recognizing contradictions
S-35 exploring implications and consequences
S-23 making interdisciplinary connections
S-25 reasoning dialogically: comparing perspectives, interpretations, or theories

Remodelled Lesson Plan *S-21*

Teachers' introduction

We recommend that the teacher spend as much time as possible on this unit. By using social studies time, teachers can increase time available for study of news. News media themselves should be the main source of material, rather than textbooks. Students may also critique parts of the text after their study of news.

Although both the original and remodelled lessons focus on newspapers, we recommend that other sources of news also be used, discussed, and compared. "What are the differences between TV, radio, magazines, and newspapers? How do these differences affect presentation of the news? What are the consequences of the differences? In what ways is reading what people have said better or worse than hearing and/or watching them? How should these difference affect use of each medium?" *S-29*

Students could compare the perspectives reflected in different news magazines, newscasts, and newspapers. Videotapes of news reports could be used to introduce students to important stories.

Our remodelled unit is divided into the following sections: 1) Preliminary work; 2) Story placement; 3) Individual items; 4) Influence of media; 5) Purposes of news; and 6) Using news in other subjects.

1) Preliminary work

The class could spend the first week or so examining the news. The teacher may want to set up heterogeneous reading groups wherein stronger readers can help weaker readers. Groups may be formed to follow ongoing stories for the duration of the unit (and beyond). Such groups can make periodic reports to the rest of the class, and the subjects can be discussed. *S-8*

Work within such groups could be divided, with interested students doing background research, and others collecting, paraphrasing and analyzing articles, and looking up unfamiliar terms in dictionaries and encyclopedias. Students not interested in following an issue may cut and categorize stories (perhaps by subject, importance, or perspective of the source). Some students could keep running tallies on such things as use of wire services, journalists' sources, reports of opinion polls, what proportion of the news is quotes, or who is quoted most often.

The class could have an exploratory Socratic discussion of what 'news' means and why it is important. The teacher could ask questions like the following: "What is news? What are newscasts and newspapers for? What do they do? *S-1* (Follow up student responses with further questions or counter examples.) What kinds of stories or events make up the news? What kinds of stories do not make the news? *S-17* Why do people listen to, watch, and read news? What do people want to know about? What do people need to know about? (Encourage multiple responses, and encourage students to draw this distinction between want and need.) What kinds of things are important for people to know? Why?" *S-24*

When students have had sufficient time to familiarize themselves with newspapers and have shared their discoveries and impressions, the teacher can begin a series of more in-depth discussions about the significance of what students have found and about news media.

2) Story placement *S-1*

Students could apply insights gained through perusal of the news and preliminary discussions by discussing placement and emphasis of news. The teacher could use questions like the following: If you were an editor, and had a stack of stories, how would you decide which to print, and which not to print? Why? Which to put on the front page and which inside the paper? Why? Which gets the biggest headline? If you were writing headlines, how would you figure out what to say? If you were a reporter, which details would you put first? Next? Last? Why? Would everyone make the same decisions? Have students discuss what kinds of stories everyone would agree are most important, least important, and which are of disputed importance. They can begin to generate criteria for judging the relative importance of news items. *S-17*

Students could compare front page stories with stories inside the paper, compare their ideas about what's most important to those of the editors, and generalize about their criteria. Ask questions like the following: "Why do you think these stories are on the front page? What, according to the editors of this paper, are the most important stories of the past week? Why, do you think, did they make these decisions? What other decisions could they have made instead? Are there stories or articles the editors thought were important, that you think are unimportant? Which stories inside of the paper do you think belong on the front page? Why? *S-12* What were the editors assuming? What could they have assumed instead? Which assumptions are better? *S-30* Why? (Similarly, students could compare different sources' coverage of specific stories.) Do any of the criteria conflict? If so, why might they conflict? Can they be reconciled? What values underlie these criteria If so, how?" *S-15*

3) Individual items *S-13*

To develop students' sense of the requirements of fair coverage, the teacher could take a lead paragraph or headline, tell students the basic idea of the story, and ask questions like the following: "To research this story fairly, what would you have to do? Where could you get the information you need? Who would you have to talk to? What questions should you ask?"(The answers could be compared to the actual story, or stories from different sources — other papers, magazines, or TV.) If the story is one of conflict, the teacher might ask: "How are the sides portrayed in the story? Are they given equal space? Is each side portrayed neutrally? Why do you say so? Are the evaluations justified? Why or why not? How could we find out? How do the terms used influence the reader? Are the terms justified?" *S-9*

Students could discuss how the alleged facts in a story can be evaluated, rather than applying the fact/opinion distinction to statements. The teacher or students could select a story, and discuss questions like the following: What facts are mentioned in this story? (The teacher may want to record these.) What is the main point? Are all of the facts relevant, or are some irrelevant? Why do you say so? *S-31* Do the facts seem complete? Are there important questions left unanswered? What? Why? Are both sides represented? How does each side represent the issue? Do they agree about how to word the issue? Give an unbiased formulation of the issue. Is the report complete/does it tell you everything you need to know to be able to judge the situation? Why? What sources are used? Are these people in a position to know what they claim to know? Why or why not? Does anyone connected with the story have a vested interest in what people believe about it? *S-16* What evidence is presented to support or undermine the truth of the claims made? What conclusions, if any, can we reach about this story? *S-33*

For work on headlines, students could take actual newspaper articles, summarize or paraphrase them, and then assess the accuracy of the headlines. *S-21* Students could suggest better headlines, and compare different headlines for the same story. *S-1*

Examination of editorials, columns, and letters to the editor provide fruitful practice in argument analysis and critique. The class could discuss questions like the following: What is the writer's main point? How does he support it? What are the key terms or ideas? Are they used properly? Why or why not? Does anything said contradict something you know? *S-34* How can we find out which is true? Does the writer cite evidence/facts? What? Where does he get them? Are they clearly true, clearly false, or questionable? Why? Are the facts relevant? Why or why not? Are some relevant facts left out? *S-33* How would someone with an opposing view answer? (Students could practice dialogical or dialectical thinking here, if they are familiar enough with the subject of the passage.) What are the strengths of this argument? The weaknesses? Does the writer make a good case? Why or why not? *S-18*

4) Influence of media *S-35*

To explore some of the effects media have on reported news, the teacher could lead a discussion about "News as a business." Point out that most money comes from advertising and that news media with larger audiences get more money from advertisers. So news emphasizes stories that sell papers and attract viewers. And to maximize profits by spending less, news media tend to use cheaper sources such as press conferences and press releases, rather than investigation. The teacher may want to explain how AP and UPI are news-gathering services to which media subscribe. These services provide most of the news used by reporters.

Since two common sources of news are the press conference and press release, the teacher may want to explain what these are. Perhaps students could watch a videotape of a press conference. Students could look for and count mentions of press releases and press conferences, discuss why people give them, who gives them, who doesn't give them, and why they are relied on heavily.

"How does profit motive affect the news we recieve?" **S-35**

5) Purposes of news S-17

At or toward the end of the unit, the class could discuss, in greater depth than in the preliminary discussion, purposes of following the news. The class can discuss the news covered during the unit. Ask questions like the following: "What were the major stories? What other stories did you see? How important are the stories we've seen? Why?" For individual stories, ask, "Is this something people should be aware of? Why or why not? Why would people find this interesting or important? How important is this? What effect did it have? On whom? Which stories do you think are the most important for people to know about? Why? What does 'news' mean?" (Discuss at length.)

During the course of this discussion, the teacher may have students review the concept of 'democracy.' If necessary, explain the phrase 'informed decision.' The class can then discuss the kinds of news citizens of a democracy need to know — background for important decisions; actions of elected and appointed government officials. (Discuss at length.)

6) Using News in Other Subjects S-23

Social Studies

Students could write news reports of historical events under study. Different students or groups of students could write the reports from different points of view, for example, the Revolutionary War from the points of view of the English, Indians, and Revolutionaries. Students could compare and evaluate the results. **S-25**

Stories followed by students could be researched using back issues and other resources for background into the history of the country, conflict, or people involved. **S-8** Study of both the news and geography could be enhanced by having students read and discuss news about areas under study in geography, or by using their geography texts and other sources to research areas mentioned in important news stories.

Politics is an especially fruitful area for using news. Students can discuss different offices and to which branch of government each belongs, distinguish aspects of government mentioned in the Constitution from those not, and discuss any Constitutional issues which arise during the unit. Students can also learn about other governments, how they work and their similarities with and differences from ours, as well as our relationships to them.

Students could also relate discussion of political action groups and public opinion to government and history. Ask, "What is this group trying to accomplish? Why? Why hasn't it been done? How are they trying to accomplish their purpose? Do you think their goals are important? Why or why not? How would you evaluate their methods?"

The subjects anthropology, sociology, psychology are also covered in the news and could be introduced or discussed.

Science

Public opinion polls could be compared with scientific studies. Students could use news reports when studying weather and climate. Such subjects as energy, the environment, health and nutrition, astronomy, and physics are covered in the news. Students can use, discuss, and evaluate various charts, graphs, and diagrams presented in news reports.

> *When the powerful tools of critical thinking are used merely at the service of egocentrism, sociocentrism, or ethnocentrism, then genuine communication and discussion end, and people relate to one another in fundamentally manipulative, even if intellectual, ways.*

Remodelling Social Studies

Introduction

The major problem to overcome in remodelling social studies units and lessons is that of transforming didactic instruction within one point of view into dialogical instruction within multiple points of view. As teachers, we should see ourselves not as dispensers of absolute truth nor as proponents of relativity, but as careful reflective seekers after truth, a search in which we are inviting our students to participate. We need continually to remind ourselves that each person responds to social issues from one of a variety of mutually inconsistent points of view. Each point of view rests on assumptions about human nature. Presenting one point of view as the truth limits our understanding of issues. Practice in entering into and coming to understand divergent points of view, on the other hand, heightens our grasp of the real problems of our lives. Children, in their everyday lives, already face the kinds of issues studied in social studies and are engaged in developing sets of assumptions on questions like the following:

> What does it mean to belong to a group? What rights and responsibilities do I have? Does it matter if others do not approve of me? Is it worthwhile to be good? What is most important to me? How am I like and unlike others? Whom should I trust? Who are my friends and enemies? What are people like? What am I like? How do I fit in with others? What are my rights and responsibilities? What are others' rights and responsibilities?

Humans live in a world of humanly constructed meanings. There is always more than one way to conceptualize human behavior. Humans create points of view, ideologies, and philosophies that often conflict with each other. Students need to understand the implications of this crucial fact: that all accounts of human behavior are expressed within a point of view, that it is not possible to cover all the facts in any account of what happened, that each account stresses some facts over others, that when an account is given (by a teacher, student, or textbook author), the

171

point of view in which it is given should be identified and, where possible, alternative points of view considered, and finally, that points of view need to be critically analyzed and assessed.

Adults, as well as children, tend to assume the truth of their own unexamined points of view. People often unfairly discredit or misinterpret ideas based on assumptions which differ from their own. In order to address social issues critically, students must continually evaluate their beliefs by contrasting them with opposing beliefs. From the beginning, social studies instruction should encourage dialogical thinking, that is, the fairminded discussion of a variety of points of view and their underlying beliefs. Of course, this emphasis on the diversity of human perspectives should not be covered in such a way as to imply that all points of view are equally valid. Rather, students should learn to value critical thinking skills as tools to help them distinguish truth from falsity, insight from prejudice, accurate conception from misconception.

Dialogical experience in which students begin to use critical vocabulary to sharpen their thinking and their sense of logic, is crucial. Words and phrases like 'claims,' 'assumes,' 'implies,' 'supports,' 'is evidence for,' 'is inconsistent with,' 'is relevant to' should be integrated into such discussions. Formulating their own views of historical events and social issues should enable students to synthesize data from divergent sources and to grasp important ideas. Too often, students are asked to recall details with no synthesis, no organizing ideas, and no distinction between details and basic ideas or between facts and common U.S. interpretations of them.

Students certainly need opportunities to explicitly learn basic principles of social analysis, but more importantly, they need opportunities to apply them to real and imagined cases, and to develop insight into social analysis. They especially need to come to terms with the pitfalls of human social analyses, to recognize the ease with which we mask self-interest or egocentric desires with social scientific language. In any case, for any particular instance of social judgment or reasoning, students should learn the art of distinguishing *perspectives on the world* from *facts* (which provide the specific information or occasion for a particular social judgment). In learning to discriminate these dimensions of social reasoning, we learn how to focus our minds on a variety of questions at issue.

As people, students have an undeniable right to develop their own social perspective — whether conservative or liberal, whether optimistic or pessimistic — but they should be able to analyze the perspective they do use, compare it accurately with other perspectives, and scrutinize the facts they conceptualize and judge in the social domain with the same care required in any other domain of knowledge. They should, in other words, become as adept in using critical thinking principles in the social domain as we expect them to be in scientific domains of learning.

Traditional lessons cover several important subjects within social studies: politics, economics, history, anthropology, and geography. Critical education in social studies focuses on basic questions in each subject, and prepares students for their future economic, political, and social roles.

Some Common Problems with Social Studies Texts

• End-of-chapter questions often ask for recall of a random selection of details and key facts or ideas. Often the answers are found in the text in bold or otherwise emphasized type. Thus, students need not even understand the question, let alone the answer, to complete their assignments.

• Timelines, maps, charts and graphs are presented and read as mere drill rather than as aids to understanding deeper issues.

• There is rarely adequate emphasis on extending insights to analogous situations in other times and places.

• Although the texts treat diversity of opinion as necessary, beliefs are not presented as subject to examination or critique. Students are encouraged to accept that others have different beliefs but are not encouraged to understand why. Yet it is by understanding *why* others think as they do that students can profit from considering other points of view. The text writers' emphasis on simple tolerance serves to end discussion, whereas students should learn to consider judgments as subject to rational assessment.

• Students are not encouraged to recognize and combat their own natural ethnocentricity. Texts encourage ethnocentricity in many ways. They often present American ideals as uniquely American when, in fact, every nation shares at least some of them. Although beliefs about the state of the world and about how to achieve ideals vary greatly, the American version of these is often treated as universal or self-evident. Students should learn not to confuse their limited perspective with universal belief. Ethnocentricity is reflected in word choices that assume an American or Western European perspective. Cultures are described as isolated rather than as isolated from Europe. Christian missionaries are described as spreading or teaching religion rather than Christianity. Cultures are evaluated as modern according to their similarity to our culture. In addition, texts often assume, imply, or clearly state that most of the world would prefer to be just like us. The American way of life and policies, according to the world view implied in standard texts, is the pinnacle of human achievement and presents the best human life has to offer. That others might believe the same of their own cultures is rarely mentioned or considered.

• Texts often wantonly omit crucial concepts, relationships, and details. For example, in discussing the opening of trade relations between Japan and the U.S., one text failed to mention why the Japanese had cut off relations with the West. Another text passed over fossil fuels and atomic energy in two sentences.

• Most texts treat important subjects superficially. There seems to be more concern for the outward appearance of things than for their underlying dynamics. Many texts also tend to approach the heart of the matter and then stop short. Topics are introduced, treated briefly, and dropped. History, for instance, is presented as merely a series of events. Texts often describe events briefly but seldom mention how people perceived them, why they accepted or resisted them, or what ideas and assumptions influenced them. Texts often cover different political systems by mentioning the titles of political offices. Most discussions of religion reflect the same superficiality. Texts emphasize names of deities, rituals, and practices. But beliefs are not explored in depth; the inner life is ignored, the personal dimension omitted.

• In many instances, texts encourage student passivity by providing all the answers. After lengthy map skills units, students are asked to apply those skills to answer simple questions. However, they are not held accountable for providing the answers on their own. Texts usually err by asking questions students should be able to answer on their own, and then immediately providing the answer. Once students understand the system, they know that they don't have to stop and think for themselves, because the text will do it for them in the next sentence.

• Graphs and charts are treated in the same manner. Students practice reading maps in their texts for reasons provided by those texts. They are not required to determine for themselves what questions a map can answer, what sort of map is required, or how to find it. Map reading practice could be used to develop students' confidence in their abilities to reason and learn for themselves, but typically isn't.

• Chart assignments can be remodelled to provide more thought-provoking work on students' parts by adding headings regarding implications, consequences, or justifications and by having students compare and argue for their particular ways of filling the charts out.

• Although the rich selections of appendices is convenient for the students, they are discouraged from discovering where to find information on their own. In real life, problems are not solved by referring to a handy chart neatly put into a book of information on the subject. In fact few, if any, complex issues are resolved by perusing one book. Instead we ought to be teaching students to decide what kind of information is necessary and how to figure out a way to get it. In addition, many of the appendices are neatly correlated, designed and labeled to answer precisely those questions asked in the text. Students therefore do not develop strategies they need to transfer their knowledge to the issues, problems, and questions they will have as adults.

• Texts often emphasize the ideal or theoretical models of government, economic systems, and institutions without exploring real (hidden) sources of power and change. The difficulty and complexity of problems are alluded to or even mentioned, but without exploring the complexity. Furthermore, texts typically do not separate ideals from the way a system might really operate in a given situation.

• Explanations are often abstract and lack detail or connection to that which they explain, leaving students with a vague understanding. Texts fail to answer such questions as: *How* did this bring about that? What was going on in people's minds? Why? How did that relate to the rest of society? Why is this valued? Without context, the little bits have little meaning and therefore, if remembered at all, serve no function and cannot be recalled for use.

Subject-Specific Problems

There are somewhat different problems which emerge in each of the areas of social studies. It is important to identify them:

History

• Primary sources, when used or referred to at all, are not examined as sources of information or as explications of important attitudes and beliefs which shaped events. Their assessment is not discussed, nor are influences which shape that assessment. Texts fail to mention, for example, that most history was written by victors of wars and by the few educated people. Much information about other points of view has been lost. Most selections from primary sources are trivial narratives.

• History texts state problems and perceived problems of the past, give the solutions attempted, and mention results. Students don't evaluate them *as solutions*. They don't look at what others did about the same problem, nor do they analyze causes or evaluate solutions for themselves. We recommend that teachers ask, "To what extent and in what ways did the action solve the problem? Fail to solve it? Create new problems?" Students could argue for their own solutions.

• When discussing causes of historical events, texts present the U.S. interpretation as though it were fact. Thus, students gain little or no insight into historical reasoning.

• When texts present negative information on the U.S., they don't encourage students to explore the consequences or implications of it.

Politics

• Traditional lessons seldom discuss the difficulty of being a good citizen (e.g., assessing candidates and propositions before voting), nor do they discuss the positive aspects of dissent, i.e., the need to have a wide-ranging open market of ideas.

• Texts tend to make unfair comparisons, such as comparing the *ideal* of governments of the U.S. and its allies to the *real* Soviet government.

• Important ideals, such as freedom of speech, are taught as mere slogans. Students read, recall, and repeat vague justifications for ideals rather than deepen their understanding of them and of the difficulty in achieving them. In effect, such ideas are taught as though they were facts on the order of the date a treaty was signed.

• Texts often confuse facts with ideals and genuine patriotism with show of patriotism or false patriotism. The first confusion discourages us from seeing ourselves, others, and the world accurately; we often don't see the gap between how we want to be and how we are. The second encourages us to reject constructive criticism.

Economics

• Texts assume a capitalist perspective on economics, and texts generally contrast ideal capitalism with real socialism.

• Texts cover economic systems superficially, neglecting serious and in-depth coverage of *how* they are supposed to work (e.g., in our system, people must make rational choices as consumers, employers, and voters).

Anthropology

• Cultural differences are often reduced to holidays and foods rather than values, perspectives, and more significant customs, giving students little more than a superficial impression of this field.

Geography

• Texts more often use maps to show such trivialities as travelers' and explorers' routes than to illuminate the history and culture of the place shown and the lives of the people who actually live there.

What ties many of these criticisms together and points to their correction is the understanding that study of each subject should teach students how to reason in that subject, and this requires that students learn how to synthesize their insights into each subject to better understand their world. The standard didactic approach, with its emphasis on giving students as much information as possible, neglects this crucial task. Even those texts which attempt to teach geographical or historical reasoning do so occasionally, rather than systematically. By conceptualizing education primarily as passing data to students, texts present *products* of reasoning. A critical approach, emphasizing root questions and independent thought, on the other hand, helps students get a handle on the facts and ideas and offers students crucial tools for thinking through the problems they will face throughout their lives.

When students begin to put their insights and understandings into a comprehensive point of view, they will naturally differ on many important points.

Students need assignments that challenge their ability to assess actual political behavior. Such assignments will, of course, produce divergent conclusions by students in accordance with the state of their present leanings. And don't forget that student thinking, speaking and writing should be graded not on some authoritative set of substantive answers, but rather on the clarity, cogency, and intellectual rigor of what they produce. All students should be expected to learn the art of social and political analysis — the art of subjecting political behavior and public policies to critical assessment — based on an analysis of important relevant facts and on consideration of reasoning within alternative political viewpoints.

Some Recommendations for Action

Students in social studies, regardless of level, should be expected to begin to take responsibility for their own learning. This means that the student must develop the art of independent thinking and study and cultivate intellectual and study skills. This includes the ability to critique the text one is using, discovering how to learn from even a poor text. And since it is not reasonable to expect the classroom teacher to remodel the format of a textbook, the teacher must choose how to use the text as given.

Discussions and activities should be designed or remodelled by the teacher to develop the students' use of critical reading, writing, speaking, and listening. Furthermore, students should begin to get a sense of the interconnecting fields of knowledge within social studies, and the wealth of connections between these fields and others, such as math, science, and language arts. The students should not be expected to memorize a large quantity of unrelated facts, but rather to think in terms of interconnected domains of human life and experience. This includes identifying and evaluating various viewpoints; gathering and organizing information for interpretation; distinguishing facts from ideals, interpretations, and judgments; recognizing relationships and patterns; and applying insights to current events and problems.

Students should repeatedly be encouraged to identify the perspective of their texts, imagine or research other perspectives, and compare and evaluate them. This means, among other things, that words like 'conservatism' and 'liberalism,' the 'right' and 'left,' must become more than vague jargon; they must be recognized as names of different ways of thinking about human behavior in the world. Students need experience actually thinking within diverse political perspectives. No perspective, not even one called 'moderate,' should be presented as *the* correct one. By the same token, we should be careful not to lead the students to believe that all perspectives are equally justified or that important insights are equally found in all points of view. Beware especially of the misleading idea that the truth always lies in the middle of two extremes. We should continually encourage and stimulate our students to think and never do their thinking for them. We should, above all, teach, not preach.

History

History lessons should show students how to reason historically and why historical reasoning is necessary to understanding the present and to making rational decisions regarding the future. To learn to reason historically, students must discuss issues dialogically, generating and assessing multiple interpretations of events they study. This requires students to distinguish facts from interpretations. It also requires that they develop a point of view of their own.

• Dates are useful not so much as things-in-themselves, but as markers placing events in relation to each other and within context (historical, political, anthropological, technological, etc.). To reason with respect to history, we need to orient ourselves to events in relation to each other. So when you come across particular dates, you might ask the students to discuss in pairs what events came before and after it and to consider the significance of this sequence. They might consider the possible implications of different conceivable sequences. Suppose dynamite had been invented 50 years earlier. What are some possible consequences of that?

• Why is this date given in the text? What dates are the most significant according to the text? To us? To others? Notice that many dates significant to other groups, such as to Native Americans, are not mentioned. All dates that are mentioned result from a value judgment about the significance of that date.

Economics

When reasoning economically, Americans reason not only from a capitalist perspective, but also as liberals, conservatives, optimists, or pessimists. Lessons on economics should stress not only *how* our system is supposed to work but also how liberals, conservatives, etc. tend to interpret the same facts differently. Students should routinely consider questions like the following: "What can I learn from a conservative or liberal reading of these events? What facts support a conservative interpretation?" They should also have an opportunity to imagine alternative economic systems and alternative incentives, other than money, to motivate human work.

Some Key Questions in Subject Areas

Instruction for each subject should be designed to highlight the basic or root questions of that subject and help students learn how to reason within each field. To help you move away from the didactic, memorization-oriented approach found in most texts, we have listed below some basic questions, to suggest what sort of background issues could be used to unify and organize instruction. We have made no attempt to provide a comprehensive list. Consider the questions as suggestions only. In most cases, some translation or specific follow-up questions would be necessary before they could be posed to students.

History

Why are things the way they are now? What happened in the past? Why? What was it like to live then? How has it influenced us now? What kinds of historical events are most significant? How do I learn what happened in the past? How do I reconcile conflicting accounts? How can actions of the past best be understood? Evaluated? How does study of the past help me understand present situations and problems? To understand this present-day problem, what sort of historical background do I need, and how can I find and assess it? Is there progress? Is the world getting better? Worse? Always the same? Do people shape their times or time the people?

Anthropology

Why do you think people have different cultures? What shapes culture? How do cultures change? How have you been influenced by our culture? By ideas in movies and T.V? How does culture influence people? What assumptions underlie my culture? Others' cultures? To what extent are values universal? Which of our values do you think are universal? To what extent do values vary between cultures? Within cultures? How can cultures be categorized? What are some key differences between cultures that have writing and those who don't? What are the implications and consequences of those differences? How might a liberal critique our culture? A socialist? Is each culture so unique and self-contained, and so thoroughly defining of reality, that

177

cultures cannot be compared or evaluated? How is your peer group like a culture? How are cultures like and unlike other kinds of groups?

Geography

How do people adapt to where they live? What kinds of geographical features influence people the most? How? How do people change their environment? What effects do different changes have? How can uses of land be evaluated? How can we distinguish geographical from cultural influences? (Are Swedes hardy as a result of their geography or as a result of their cultural values?) Which geographical features in our area are the most significant? Does our climate influence our motivation? How so? Would you be different if you had been raised in the desert? Explain how.

Politics

What kinds of governments are there? What is government for? What is my government like? What are other governments like? How did they come to be that way? Who has power? Who should have power? What ways can power be used? How is our system designed to prevent abuse of power? To what extent is that design successful? What assumptions underlie various forms of government? What assumptions underlie ours? On what values are they theoretically based? What values are actually held? How is the design of this government supposed to achieve ideals? To what extent should a country's political and economic interests determine its foreign relations? To what extent should such ideals as justice and self-determination influence foreign policy decisions? Take a particular policy and analyze the possible effects of vested interests. How can governments be evaluated? How much should governments do to solve political, social, economic, etc., problems?

Economics

What kinds of economies are there? In this economy, who makes what kinds of decisions? What values underlie this economy? What does this economic system assume about people and their relationship to their work — assume about why people work? According to proponents of this economic system, who should be rewarded? How can economic systems be evaluated? What problems are there in our economy according to liberals? Conservatives? Socialists? What features of our economy are capitalistic? Socialistic? Communistic? How does ideal capitalism, socialism, communism work?

Unifying Social Studies Instruction

Although it makes sense to say that someone is reasoning historically, anthropologically, geographically, etc., it does not make the same sense to say that someone is reasoning socio-scientifically. There is no *one* way to put all of these fields together. Yet, understanding the interrelationships between each field and being able to integrate insights gained from each field is crucial to social studies. We need to recognize the need for students to develop their own unique perspective on social events and arrangements. This requires that questions regarding the interrelationships between the fields covered in social studies be frequently raised and that lessons be designed to require students to apply ideas from various fields to one topic or problem. Keep in mind the following questions:

What are people like? How do people come to be the way they are? How does society shape the individual? How does the individual shape society? Why do people disagree? Where do people get their points of view? Where do I get my point of view? Are some people more important than others? How do people and groups of people solve problems? How can we evaluate solutions? What are the relationships between politics, economics, culture, history, and geography? How do each of these influence the rest? How does the economy of country X influence its political decisions? How can governments, cultures, and economic systems be evaluated? Could you have totalitarian capitalism? Democratic communism? Are humans subject to laws and, hence, ultimately predictable?

In raising these questions beware the tendency to assume a "correct" answer from our social conditioning as Americans, especially on issues dealing with socialism or communism. Remember, we, like all peoples, have biases and prejudices. Our own view of the world must be critically analyzed and questioned.

Try to keep in mind that it takes a long time to develop a person's *thinking*. Our thinking is connected with every other dimension of us. All of our students enter our classes with many "mindless" beliefs, ideas which they have unconsciously picked up from T.V., movies, small talk, family background, and peer groups. Rarely have they been encouraged to think for themselves. Thinking their way through these beliefs takes time. We therefore need to proceed with a great deal of patience. We need to accept small payoffs in the beginning. We need to expect many confusions to arise. We must not despair in our role as cultivators of independent critical thought. In time, students will develop new modes of thinking. In time they will become more clear, more accurate, more logical, more open-minded — if only we stick to our commitment to nurture these abilities. The social studies provide us with an exciting opportunity, since they deal with issues central to our lives and well-being. It is not easy to shift the classroom from a didactic-memorization model, but, if we are willing to pay the price of definite commitment, it can be done.

> *Though everyone is both egocentric and critical (or fairminded) to some extent, the purpose of education in critical thinking is to help students move away from egocentricity, toward increasingly critical thought.*

War

Objectives of the Remodelled Plan

The students will:
- discuss the consequences of technology on war
- discuss the moral implications of war, evaluating actions and policies

Standard Approach

When covering wars, texts often mention the technology available or which developed during each war. Texts provide explanations of the causes and results of wars covered.

Critique

Connections are rarely made between the technology of war and the outcomes. There are few discussions of war strategies, or the social changes that occur after them. Some texts point out that technology changes war. One does not get the sense from most texts that people are involved in war, and that war affects people. The students are not given any indication of what war is like for any of the parties. Students don't discuss the moral implications of certain kinds of weapon technology, like nerve gas, germ warfare, nuclear missiles, and napalm. Students miss the opportunity to think independently about how to avoid World War III. They do not consider the ways in which we wage war and how that has changed over time, partly as a result of technology. Students do not consider the significant question of ethics of war or causes of war.

Strategies Used to Remodel

S-35 exploring implications and consequences
S-20 analyzing or evaluating actions or policies
S-10 refining generalizations and avoiding oversimplifications
S-17 questioning deeply: raising and pursuing root or significant questions

Remodelled Lesson Plan

Students could develop more insight into the effects of technology on war by discussions like the following: Consider a medieval war and discuss the technology that was available. How did the technology affect the way the war was fought and the effects it had? Now compare that with a 19ᵗʰ Century war. **S-35**

How do humans wage war? Why? What are some ways we could use technology to avoid war? Why do you think this would prevent war? How might technological advances cause war?

Is it morally acceptable to do whatever it takes to win a war? Why or why not? What weapons or techniques of war are unjustified? (Students could discuss biological warfare, defoliation, etc.) **S-20** What might be some exceptions? Why are they exceptions? **S-10** Write a code of honor for yourself that includes wartime behavior toward the enemy. Think about this in terms of types of weapons, targets, when to wage war, who to protect, etc.

Other discussion on war include pursuing questions like the following: Why are there wars? Is there one sort of cause, or many kinds of causes of wars? (Have students consider specific examples and possible counter-examples.) Does anyone think war is good? Why do many people believe war is necessary? What would people have to do to stop war? What kinds of effects do wars have on the people involved in them? **S-17**

What kinds of wars are there? What are the differences between fighting wars in your own country and fighting wars elsewhere?

When, if ever, is going to war justified? Are all parties responsible for being in a war? Can you think of a war that was clearly only one side's fault? When, if ever, is violence justified? **S-20**

Teachers who don't learn how to use basic critical thinking principles to critique and remodel their own lesson plans probably won't be able to implement someone else's effectively. Providing teachers with the scaffolding for carrying out the process for themselves, and examples of its application, opens the door for continuing development of critical thinking skills and insights.

Women

Objectives of the Remodelled Plan

The students will:

- develop their perspectives on women's work and roles throughout history

Standard Approach

> Texts now generally include passages about famous or important women. Some women are portrayed as important to U.S. history. The subject of suffrage is fairly complete. Many texts mention the legal, social, and economic status of women in other times and places.

Critique

Individual women are usually discussed when they have taken on roles typically reserved for men or when they are complaining about equality. Woman's traditional importance to home and family are barely touched upon. Although women of the past who stood out are mentioned, there is little characterization of typical women. History is a history of man's actions and ideas, with women making only minor and infrequent contributions. While women are discussed in almost every text as individuals and as a movement, the importance of traditional women's roles and work is almost totally overlooked.

The texts list as the causal factors for female demands: smaller families, more convenience foods, and better household appliances. The women had more time, so they began to complain about the status quo. This of course denies evidence of women's frustrations at discrimination throughout history.

The texts often seem to imply that women's issues are all taken care of, that the problems are all in the past. The reader is left with the impression that women are no longer discriminated against, that they have fought for their equal rights and have won them.

Strategies Used to Remodel

S-12 developing one's perspective: creating or exploring beliefs, arguments, or theories
S-21 reading critically: clarifying or critiquing text
S-29 noting significant similarities and differences

Remodelled Lesson Plan *S-12*

What women have we studied in history? Why? What did most women do? Why? How did that affect "men's world?" Why were these activities not mentioned? Should they have been? How important were the things that were "women's work?" Why did women do these kinds of things?

Ask students about their family history. Have them do a family history concentrating on their maternal lineage. They can talk to women of past generations and ask them what they remember about the previous generations. "Talk to the oldest woman you know and find out about her life. As a class, share all of these women's stories. What can we learn about women's lives from this study?"

What accounts for the recent changes in how people perceive gender-related roles? What problems have these changes produced? Why?

What have we learned that the text did not cover? How could the text have been written better? *S-21*

Whenever studying another society or time, students could discuss kinds of things women did. When this has been done for a wide variety of cultures and times, students could try to explain common features among them. *S-29*

> *Do not to spend too much time on the general formulations of what critical thinking is, before moving to the level of particular strategies, since people tend to have trouble assimilating general concepts unless they are made accessible by concrete examples.*

Landforms

Objectives of the Remodelled Plan

The students will:

- infer how various landform patterns can influence culture, industry, and trade, thereby pursuing root geographical questions
- think of some ways people might mitigate this influence

Standard Approach

Landforms are taught by description. There are different landforms, and here they are. One activity asks students to describe landforms as seen by pioneers coming to the Western part of our country.

Critique

Texts often stay at the descriptive level; the texts merely explicate categories of landforms. Students do not first consider physical maps, and discuss what they see. There is little connection to people, their attitudes, their behaviors. Where these things are mentioned, the approach is didactic rather than critical or tending to encourage autonomous thought. Students do not practice thinking geographically.

Strategies Used to Remodel

S-1 thinking independently
S-35 exploring implications and consequences
S-17 questioning deeply: raising and pursuing root or significant questions
S-5 developing intellectual humility and suspending judgment
S-8 developing intellectual perseverance

Remodelled Lesson Plan

Have the students make up a country or choose one that already exists. If they make up a country, have them compare that country with one that already exists to make sure that they include all of what needs to be included, such as mountains, valleys, rivers, flatlands, lakes, etc. **S-1** Then, in either case, have them explore the implications that follow from different landforms in combination with different populations and economies. For example: 1) A dry desert necessitates finding water whenever it is available; hence, nomadic cultures. 2) People living on an island will probably eat fish and use boats for transportation. **S-35** You might include some library research in this assignment that involves them in discovering and analyzing facts about populations and landforms.

Students can then explore root geographical questions in an extended discussion. "Where would you put airports, factories, farms? Why might some areas be overcrowded? Why would they be popular? Why might some other areas be unpeopled? Why would these be unpopular? Where would travel and trade be easy? Hard? Why? Where would it be easy to agree on boundaries? Hard? Why? How did landforms affect your decisions and explanations? How could you overcome some of the obstacles some landforms present?" **S-17**

What do you know now about landforms that is useful? Why is it useful? What other questions do you have about landforms? **S-5** How could you answer them? **S-8**

Before reading their texts on a particular region, students could first predict how the people there are influenced by and respond to the geography. **S-1**

Lesson plan remodelling as a strategy for staff and curriculum development is not a simple one-shot approach. It requires patience and commitment. But it genuinely develops the critical thinking of teachers and puts them in a position to understand and help structure the inner workings of the curriculum.

Maps

Objectives of the Remodelled Plan

The students will:
- analyze the concept of a map
- discuss the purposes for maps
- explain why symbols are used on maps, and why particular symbols may have been chosen
- think independently in order to make maps
- practice independent thought by using maps to understand the countries they study

Standard Approach

The following skills are generally covered in materials regarding maps: latitude/longitude calculations, identification of different kinds of maps, and calculations of scale and elevation. The other main topic covered is the problem of making a flat map to represent a globe; several different world map projections and their limitations are explained.

Critique

Texts provide little on the concept of maps and map theory. There is no adequate development of the concepts 'map' or 'model.' Students are *told* about a map's legend, and the symbols locating specifics on the map, but are not asked to consider why symbols need to be used, or why the particular symbols were chosen. They do not evaluate choice of symbols. Map projections are presented without any opportunity for independent thinking; they are just listed with their good and bad qualities.

There is no discussion as to how to choose maps for particular purposes, nor are students offered any atlas skills. It is more important for students to be able to find and use the kinds of maps they need for particular purposes, and to be able to read new kinds of maps, than to or simply locate listed places on a given map.

Strategies Used to Remodel

S-9 developing confidence in reason
S-14 clarifying and analyzing the meanings of words or phrases
S-1 thinking independently
S-19 generating or assessing solutions
S-15 developing criteria for evaluation: clarifying values and standards

Remodelled Lesson Plan S-9

You might begin by first asking students what a model is. Ask them to make a list of all the different kinds of models they can think of. "What do these models have in common?" The students might say they represent something, they have to be a certain size, they look like something else, etc. Ask students what a model of the Earth is called. They may say map or globe. Look at a variety of maps with the class. (Street map, map for tourists, celestial map, floor plan.) Ask them what they notice. "What does each represent? What is each used for? What do the maps have in common? Why? How does this particular difference serve the function of the map, or arise from the nature of the place and from features it represents? Compare maps to verbal descriptions. Why do you think we use symbols on maps? Why has someone chosen these particular symbols?" *S-14*

Ask students how they would go about making a map of the world. "What are some of the problems we might run into? What would you want to consider when making a flat representation of a sphere? Look at different kinds of maps of Earth. Are they all the same? How are they different? Make your own map of the Earth. Compare it with those of other students. What can you learn from looking at all of the maps?" *S-1*

You may want to have students use art time to make maps of countries, states, towns, their school, their bedrooms. "Which maps will have which features? Why? How do you decide? Where should you put each feature? How far away from other features? How can you make clear what each represents? What do you want your map to show? What purposes could it serve?" *S-19*

Make a personal atlas yourself, and a classroom atlas as a group. Which maps belong in which atlas? How did you decide? What were you assuming that led you to make that decision? *S-15*

Have students write test questions and answer keys (on copies of various kinds of maps) and select some for a map-use test. *S-1*

Fostering independent thought throughout the year *S-1*

When discussing specific countries and periods of history, have students read and discuss population distribution, physical, political, linguistic, and land use maps before reading their texts. They could also discuss such things as trade routes and difficulty or ease of travel, noting what other groups are nearby, etc.

Whenever they are about to use a map to pursue a question or problem, first ask them what kind of map they need, and how and where to find it.

Stereotyping

Objectives of the Remodelled Plan

The students will:

- develop critical insight into the sociocentric phenomenon of stereotyping
- discuss the evidence for or against various stereotypes
- explore why stereotyping is so difficult a problem, due to its unconscious nature
- examine American media to determine the stereotyping common in the U.S.
- find out some of the stereotyping typical of their peer groups

Standard Approach

Many texts include discouraging stereotyping as part of their objectives. According to texts, stereotypes are negative and harmful beliefs about people usually based on false ideas about the ethnic groups to which they belong, or their gender. Texts mention common stereotypes and discourage students from using them.

Critique

One of the biggest obstacles to understanding people, and learning history, politics, sociology and psychology is oversimplification in the form of stereotyping. Texts address stereotypes in a category by themselves, rather than as one sort of poor reasoning. Stereotypes, like any beliefs, can be evaluated by examining *evidence*.

The standard approach is didactic in that students are informed that stereotyping is wrong, and so are unlikely to see themselves as engaging in it. Thus students do not discover their stereotypes, evaluate them, or evaluate their effects. Students should decide what, exactly, is wrong with stereotyping, by considering the evidence for and against conclusions of that nature. There is no hint that people might not be aware of stereotyping, that it may be unconscious, that people might not be able to admit that they do this. Students are not encouraged to explore how having a preconceived notion can affect perceptions.

Furthermore, texts unnecessarily restrict the concept, leaving out many common stereotyped notions — both positive and negative — of such people as: computer nerds, doctors, criminals, government officials, musicians and movie stars, blue collar workers, political radicals, yuppies, welfare recipients, etc.

By developing students' insight into sociocentricity and having them examine generalizations, this lesson helps students develop intellectual good faith.

Strategies Used to Remodel

S-7   developing intellectual good faith or integrity
S-2   developing insight into egocentricity or sociocentricity
S-10 refining generalizations and avoiding oversimplifications
S-9   developing confidence in reason
S-13 clarifying issues, conclusions, or beliefs
S-35 exploring implications and consequences
S-12 developing ones' perspective: creating or exploring beliefs, arguments, or theories
S-33 evaluating evidence and alleged facts

Remodelled Lesson Plan s-7

Consideration of this topic might begin with cliques and stereotypes students have of other students: How do you group or categorize the people you see around? Describe people in each group. How do you know so much about these people? On what evidence do you base your ideas? How do categories help us think about people? How can they mislead us? **S-10** How do you feel about the idea that others may have you classified? Why? **S-2**

To have students discuss the quality of evidence for and against their beliefs about those groups, ask: "What can and can't you say about groups of people? What evidence is needed to support this conclusion? That conclusion? What could account for that evidence? What evidence counts against it? **S-13** How can all of the evidence be accounted for?" **S-10**

Look at newspapers, news magazines, and popular culture for examples of stereotyping. Keep records of your findings. What do your findings say about our American perceptions? How might these perceptions affect the kinds of personal decisions we make? Decisions as a country? **S-35**

Students could discuss stereotypes presented on TV and in movies, and reasons for those portrayals. Have students name shows and movies. Ask, "What are the characters like? What types do they represent? Is anyone really like that? In what ways? In what ways are real people different?" **S-10**

Why do people generalize this way? Where do they get these ideas? Why do they keep them? Why is it hard to give up stereotyped notions? How could we combat this in ourselves? How do we know if our perceptions of others are accurate? **S-12**

Students could design a study or a poll to discover stereotypes held by their fellow students. What do we need to know? How can we get the information? What should we do first? Why? Then what? How can we be sure our information is accurate? How will we know when a person is being honest? How will we know if they are being honest with themselves? How could a person not be honest with himself? How would this complicate our study? How should we organize the information so that it is meaningful? **S-33**

Before studying a country or group of people, students could list ideas and images they associate with them. Later, students could critique those impressions in light of what they have learned. **S-2**

Oil

Objectives of the Remodelled Plan

The students will:

- explore the significance of oil in various respects, discovering interdisciplinary connections
- consider the implications and consequences of oil possession and use on different countries and from a variety of perspectives

Standard Approach————————————

> Texts generally state that petroleum oil is the most important mineral deposit of our century, that we can find where the largest deposits of oil are located, or what percentage of the world's energy supply is derived from oil at any point in history. One text considers the effect of oil on Saudi Arabians: a farmer may now be in the oil business, a poor family may now be rich, and this family's son may now be able to go to college. Some texts mention OPEC and the energy crisis of the 1970's.

Critique

Oil makes a good topic, due to its economic, political, and environmental significance. Students should explore the implications and effects of widespread use of oil. Study of oil provides background information crucial for understanding domestic politics, international relations, economics, and environmental concerns, and is a good example of the overlap of these areas.

Students are *told* that oil is an important mineral, rather than being allowed to come to that conclusion on their own by exploring its significance. There is no discussion of perspective; students do not sort out different attitudes on oil use and how to meet energy needs.

Strategies Used to Remodel

S-23 making interdisciplinary connections
S-1   thinking independently
S-13 clarifying issues, conclusions, or beliefs
S-35 exploring implications and consequences
S-17 questioning deeply: raising and pursuing root or significant questions
S-25 reasoning dialogically: comparing perspectives, interpretations, or theories
S-5   developing intellectual humility and suspending judgment

Remodelled Lesson Plan

This topic provides an opportunity for students to research various aspects — oil location and available amounts, the effect of oil on oil-rich developing countries, oil as an international point of contention, environmental concerns. **S-23** Students can share their findings when relevant in the discussion. Ask them what fields of study they have to pursue to learn about oil and its effects on people. **S-1**

Why is oil important to people? Would everyone agree? Who might not? Would people have agreed with you in 1800? 1600? BC? 1900? Find times in history where the importance of oil changed. Why did it change? **S-13**

To explore the significance of owning oil, have the students consider Saudi Arabia. Would all Saudis agree about the importance of oil? How about the newly rich? The old rich? The poor? The rulers? The religious leaders? Why is oil so important to Saudi Arabia? How has it affected their culture? Find other countries which have been affected by oil to that extent. Look at countries with a great deal of oil as well as those with very little oil. **S-17**

Have students discuss differences in oil use among several countries and discuss the causes for and implications of these differences. Why does this country use so much (so little) oil? And why is that? How does that affect that country? Its citizens? Its relationships to other countries? **S-35**

What reasons are there to lessen or end our dependence on oil? What reasons are there against doing so? What problems does use of oil cause? Who is affected? How? Who is helped? Harmed? Who would be hurt if we changed to using other kinds of energy? How could everyone's needs be met? How would you solve the problems caused by extensive use of oil? **S-25**

How has oil affected our foreign policy? Which oil rich countries are our friends? Enemies? Neither? Why? How should we treat countries that supply us with oil? What if they want to cut us off? **S-35**

Why did I focus on oil in this lesson? What do you think my purpose was? Why do you think so? What are some significant questions surrounding oil? How could we research them? **S-5**

Natural Resources

Objectives of the Remodelled Plan

The students will:

- clarify the concept of natural resource and the values underlying the concept
- explore the implications and consequences of having natural resources, including using, misusing, and not using them
- consider what it means to be successful as a country

Standard Approach

Most of the information is presented in map form, with the main emphasis on the location of various resources.

One text offered a short discussion on conservation, and several offered alternative forms of energy and the concept of energy itself as a natural resource. One text was interested in the role natural resources play in the formation of a world leader, emphasizing that, although nature gave us rich natural resources, we had to use them well to become productive and powerful.

Critique

It is less important for students to know who has what than it is for them to learn how to find such information when they need it, and to understand the implications of having and not having or using and not using various natural resources. Additionally, examples covered in the book should be used as opportunities for discussion of deeper issues, especially as they relate to ecology, geology, economics, politics, anthropology, technology, and history.

The implications of various mineral deposits and other natural resources on history and culture are inadequately drawn out. There is far too much emphasis on who has what, and too little on how and why people use their resources, and on the long term effects. Few implications are brought out concerning modern forms of energy. Using resources is assumed to be what all intelligent nations do to get ahead, and no other view is examined or evaluated.

Claims that "Nature gave us bountiful resources" could be explored and compared to another point of view — that nature didn't give them to us. They were here, and we got them because we came here and took them.

Strategies Used to Remodel

S-14 clarifying and analyzing the meanings of words or phrases
S-15 developing criteria for evaluation: clarifying values and standards
S-1 thinking independently
S-21 reading critically: clarifying or critiquing texts
S-9 developing confidence in reason

Remodelled Lesson Plan

Students could begin by analyzing the key concept. "What kinds of things are called natural resources? What aren't? Why? What qualifies something as a natural resource? **S-15** What are natural resources used for? Why is this important to know about? **S-14**

How could we find out who has what resources? What role have natural resources played in history? How could we find out? **S-1**

"What effects does our use of natural resources have? How can we find out? What does 'use wisely' mean? As opposed to what? How can use of resources be evaluated?" For each example, ask, "Why would this be called wise? Unwise? Why was this done? Not done? In what ways do we 'use them wisely'? How do we not? How has our use of resources hurt us? Why have we done this? Why does (name a country) export rather than use (name a resource)?" (Discuss at length.) **S-15**

"Why have we made more use of natural resources than developing countries have or did? Who should control how natural resources will be used? Why? Who does now?

Ask, "What is progress? What issues involve this concept?" If the text uses the concept 'success,' students could develop a concept of success as it applies to a country and a means of evaluation. Then they can discuss what fits this ideal. "How did the book attribute success? Why? Do those things go with success?" **S-14**

Continue probing into the assumptions of the text. "What does it mean to say that 'Nature gave us these resources?' What does it assume? Imply? How else could we describe why we have the resources we do? What does that assume? Imply? Why did the text choose that way of speaking?" **S-21**

To develop students' confidence in their ability to think independently, the teacher could have them study resource maps and predict areas of conflict, whenever they are about to study an area or country **S-9**

> *It is better to use one clearly understood strategy than to attempt to use more than you clearly understand.*

Preamble to the Constitution

Objectives of the Remodelled Plan

The students will:

- grammatically analyze the Preamble to the Constitution
- clearly state the ideals exemplified by the Preamble and describe what kind of government would fulfill them
- evaluate it for its mode and form of expression
- write the essential meaning in their own words
- memorize it

Standard Approach

In most eighth grade history classes, students are required to memorize and recite the Preamble to the Constitution.

Critique

Memorization without comprehension accomplishes very little. While it is nice to exercise students' memories, we could do this while exploring its content at length. Without a discussion of the Preamble, no real thinking is taking place. Students will find memorizing easier once they grasp the grammatical structure and meaning of the passage.

The following remodel provides a detailed application of the strategy critical reading.

Strategies Used to Remodel

S-21 reading critically: clarifying or critiquing text
S-35 exploring implications or consequences
S-15 developing criteria for evaluation: clarifying values and standards
S-23 making interdisciplinary connections
S-1 thinking independently
S-11 comparing analogous situations: transferring insights to new contexts

Remodelled Lesson Plan S-21

Read the Preamble to the students, while they copy it. Have the class or groups of students go over it phrase by phrase, looking up unknown words, and clarifying it. The class as a whole could do a grammatical analysis of it. (How many sentences are here? What is the subject? 'We.' Who is meant by 'we'? What do "we" do? "We in order to . . . " makes no sense. Is this a sentence? Can it stand by itself independently? "In order to" means, "We're doing (something) because we want to accomplish these goals." What is that something? What are "we" doing? "We establish." "We ordain." Are these complete sentences, or do the verbs require objects? "We establish this Constitution," "We ordain this Constitution," etc.)

Have students explore what each purpose means and requires. Ask them what this implies for a system of government. **S-35** "What kind of government did the framers intend? What would a government have to do to fulfill the framers' ideals?" **S-15**

Have students rewrite the Preamble in their own words until they have a few clear sentences and really understand it.

What exactly were the authors of the Constitution doing? (Bringing into being a government and defining its powers, forms, and limitations.) Why was it written? Does it accomplish its intent? Compare these ideals with the way our government functions in 1988. Find examples in newspapers to illustrate your points.

To explore the worth of the Preamble as a piece of writing, have students notice the vocabulary in and style of it, and compare it to everyday speech and writing and with their paraphrases. The teacher could substitute phrases in the Preamble for phrases which subtly or drastically change the meaning, or which are less clear or less eloquent than the original. (For example, for "to form a more perfect union," substitute "to get along better together." Have students compare your phrases with the originals.) Evaluate the Preamble as a piece of writing. **S-23**

The assignment of memorizing it could now be given.

Another discussion could have students evaluate the Preamble's meaning. "Do you think the writers left anything out of this paragraph? If so, what? Why is that important? Is anything included that you disagree with? What? Why do you disagree? How would you rewrite that part?" **S-1**

Write your own Preamble reflecting your ideals. Do this for a country, and for your school. **S-11**

Every trivial lesson you abandon leaves more time to stimulate critical thinking.

Climate

Objectives of the Remodelled Plan

The students will:
- discuss the effects of weather and climate on people
- consider how people respond to overcome these limitations, analyzing and assessing solutions
- evaluate the effects of human efforts to overcome climate
- deeply question the importance of studying climate
- engage in a dialogical discussion regarding the effect of climate on a culture's character

Standard Approach———

Climate is defined in texts as a pattern of weather in a particular area. It includes: temperature range; humidity; average amount of precipitation, its kind, and when it occurs; and number of sunny days normal for the different seasons. The books show how maps can show the climate in various places. The texts also explain regions as areas with a particular kind of climate in common. Some describe wind patterns and clouds. Most discuss the effects of climate on life, especially humans. The climate in which we live may limit what we can do. But we invent ways to overcome these limitations, such as irrigation, fire, ice machines, etc.

One text also includes a discussion on the effect climate has on people. We learn how Aristotle believed that people who live in a hot climate will be one kind of person, while people who live in a cold climate will be the opposite. Strabo, on the other hand, points out that, although Athens and Sparta both have similar climates, they have very different kinds of people from one another. However, this text allows, climate does affect the clothes we wear, the houses we build, the crops we grow, and our population distribution.

Critique

These lessons miss opportunities to encourage independent thought. The students could themselves consider how climate affects us, how it limits us, how we can overcome it, and so on. But texts generally pose these kinds of questions and then immediately answer them. This didactic treatment of climate is typical.

The Earth and people are generally presented as adversaries, with the text implicitly approving humans. Man the conqueror tames the effects of climate. Students do not discuss this view or evaluate the consequences of our actions.

The students do not question the importance of knowing about climate and so gain little insight into root questions of geography.

The text that presented the disagreement between Aristotle and Strabo denied students a chance to think the issue through for themselves and compare the two theories, by immediately presenting them with "correct answers."

Strategies Used to Remodel

S-4 exploring thoughts underlying feelings and feelings underlying thoughts
S-35 exploring implications and consequences
S-19 generating and assessing solutions
S-17 questioning deeply: raising and pursuing root or significant questions
S-1 thinking independently
S-13 clarifying issues, conclusions, or beliefs
S-28 thinking precisely about thinking: using critical vocabulary
S-25 reasoning dialogically: comparing perspectives, interpretations, or theories

Remodelled Lesson Plan

You might begin by asking students how they feel about weather. "Do different types of weather make you feel different ways? How does weather affect us? Why do you think that is? **S-4** How can weather modify our behavior or decisions? What is weather? Are there patterns to it? Describe them." Explain that these patterns are our climate, that climate is the typical pattern of weather.

"How does climate limit us? Our culture? Others? How? Why? (Probe students' responses to bring out their reasoning.) How is climate used by or helpful to us? How do we generally respond to the limitations imposed by climate? Is this the only response we could give? What are some other options? Why do you suppose we choose the responses we do? What are the effects of our responses? **S-35** Are any other responses more reasonable? Why? **S-19** Is there an ideal climate?" Students could then read the text and compare points made in it to those raised in the discussion. Students could contrast the values of "taming the environment" and "living with the environment." **S-4**

"Consider what you have just learned about climate. What kind of important issues does this introduction help you to approach? Why should we be familiar with the climates of the world? What does knowing about a particular climate tell you about the people who live in it?" **S-17**

To have students compare the two theories about the influence of climate, you could begin by offering Aristotle's idea and asking the students what they think. **S-1** "What sorts of differences did Aristotle have in mind? Why did he say this?" Offer Strabo's rebuttal. Ask students what they think now. "What else could Strabo have said? What could Aristotle reply? What could Aristotle reply today? How could this idea be verified or refuted? What would someone need to do? What evidence would count for it? Against it? **S-13** What does your understanding of social studies and knowledge of geography tell you about this dispute? Have you learned of evidence relevant to this issue — groups of people that support or undermines Aristotle's theory? **S-28** Would that evidence prove the claim

197

or could something else account for that evidence? How could those factors be prevented from influencing this study? Finish the conversation between the two philosophers. If you were to walk in on the conversation, what would you say to Aristotle? To Strabo?" *S-25*

Students could write an essay giving and supporting their own theories.

Getting experience in lesson plan remodelling: How can I take full advantage of the strengths of this lesson? How can this material best be used to foster critical insights? Which questions or activities should I drop, use, alter or expand upon? What should I add to it?

The Cold War

Objectives of the Remodelled Plan

The students will:
- practice intellectual courage by considering the Cold War from multiple perspectives
- develop intellectual good faith by applying the same standards to the U.S. and U.S.S.R.
- raise and clarify questions regarding particular Cold War incidents

Standard Approach

Texts trace the rise of hostilities between our government and that of the Soviet Union. They generally mention Soviet expansion in Europe, the Berlin Wall, the Cuban Missile Crisis, The Warsaw Pact and NATO, Soviet support of revolutionaries throughout the world, and U.S. aid to non-communist countries.

The U.S.S.R. forces countries to become communist and puts communist leaders in power, while the U.S. fights to keep countries from becoming communist by supplying food, money, and help to fight communism. Since the communists use poverty to incite communist revolutions, the U.S. gives assistance to improve those conditions and thus strengthen the country against communism.

Critique

Predictably, treatment of the Cold War is generally biased. In each case covered, they want to oppress, we want to free; they take over or interfere with, we offer aid and assistance; their friends are dictatorships and tyrannies, ours are democracies. Students are given little or no idea of how other perspectives conceptualize the Cold War or the superpowers. Students should come to understand how others see us and the world, and come to their own conclusions on specific events. Every country's foreign policy can stand some improvement. Ours is no exception.

This entire remodel helps students develop intellectual courage and integrity.

Strategies Used to Remodel

S-6   developing intellectual courage
S-7   developing intellectual good faith or integrity
S-21   critical reading: clarifying or critiquing text
S-25   reasoning dialogically: comparing perspectives, interpretations, or theories
S-13   clarifying issues, conclusions, or beliefs
S-12   developing one's perspective: creating or exploring beliefs, arguments, or theories
S-20   evaluating actions or policies
S-11   comparing analogous situations: transferring insights to new contexts
S-26   reasoning dialectically: evaluating perspectives, interpretations, or theories

Remodelled Lesson Plan s-6

Ask students to read whatever their text has on the subject of the Cold War. Have them clarify and critique their texts with questions like the following: "What does the text say about the Cold War? Whose fault is it? What assumptions are made in the text? As this text is written, is there a clear 'good guy' and a clear 'bad guy?' From what perspective is this text written? How can you tell? What is the point of view presented in the text? What must the authors believe to present this point of view? What else might a person think? How could the text be written to reflect another point of view? How would a text written from a Soviet perspective present similar material? What would such a perspective assume? *S-25* What other points of view are possible?" Students could pick two paragraphs to rewrite from another point of view. *S-21*

Ask, "How does the U.S. government distinguish countries — what categories are used? Why? What categories does the U.S.S.R. use? Why? How are the U.S. and the U.S.S.R. different in their foreign policies? What do U.S. and U.S.S.R. foreign policies and perspectives have in common? How should foreign policy be evaluated? Do countries have the right to involve themselves in how other countries are run? Why or why not? If they do, when? In what ways?" *S-20*

Have students (or groups of students) focus on one incident or conflict at a time, list the parties involved, and discuss each. "What happened? What reasons were given? How could we figure out if those were the real reasons? What should have been done?" The class could compare two or more similar incidents and responses to them. *S-29* Students should be encouraged to apply the same standards to each country. ("Do any differences between these two situations warrant different evaluations of these actions?") *S-7*

Have students raise questions the text doesn't answer. Ask questions to help the students to refine their questions: "Why do you raise that question? Why does that seem significant to you? What would this answer imply? How could this question be settled? What points of view need to be considered?" *S-13*

Students could locate Vietnam and Afghanistan on maps and compare the two wars. *S-29* Students could interview adults regarding their views about the war in Vietnam. Students could begin with such questions as, "What did you think of the war then? Why? What did you think of those who disagreed with you? Have your views changed? Why?" Have them probe the interviewees' responses. Students could then discuss the views they collected. *S-25*

Students could also research news accounts of the war and anti-war protest. What, if anything, was settled? What issues remain?

Organize a conference on whether we should increase aggressions in Vietnam (1968) or pull out (or something else altogether). Each student can take a particular perspective from which to argue. Have the student conduct a similar meeting about a current issue. *S-11*

Have groups of three students take turns arguing from three different perspectives in a dialectical discussion regarding a dispute between the U.S. and the U.S.S.R. mentioned in the text. They could trade positions and thus argue each side. Have the students evaluate the arguments they have generated. *S-26*

To think critically about issues we must be able to consider the strengths and weaknesses of opposing points of view. Since critical thinkers value fairmindedness, they feel that it is especially important that they entertain positions with which they disagree.

The Causes of the Civil War

Objectives of the Remodelled Plan

The students will:
• consider the causes of the Civil War from various perspectives, reasoning dialogically
• evaluate slavery
• compare arguments for slavery with arguments used in analogous situations
• critique several texts in their presentation of this issue

Standard Approach

Texts generally ascribe the outbreak of the Civil War to the issue of slavery. Several of the texts indicated the concern of Clay, Webster, and Lincoln for the integrity of the Union. One mentioned Buchanan's decision that, although states have no Constitutional right to secede, the federal government has no power to force the states to remain in the Union.

Critique

As always, study of war provides an opportunity for dialogical and dialectical thinking. Unfortunately, texts typically treat the subject didactically. The cause of a war is presented as a fact on the same order as a date, rather than as an inference that must be reasoned to. A fairminded approach to determining the causes of wars requires consideration of explanations from all relevant perspectives. The explanation given by the winner should not be assumed.

Although texts tend to overemphasize slavery, they fail to explore the concept deeply. They say the South wanted slavery and many people in the North were opposed to slavery, some of them violently so. There is little or no attempt to understand the positions for or against slavery; to characterize the kinds of thinking that allowed some people to own other people or the principles on which others based their disapproval. Texts failed to examine the view of the Blacks that allowed them to be dehumanized. On the other hand, there is little development of any other concerns in the North. Economic issues, for instance, were neglected.

The questions in the texts are typically surface questions; for example, students are asked to look at a map and describe what is illustrated. Most of the questions can be answered by repeating the text, and thus require no critical thought whatever.

Finally, no text addressed any exciting root issues or drew connections between issues of the Civil War and contemporary problems and issues, thus failing to lay the groundwork for deeper understanding of subsequent events.

Strategies Used to Remodel

S-1   thinking independently
S-17 questioning deeply: raising and pursuing root or significant questions
S-25 reasoning dialogically: comparing perspectives, interpretations, or theories
S-11 comparing analogous situations: transferring insights to new contexts
S-21 reading critically: clarifying or critiquing text
S-6   developing intellectual courage
S-20 analyzing or evaluating actions or policies

Remodelled Lesson Plan

To encourage independent thought, before students read their texts, ask them to consider the Mid-1800's as they have studied that period, using timelines and maps to supplement discussion. Ask, "What was going on in the country? What changes were happening? What problems? What conflicts?" They should mention slavery, new states and territories, gold and the move west, industry, relations with Europe, trade, relations with Native Americans, etc. **S-1**

"What kinds of opinions were being expressed? Who expressed them? What were the lines of reasoning behind them? **S-25** What kinds of interests, values, ideas might have been behind each of the positions? How can we classify these opinions and positions? What categories can we find? How can we show our classification system? What does it show?" Here the teacher could have students use such techniques as charts, graphs, semantic maps, political maps, logic trees. Students can discuss the reasons for or implications of any patterns they notice. **S-17**

Causes of the War

Have students compare determining the cause of a war to determining who started an argument. **S-11** "How would the North attribute the cause of the war? Who's fault would they claim it to be? What would the South say? **S-6** What does the text say? From what point of view is the text written? **S-21** Does it present opposing views? How could an issue like this be settled? Would most wars have *a* cause, or many? What differences between North and South may have contributed to the war? What were the differences? (Could this difference be a contributing factor? How?) Why was this reason given as the cause of the war? Whose fault does it imply? Was the war just?" **S-17**

Evaluating Slavery

"Do you think slavery is justified? How could Southerners defend it? **S-6** "If students don't know, point out that many didn't believe Blacks were capable of taking care of themselves and were convinced that slavery was necessary for their economy. "Who was responsible for the slavery in the U.S. South? Did the

Federal government have the right to outlaw slavery in every state? Where do states' rights end? Why?" **S-20**

If not discussed previously, ask, "Where did the slaves come from? How did they get here? Why?" **S-17** If students have the background, they could compare conditions of American slaves with slaves in other times and places. **S-11**

Students could compare pro-slavery arguments with arguments used elsewhere and at other times by those who oppress groups of people (e.g., Apartheid, colonialism, imperialism. "Where else have these reasons been used? By whom? About whom? Why? Based on what evidence? What were the results of acting on that belief?" **S-11**

Finally, read several texts with the students and invite them to critique each presentation of the issues leading to the Civil War. **S-21**

The reader should keep in mind the connection between the principles and applications, on the one hand, and the character traits of a fairminded critical thinker, on the other. Our aim, once again, is not a set of disjointed skills, but an integrated, committed, thinking person.

China

Objectives of the Remodelled Plan

The students will:
- evaluate evidence for the approximate age of a culture
- recognize ethnocentrism in others, in themselves, and in the text
- transfer insight into aspects of Chinese history to analogous situations
- analyze the teachings of Confucius and Lao-Tzu

Standard Approach

China is described as the oldest culture, with a civilization reaching back for at least 3,500 years. China is described as an ethnocentric society, basically due to its isolation throughout history. Some texts mentioned the various dynasties, sometimes briefly discussing one or two. One text focused on Shih Huang Ti, an early ruler. China of the Chou dynasty is compared to ancient Egypt. The climates and populations of China and the United States are compared. Recent Chinese history is mentioned: the Opium War with Great Britain, the revolt of the Emperor's army in 1911 and the underlying causes, the conflict between Chiang Kai-Shek of the Nationalist Party and Mao Tse-tung of the Communist party, including Japan's invasion of China and Mao's system of social control in which community is more important than the family. Most texts mention the Wall and its purpose.

Nearly every text includes a section on Confucius. Some texts also mention Lao-tzu (the founder of Taoism) and contrast his views with those of Confucius.

Suggested activities include: fact recall (reading a timeline of the dynasties), defining vocabulary words, and map reading (listing bordering countries and areas of high population density).

Critique

Study of ancient China provides an example of an old and powerful culture very different from ours. It is also a case of an area that mainly had only one big power, unlike much of Mediterranean history. Furthermore, since China was strong, understanding its influence on East Asia is necessary to understanding East Asia. But the main value of study of any country and time is to develop students' ability to think historically and anthropologically and to begin to have them consider whatever basic historical forces, events, and aspects of culture are mentioned in their texts.

Texts generally emphasize details. Chapters are largely filled with fact after fact, with little or no analysis. Analyses that are given are generally too brief and often too superficial to mean much to students. For example, they may explain the break in economic linkage between China and Russia in one sentence, giving as the reason the Soviets' sudden departure from China.

Often, end-of-chapter questions demand little more than simple recall. "What are China's natural barriers? What is loess? How is it formed?" Timelines and map activities merely require students to read them. Students do not discuss the implications of what they see. Often, questions imply the desired answer such as in the following example: "Do we even try to cultivate slopes as the Chinese do? Why or why not?"

One text dealt effectively with the Mongol invasion, giving a detailed and reasonable explanation, but ended the section with the implication that it was insignificant that the Mongols had invaded and were ruling China, since they had acquired many Chinese customs. Students could compare this case with invasion by those of alien culture and/or discuss whether it made a difference, and of what sort.

By emphasizing *Chinese* ethnocentrism, and ignoring American ethnocentrism, many texts inadvertently support student ethnocentrism. One activity had students reflect on ways in which our pro-American bias shows in the media. Another asked students to look at a China-centered map and a U.S.-centered map, and infer attitudes from these. Such activities can be extended with in-depth discussion of why people have these attitudes and various ways ethnocentricity is manifested.

Brief study of the philosophers can provide insight into the culture, as well as opportunity for dialectical thought. Such discussion requires going beyond paraphrase, and into discussion of the ideas; whether compatible with each other, evaluating them, or probing contradictions between or among others.

Strategies Used to Remodel

S-9 developing confidence in reason
S-33 evaluating evidence and alleged facts
S-13 clarifying issues, conclusions, or beliefs
S-11 comparing analogous situations: transferring insights to new contexts
S-20 analyzing or evaluating actions or policies
S-2 developing insight into egocentricity or sociocentricity
S-18 analyzing or evaluating arguments, interpretations, beliefs, or theories
S-26 reasoning dialectically: evaluating perspectives, interpretations, or theories

Remodelled Lesson Plan

You could begin by asking students (or having them write as a homework assignment) what they know about China. Throughout the lesson, students could make a timeline, with periods and events in China above, the Mid-east and Europe below. Students can look at various kinds of maps, list their observations, and make inferences regarding the significance of what they find. **S-9**

Then have them read their texts, and ask for the main points covered. "What does the text say? Why did it mention these points? What is the most important thing to learn from this chapter? Is there anything you want to know about? How could you find out?"

To develop students' insight into anthropological reasoning and clarify the claims regarding China's age, you could ask, "How do we know how old a culture is? What kinds of things would we find in China to illustrate that China has the oldest culture? Why would these show us how old China is? How would they show us how old Chinese culture is compared to other cultures? **S-33** Is it significant that Chinese culture is so old? Why? Would it be more significant to the Chinese or to us? Why do you think so?" **S-13**

What would you need to do in order to understand Chinese history and culture? Compare Chinese history, culture and ideas with other countries In what ways was China ahead of Europe? Behind?

Students can compare any wars mentioned in their texts to other wars they have discussed. "Who started this war? What motivated them? What would you say caused this war? Why did that occur? What wars that you know about are like this one? In what ways? In what ways are they different? Is there anything you know about that other war that you can apply to understanding this war? What? What does that tell you about this war? What that you know about this war can you apply to better understand other wars you know something about?" **S-11**

• What was it like to live near the place the Wall is, before the Wall was built? What motivated the building of the Wall? What effects did the Wall have on the society? What was it like to build it? **S-20**

• Why does this text discuss China's ethnocentrism? What evidence do they have of it? What explanation do they give? What reasons have they for feeling superior? How do you think the Chinese thought of other people? How do you think they thought of themselves? **S-2**

• What have we learned about Asia? How could we characterize China's relationship to the rest of Asia?

If the text mentions Confucius and Lao-tzu, students could analyze their ideas with questions like the following: What did each say? What do you think they meant? Have you thought or heard similar ideas? What would they agree about? Disagree about? If you lived your life according to Confucius, how would you live? How would your study of Confucius affect how you live your life? Lao-tzu?What is Confucius' basic idea? Lao-tzu's? What specific differences are there between these two thinkers? Can their insights be reconciled? Why are they important? **S-18** Students could write a dialectical discussion between followers of Confucius and Lao-tzu, and evaluate it. **S-26**

Nigeria

Objectives of the Remodelled Plan

The students will:
* explore reasons for British colonization of Nigeria and evaluate it
* explore its consequences
* construct the perspectives of different people involved
* discuss causes for Nigeria's present problems, thus practicing historical reasoning

Standard Approach

Some texts introduce the history of Nigeria tracing British colonialism. After the Boer wars, the British moved north into Central Africa, including Nigeria. After WWII, most of Africa was independent. Nigeria, in particular, gained its freedom in 1960, deciding to keep the name given them by the British. Along with other former British colonies, Nigeria joined the Commonwealth of Nations. When the British took over, Nigeria was a land of various different groups with quite different ways of life and languages. They were very hard to hold together in one nation. Their civil war between 1967 and 1970 brought the West and East together. Even today there are communication problems in Nigeria, due to their many languages and customs. In addition, the discovery of oil in Nigeria in 1958 brought changes such as big cities, traffic jams, clogged harbors, limited telephones and gas stations, and housing shortages. Nigeria's problems are hard to solve.

Critique

Study of Nigeria can illustrate how understanding the history of a place is necessary to intelligently discussing its present problems. Here, the original cultures and groups and their differences, colonialism, developing countries and their relationships to developed countries are key elements.

Typically, texts stick to the bare facts, (though once able to feed itself, Nigeria must now import much of its food; Nigerians decided to keep the name 'Nigeria;' Nigeria had a civil war) with little or no explanation of reasons, causes, implications, or evaluations. Many of the details approach deeper issues, but they are not adequately explored or explained.

The concept of colonialism is seriously underdeveloped. The world views and attitudes that allowed and justified colonialism, the reasons underlying it, its effects on culture and development are ignored. Some texts do not really discuss colonization much at all, especially not the opinions of the colonized, except to say that everyone would rather be free like we are. Students are not asked to consider why. Little attempt is made to understand the differences between the many points of view represented in this slice of history. For example, what of the British who were appalled at colonialism, or the tribes and individuals in Africa who welcomed British and western ways? One can't understand colonialism without understanding events and social structures in colonizing powers that supported it.

The fact is offered in one of the texts that Nigeria used to produce nearly all of its food, but now is forced to import much of it. Although the book acknowledges that this is a serious concern, it did not refer to any causes of this situation. The text did not draw out any of the implications if this trend continues, how to reverse this trend, or how it could have been avoided. The students are not invited to wonder how egocentrism, sociocentrism, or differing points of view and culture might have helped to cause this problem and interfere with its solution. Nor do students consider the ways other countries interfere with developing countries' attempts to improve. Nigeria is treated in isolation from the rest of the world.

Texts generally confuse development and modernization with becoming like the U.S., thus failing to recognize the potential variety of forms of development and progress. Other countries must learn from us; we have little to learn from them.

Strategies Used to Remodel

S-32 making plausible inferences, predictions, or interpretations
S-1 thinking independently
S-35 exploring implications and consequences
S-12 developing one's perspective: creating or exploring beliefs, arguments, or theories
S-15 developing criteria for evaluation: clarifying values and standards
S-20 analyzing or evaluating actions or policies
S-8 developing intellectual perseverance

Remodelled Lesson Plan

Students could begin by looking at physical, political, and linguistic maps of Africa and West Africa, describing observations, and making inferences. **S-32** When students have read the material, they could do a timeline of events in Africa and Europe.

Interested students could research Nigeria, other colonies, and the colonizing countries, before this section is covered. They could report to the rest of the class during discussion. At the very least, English history of the time should be studied or reviewed, in order to provide background for understanding colonialism. "What do we know of England at the time? How powerful was England? Why? What does this tell us about why England had colonies? What did England get from its colonies? How did it treat its colonies? Why?" **S-17**

Students could compare West African cultures with Great Britain and other European countries.

Who drew Nigeria's boundaries? Would Africans have drawn the same boundaries? What have been long term effects of the way Europeans drew boundaries in West Africa?

How did the British characterize West Africans and colonization? What different kinds of English people were in Africa? Why? What kinds of relationships did they have with native Africans? What reasons did the British government give justifying colonization? How about the Nigerians? Why did the British colonize this area? What different groups might have had opinions on this subject in the U.K.? In Nigeria? Elsewhere? Did England have the right to rule? Should the English have done anything differently? *S-20*

Why did Nigeria gain independence? Compare this to other examples of colonies gaining independence.

What problems does Nigeria face? What are the causes? What features of Nigeria have most influenced its history? What historical facts influence Nigeria presently? Why is Nigeria not producing enough food? *S-1* What has changed? Why? Should other people be worried about this problem? What will happen if this trend continues? How can this be avoided? What would you advise the Nigerians to do? What would happen then? *S-35* Is this what you really want to happen? What would a solution require? With what kinds of knowledge are experts from here and Europe most needed? African experts most needed? Whose knowledge has been most relied on? What kinds of knowledge has been lost?

Why are some countries at a subsistence level? Why is farming poor, medical care scarce, health education poor, and income so low? Should a country want to change this? Why? Why might they? Why wouldn't they? Who might want things to change? Who might not? Does anyone benefit from this situation? What could keep a country from changing when they want to? What could make them change against their will?

Ask students to describe the standard of living in Nigeria. Is it the same for everybody? How many different kinds of living situations can you think of? What was life like before the British arrived, during the British rule, and in the independent Nigeria (at the beginning and now)? When was the quality of life best? In what ways? In what ways worse? For whom? Were other times better for other people? Who? Why do you think so? What are you assuming when you say that life is better? In what ways? In what ways worse? When is it better? When is it better for poor people? When is it better for rich people? Is this true everywhere, in any country, in any culture? *S-12* Have students develop criteria for classifying living arrangements in terms of subsistence, developing economies, and industrial economies. *S-15*

What were the long-range affects of colonialism on Nigeria? Do you think colonialism was justified? What, if anything, should the British have done differently? *S-20* Discussion of colonialism could be extended by having students discuss whether any group of people has the right to rule over others. The issue can be raised, and students reminded of this chapter, whenever relevant during the course of the year. *S-17*

To more fully explore the idea of historical thinking with respect to Nigeria, the teacher could ask,"What perspectives would we need to study in order to develop a complete and fairminded view of Nigerian history? (Different Nigerian groups/cultures, pro- and anti-Western Nigerians, pro- and anti-colonial British.) How would one gain expertise on Nigeria? *S-8*

Progress and Technology

Objectives of the Remodelled Plan

The students will:
- clarify the words 'progress' and 'technology'
- clarify and critique the use of the terms in their texts
- compare the relative values of technological and other kinds of progress
- describe and rank technological advances
- exercise fairmindedness regarding the value of technology and progress and each level of technological development

Standard Approach

Texts generally use or rely on the notion that the story of history is the story of progress. Often this claim is backed up with discussions of technological advances and the advantages they bring. Sometimes texts refer to such ideas as progression toward greater freedom, opportunity, and justice.

Texts outline stages of development: hunting/gathering; agricultural/commercial; urban/industrial; and scientific/technological. They sometimes point out that there seems to be an increasing rate of change, especially in the technological era. 'Technology' is defined as the use of science. One text called it "all the tools of society and skills to use them." Several inventions and some of their effects on society are noted. A progression of increasingly complex systems of managing time and energy are represented to show our human advancement.

One text has students rank types of technology for their relative importance, for example:

Rank	Item	Reason for Rank
1	running water	drink, cook, wash

Critique

The concept of progress runs through many lessons. It is often left vague, more often limited to technical and material progress. Students have little or no opportunity to explore the broader concept and contrast it with the narrower use common in texts. Texts tend to assume that developing countries will develop into societies like ours, rather than in their own unique ways. They also frequently seem to assume that technological advancement is always progress in a positive sense. Such lessons or discussions could foster consideration of multiple perspectives and encourage flexibility of thought.

Typical presentations presume a hierarchy of different kinds of society, and assume that the kind most like ours is the most advanced and, therefore, unquestionably the best. Texts tend to emphasize positive aspects of technological development and downplay the negatives. Students should know that some people prefer aspects of hunting/gathering and agricultural societies to ours. Texts insufficiently illuminate the vast differences in lifestyles, cultures, and viewpoints of people with less technological societies. Texts often mention the rate of increasing change, with little discussion of implications or consequences.

Activities like the chart mentioned above can be remodelled to provide a more complete and thought-provoking activity by adding headings which require justifications, implications, or consequences.

Strategies Used to Remodel

S-12 developing one's perspective: creating or exploring beliefs, arguments, or theories
S-15 developing criteria for evaluation: clarifying values and standards
S-29 noting significant similarities and differences
S-14 clarifying and analyzing the meanings of words or phrases
S-21 reading critically: clarifying or critiquing texts
S-7 developing intellectual good faith or integrity
S-3 exercising fairmindedness
S-4 exploring thoughts underlying feelings and feelings underlying thoughts
S-32 making plausible inferences, predictions, or interpretations

Remodelled Lesson Plan S-12

Students could consider the word 'progress.' "What does 'progress' mean for a person? A country? The world? How can you tell if a change is progress, as opposed to other kinds of change? **S-15** What kinds of progress are there? Is achieving a peaceful world progress? Is this the same sense or a different sense of 'progress'? **S-29** What else would be progress? What sorts of progress seem most important to you? Can forms of progress be ranked? By what criteria? (Have students distinguish unanimous from disputed examples or criteria.) In what ways was the invention and widespread use of the printing press progress? **S-14**

What does the word 'progress' mean in your text? Where is it used? In what context? To what does it refer? What does this word imply? **S-21**

Is technology a prerequisite for progress? Can technology ever hinder progress? How?

Students could review or research and then discuss the differences between hunting/gathering, agricultural, and urban societies. "How would the day in the life of the average person differ? Why might people in hunting/gathering societies prefer their way of life to ours? Those in predominantly agricultural societies? What aspects of our kind of society might they dislike? **S-7** Why? What aspects might they wish for? Why? How might their perspectives and expectations differ? How are the character of life and the character of the technology and the economy related? How quickly does the character of life change in each kind of society? What is attractive about each? Unattractive? Which would you prefer? Are there ways of combining the best features of each? **S-3**

Where do you think people are going regarding technology? Why do you think so? Consider recent important innovations. How has each played a role in changing life for individuals? Evaluate each.

Is humanity progressing? Why do you say this? How do you know? What are good goals to progress toward? How could you decide? Who would agree with you? What would they say? What would they say? How would you respond? Who might disagree with you? What else could be said?

Imagine life without technology. How would such a life be different? Are there any ways in which it would stay the same? Why do you think so? Is it truly possible to have no technology? What is the lowest technological level possible for a human culture? Why do you think so? Why might someone not approve of our level of technology? Why might someone prefer living with much less technology? *S-3*

What do the terms 'developed' and 'developing' imply? What values does use of these terms presuppose? *S-14* What words might a hunter/gatherer use? *S-3*

How does the increasing rate of change affect a society? How do you feel about it? Why does it make some people excited and hopeful and others worried or angry? *S-4*

The ranking chart could be reworked to look like this:

Rank	Item	Use	Value	Defense
1	running water	drink, cook, wash	survival health	may have trouble finding water otherwise; sitting water can spread disease.

A final column could be called "Consequences."

Of each item in the chart, students or groups of students could discuss questions like the following: Why is this progress? How does it affect people's lives? Does it have negative consequences? What? How could they be lessened? Is this worth the cost? Students could share and discuss their rankings and justifications and consequences, and argue among themselves where they disagree. *S-15*

Ask what a standard of living is. "What is a good life?" Students could write a short paper on the highest quality of life. (This could be assigned in language arts as preparation for the lesson.) "What does a person need to be happy? To be mostly happy? To be very, very happy? If we did this survey all over the world, do you think we would get similar answers? Why or why not? What might be the same? What might be different?"

To clarify the idea of subsistence living, students could write a paper from the view of a homeless person in an American city. What would his or her day be like? What would this person do for money, food, a place to sleep, clothes, shelter from rain, to pass the time of day? What would you do? What else would you need to worry about? What would life be like if a whole country lived at a subsistence level? Would the homeless person be better or worse off? *S-32*

As a concluding activity, the teacher could give students copies from several texts of passages referring to the concept 'progress.' Students could critique them, combine the best points in each with their own ideas, and write a better section on progress. *S-21*

Economic Systems

Objectives of the Remodelled Plan

The students will:

• compare and evaluate economic ideals and practices of the U.S. and U.S.S.R.
• examine assumptions underlying economic systems
• compare our attitudes about the U.S.S.R. with our attitudes about similar systems, systems like ours, and completely different systems

Standard Approach

> The students are told that, although the U.S. and the U.S.S.R. have similarly good resources, their economies are quite different. The U.S. is characterized by individuals deciding how to spend their money, while in the U.S.S.R. the government decides or commands what shall be produced, and controls land, farms, factories, and industry. Prices in the U.S. are governed by supply and demand, while the Soviet government may set prices to discourage the purchase of certain items. The market economy shows producers that Americans want many consumer goods for their own use. In our free enterprise system, people choose jobs and careers, what to buy, sell, and produce, what to pay and charge. Businesses are run for profit. In the U.S.S.R. many of these decisions are made by the government, not by each individual.
>
> One text offers a chart to show the number of hours a worker in the U.S. and the U.S.S.R. would have to work in order to earn enough to purchase various luxury items. Salaries in the U.S.S.R. are lower than those in the U.S., yet education and skills are rewarded with money, housing, good meats, and cosmetics. The U.S. government does play a role in the U.S. economy, but only to protect consumers and oversee trade with other countries. The government in the U.S. also functions as a buyer/consumer, as a market itself. If our government does anything more directive, it is usually because enough people request help. We take for granted a lifestyle that is only available to the rich in other countries.

Critique

Students studying lessons like this need to grasp how capitalism is supposed to work, the mechanics of it, the view of man and economics on which it is based, and how to evaluate departures from those ideals. They should come to understand communism and how it is supposed to work, what conception and ideals underlie it, and how to evaluate departures therefrom. Texts give abstract principles but little sense of how capitalism is supposed to work and what is required to keep it going; for example, rational consumers and employers, and a government which is neutral toward particular businesses and which prevents businessmen from abusing each other or the public.

The comparison of the two systems is rife with ethnocentricity. It is also full of misleading information. Sometimes texts almost make it sound as though each American individually designs the economy. There is no mention of the factors that inhibit millions of people from participating freely and equally, or other factors in our society which conflict or interfere with ideal capitalism. There is little opportunity for independent thought, as students are told what values and aspirations to have. Students do not have an opportunity to begin to consider different American viewpoints regarding economic problems we face. The texts present only two positions, two choices, us and the good life, or them and oppression. There is little attempt to treat the concept of communism as a communist, or even a neutral party, would. Although one text acknowledged that the U.S.S.R. offers its citizens free education, medical care, and vacations, nothing else was said supporting the ideals or practices of the U.S.S.R.

Strategies Used to Remodel

S-6   developing intellectual courage
S-1   thinking independently
S-29   noting significant similarities and differences
S-30   examining or evaluating assumptions
S-27   comparing and contrasting ideals with actual practice
S-10   refining generalizations and avoiding oversimplifications
S-25   reasoning dialogically: comparing perspectives, interpretations, or theories
S-3   exercising fairmindedness
S-2   developing insight into egocentricity or sociocentricity
S-35   exploring implications and consequences

Remodelled Lesson Plan s-6

Capitalism

When students have read their texts, they can discuss the negative opinion of the U.S. toward the U.S.S.R. and the negative opinion of the U.S.S.R. toward the U.S. and compare the countries. How is their government different from ours? Their economy? Their industry? **S-1** Students can then begin in-depth analysis of capitalism.

What are the goals of capitalism? For owners? For workers? For consumers? Do these goals conflict? How does the system address the conflict? On what assumptions about people is this system based? What does this system assume about why people work, produce, and create? What evidence is relevant to settling that question? What is your position? Why? **S-30** How is a capitalist economy supposed to provide the best goods and services for the best prices? Why would this system have that result? What does this system assume about how people decide which goods and services to use? What employees to hire? How should these decisions be made?

Now that the ideal system has been set out, students can begin to distinguish actual practice from those ideals. How is our government supposed to protect consumers? From whom? What would producers do? Why? What are some possible economic choices individuals make? What kinds of decisions can your parents make? Not make? *S-10* How do people make economic decisions? How do they decide which brand of a particular product to buy? What role does advertising play in our system? What role should it play? What kinds of forces, factors, attitudes, and habits interfere with the free working of market forces? Do Americans decide what job to take, how much they will be paid? How do individuals help to decide? What are the limitations of our freedom to decide issues for ourselves? Are these deviations from ideal capitalism good, or should they be prevented? If so, how? What interferes with Americans' freedom to determine their careers? *S-27*

Emphasize that no country has a pure version of any economic system. You could talk about some of the aspects of socialism in our economy. You might mention (or have students mention) Social Security, Medicare, or note that government-controlled postal and passenger rail services in the U.S. are further examples of aspects of socialism in our economy. Ask, "In what ways are these 'socialist' in nature?" *S-10*

A written assignment here might be: Explain the goals of capitalism. Consider such things as: fairness, and whether the goals are easy or hard to achieve.

Have students "play capitalist" in a genuinely free market economy, to discover such ideas as supply and demand, etc. They could then discuss and compare their experiences with real situations (e.g., students are given capital and resources to start with).

Socialism

You might list the essential features of socialism for clarity, including some of the benefits that socialism ideally provides, such as comprehensive health care, free education through university level, guaranteed employment, etc. *S-3* For example, ask, "What might be some implications of the features of socialism? How are the services, such as free medical care, paid for? *S-35* What would life be like for a person living under socialism? How would it be different from capitalism? The same? Where is socialism practiced? What are some of the goals and ideals of socialism? What do you think of them?"

When examining our own system, we saw how the form of capitalism we have departs from ideal capitalism. What do you think is true for the Soviets? What evidence do you have for your answer? Where could we get information like this? What do we have to watch for in our information? How could our negative feelings for the U.S.S.R. influence the information we find? *S-16* Why are there unions in some socialist countries? What problems do socialist countries face? Is the U.S.S.R., for example, a classless society? What would be some examples of how class distinctions persist in the Soviet Union? Why? *S-27*

Comparison of the Economic Systems

What problems does each system face? What sort of people does each system claim to reward the most? Actually reward? What sort of people do you think should be rewarded most? Why? What sort of a society would that produce? How could such a system be implemented? **S-1**

What can make each system go wrong? Do you approve of the goals? Have they been achieved? To what extent? Why or why not? **S-27**

How can we find American opinions on other systems of economies and governments? Devise a method to measure American opinion. (Through media or by surveying adults.) Show this information on a chart or graph. Why do most Americans disapprove of communism and socialism so strongly? Notice how we feel about the U.S.S.R. itself. How does this compare to how we feel about countries with systems similar to the U.S.S.R., more similar to us, completely different from both? Who do we like best? Least? How would the U.S.S.R. probably make a scale? Who might they like most and least? Why? How can you explain these differences? **S-2**

Several concluding activities could now tie the lesson together. One would be to assign students to role play defenders and critics of both systems. They could compare the assumptions, basic concepts, and values of each. **S-25**

A written assignment might be given as follows: "People who emigrate from the U.S.S.R. to the U.S. sometimes have difficulty adjusting to our economic system. Could you predict what some of those difficulties might be and why it could be hard for them to adapt?" (The assignment could be reversed for an American taking up residence in the Soviet Union.) **S-3**

Students could write analyses and assessments of their texts.

> *The highest development of intelligence and conscience creates a natural marriage between the two. Each is distinctly limited without the other. Each requires special attention in the light of the other.*

The Constitution

Objectives of the Remodelled Plan

The students will:

- learn some functions of the three branches of U. S. government
- clarify claims in their texts by exploring root issues regarding government and the distribution of power in our government
- compare ideals of the Constitution with actual practice
- develop criteria for evaluating political candidates
- through Socratic questioning, understand the reasons for and assumptions underlying rights guaranteed under the Bill of Rights
- develop their perspectives on human rights, and functions and limits of government
- transfer insight into the Constitution to current events

Standard Approach

> The history of the Constitution, as well as some of its present day applications, is presented. Main themes and concepts are explained such as federalism, separation of powers, judicial review, the Bill of Rights, how a bill becomes law, and democracy. Students are asked to consider the role of these concepts in current American politics. Typical end-of-chapter questions are, "Why did our leaders call the constitutional convention? What were the four main compromises? What were the main arguments for the opponents and the supporters?" Other questions ask for explanation and evaluation, such as, "What is meant by the statement 'The government is you.'? Do you agree with the statement? State your reasons." Vocabulary enrichment involves having the students look up words and put them into sentences.

Critique

We chose this lesson because understanding the Constitution is crucial to citizenship in a democracy. Students should explore the ideas underlying important aspects of our government: how it is supposed to work, why it was structured the way it was, how the structure is supposed to preserve citizens' rights, how it could fail to do so, and why rights are important to preserve. Critical education demands clear and well-developed understanding of these points. When understanding is superficial or vague, hidden agendas and mere associations guide thought and behavior. Slogans substitute for reasons, prejudices for thought. Citizens become willing to accept the appearance of freedom, equality under the law, and democracy, rather than insisting on their realization.

The greatest flaw with the standard approach is its lack of depth; not nearly enough time is given to fostering understanding of this important document. The relative importance of different material should be reflected in the text space given and time spent on it. Spending insufficient time on such important ideas leads texts to treat them superficially or vaguely. Students have little opportunity to understand key ideas fully, see the whole picture, appreciate reasons for important parts of the Constitution, or develop their perspectives on government, human relations, and how to preserve their rights.

Texts generally ask too few questions, have little extended discussion, and ask too many questions which are trivial, or simple recall. Some of the suggested explanations and answers are generally sorely incomplete, vague, confusing, or fail to answer the questions. To simply tell students that our government's system of checks and balances helps protect people's freedom does little to help students understand that system or how it is supposed to work.

Important explanations are undeveloped, fail to probe the reasons. Texts offer abstract and unclear explanations, and then merely require students to reiterate them. Often the answers to the end-of-chapter questions are tagged by bold face in the text. Students are encouraged to substitute reiteration for understanding; to accept apparently unconnected answers as adequate explanations, for example, that the right to trial was thought important because it was denied by the British.

Similarly, regarding the Bill of Rights, texts fail to answer the important questions: Why did people think these rights should be written down? What is the advantage? Why write them into the Constitution? Does writing them into the Constitution guarantee they won't be violated? Crucial questions and connections are left unanswered. Neither texts nor students clarify the various Constitutional rights, leaving them in the realm of empty slogans.

Strategies Used to Remodel

S-21 reading critically: clarifying or critiquing texts
S-17 questioning deeply: raising and pursuing root or significant questions
S-7 developing intellectual good faith or integrity
S-27 comparing and contrasting ideals with actual practice
S-15 developing criteria for evaluation: clarifying values and standards
S-19 generating or assessing solutions
S-24 practicing Socratic discussion: clarifying and questioning beliefs, theories, or perspectives
S-13 clarifying issues, conclusions, or beliefs
S-30 examining or evaluating assumptions
S-12 developing one's perspective: creating or exploring beliefs, arguments, or theories
S-26 reasoning dialectically: evaluating perspectives, interpretations, or theories
S-14 clarifying and analyzing the meanings of words or phrases
S-35 exploring implications or consequences
S-11 comparing analogous situations: transferring insights to new contexts

Remodelled Lesson Plan

Introduction to the Constitution

When the passages about the Constitution and whatever portions of the document students can read have been read, allow students a chance to get the "big picture," by asking, "What is this document for? What is its purpose? What basic points does it cover?" (It defines the three branches of Federal Government, describes how offices are filled, lists duties of and limits on each branch.) You might read the Preamble to the students and discuss it with them. (See the lesson on the Preamble.) The class could do similar analyses of portions of the Constitution. You could then tell the students about some of the details left out of their texts. Students could reiterate the veto and override process, and discuss what protection it gives. **S-21**

Separation of Powers, and Checks and Balances S-17

Discussion of the previous point can lead into a discussion of the separation of powers and checks and balances. To probe these ideas in depth, thereby making the reasons for our system of government clearer, you could ask, "Have you ever been in a situation where someone had too much power or abused power? Why was that a problem? How could the problem be solved? How did the authors of the Constitution try to solve it? Why not give all of the power to one branch, say, the Executive? Why can't the President declare war? Why have each branch have some power over the others, rather than giving each branch complete control over its duties? What does the text say in answer to this question? What does its answer mean? How could concentrating power lead to loss of people's rights? **S-21** Make up an example which shows how a system like this could prevent abuse of power. This separation of powers and system of checks and balances is the ideal. What could make it go wrong? How could the President start a war without Congressional approval? Has this ever happened? Should it ever happen? **S-7** Why or why not?Make up an example of how it could go wrong. (Using the checks and balances unfairly, or not using them at all.) Why would that be bad? **S-27** What has to happen to make it work right? What should we look for in our leaders? What sort of people should be chosen? (e.g., when voting for President, voters should consider who the candidate would appoint to important offices or whether the candidate is a good judge of character. Perhaps members of Congress who abuse or fail to use checks on the President should be reconsidered.) **S-15**

The class could also relate some of the above ideas to a specific historical or current issue regarding abuse of power or charges of abuse of power. The students could also try to come up with alternative solutions to the problem of abuse of power and compare their solutions with those in the Constitution. **S-19**

The Bill of Rights S-24

Students could generate a list of the rights covered. To foster in-depth understanding of the meaning and importance of the Bill of Rights, the teacher could conduct a Socratic discussion clarifying and analyzing each right with questions like the following: What does this right mean? What does it say people should be allowed to do? How could it be violated or denied? **S-13** Why might people try to take it away? How important is it? Why? Why would not having this right be bad? How would it hurt the individual? Society? Are there exceptions to this right? Should there be these exceptions? Why or why not? **S-17**

The class could also discuss the underlying ideas and assumptions behind the Bill of Rights, especially the First Amendment rights. (The importance of following conscience, especially regarding political and religious beliefs; the belief that when everyone can discuss their ideas and consider all alternatives, the best ideas will prevail or compromise can be reached; people who do no wrong shouldn't have to be afraid of their government; even people who do wrong have rights; trials in which both sides argue before a jury of impartial citizens will best render justice; government has an obligation to be fair to citizens and not make arbitrary or unjust laws; etc.) **S-30** You might ask, "Why did some people want these rights written down? What are the advantages? Are there disadvantages? Are there important rights omitted? Should they be added to the Constitution? Why or why not?"

For this activity, the teacher could split the class into groups, each of which could discuss one or two rights. One member of each group could then report to the rest of the class.

Human Rights Throughout the World **S-12**

The class could also discuss these rights with respect to people all over the world, and so begin to forge their own perspectives on international politics, human nature, and the role of the U. S. as a world power. Ask, "Do you think everyone all over the world should have these rights? Why or why not?" (You may need to point out that not every country has these rights: In some countries you can be put in jail for disagreeing with your government leaders, even if you don't advocate violence; you can be taken by the police or soldiers, kept, tortured and even killed without ever having a trial; you can be arrested for practicing your religion or for not following the rules of the official religion; etc.) Students could then talk about what, if anything, our government should do about these countries. How should we treat such countries? Should we give them aid or withhold it? What kind of aid? Should we tell them we want them to change, or is it none of our business? What if most of the people of the country voted for the leaders that do these things? If people want to escape these countries, should we let them move here and become citizens? Why do some Americans object to this idea? **S-7** Teachers familiar with the U.N. Declaration of Human Rights could mention it here. If students express different points of view, the teacher could conduct a dialectical exchange by having students defend their views, clarify key concepts, explore assumptions, and note where the perspectives conflict. **S-26** As always in such a discussion, encourage students to listen carefully to, and note strengths in, perspectives with which they disagree.

Purposes and Limits of Government **S-17**

The lesson could also be used for a discussion probing the purposes and limits of government and deepening students' understanding of government and our Constitution. The Preamble could be re-read to initiate discussion. The following questions could be used to develop an analogy with, say, student government, if the school or class has one: Why do we have student government? What does it do? Are you glad there is student government? Why or why not? Why did the writers of the Constitution believe they had to start a government? Do you agree with them? Why or why not? What does government provide for us? (The class could use a list of Federal Departments to generate some ideas.) How could we have these things without government, or why couldn't we have them without government? What is our government *not* supposed to do? Why?

Students could discuss the concepts 'fair' and 'unfair laws,' or 'just' and 'unjust laws,' with questions like the following: Give me examples of unjust laws. (Discuss each at length — Does everyone agree it is unjust? Why is it unjust?) Why was each made? What justification was given for each law? Then students might summarize the differences between just and unjust laws. *S-14*

Students could compare possible reactions to unjust laws, and the consequences of these reactions. Encourage them to include examples in their discussion. You may use questions like the following: What can people do when their laws are unjust here? Elsewhere? What have different people done? What happened next? Why? *S-35* Students could compare alternatives and their results, for both the individuals and countries. *S-19* Do people have the right to break unjust laws? Why or why not? When? Under what circumstances? If a government has many unjust laws, should other governments do anything about it, or is it none of their business? Why? What, if anything, should be done? What might the people in the unjust government say? Would they think of themselves as unjust? Should we help governments that seem to us to be unjust? *S-12*

Current Events *S-11*

The lesson could also be linked to a unit on the news. The class, or groups of students who could report to the class, could find newspaper articles about major bills being debated or passed, Supreme Court decisions, a Cabinet or Supreme Court nomination, or debates on foreign affairs. The class could outline both sides of the issue, pinpoint the relevant part of the Constitution, and discuss the implications of different possible outcomes. If the issue revolves around interpreting the Constitution, the class could discuss why there is no agreed-upon interpretation. Students could also distinguish aspects of the issue involving the Constitution from aspects which have become part of our government but are not set out in the Constitution.

8

Remodelling Science Lessons

Introduction

Understanding a critical approach to science education is often challenging, since many of us who teach science have ourselves been taught science in a "non-critical" way. Rather than tackle the critical approach to science education headlong, let us begin by understanding what a critical approach is *not*. Too often, science teaching places an overly-strong emphasis on a narrow mastery of the conventional explanations and techniques of established science. Sometimes this means asking students to memorize facts, definitions, diagrams, and so forth. More often, however, students are not required actually to memorize information, but they are asked to master a wide array of standard information and explanations, and they are asked to learn to solve a long list of standard problems or answer standard questions in the physical sciences, life science, or earth science. The emphasis in many textbooks is on preparing students to answer questions like the following, all of which are paraphrased from middle school science texts:

- What are the three kinds of volcanoes, and how are they formed?
- What is an element? a molecule? a compound?
- What are the three parts of a transformer? What kind of electricity does a transformer use?
- How are antibiotics produced? Do antibiotics cure all diseases?
- Which organ of the body pumps blood? The movement of blood is called _____.

While many of these questions represent information which might be of interest or of use to middle school students, mastery of this kind of information does not constitute the most powerful approach to science education. Teaching for a critical understanding of science involves additional elements. Let us go on and see what these elements are.

One of the very important goals of science education should be to help students understand how scientists establish their scientific beliefs. In other words, how do scientists establish the knowledge of the world which we want students to learn? By exploring this question, students can come to a more fully-informed understanding of where the very involved and beautiful explanations of professional science have come from. They will begin to see that science does not arise in some impersonal way from experiments, but that human thought, in both logical and intuitive forms, plays as important a role as experimental data. In this way, they can see that scientific understanding is often powerful, but also fallible. Thus, they can become more critically aware "consumers" of the claims of science which we can read about in the newspapers every day. But perhaps even more importantly, students can be moved to an attitude of intellectual autonomy, the sense that they, too, can interpret their world through their own clear observation and critical thought. One attribute of critical thinkers is that they exercise independent thought and recognize that, at times, it is possible to come to an understanding of the world independent of authorities. Science education should combat the widespread belief that "It's someone else who does and understands science."

One important way to teach students about how scientists establish their knowledge is to allow students to investigate actual questions in the laboratory. Many typical texts, however, take all the initiative out of the "investigation" by presenting a detailed list of procedures to be followed, the steps to take in thinking about observations, even what students should observe and what they should conclude. To learn from a laboratory investigation or other kinds of inquiry activities, students should understand its purpose and should have some opportunity and responsibility to plan the approach and to interpret data or observations. Of course, teachers play an important role in student inquiry through their guidance and structuring, but it is possible to give students the responsibility of designing parts of investigations and interpreting their own data. Some of the remodelled lessons which follow point out ways to do this. In general, students can determine what data they need; design their own data tables; conduct experiments; think about their own interpretation of their data; and discuss their interpretations with classmates who might agree or disagree.

This is a key point in a critical approach to student inquiry: scientific thinking is not a matter of running through a set of steps called the "scientific method." Rather, it is a kind of thinking in which we move back and forth between questions, answers to those questions, and experiments which test those answers. "What do I think about this? If that's so, what will happen when I try ...? Why didn't this come out the way I expected?" In this process, we engage many of the attributes and skills of critical thinking. We must not make snap judgements; we must pose question clearly; we must see the implications of ideas clearly; we must listen as someone comes to a different interpretation of what we have observed.

In order to help students understand the basis for scientific knowledge, it is not enough to introduce them to something called "the scientific method," although science textbooks often devote a few pages to this topic. One of the problems with this approach is that there is no one method which all scientists follow. For instance, the work of a theoretical physicist who speculates about the fundamental nature of matter is different than that of the ornithologist trying to understand the behavior of birds. The physicist relies heavily on abstract mathematics, logical considerations, and even a sense of aesthetic judgment, while the ornithologist observes the natural environment very carefully and tries to find a pattern in his observations. So these two scientists use a very different set of "tools" in their work. Some scientists do experiments, but not all do. As an example, chemists can go into the lab and try a reaction in a variety of conditions; in this way they can test a theory about reactions. But evolutionary biologists cannot see what would have evolved if the situation had been different; they can only look at various kinds of evidence left behind by what has already happened. So these two kinds of scientists must work in different ways, with one able to perform experiments in the laboratory and the other unable to experiment, but forced to rely on historical data.

Science is more than a way of thinking, however. Science includes a vast array of interlocking factual information, concepts and theories which provide us with one particular way of understanding ourselves and the world. In this introduction we will discuss two key features of a critical approach to teaching science content. First, that a critical understanding of science content emphasizes understanding of the fundamental ideas of science and their relationships rather than shallow understanding of lots of material. Second, that teaching for a deep understanding must include the recognition that students come to our classes with already well-established intuitive ideas about many areas of science.

The debate about coverage versus depth is an old one. While there may be reasons to emphasize a brief treatment of many science subjects, advocates of the critical approach to science teaching argue that students will understand science better and become better thinkers generally if they come to a deeper understanding of the central ideas of science. Since it takes time for students to grasp the implications of ideas and to see the connections between scientific concepts and explanations, we must spend more time on selected material. While it is beyond the scope of this introduction to outline the most important ideas in middle school science, we do encourage you to review your own teaching to assure yourself that you are providing students the time and experience they need to reach a deep understanding of the ideas central to the science you teach.

Our second point involves the preconceptions that students have concerning the science topics we teach. It is essential that science educators recognize that students of all ages have their own ideas about the world around us. From our earliest years on, we develop ideas about the growth of plants, the motions of pendulums, how birds can fly, and many more everyday experiences. These preconceptions play a very strong role when we teach for the deep understanding implied by a critical approach to science education. It is not enough to present the established knowledge of science. Every science teacher has experienced giving a clear and articulate explanation only to find, with a sinking feeling, that his or her students did not "get it." Jack Easley, the author of a series of penetrating articles on mathematics and science education, tries to explain this experience when he says, "cognitive research shows that young children develop and test alternative rational explanations which authoritative exposition can't displace."[1] A critical approach to science teaching recognizes that students must first articulate their own beliefs if they are to modify their beliefs in the light of their school experiences. Science teaching must begin by helping students to clarify and state their preconceptions so that they can go on to develop the deeper, more accurate understanding which is the goal of the critical approach to science education. Some of the remodelled lessons which follow suggest ways in which this might be accomplished.

[1] Jack Easley, "A Teacher Educator's Perspective on Students' and Teachers' Schemes: Or Teaching by Listening," Presented at the Conference on Thinking, Harvard Graduate School of Education, August, 1984, p. 1

Bugs' Bodies

Objectives of the Remodelled Plan

The students will:

- consider their preconceptions about insect anatomy while they build models of insects
- after learning more about insect anatomy, they will rebuild their models to incorporate their new understanding thereby examining, evaluating and modifying their assumptions

Standard Approach

In a brief discussion of insects, texts introduce the structures common to all insects. They name the three main parts of the body and give the number of legs, eyes, antennae.

Critique

Such brief text passages present some simple information about the structure of insects. They give us an opportunity to discuss techniques of science teaching which recognize that students have preconceptions about the subjects we teach.

It is important to remember that our students often have ideas about the subjects we are teaching. Students at this level will usually have some preconceptions about insects. They have ideas about what insects are and are not (most will not identify insects as animals), what they do, how they are built. Here are some important points to consider:

• Children do not come into our classes as "blank slates" ready to receive instruction. Rather, they often have well-developed, but somewhat incorrect, concepts already. These preconceptions strongly affect the understanding children come to when they learn science in school.

• Children's preconceptions are often interesting and creative ways to make sense of the various things children have themselves observed or have been told in or out of school. Children's preconceptions are not "learned" as a single idea, but are *constructed* in the child's mind as he or she actively tries to make sense of many experiences and pieces of information from both schooling and out-of-school experiences.

• Since these preconceptions often do "make sense" to some degree, especially in the child's viewpoint, it is difficult to change them. Often we as teachers think, "I said it clearly and correctly. Why didn't they get it?" We forget that children's' preconceptions are very resistant to change, and we often need to take an approach designed to help children modify the pre-conceptions they have already constructed.

Since children do come into our classes with their own preconceptions, how can we best teach science so that students form a more accurate and complete understanding of things? In teaching science concepts, we need to adopt a style of teaching somewhat different than we might use for other subject matter. The principles of effective didactic instruction, while sometimes useful when we are teaching information or well-defined skills, aren't the ticket here, because this particular model of instruction doesn't address two necessary features of good science teaching. In science teaching, we must first take into account students' *prior* knowledge and, second, we must shape instruction so that the students consider what they already know and then become actively involved in modifying their understanding to make it more complete and accurate.

In the lesson on bugs or any other science lesson, we should stress the connection between what the children are learning in school and their everyday experience. There are at least two important reasons for doing this. First, we all hope that school learning can help children understand their everyday lives; this should be one of the main goals of schooling. Often we try to use this connection to motivate our students to learn. But there is another reason to help students realize that they already have ideas about the science topics they are studying, and this idea is closely related to our discussion of students' preconceptions. Too often students seemingly compartmentalize their ideas into "school ideas" and "ideas about real life." In order for school science to help students make their views of the world more accurate and complete, we must break down the division between school ideas and real life ideas. Since much of good science instruction involves helping students refine their preconceptions, it is very important to set up situations which encourage students to look in their "real life compartment" for their existing ideas on the topics they are studying.

Strategies Used to Remodel

S-1 thinking independently
S-30 examining or evaluating assumptions

Remodelled Lesson Plan

Let's look at a lesson on bugs to understand how these ideas might work. While no single example can provide a complete illustration, this lesson on "How Bugs' Bodies Are Built" will give us an example. We should start our lesson with an activity designed to help the students recognize that they already have some ideas on bugs' bodies. While it might work just to have a discussion, there are better ways. In the case of our lesson on bugs, we could begin by having the students build models of bugs in "Mr. Potatohead" fashion. **S-1** In doing this, they must recognize and act on their preconceptions about how bugs' bodies are built. For instance, many students might think that bugs have eight legs, and their models would represent this.

After the class built their models (maybe even working in groups in order to share their individual preconceptions socially), the teacher would provide some information about bugs. This could take place in any number of ways, including all the traditional methods of instruction. The "principles of effective didactic instruction" provide helpful ideas for organizing these kinds of informational presentations. Then, following this direct instruction, the students would go back to their bug models, discuss with each other how real bugs differed from their model bugs and perhaps make a new version or modify the old one. By going back to the original model to make corrections, the students will confront their old ideas about bugs. In this active way, their preconceptions about how bugs bodies are built will be changed to be more accurate. **S-30**

227

Scientific Reasoning: Do Snails See?

Objectives of the Remodelled Plan

The students will:

- clarify their preconceptions on the "sightedness" of snails
- clarify the key question by proposing experiments to provide evidence
- clarify, through discussion, that the interpretation of experiments involves assumptions

Standard Approach

In a brief discussion of mollusks, the garden snail is cited as an example ,and the statement is made that, "Attached to the body are two pairs of tentacles and a pair of eyes." More information about snails is then given.

Critique

Science texts often present a great amount of information without helping students understand why scientists hold this knowledge. This passage gives us the opportunity to discuss ways to help students understand how scientific knowledge is justified.

Science instruction in the life sciences, from which this example is drawn, often includes much information on the processes and physiology of cells and organisms. To some extent, this is appropriate. Too often, however, we forget that science education should include experience with the ways in which scientists establish their beliefs — in this case, about whether snails have eyes. As students grow in their ability to understand how scientific ideas are established, they will become more critically informed "consumers" of scientific knowledge and better able to distinguish well-grounded scientific belief from ill-grounded beliefs which pose as science. They will also develop the attitudes and skills needed to become intellectually more autonomous and able to come to their own understanding of the world based on personal experience and critical thought.

Strategies Used to Remodel

S-9   developing confidence in reason
S-24 practicing Socratic discussion: clarifying and questioning beliefs, theories, or perspectives
S-13 clarifying issues, conclusions, or beliefs
S-10 refining generalizations and avoiding oversimplifications

Remodelled Lesson Plan s-9

We might start this lesson with a discussion of snails and their behavior in order to expose students' preconceptions. "Do you believe snails can see? What makes you believe this?" Often, students will express a range of opinions on the "sightedness" of snails. Some reasons for holding their beliefs could be called "theoretical." For example, some students will say that all animals have eyes, therefore snails must have eyes. Others will say that those stalks on snails heads look like eyes so they must be eyes. Other students will have reasons for their beliefs which could be called "experimental" in the sense that they are based on observational evidence. Examples of this might be citing the fact that snails are active at night, when it is dark, so they must be able to tell light from dark. All these reasons provide a context for us to practice many of the critical thinking micro-skills, such as examining assumptions, examining evidence, and making plausible inferences through questions like the following: "Can you be sure they are eyes just because they look like eyes? Are you sure that all animals have eyes? Snails do come out at night, but that might be because it is cooler out. If that were so, could you still be sure that they were telling light from dark?" **S-24**

After questioning students about their present beliefs and reasons, we could turn to experimental ways to explore these ideas. It would be ideal if students could actually observe snails as they tested their ideas, but discussion may be the only possibility. We could start by asking "What would be the difference in the snails' behavior if they could see or if they couldn't see?" **S-13** Perhaps a student would respond that snails would back away from a bright light. We could ask, "Would shining a flashlight at a snail and observing its behavior *prove* that the snail either could or couldn't see?" Depending on the particular responses which students made, you might suggest 1) that the light also is hot, and that might be what the snail sensed; 2) that the light might not be bright enough to affect snails; 3) that snails might *like* bright lights and might have moved toward the light. **S-10** While some of these possibilities seem a little farfetched, they do illustrate that experimental proof in science is complex and that the implications of an experiment depend on assumptions.

Discussions of this sort also give students practice in listening to the arguments of others. Through this kind of discussion, we can help students to critically examine how they, and scientists in general, might establish reasons for holding their beliefs. In this way, students can come to see scientific knowledge as the result of thought and evidence working together, and they will also begin to understand that evidence is *interpreted* in order to arrive at knowledge. Scientific knowledge does not arise unambiguously out of experiments.

The Air We Exhale

Objectives of the Remodelled Plan

The students will:
• interpret observations made after blowing air on a glass plate
• discuss the conclusions they can draw from their observations

Standard Approach

Texts state that body cells need oxygen and then briefly outline the movement of oxygen into the lungs and into the blood. They explain that waste substances from the cells enter the blood, move to the lungs and are then exhaled. Some texts suggest that students blow on a flat piece of glass and observe what they see. They are informed that there are small droplets of water. They are then asked where the water came from and are told that water is one of the waste materials from the body and that the air we exhale contains water vapor.

Critique

While texts try to provide some activities for students to perform, they tell students what they should observe and provide the "correct" interpretation. This approach may actually inhibit the students' sense of critical thinking by suggesting that, in school at least, questions are not really meant to be thought about.

Such lessons attempt to help students understand a very fundamental idea: that the air we breathe out is different in some way from the air we breathe in and that this difference has to do with what the body needs and the waste products it produces. The standard approach tries to base this assertion on some simple observations which students could make. However, several opportunities for engaging the students in critical thought are missed. Probably the most obvious opportunity is that when students have been directed to try a test for water vapor or for carbon dioxide, they are told immediately what they are supposed to observe. While there are obvious practical reasons for this approach, it does have the effect of undermining the student's sense of independence. Why should students try something for themselves if the texts tell them what they are supposed to observe? Or, if some students' observations do not agree with what the text tells them they will see, what should they think about this? Students either should be told what happens without having been asked a purely rhetorical question, or, better, they should actually try it for themselves. In this way, their intellectual independence is strengthened.

Blowing on a glass plate and interpreting what is seen presents several opportunities for developing critical thinking. The way texts use activities like this is a little problematic, since the implication is that the condensation on the plate provides evidence that water is a waste product from the body. The text does not state this directly, but it also does not clarify what evidence this observation actually does provide. It would be difficult to provide evidence to students which proves that water is a waste product, but we could encourage them to think critically about the simple observations that are suggested by the text.

Furthermore, the reasoning and evidence are incomplete, encouraging students to make a poor inference. To conclude that the water comes from us, the air breathed out must be compared to the rest of the air in the room.

Strategies Used to Remodel

S-1   thinking independently
S-32 making plausible inferences, predictions, or interpretations
S-13 clarifying issues, conclusions, or beliefs

Remodelled Lesson Plan *S-1*

We could begin by asking students to breathe on a glass plate. Condensation will be visible if they observe quickly after breathing on the glass. The following questions will suggest a line of reasoning: "What do you observe? Have you observed anything like this before? What do you think it is?" The teacher can help students establish that this is water. "Is there water in the air around us? Where does the water come from?" **S-32** At this point, it would be helpful to establish that the water we observe on the glass is present in our breath but not in the air around us. "How could we test the air in the room to see if water will condense on the glass? **S-13** By fanning hard with your hand you can force air over the glass plate. What do you see now?" Through this line of reasoning, we hope to establish that our breath contains water vapor which the air in the room does not contain. "When we breathe on a glass plate, we see water condensed on the plate, but when we fan about the same amount of air over the plate, we don't see any condensation. From this, what can we say is different about the air we breathe out compared to the air in the room?" **S-32** Through this line of questioning, we are trying to establish that there is water in the air we exhale which will condense on a glass plate, while there is not enough water in the air around us to condense if we fan air over a plate. In this way, we illustrate to students the line of reasoning we must take to show that the air we exhale is different from the air we inhale. We have not yet shown that this difference is a waste product from our cells, but we can suggest this to students.

Simple Machines

Objectives of the Remodelled Plan

The students will:

- design a series of questions concerning simple machines which can be answered through the use of data which they can collect, thus thinking independently
- determine the information they need to answer their questions by clarifying them
- make measurements and record data
- provide answers to questions based on the logical use of their own data

Standard Approach

Typical lessons are designed to have students compare the effects simple machines have on the force required to move objects. In one such lesson, students are directed to copy a data table and then make several measurements. They are to 1) use a spring scale to lift a cart, 2) use a pulley to lift the cart and measure the force with the scale, 3) set up an incline and pull the cart up with the spring scale, thereby measuring the force needed, and 4) use the incline and pulley together and measure the force needed. They are then asked questions concerning the effects of pulleys and inclines on the force needed to move objects.

Critique

The main problem with such lessons, from the point of view of encouraging critical thinking, is that students are directed to perform a series of measurements *without* first conceiving a question or planning a strategy. The point of the activity unfolds only through the question in the "Conclusions" part of the activity, which is located at the end. The problem with this design is that students are asked to engage in a series of measurements which have no apparent relationship to any particular question. In addition, by asking students, as in the above mentioned lesson, to copy a particular data table (for which a model is given in the text), no chance is given for students to invent a way to organize the data they are about to gather. Again, this strategy removes another opportunity for students to organize their own approach to answering a question.

Both pulleys and inclined planes are simple machines with which 6th - 9th grade students may have had experience. Thus, this activity presents an opportunity for bringing out students' preconceptions. This could be done by asking students to name ways in which these simple machines are used in everyday life. Students should also be asked to predict and record their predictions concerning the effects of these simple machines *before* doing the actual measurements. Predicting the outcome of situations is an important way to bring students' prior knowledge into school activities.

Students should also be asked to give ways in which these simple machines are used in everyday life. While one effect of this kind of question is simply motivation, another important effect is drawing out students' *preconceptions* on these simple machines. Often students, mentally and unconsciously, separate their understanding into "in school" and "out of school" compartments. Thus it is important, in order to help students form a logically integrated understanding, to point out to them that they have already developed ideas on particular school subjects. These preconceptions form the basis for a better-developed understanding of simple machines, which we hope to encourage through activities such as this one on the effects of pulleys and levers.

Strategies Used to Remodel

S-1   thinking independently
S-13 clarifying issues, conclusions, or beliefs
S-33 evaluating evidence and alleged facts
S-5   developing intellectual humility and suspending judgment

Remodelled Lesson Plan

The most important aspect to remodelling this activity is to begin with questions for the students. "How do people use an inclined plane (or a pulley) to help them do something? What is it about an inclined plane (or pulley) that makes it useful?" **S-1** These kinds of questions lead naturally to asking students to design a way to measure how the force needed to hold the cart when it hangs vertically compares with the force needed to hold it on the incline. As part of this process, the students must clarify their questions so that they are answerable through use of the data they can compile. "What, exactly, are we trying to find out? How can we do so? What will that show?"**S-13** In this way, the activity would be *designed by the students* rather than performed as a kind of "cookbook" activity from the text.

In the same vein, students should not be given a data table to copy; they should be asked to design ways to record their data so that they could make the comparisons in which they are interested. **S-1** Starting with a question rather than a list of directions requires students to generate their own procedures by clarifying possible questions and recognizing what kinds of data will allow them to give a reasoned answer to the questions posed. Why did we do this? What happened? What does that show? Could another explanation account for our findings?**S-33**

Asking students to make predictions is an important technique for bringing out their preconceptions. You might demonstrate weighing the cart directly and then, placing it on the incline, ask students "How much force do you predict it will take to hold this cart on the incline? How do you think the force to hold the cart will change if we make the ramp steeper?" You could also probe their theoretical understanding by asking "What is it about an inclined plane that makes it work this way?" **S-1**

Having made predictions, the students must suspend their own preconceptions as they take data and logically analyze their data. Thus, they must suspend final judgement on the questions they have posed until they carefully evaluate the direct evidence they have collected. **S-5**

Thinking critically involves the ability to reach sound conclusions based on observation and information. Critical thinkers distinguish their observations from their conclusions and situations from interpretations.

The Wave-Particle Theory of Light

Objectives of the Remodelled Plan

The students will:
* explore and clarify the nature of models and the use of model in science through discussion
* note significant similarities and differences between models and what they represent
* develop confidence in reason by proposing a model to explain a physical observation
* interpret an observation with light in terms of the wave model of light

Standard Approach

In introducing the electromagnetic spectrum, texts will mention the wave-particle theory of light. Students are told that if they look at a distant light source through a pinhole in a card, the pattern of light they observe is larger than the actual size of the pinhole. They are told that this "strange effect can be explained if light is thought of as a series of waves." They are then told that other kinds of experiments give different results. These experiments show that light always transfers energy in the form of small particles." The students are told that these light particles are called photons. The passage concludes by saying the *wave-particle theory of light* is the name of the theory that results from combining these two different kinds of experimental results.

Critique

This brief passage raises several questions: how models are used in science; why diffraction through a pinhole indicates that light acts like a wave; what "transfers energy in the form of small particles" means; what it means for light to act as a wave in some experiments and as a particle in others. Most of these issues cannot be dealt with successfully in a brief introductory passage. (In fact, such passages suggest considering whether these issues should be addressed this briefly if the result is to raise issues which students cannot understand.) It is possible, though, to help students understand the role of *models* in science and, for this reason, this remodelling discussion will focus on the use of models in science.

Strategies Used to Remodel

S-14 clarifying and analyzing the meanings of words or phrases
S-29 noting significant similarities and differences
S-9 developing confidence in reason
S-32 making plausible inferences, predictions, or interpretations

Remodelled Lesson Plan

The discussion could begin by raising the issue of models in general. The most familiar use of the word 'model' to students is probably as in 'model airplane,' a small representation of a larger object. The following questions will help students discover some features of models. "How is a model airplane like an actual airplane? How is it different? What does a model of an airplane enable you to do? What kinds of things does a real airplane do that a model cannot do?" Through these kinds of questions, we try to help students clarify their own thinking about this simple kind of model. **S-14**

Next, we could introduce models which are more abstract than simple model airplanes. Most students have had experience with some kind of map, and we will use this to extend the idea of a model. After reminding the students about road maps, perhaps by showing them a road map of your state as an example, you could ask them to think of the ways in which this map is a model and how this map model differs from an airplane model. "Is the map a complete picture of your state? Could you use the map to find out everything you might want to know about your state?" These kinds of questions will help students understand that a map is a useful representation of some aspects of your state in which people might be interested. The map is not a complete, accurate representation of every aspect of your state, but it does help us understand and use the road system. We would probably make a different kind of map if we wanted to understand how the hills and mountains of the state worked to form river systems, for instance. The following kinds of questions will encourage students to explore the usefulness of maps. "What does this road map tell us? What does it help us do? Is this map a miniature model of our state? Are there things in our state which aren't shown on this map? Why are these things left off?" The point of these questions, and many other possible questions, is that maps (or models in general) are not complete representations but are designed to help us understand some particular aspect of the thing we are studying. **S-29**

In the case of maps, we make a small model of a large object. In much of science we do the opposite — we make a large model of small things like atoms, for instance. But these models in science have many of the same features of the models and maps we have been discussing.

Sometimes in our science teaching, we can describe something or let students experience it directly and then ask students to invent some kind of model. For example, after watching a drop of ink slowly diffuse through a glass of water, students could try to invent the best model they can to explain what they saw. **S-9**

In the case of a model for light, we can let students observe diffraction through a pinhole, as the original lesson points out. The students can also be shown pictures of water waves bending around objects — breakwaters in a harbor, for instance. You could ask, "If light acted like these kinds of waves, what would we expect to see when light travels through pinholes and into our eyes?" **S-32**

Through questions like this, you can lead students to understand possible implications of the pinhole in the card activity mentioned in the original text passage. In this way we can begin to help students understand what it means to say "lights acts like a wave" or that "we can use a wave model of light."

The text goes on to mention the particle model for light. Unfortunately, the evidence leading to this model is much more difficult to observe and interpret. We cannot present this evidence to students. In this remodelling discussion, we have, however, seen an approach which helps students understand what models are and how they are used in science. We have also taken a brief look at some of the evidence which is best interpreted thorough the wave model of light.

Your first remodels should use those skills or insights clearest to you. Other principles can be integrated as they become clear.

Newton's Second Law of Motion

Objectives of the Remodelled Plan

The students will:
- make plausible predictions about motions of objects
- analyze their experiences regarding motions of objects
- clarify the concepts of force, friction, and mass through discussions and questions about common experiences

Standard Approach

Texts often approach teaching Newton's Second Law of Motion by using examples of frictionless surfaces, such as a hockey puck on ice. They then state that experiments in such situations have shown that doubling the force will double the acceleration. Some texts introduce the mass of an object as the ratio between the force and acceleration, and provide a summary of Newton's Second Law: "When a force is applied to an object, the object accelerates in the direction of the applied force. The acceleration is greater when the force is greater. The acceleration is less when the mass of the object is greater."

Critique

Newton's Second Law is very difficult for students to understand, since it apparently contradicts many of our everyday experiences. For instance, frictional forces are so much a part of everyday life that students rarely have the opportunity to experience frictionless motions. The text misses an important opportunity for students to come to terms with this aspect of their experiences. Also, the definition of 'mass' as force divided by acceleration is much too abstract to be of use to students at this level.

This lesson gives us the chance to raise the question of the *appropriateness* of presenting particular science concepts to 6ᵗʰ -9ᵗʰ grade students. It is appropriate for these students to try to understand the motion of objects in terms of their own experience and in terms of the ideas of scientists who have studied motion. Newton's Laws, though, present a highly abstract and condensed way of understanding motion. Many of the important aspects of Newton's Laws are often not apparent in everyday life, and therefore, students' preconceptions about motion are often quite at odds with the abstractions of Newton's Laws. Briefly, what are some of the preconceptions students have which apparently contradict Newton's Laws?

The First Law states, "Objects move in a straight line at constant speed unless a force is acting on them." Since everyday motions are always subject to forces, especially frictional forces, children are without the kinds of experience which would enable them to have "experienced" the First Law. As a different example, many middle school and older students think that if a stone whirled overhead in a circle on a string is released, the stone will follow a kind of curved path (when viewed from above). Their preconceptions on this kind of motion are entirely at odds with the prediction of the First Law that the stone will follow a straight line.

The Second Law deals with the relationship between force, *mass*, and *acceleration*. Again, this presents difficulty for students, since our everyday experience leads us to see motions in terms of force, *weight*, and *speed*. Based on everyday experience, most students believe that the harder you push something, the faster it goes. We develop these preconceptions from experiences like pushing heavy objects across the floor. While the confusion of weight for mass is not a relatively important issue for middle school students, the spirit of the Second Law is lost when we relate forces to *speeds* rather than to *accelerations*.

Strategies Used to Remodel

S-12 developing one's perspective: creating or exploring beliefs, arguments, or theories
S-1 thinking independently
S-14 clarifying and analyzing the meanings of words or phrases

Remodelled Lesson Plan **S-12**

We begin remodelling this lesson by changing its goal somewhat. Instead of trying to teach Newton's Laws, we try to do two things: 1) we try to help students articulate their preconceptions about the motion of objects; and 2) we try to challenge students in a way which encourages them to modify their understanding to arrive at a more powerful, all-encompassing view of their experiences, thus developing their perspectives. If we can accomplish these goals, we will help prepare them for a critical understanding of the abstract statement of Newton's Laws later in their education.

As an example, let us begin with the relationship between force ("pushes and pulls" to students) and motion. We could have students consider two extreme situations: pushing a car along a road and pushing an object over a very smooth, frictionless surface. (Use a situation your students might have experienced like a frozen lake, an air hockey table, sliding on a smooth or wet floor, etc.) "What happens when we stop pushing? Why?" **S-1** Through questions like this, we are trying to challenge one characteristic preconception which is that something moving requires a continuing force. Our strategy is to cause students to consider the difference between high-friction and low-friction situations. Also have them consider the force required 1) to *stop* moving objects, and 2) to change their direction. Through this strategy, we hope that students will see changing motion (in speed or direction) as the result of external force acting on the object. This is one of the difficult points in Newton's Laws for beginners.

Another major point in Newton's Second Law is the mass of an object. While the texts' definition of mass as "the ratio of force to acceleration" is technically correct, it is not an appropriate definition for students at this level. At this age, students should learn science by considering concrete ideas. While force and, to some extent, acceleration are concepts with which students have direct experience, the idea of a *ratio* of these quantities is too abstract for students to understand in a critical sense. It is probably better to refer to the mass of an object as "the amount of matter." Students often confuse the *mass* of an object with the *frictional force* associated with moving it. Big objects, like pianos, are difficult to move around due to friction. It is, however, surprisingly easy to move a small boat weighing about as much as a piano, since the frictional force opposing the motion of a boat in the water is very small. Through questions involving large objects and small objects, along with high- and low-friction situations, we can clarify students' understanding of mass of objects. **S-14**

Ask students, "Why is it harder to move objects on rough surfaces than smooth or slippery surfaces? Why is it harder to start an object moving on a smooth surface, than it is to *keep* it moving? Why is it harder to stop a bulky object than one with less matter? A faster object than a slower one?"**S-1**

Macro-practice is almost always more important than micro-drill. We need to be continually vigilant against the misguided tendency to fragment, atomize, mechanize, and proceduralize thinking.

9 Beginning to Remodel: From Teachers in the Trenches

Introduction

A s teachers are developing their skills in lesson remodelling, some are sending us samples of their work. It is, of course, a pleasure for us to see teachers in the field making lesson plan remodelling a reality. We are indebted to those who have sent us remodels. We have included several of these remodels to give you the opportunity to see a variety of approaches to lesson plan remodelling and to encourage you as educators to implement your creative ideas effectively through the structure presented in the handbook. As you can see, critical thinking can and should be applied to any and all dimensions of learning, from chemistry to physical education.

The following, then, demonstrate some of the "first effort" remodels we have received. We welcome other contributions.

Soccer Tactics

by Joan M. West, Victorian Ministry of
Education, Australia

Objectives of the Remodelled Plan

The students will:

- participate in a previously planned fitness program specific to the requirements of soccer
- develop attacking and defensive strategies in soccer, thus thinking independently
- assess their solutions and actions
- develop and participate in modified games which will apply the devised strategies
- devise and participate in soccer ball skills practices

Original Lesson Plan

> Students analyze two specific aspects of the game of soccer — distance and player size — which affect the game outcome and hence influence strategy. In response to teacher-posed problems, small groups of students devise their own solutions within the limitations of their skill, fitness, rules of the game, and problem solving abilities.

Critique

This lesson is used to illustrate the "divergent" teaching style which is the *least* teacher-directed model discussed in one of the "classic" physical education instructional strategies texts. In the opening section of the lesson, pairs of students explore the implications of situations set up by the teacher. The students lose the chance to imagine their own situations, explain the problems which could occur, and devise possible strategies. By presenting the students with the two variables to be explored, this lesson misses a key step — that which provides the opportunity for students to discover the factors that they consider are important in the game outcome. From this point, small groups could design and try out strategies to either overcome or maximize these factors.

Strategies Used to Remodel

S-1 thinking independently
s-31 distinguishing relevant from irrelevant facts
S-19 generating or assessing solutions
S-20 analyzing or evaluating actions or policies

Remodelled Lesson Plan *S-1*

The lesson starts with a soccer-specific warm-up activity, devised in previous lessons by the students, which includes practice of dribbling, tackling, and passing in small groups. Students also pair up and then practice against other pairs. Discussion then follows in those small groups when students themselves identify and justify key factors which influence win-lose situations. *S-31*

Students devise and participate in practice situations for strategies which either overcome or maximize those variables. How, exactly, does this factor influence the game? Why? What problems can this cause? How? How could this problem be solved? What effect would that have? Which solution is best for which situation? *S-19*

This practice is followed by discussion in which the students assess the strategies' effectiveness. How did each proposed solution work? Which helped solve the problem? Did any create additional problems? Why? Which solution is best for which situations? *S-20*

When rule violations occur, in particular dangerous play, the teacher could direct the discussion to students' assessing the consequences of such behavior. Why did this happen? Why do players do this? What effect does this have? How can we all help prevent this from happening in the future? *S-20*

In closing the lesson, students and teacher could return to the original questions: Which factors influence the game outcome? What strategies can you use to maximize or minimize them? Students have the opportunity to explain the specific situations in which they identified key variables.

> *It should not be assumed that there is a universal standard for how fast teachers should proceed with the task of remodelling their lesson plans. A slow but steady evolutionary process is much more desirable than a rush job across the board.*

Mixtures

by Sister Isabel Clark, Academy of the
Visitation, St. Louis, MO

Objectives of the Remodelled Plan

The students will:
- compare and contrast mixtures, compounds, and suspensions
- recognize properties of mixtures, in order to analyze the word
- discuss properties with partners to clarify
- compare the scientific and ordinary concepts 'mixture'

Original Lesson Plan

This lesson focuses on mixtures, emphasizing the differences between mixtures and compounds.

Before having the students read the section about mixtures, ask them to brainstorm common examples of mixtures. (Some suggestions are gravel, cereal with milk, and a tossed salad.) From the examples, help the students develop an operational definition of a mixture. Revise the definition after the students have read the section.

Critique

This lesson offers an opportunity for students to work out their own definition of a mixture, but the brainstorming technique suggests that they already know what a mixture is. We suggest that samples of real mixtures as well as two compounds that they have already studied and one suspension be used instead of the brainstorming. By working with real materials, the students are in touch with the concrete object to observe. The introduction of a third substance, namely a suspension, gives the student a substance that is similar but retains other properties that will lead the student on to the next part of the lesson.

Strategies Used to Remodel

S-29 noting significant similarities and differences
S-14 clarifying and analyzing the meanings of words or phrases
S-17 questioning deeply: raising and pursuing root or significant questions

Remodelled Lesson Plan

This lesson requires preparation of materials for students who will work in groups of four at 6 tables for four. Set out plastic or paper cups of each of the following mixtures for each table: sand and gravel, cereal with milk, tossed salad, and other mixtures. Then prepare two cups for each table with a compound in each cup, such as water and sugar, which were used in the last lesson. To this add one cup of oil and vinegar salad dressing as a suspension which will be used in the next lesson.

Ask students to work in groups of four. Tell them that one way that chemists would group the cups is by how the different substances are combined in each cup. Have them sort and compare the cups and discuss their groupings. Or tell them to examine and observe the contents of each cup and identify it as compound, mixture or other. The two compounds, sugar and water were used in the last lesson. As they compare the cups, some should discover the key property of mixtures, namely that they are combinations of substances that are not chemically combined and so can be separated. **S-29** Each student in the group should be ready to state what cups contain mixtures and defend that position. Tell them to test for mixtures by separating the substances in the cups. A written statement defining 'mixture' from the group should be made to give to the entire class. Thus, each group can see how they are like the others and can help to refine the final definition. Students could then propose other potential mixtures. **S-14**

Spend some time on the substance that is the suspension. If some groups thought it was a mixture, ask them to defend their positions. Clarify the definitions for further distinctions for the students who might not make the distinction on their own. **S-29**

After reading their texts, students could compare the scientific and ordinary concepts 'mixture.' (For example, though people would usually call cake batter a mixture, chemists wouldn't.) **S-29**

Students could also propose reasons why chemists would find these categories important. **S-17**

Getting experience in lesson plan critique: What are the strengths and weaknesses of this lesson? What critical principles, concepts, or strategies apply to it?

Human Treatment of Whales

by Noreen Miller, School District #12, Denver, CO & Lanai Wallin, Skyview Elementary, Denver, CO

Objectives of the Remodelled Plan

The students will:

- raise and pursue significant questions regarding our relationships with animals
- evaluate actions
- examine their assumptions through Socratic discussion

Original Lesson Plan

> This is a seatwork lesson on a newspaper article about four whales at Sea World who attacked their trainers — the trainers are suing. It is usually taught with emphasis on coding. That is, the students mark their copies of the article with an A for agree, D for disagree and I for interesting.

Critique

Although the usual manner of reading a newspaper article for an opinion is fast and efficient, it is a superficial approach to understanding belief systems. The lesson as stated would not establish why the students agree or disagree or the nature of the reasons for their thinking. The issues being raised need to be clarified, as do the assumptions underlying the students' beliefs. A seminar and dialogue using critical thinking would be more useful, as it would help students clarify their reasoning processes.

In the particular Socratic dialogue with fifteen students who had been trained in seminar techniques, some of the students also raised additional points such as: the people at Sea World are not well trained; these people should have studied the whales first; more research is needed; research under controlled conditions is different than field research; Sea World is run for profit.

Strategies Used to Remodel

S-17 questioning deeply: raising and pursuing root or significant questions
S-21 reading critically: clarifying or critiquing texts
S-20 analyzing or evaluating actions or policies
S-24 practicing Socratic discussion: clarifying and questioning beliefs, theories, or perspectives
S-18 analyzing or evaluating arguments, interpretations, beliefs, or theories

Remodelled Lesson Plan s-17

Have the students read a newspaper article such as the one about four homicidal whales and their trainers. Ask them to think about the conflicts that are posed, both the obvious one and the more subtle ones, if they see any. Have them share the conflicts that they found. Then ask them to state in complete sentences the conflicts they discovered. Have them give their initial responses and reasons. **S-21**

Raise key questions, such as: "Who was responsible for what happened? Why? What should happen now?"

Discussion could move in the direction of more general and basic questions. "How do human beings relate to animals? What different relationships are there? What responsibilities, if any, do we have toward animals?" (Have students consider pets, stray animals, animals in zoos, in the wild, and animals that we eat.) Another question might be, "Is it necessary to conduct research on animals? If so, under what conditions can we accept such research? If not, what can we do instead of using animals for research?" **S-20**

Probe for further issues by asking questions such as, "Is it fair to put animals into captivity?" A possible student response could be, "No, because it makes them unhappy." The teacher could probe this answer in the following manner: "Are all animals in captivity unhappy? How can we as human beings know whether an animal is happy or unhappy? Do the needs of human beings ever take precedence over the happiness of animals?" **S-24**

After some discussion, ask the students to state some of the important issues that they have discovered. Write them on the board.

Begin to Socratically question the class as a whole about their responses to the issues raised. Probe them for the assumptions that underlie their belief systems by asking such questions as: "Do animals have rights? What is the status of a human being in comparison to an animal? Is it acceptable to confine animals just because it has been common practice to do so? Can humans kill and control animals without any negative consequences?" **S-24** By questioning students about the basis for their agreement or disagreement with a belief, they will gain practice in seeing their thought processes at work. They will better understand the reasons for their beliefs and the assumptions that underlie them. During the discussion, note related issues that are raised and come back to them later in the lesson or at another time.

When students disagree, encourage them to argue back and forth, trying to convince each other. Have students evaluate the arguments given. For example, you could ask, "Of all of the reasons given for (conclusion), which are the strongest? Weakest?" **S-18**

Myths

by Virginia Reilly, St. Apollinaris School,
Napa, CA

Objectives of the Remodelled Plan
The students will:
- deeply question the meaning of a particular myth
- discuss the literal meaning of the myth
- apply their understanding of the myth they have studied to myths of other cultures
- explore why myths appear in the literature of so many cultures

Original Lesson Plan

> Skills Unit 31 focuses on myth and legend recognition. The children are directed to read a story about why Ra-wen-io, maker of all things on earth, gave rabbit long back legs and long ears and why he gave owl a short neck and big eyes. Upon finishing the story, children are asked to answer factual questions about the story and to consider the definition of myth and legend. They are then asked to read a Hawaiian story about Pele and how she became goddess of volcanoes. Again factual questions are asked. In addition, children are asked to identify the story as myth or legend. The unit concludes with a lesson on legend identification.

Critique

I will focus on the myth aspect of the lesson. Even though many sixth graders would be unable to recite definitions of myth and legend and identify a given story as one or the other, they have long been acquainted with myths and legends. Certainly it is important that children have the language of literature and be able to recognize different forms of literature, but that is not enough. Skills Unit 31 has for its main task myth recognition, but it fails to consider the worthier task of myth and its relationship to reality, seen and unseen.

In the section titled "Introducing the Skill Lesson," the teacher is told the scope of the lesson and what to say and do.

> Read the title. Explain that in this lesson pupils will read about two very old types of literature — the myth and the legend. The lesson will help them understand the difference between the two and will help them recognize each when they read or hear such tales.

Such is the scope of the lesson. Not only does it fail to encourage critical thinking in the student, but it likewise discourages the teacher from thinking critically. Neither teacher nor student is

248

called upon to become actively involved in this lesson; rather they are told to do trite, uninteresting tasks.

After reading the first myth, the children read the following in their text:

> The story you have just read is an American Indian myth. A myth is a very old story handed down among people. It may be about some gods or goddesses. It often explains something about nature, such as why there is thunder and lightning.

The children have been given a definition of myth; they are not encouraged to explore for themselves the meaning of myth, an exercise more valuable because it engages their curiosity and taps their desire to know and understand. The lesson continues, and children read another story about gods and goddesses, after which they are asked to identify the story as legend or myth, a task which children complete successfully as the definition of myth in the text uses the key words, gods and goddesses. Thus the lesson of myths is completed without ever having explored myth and its meaning.

Strategies Used to Remodel

S-17 questioning deeply: raising and pursuing root or significant questions
S-35 exploring implications and consequences
S-14 clarifying and analyzing the meanings of words or phrases
S-11 comparing analogous situations: transferring insights to new contexts

Remodelled Lesson Plan S-17

The remodelled lesson, by having students discuss root questions, would explore myth and its meaning. Instead of defining myth for the children and having them apply that definition to stories they read, I would begin by telling the children that they are going to read an Indian myth. A discussion of the Indian myth in particular and of myth in general would follow. What part of the myth seems unbelievable? Does the myth deal with reality? What reality does the myth explain? What are the obvious, seen realities that the myth explains and the less obvious but unseen realities that the myth implies? **S-35** Why does the myth describe a creator and creatures? How is that relationship developed through the actions of Ra-wen-io, rabbit, and fox, and what is implied about their relationships? Do myths reveal reality as it is or as a society perceives it to be? Why do people tell myths? What do myths reveal about the tellers of myths and their beliefs? **S-17**

The lesson would be extended over a period of time during which myths from other cultures would be read, discussed, and compared. How do the details of myths differ? Why do they differ? Are myths alike in any way? How? Why? Why are myths an important part of the literature of many cultures? **S-14**

The lesson would conclude with a written essay in which the children would be asked to compare and contrast two myths, one which had been discussed in class and one which they would read for the first time. **S-11**

Johnny Tremain

by Michael Cecil, Nipher Middle School, Kirkwood, MO

Objectives of the Remodelled Plan

The students will:

- question perspectives on an incident in a historical novel
- make interdisciplinary connections between the dramatic and historical
- analyze the author's socio-political beliefs
- evaluate source credibility by examining claims regarding potential vested interest

Original Lesson Plan

Objective: Gain further understanding about the historical period through the study of a work of fiction. Content matter: *Johnny Tremain* by Esther Forbes.

Students are directed to pay attention to descriptive details, comparing pre- and revolutionary times to today. Lessons direct students to focus on food, dress, transportation, and communication. Students are directed to pick a topic and do a poster or model on it: e.g., ships of the late eighteenth and mid-twentieth centuries. The intent is to have students realize what it would have been like to be a teenager during earlier times. The skill of comparing and contrasting is the primary tool in analyzing the material.

Critique

No direction is given to discuss the author's presentation: whether the presentation limits or expands student perspective, such as examining what is not stated directly in descriptive narrative nor in character dialogue. Thus, the directed conclusions may be superficial. The only event examined further is the firing of the first shot at Lexington. Even at that, the quibble over who fired it takes on disproportionate importance and reinforces already-held assumptions about good guy/bad guy labeling. The novel provides numerous opportunities for in-depth critical examination of the socio-economic circumstances, thus providing greater depth in understanding the characters' actions and the reader's assumptions about judging those actions. However, I'll cite a specific instance and describe an approach for gaining greater understanding of the period and the author's assumptions about the period.

Strategies Used to Remodel

S-23 making interdisciplinary connections
S-27 comparing and contrasting ideals with actual practice

S-18 analyzing or evaluating arguments, interpretations, beliefs, or theories
S-24 practicing Socratic discussion: clarifying and questioning beliefs, theories, or perspectives
S-16 evaluating the credibility of sources of information
S-4 exploring thoughts underlying feelings and feelings underlying thoughts

Remodelled Lesson Plan

Johnny Tremain burns a hand while attempting hurriedly to finish a silver piece commissioned by John Hancock. Johnny's carelessness is a direct result of the law prohibiting working on the sabbath. This would be an excellent opportunity to discuss the separation of church and state. Why was this law passed? What is the relationship here? Who officially passed laws in Boston? Who influenced the lawmakers? How did the framers of the U.S. Constitution deal with this issue? In contemporary U.S., are religious values of specific religions reflected in law? How does this happen if church and state have been directed by the Constitution to remain separate? **S-27** What are the results? **S-23** How does the author probe such questions? Does the presentation unfairly favor certain conclusions? On what assumptions might these be based? **S-18** Such questions would be pursued though small group work and large group Socratic discussion.

There is yet another aspect of the hand-burning incident that bears scrutiny. Johnny's injury is not tended by a doctor, but rather by a midwife because the doctor is considered likely to expose their sabbath violation to the authorities; the unsanctioned midwife is not. Why? The implications and causes of the situation are never explored in the lesson directions, or by the author. In fact, Forbes is clearly supportive of the doctor, as witnessed by the negative physical description (the midwife being reduced to an ugly hag) and the prominence of the doctor's judgment (given later when the doctor discovers that Johnny's hand has been rendered nearly useless through the midwife's incorrect treatment).

The students need to be ushered through Socratic discussion to probe beyond this one-sided presentation, to grapple with questions, such as: Why would the doctor have been more likely to bring punishment on Johnny and the family for violating the sabbath law? What would the doctor and midwife have lost or gained from turning them in? Does this reveal societal attitudes about medicine, or is the doctor simply a more responsible, law-abiding citizen? Why did the midwife make such an obvious mistake in wrapping the wound? Was she incompetent? Why? Did the doctor and midwife have equal access to training and supplies? Was the midwife better equipped than the doctor to deal with some medical problems? Which ones? Why? How many women were legal doctors at that time? What does this say about the attitudes of the time? **S-24**

Who does the author place in the more favorable light? How? What can we infer about the author's attitudes and assumptions from the way the story was presented? How does she establish the doctor as the more credible source of medical judgment? **S-16** Does the doctor's role as one of the Sons of Liberty affect your emotional trust of his medical pronouncements? Why? What literary effect does this presentation have? **S-4**

To satisfactorily answer any of the above questions, the students would be directed to do additional reading, individually or in small groups. The students would also benefit from discussing what additional information Forbes could have provided to create a more even-handed account or a more critical assessment of the historical period. Students can then discuss how such a presentation would affect the work as literature. **S-23**

Despite the detail with which we have delineated the strategies, they should not be translated into mechanistic, step-by-step procedures. Keep the goal of the well-educated, fairminded critical thinker continually in mind.

Cause and Effect

by JoAnne Rains, Laurens County
District # 55, Clinton, SC

Objectives of the Remodelled Plan
The students will:
- clarify and analyze a problem
- explore the main character's feelings
- assess solutions
- transfer insights into causes of the problem to their lives

Original Lesson Plan

> This is a three-page skill lesson dealing with cause-effect and sequence relationships. I will only address the first page which teaches recognition of cause and effect. The students are to read a half-page story about Ramona, who plans to take her dog, Pedro, to obedience school. Dad calls to tell Ramona that, because he has a flat tire, she would have to call Grandmother to take her to the obedience class. When Grandmother is not home, Ramona becomes upset until Aunt Dolores walks in the front door.

Critique

This lesson was one that I seriously considered throwing out, but, since it was the only exposure to the cause/effect terminology in the student textbook, I decided to remodel it.

The reasons for recognizing cause and effect were never explored. The lesson certainly missed a good opportunity to explore and discuss Ramona's feeling upset. The authors oversimplified both the concept and the discussion. They pointed out *their* ideas of cause and effect in the student textbook directly following the story without giving students a chance to discover them for themselves. The questions suggested in the teacher's edition are either factual or can be answered by yes or no with no opportunity for critical thinking on the part of the student.

Strategies Used to Remodel

S-13 clarifying issues, conclusions, or beliefs
S-10 refining generalizations and avoiding oversimplifications
S-4 exploring thoughts underlying feelings and feelings underlying thoughts
S-19 generating or assessing solutions
S-11 comparing analogous situations: transferring insights to new contexts

Remodelled Lesson Plan

Introduction

I would begin the class by having the students read the story. I would then give various students the opportunity to retell the story in their own words. As they are talking, I would write "**Cause** ←→ **Effect**" on the board.

The problem *S-13*

I would define and isolate (or clarify) the problem by asking the following questions:

- Who is involved?
- What is at issue here (what is involved)?
- What is the cause (why did it happen)?
- What is Ramona's problem?
- How do you know this is the real problem?
- Name *every* factor that contributed to her problem. **S-10**

By helping the students to isolate the cause before the problem is defined, I find that there is less chance for the student to confuse the symptom with the problem.

The feelings S-4

After the problem has been identified and defined, I would use one or more of the affective strategies to encourage the students to examine Ramona's feelings. This could be accomplished by asking the following questions.

- What did Ramona feel when her dad called and told her he could not take her to the dog's obedience class?
- Why did Ramona feel this way? What did she think?
- At what point did Ramona become more upset?
- Why did this make a difference?
- Who or what was responsible for Ramona's feelings?

Through these questions, the students have explored in-depth what Ramona's feelings were and why she felt that way, and then they have evaluated her feelings. As a transition to "solution and transfer," I would ask: "How does the problem, as we have defined it, relate to Ramona's feelings?"

The cause can be restated by asking:

- What actually caused this problem?
- What was the effect (what actually resulted) because of this problem?

To assist the students in looking for multiple problems, causes, etc., I would then ask them to look for other cause and effect relationships in the story.

The solutions and transfer

To encourage the students to look for alternatives in their own problem solving, I might ask, "What could Ramona have done if Aunt Dolores hadn't come? How would that have helped? Would it cause other problems? Which solution is best?"**S-19** After this discussion, I would use a classroom situation as an example of cause and effect, then allow the students, through questioning and discussion, to determine the cause and effect. I would encourage the students to use questions similar to the ones asked in the "Ramona Story." To wrap up the lesson, I would let the students share their own real-life examples of cause and effect. My emphasis here would be on their recognition and exploration of alternative solutions in their own lives. **S-11**

Note: My 7th and 8th grade classes usually become so involved in these real-life situations that they often need to carry this lesson over to a second day.

The Soviet Perspective

by Bethanne T. Jacobson, Upper St.
Clair High School, Washington, PA

Objectives of the Remodelled Plan

The students will:
- develop intellectual good faith and courage by exploring their perspectives on the Soviet Union
- evaluate the credibility of various sources of information
- reason from within the Soviet perspective

Original Lesson Plan

The students begin by reading the unit on the Soviet Union. Extensive map work is included, locating most of the major features of the Soviet Union. Students are given a specific topic connected with the Soviet Union and give an oral presentation to the class. Daily class time is normally a short class lecture followed by teacher-led discussion of assigned reading. Map work is in the form of worksheets. Prior to the exam, a review is done in the form of a "Geography Bee" with the students in two teams. (The winning team gets to skip one assignment in the next unit.) The unit concludes with a written subject/objective exam and map test.

Critique

This lesson offers little to the student in the way of critical thinking. It is (unfortunately) a typical lesson plan for a majority of today's social studies teachers. The lecture aspect does not allow the students to interact, think, evaluate, or reason. They simply memorize the necessary information and then spit the information back out to the teacher on the exam. The exam does have an objective section in which, if the students had the ability (and few do unless allowed to use it), they could evaluate and argue points of view. The teacher-led discussion, again, does not allow the student to take the lead.

My remodelled lesson plan involves the students in decisions. It allows the student to critically analyze the text and other sources of information. The students are asked to take the perspectives of Soviet citizens and try to visualize life from their point of view.

Strategies Used to Remodel

S-7 developing intellectual good faith or integrity
S-4 exploring thoughts underlying feelings and feelings underlying thoughts
S-2 developing insight into egocentricity or sociocentricity

256

S-10 refining generalizations and avoiding oversimplifications
S-12 developing one's perspective: creating or exploring beliefs, arguments, or theories
S-28 thinking precisely about thinking: using critical vocabulary
S-16 evaluating the credibility of sources of information
S-3 exercising fairmindedness
S-5 developing intellectual humility and suspending judgment
S-6 developing intellectual courage

Remodelled Lesson Plan S-7

The class could begin with a brainstorming session. Students would be asked to explore their beliefs about the Soviet Union and Soviet life in general. Ask, "When someone mentions the country, the Soviet Union, what comes to your mind? How do you feel about it? **S-4** What do you think everyday life for a student in the U.S.S.R. is like? Do you think the kids like to do any of the same things you do for fun? What do you suppose they study in school? How do you think they feel about school? What kinds of problems do you suppose they have? What have you read or heard about the Soviet Union? Where? Did it come from a Soviet? Would a Soviet say the same things? **S-2** What would a Soviet critical of his country say? **S-10** One who approved of his country? What else do you know about the U.S.S.R.? About the government, employment, social programs, entertainment?" **S-12**

Following this session, the students can read the text and one other source for comparison. The next few days could be spent evaluating the text and other sources using the ideas brought out from the brainstorming session on the first day. Students can explore their attitudes towards Soviets by considering some of the following questions: Why do you suppose that you have the opinions that you do about Russians? Where did your beliefs come from: your parents, friends, school, media, the government? Which of these is in a position to know? Do any of these have an interest in distorting evidence about the Soviet Union? Why or why not? **S-2** How long have you had those beliefs? Have you talked to any Soviet people personally? How do you think Soviet people form their opinions about people in the United States? Do you suppose their opinions are accurate? How can one find the truth about any group of people? What kind of evidence would you need? What is bias? **S-28** How can one determine if someone else is biased? **S-16**

The next several days would be a combination of brief lecturing, followed by teacher- and student-led discussions. The student-led discussions would be on a specific area of interest to the students which they have chosen.

The final few days would be spent in role playing . Different situations would be given to the students e.g., "You and your neighbor are Soviet citizens. A new American friend has come to stay in your home for one week." The three students would carry on a dialogue addressing the differences and similarities between the two cultures. For example, the American friend might ask, "What do you like to do for fun here? What kinds of stores are in your neighborhood? Do most people own their own houses and cars? Would you rather be an American? Do you really have to wait in long food lines? "The Soviets might be interested to know the following: "What is your school like? What classes do you take? Do many young people work while going to school? Are you guaranteed a place to live and a job when you get out of school? Who pays for your education after high school?" **S-3** An effective role play can do much to make real the people of a country on the other side of the world. The students may be surprised at the nature and extent of their biases against a people about whom they have actually known so little. **S-5**

For further follow-up discussions, the teacher could raise questions like the following: Are you now aware of some biases that you have been holding? What are they? What other biases do Americans have towards the Soviet Union? **S-6** What types of biases do you suppose the Soviet people would have toward us? What are the possible consequences of holding biased beliefs? **S-7**

If your school is multi-ethnic, an interesting follow-up would be to invite some Soviet students to speak with the class about their reality in the U.S.S.R. and some of their perceptions of the American people. If having Soviets come in to speak is unfeasible, you may want to research taped interviews of Russian people and have students view them and compare their original beliefs with what they have learned.

Human Migration

by Chris Langley, Lone Pine USD, Lone Pine, CA

Objectives of the Remodelled Plan

The students will:
- come to understand in detail Baluchi nomadic life, comparing it to their own
- develop empathy with Iranian nomadic life styles, exercising fairmindedness
- identify complex factors of modern migratory patterns in the U.S.
- relate human migration to their personal lives and the future

Original Lesson Plan

> The lesson discusses the reasons people have for migrating, including the search to find food, resources and better opportunities or because they are forced to migrate. The lesson introduces the concept and vocabulary of nomads. It also discusses historical famines and the effect they had on forcing people to move. The text discusses migration for better opportunities and briefly examines colonization. Forced migrations and the concept of refugees are briefly mentioned, and then the text considers present-day migrations. Movement to cities and warmer climates are mentioned. The teacher's edition suggests discussing modern forced migrations and recalling from the reading some of the facts concerning the reasons for migration given in the text.

Critique

The "Human" part of migration

This lesson deals with the reasons for migration. Several theories that are complex in nature are given to the teacher. One concept deals with the idea of "intervening opportunity." It suggests that the ways people look at distant opportunities are effected by the intervening opportunities. A second passage briefly looks at the "push" and "pull" factors. Little effort is made to relate these theories in the text. Rather simple examples in factual form are listed. Migration is generally pictured in this as negative, only undertaken under duress. An underlying assumption is that migration is either a primitive socio-economic phenomenon or evidence of poorly-run governments or natural disaster. No effort is made to relate the factors to human lives, to see the multi-faceted pluses and minuses in lives, or to ever place the nomadic life in a positive light. The Baluchis of southeast Iran had a semi-annual nomadic cycle where in the winter and spring they tended their herds in the mountains and in summer went to the south to harvest dates. The Shah, and before him his father, saw nomads as an embarrassment to a modern industrial country and they followed a forced plan of resettlement. This resulted in depriving these people of their traditional food sources, and they starved. When they resisted, the government flew in aircraft and machine-gunned them during their traditional migrations.

The traditional pattern of life for the Baluchi was one of pride, grace and cultural integrity. Living simply and close to nature gave them a way of life without the stress and materialism often associated with modern industrial city life.

The Multiple Perspectives of Colonization

The text makes it sound as if the only motivation for colonization was seeking a better place to live. Little detail about this motivation is given. Nor is any consideration given to the push and pull factors in colonization. Many motivations for countries to support and pursue colonization are ignored. The exploitation of the local peoples, the destruction of traditional life patterns and the power struggles that resulted between the nations of Europe are overlooked. Instead this migratory pattern is seen simply as people looking for personal opportunities, freedom and a new way of life.

The Conflicts of Modern Migrations

The text again makes it sound as if the factors in modern migration, the move to cities and warm climates, are simple. People move to cities for jobs, but no mention is made of the negatives in the cities, both historically and today, including high unemployment in cities, lack of training of new workers, and typical urban problems such as crime, overcrowding and smog. The effect that this migration has on farms and rural areas is not even explored.

Children in my area need to come to terms with these factors. I live in a very rural area which presents excellent living conditions but limited job opportunities. Often the students I work with think simply going to L.A. after graduation will solve all their problems. They often lack the social skills, and educational training or perspectives to migrate successfully to the urban areas.

Suggestions for Improvement

Generally the factors discussed in motivating migration are oversimplified, and traditional migration patterns, particularly in the U.S., are seen as simply going from bad economic situations to positive ones. The complexity of the issue is ignored completely.

The remodelled plan is focused on the people of traditional migratory patterns and the nomads. It helps the children to see the qualities of their own lives. In considering modern migration from rural to urban settings, their thinking needs to be extended to see the many issues both motivating and limiting these movements.

Strategies Used to Remodel

S-29 noting significant similarities and differences
S-3 exercising fairmindedness
S-21 reading critically: clarifying or critiquing texts
S-10 refining generalizations and avoiding oversimplifications
S-24 practicing Socratic discussion: clarifying and questioning beliefs, theories, or perspectives

Remodelled Lesson Plan

My remodelled lesson plan basically follows the organization and sequence of the original lesson, but it has two major focuses. The first focus is on the migratory patterns of nomads in traditional society first, and then upon modern migratory patterns that the children would be more familiar with.

The traditional migratory pattern of the Baluchi in Iran

As a Peace Corps volunteer in Iran, I spent much time with the nomadic Baluchi tribes of southeastern Iran and Pakistan. I would begin by showing movies and bringing in various artifacts of the Baluchis, including a wedding coat, a camel saddle bag and articles of clothing. Through discussion and demonstration, I would clarify exactly what a migratory pattern was, in this case being a seasonal migration between high pastures and low date palm orchards. I think it is important for the students by their own examination and discussion to understand how the life style limits their belongings and how it places certain controls on social patterns including marriage and the education of the children. Once the students had a clear understanding of the meaning of nomads and migration, they would need to examine in detail how the Baluchi life was similar to and different from their own. We would examine some important values in our own culture and compare them to how the Baluchis dealt with similar issues. Of particular interest to these students would be arranged marriages and the youthfulness of the brides, the separation of the sexes and materialism or possessions. I would stress that models of living and reality itself are complex and self-sufficient, showing how their ways and ours are different but one way is not good and another bad. **S-29** Because the social structure of the Middle East (and particularly Iran) is often viewed negatively here, this aspect will be quite challenging.

Once the students understand this aspect of the lesson, I would take them on to actually act out or plan a nomadic life style. Considering the plight of the homeless might be helpful here if it does not confuse the issue, but I think if the children have any awareness of this social issue, it needs to be addressed. The children would figure out what it would feel like to be nomadic, what belongings they would choose, and what modes of transportation they could adopt. Other social issues could also be experienced, including arranged marriages and separation of the girls from the boys. The goal here would be to have the students understand the lifestyle from the nomadic point of view. Then I would discuss with them the forced settlement plan adopted by the government and have the children see the thinking from the Baluchi's point of view and the government's. **S-3**

By now, hopefully, I would have pointed out some of the positive aspects of the nomadic life style and the children would be ready to critique the text and identify some of the assumptions the text makes. **S-21** This seems very important to me because the students I generally teach seldom consider that a text could be wrong, incomplete or misleading.

The process of identifying migratory patterns

The process of identifying assumptions would continue on to the second part of this lesson plan considering modern migratory patterns. Particularly we would explore the movement from rural living to urban living. We would need to discover the complexity of this issue, the various factors leading people to move to the city and what happens to them there. The assumption in my classroom generally, and also, though less so, in the text, is that life is better in the city. Through question and answer and research, the students would come to avoid the oversimplification found in the text. *S-10*

Finally, I would conclude this lesson with a Socratic discussion of why people leave Lone Pine (my town) to move to various urban settings (primarily Los Angeles). Important issues to be brought out would be motivation, preparation for a successful move, goals, quality of life, and impact on the city, more so on the local rural areas of the young moving away. Polling the students on their short-range and long-range goals would provide an interesting and enlightening closure activity for the class. *S-24*

10 The Greensboro Plan: A Sample Staff Development Plan

Greensboro, North Carolina is a city of medium size nestled in the rolling hills of the Piedmont, near the Appalachian Mountains. The school system enrolls approximately 21,000 students and employs 1,389 classroom teachers. Students in the Greensboro city schools come from diverse economic and balanced racial backgrounds. Forty-six percent of the students are White. Fifty-four per cent of the student population is minority; 52% is Black and 2% is Asian, Hispanic, or Native American. Every socio-economic range from the upper middle class to those who live below the poverty line is well-represented in the city schools. However, almost 28% of the student population has a family income low enough for them to receive either free or discounted lunches. Although our school system is a relatively small one, Greensboro has recently implemented a program that is beginning successfully to infuse critical thinking and writing skills into the K-12 curriculum.

The Reasoning and Writing Project, which was proposed by Associate Superintendent, Dr. Sammie Parrish, began in the spring of 1986, when the school board approved the project and affirmed as a priority the infusion of thinking and writing into the K-12 curriculum. Dr. Parrish hired two facilitators, Kim V. DeVaney, who had experience as an elementary school teacher and director of computer education and myself, Janet L. Williamson, a high school English teacher, who had recently returned from a leave of absence during which I completed my doctorate with a special emphasis on critical thinking.

Kim and I are teachers on special assignment, relieved of our regular classroom duties in order to facilitate the project. We stress this fact: we are facilitators, not directors; we are teachers, not administrators. The project is primarily teacher directed and implemented. In fact, this tenet of teacher empowerment is one of the major principles of the project, as is the strong emphasis on and commitment to a philosophical and theoretical basis of the program.

We began the program with some basic beliefs and ideas. We combined reasoning and writing because we think that there is an interdependence between the two processes and that writing is an excellent tool for making ideas clear and explicit. We also believe that no simple or quick solutions would bring about a meaningful change in the complex set of human attitudes and behaviors that comprise thinking. Accordingly, we began the project at two demonstration sites where we could slowly develop a strategic plan for the program. A small group of fourteen volunteers formed the nucleus with whom we primarily worked during the first semester of the project.

Even though I had studied under Dr. Robert H. Ennis, worked as a research assistant with the Illinois Critical Thinking Project, and written my dissertation on infusing critical thinking skills into an English curriculum, we did not develop our theoretical approach to the program quickly or easily. I was aware that if this project were going to be truly teacher-directed, my role would be to guide the nucleus teachers in reading widely and diversely about critical thinking, in considering how to infuse thinking instruction into the curriculum, and in becoming familiar with and comparing different approaches to critical thinking. My role would not be, however, to dictate the philosophy or strategies of the program.

This first stage in implementing a critical thinking program, where teachers read, study, and gather information, is absolutely vital. It is not necessary, of course, for a facilitator to have a graduate degree specializing in critical thinking in order to institute a sound program, but it is necessary for at least a small group of people to become educated, in the strongest sense of the word, about critical thinking and to develop a consistent and sound theory or philosophy based on that knowledge — by reading (and rereading), questioning, developing a common vocabulary of critical thinking terms and the knowledge of how to use them, taking university or college courses in thinking, seeking out local consultants such as professors, and attending seminars and conferences.

In the beginning stages of our program, we found out that the importance of a consistent and sound theoretical basis is not empty educational jargon. We found inconsistencies in our stated beliefs and our interactions with our students and in our administrators' stated beliefs and their interaction with teachers. For example, as teachers we sometimes proclaim that we want independent thinkers and then give students only activity sheets to practice their "thinking skills;" we declare that we want good problem solving and decision-making to transfer into all aspects of life and then tend to avoid controversial or "sensitive" topics; we bemoan the lack of student thinking and then structure our classrooms so the "guessing what is in the teacher's mind" is the prevailing rule. We also noted a tendency of some principals to espouse the idea that teachers are professionals and then declare that their faculty prefer structured activities rather than dealing with theory or complex ideas. Although most administrators state that learning to process information is more important than memorizing it, a few have acted as if the emphasis on critical thinking is "just a fad." One of the biggest contradictions we have encountered has been the opinion of both teachers and administrators that "we're already doing a good job of this (teaching for thinking)," yet they also say that students are not good thinkers.

While recognizing these contradictions is important, it does not in and of itself solve the problem. In the spirit of peer coaching and collegiality, we are trying to establish an atmosphere that will allow us to point out such contradictions to each other. As our theories and concepts become more internalized and completely understood, such contradictions in thought and action become less frequent. In all truthfulness, however, such contradictions still plague us and probably will for quite a while.

We encountered, however, other problems that proved easier to solve. I vastly underestimated the amount of time that we would need for an introductory workshop, and our first workshops failed to give teachers the background they needed; we now structure our workshops for days, not hours. There was an initial suggestion from the central office that we use *Tactics for Thinking*. as a basis, or at least a starting point, for our program. To the credit of central office administration, although they may have questioned whether we should use an already existing program, they certainly did not mandate that we use any particular approach. As we collected evaluations of our program from our teachers, neighboring school systems, and outside consultants, however, there seemed to be a general consensus that developing our own program, rather than adopting a pre-packaged one, has been the correct choice.

Finally, teachers became confused with the array of materials, activities, and approaches. They questioned the value of developing and internalizing a concept of critical thinking and asked for specifics — activities they could use immediately in the classroom. This problem, however, worked itself out as teachers reflected on the complexity of critical thinking and how it can be fostered. We began to note and collect instances such as the following: a high school instructor, after participating in a workshop that stressed how a teacher can use Socratic questioning in the classroom, commented that students who had previously been giving unsatisfactory answers were now beginning to give insightful and creative ones. Not only had she discovered that the quality of the student's response is in part determined by the quality of the teacher's questions, she was finding new and innovative ways to question her students. Another teacher, after having seen how the slowest reading group in her fourth grade class responded to questions that asked them to think and reflect, commented that she couldn't believe how responsive and expressive the children were. I can think of no nucleus teacher who would now advocate focusing on classroom activities rather than on a consistent and reflective approach to critical thinking.

As the nucleus teachers read and studied the field, they outlined and wrote the tenets that underscore the program. These tenets include the belief that real and lasting change takes place, not by writing a new curriculum guide, having teachers attend a one day inspirational workshop at the beginning of each new year, adopting new textbooks that emphasize more skills, or buying pre-packaged programs and activity books for thinking. Rather, change takes place when attitudes and priorities are carefully and reflectively reconsidered, when an atmosphere is established that encourages independent thinking for both teachers and students, and when we recognize the complex interdependence between thinking and writing.

The nucleus teachers at the two demonstration schools decided that change in the teaching of thinking skills can best take place by remodelling lesson plans, not by creating new ones, and they wrote a position paper adopting Richard Paul's *Critical Thinking Handbook*. This approach, they wrote, is practical and manageable. It allows the teacher to exercise professional judgment and provides opportunity for teachers to gain insight into their own teaching. In addition, it recognizes the complexity of the thinking process and does not merely list discrete skills.

The primary-level teachers decided to focus upon language development as the basis for critical thinking. Their rationale was that language is the basis for both thinking and writing, that students must master language sufficiently to be able to use it as a tool in thinking and writing, and that this emphasis is underdeveloped in many early classrooms. This group of teachers worked on increasing teacher knowledge and awareness of language development as well as developing and collecting materials, techniques and ideas for bulletin boards for classroom use.

By second semester, the project had expanded to two high schools. This year, the second year of the program, we have expanded to sixteen new schools, including all six middle schools. Kim and I have conducted workshops for all new nucleus teachers as well as for interested central office and school-based administrators. Also, this year, at three of the four original demonstration sites, workshops have been conducted or planned that are led by the original nucleus teachers for their colleagues.

It is certainly to the credit of the school board and the central administration that we have had an adequate budget on which to operate. As I have mentioned, Kim and I are full-time facilitators of the program. Substitutes have been hired to cover classes when teachers worked on the project during school hours. We were able to send teachers to conferences led by Richard Paul and we were able to bring in Professor Paul for a very successful two-day workshop.

Our teachers work individually and in pairs, and in small and large groups at various times during the day. A number of teachers have video-taped themselves and their classes in action, providing an opportunity to view and reflect on ways that they and their colleagues could infuse more thinking opportunities into the curriculum.

Essentially, we have worked on three facets in the program: 1) workshops that provide baseline information, 2) follow-up that includes demonstration teaching by facilitators, individual study, collegial sharing of ideas, peer coaching, individual and group remodelling of lesson plans, teachers writing about their experiences both for their personal learning and for publication, team planning of lessons, peer observation, and 3) dissemination of materials in our growing professional library.

We are expanding slowly and only on a volunteer basis. Currently, we have approximately seventy nucleus teachers working in twenty schools. By the end of next year, 1988-1989, we plan to have a nucleus group in each of the schools in the system. Plans for the future should include two factions: ways for the nucleus groups to continue to expand their professional growth and knowledge of critical thinking and an expansion of the program to include more teachers. We plan to continue to build on the essential strengths of the program — the empowerment of teachers to make decisions, the thorough theoretical underpinnings of the program, and the slow and deliberate design and implementation plan.

Our teachers generally seem enthusiastic and committed. In anonymous written evaluations of the program, they have given it overwhelming support. One teacher stated:

> It is the most worthwhile project the central office has ever offered. . . . Because
> - it wasn't forced on me.
> - it wasn't touted as the greatest thing since sliced bread.
> - it was not a one-shot deal that was supposed to make everything all better.
> - it was not already conceived and planned down to the last minute by someone who had never been in a classroom or who hadn't been in one for X years.
>
> It was, instead,
> - led by professionals who were still very close to the classroom.
> - designed by us.
> - a volunteer group of classroom teachers who had time to reflect and read and talk after each session, and who had continuing support and information from the leaders, not just orders and instructions.

11 What Critical Thinking Means to Me: Teachers' Own Formulations

C ritical thinking is a process through which one solves problems and makes decisions. It is a process that can be improved through practice, though never perfected. It involves self-discipline and structure. Sometimes it can make your head hurt, but sometimes it comes naturally. I believe for critical thinking to be its most successful, it must be intertwined with creative thinking.

Kathryn Haines
Grade 5

Thinking critically gives me an organized way of questioning what I hear and read in a manner that goes beyond the surface or literal thought. It assists me in structuring my own thoughts such that I gain greater insight into how I feel and appreciation for the thoughts of others, even those with which I disagree. It further enables me to be less judgmental in a negative way and to be more willing to take risks.

Patricia Wiseman
Grade 3

Being able *and* willing to examine all sides of an issue or topic, having first clarified it; supporting or refuting it with either facts or reasoned judgment; and in this light, exploring the consequences or effects of any decision or action it is possible to take.

Kim V. DeVaney
Facilitator, WATTS

All of us think, but critical thinking has to do with becoming more aware of *how* we think and finding ways to facilitate clear, reasoned, logical, and better-informed thinking. Only when our thoughts are backed with reason and logic, and are based on a process of careful examination of ideas and evidence, do they become critical and lead us in the direction of finding what is true. In order to do this, it seems of major importance to maintain an open-minded willingness to look at other points of view. In addition, we can utilize various skills which will enable us to become more proficient at thinking for ourselves.

Nancy Johnson
Kindergarten

Critical thinking is a necessary access to a happy and full life. It provides me the opportunity to analyze and evaluate my thoughts, beliefs, ideas, reasons, and feelings as well as other individuals. Utilizing this process, it helps me to understand and respect others as total persons. It helps me in instructing my students and in my personal life. Critical thinking extends beyond the classroom setting and has proven to be valid in life other than the school world.

Veronica Richmond
Grade 6

Critical thinking is the ability to analyze and evaluate feelings and ideas in an independent, fairminded, rational manner. If action is needed on these feelings or ideas, this evaluation motivates meaningfully positive and useful actions. Applying critical thinking to everyday situations and classroom situations is much like Christian growth. If we habitually evaluate our feelings and ideas based on a reasonable criteria, we will become less likely to be easily offended and more likely to promote a positive approach as a solution to a problem. Critical thinking, like Christian growth, promotes confidence, creativity, and personal growth.

Carolyn Tarpley
Middle School
Reading

Critical thinking is a blend of many things, of which I shall discuss three: independent thinking; clear thinking; and organized Socratic questioning.

As for the first characteristic mentioned above, a critical thinker is an independent thinker. He doesn't just accept something as true or believe it because he was taught it as a child. He analyzes it, breaking it down into its elements; he checks on the author of the information and delves into his or her background; he questions the material and evaluates it; and then he makes up his own mind about its validity. In other words, he thinks independently.

A second criterion of critical thinking is clarity. If a person is not a clear thinker, he can't be a critical thinker. I can't say that I agree or disagree with you if I can't understand you. A critical thinker has to get very particular, because people are inclined to throw words around. For example, they misuse the word 'selfish.' A person might say: "You're selfish, but *I'm* motivated!" A selfish person is one who systematically *ignores* the rights of others and pursues his own desires. An unselfish one is a person who systematically *considers* the rights of others while he pursues his own desires. Thus, clarity is important. We have to be clear about the meanings of words.

The most important aspect of critical thinking is its spirit of Socratic questioning. However, it is important to have the questioning organized in one's mind and to know in general the underlying goals of the discussion. If you want students to retain the content of your lesson, you must organize it and help them to see that ideas are connected. Some ideas are derived from basic ideas. We need to help students to organize their thinking around basic ideas and to question. To be a good questioner, you must be a wonderer — wonder aloud about meaning and truth. For example, "I wonder what Jack means." "I wonder what this word means?" "I wonder if anyone can think of an example?" "Does this make sense?" "I wonder how true that is?" "Can anyone think of an experience when that was true?" The critical thinker must have the ability to probe deeply, to get down to basic ideas, to get beneath the mere appearance of things. We need to get into the very spirit, the "wonderment" of the situation being discussed. The students need to feel, "My teacher really wonders; and really wants to know what we think." We should wonder aloud. A good way to stimulate thinking is to use a variety of types of questions. We can ask questions to get the students to elaborate, to explain, to give reasons, to cite evidence, to identify their points of view, to focus on central ideas, and to raise problems. Socratic questioning is certainly vital to critical thinking.

Thus, critical thinking is a blend of many characteristics, especially independent thinking, clear thinking, and Socratic questioning. We all need to strive to be better critical thinkers.

Holly Touchstone
Middle School
Language Arts

Critical thinking is wondering about that which is not obvious, questioning in a precise manner to find the essence of truth, and evaluating with an open mind.

As a middle school teacher, critical thinking is a way to find out from where my students are coming (a way of being withit). Because of this "withitness" produced by bringing critical thinking into the classroom, student motivation will be produced. This motivation fed by fostering critical thinking will produce a more productive thinker in society.

Thus, for me, critical thinking is a spirit I can infuse into society by teaching my students to wonder, question, and evaluate in search of truth while keeping an open mind.

Malinda McCuiston
Middle School
Language Arts, Reading

Critical thinking means thinking clearly about issues, problems, or ideas, and questioning or emphasizing those that are important to the "thinker." As a teacher, I hope to develop Socratic questioning so that my students will feel comfortable discussing why they believe their thoughts to be valid. I hope that they will develop language skills to communicate with others and that they will be open to ideas and beliefs of others.

Jessie Smith
Grade 1

The spirit of critical thinking is a concept that truly excites me. I feel the strategies of critical thinking, implemented appropriately in my classroom, can enable me to become a more effective teacher. By combining this thinking process with my sometimes overused emotions and intuitive power, I can critically examine issues in my classroom as well as in my personal life. I feel it is of grave importance for us as educators to provide a variety of opportunities for our students to think critically by drawing conclusions, clarifying ideas, evaluating assumptions, drawing inferences, and giving reasons and examples to support ideas. Also, Socratic dialogue is an effective means of enabling the students to discover ideas, contradictions, implications, etc., instead of being told answers and ideas given by the teacher. Critical thinking is an excellent tool for the teacher to help the students learn how to think rather than just what to think. Hopefully critical thinking will help me be a more effective teacher as well as excite my students.

Beth Sands
Middle School
Language Arts

Critical thinking is what education should be. It is the way I wish I had been taught. Although I left school with a wealth of facts, I had never learned how to connect them or to use them. I loved learning but thought that being learned meant amassing data. No one ever taught me how to contrast and compare, analyze and dissect. I believed that all teachers knew everything, all printed material was true and authority was always right. It took me years to undo the habits of "good behavior" in school. I want to save my students the wasted time, the frustration, the doubts that I encountered during and after my school years. And teaching and using critical thinking is the way to do that.

Nancy Poueymirou
High School
Language Arts

For me, critical thinking is a combination of learning and applying a data base of learning to evaluate and interrelate concepts from diverse academic disciplines. Critical thinking is understanding that knowledge, wisdom, and education are not divided into math, science, English, etc. It is the fairness of tolerance combined with a strong sense of ethics and morals. It is the fun of feeling your mind expand as you accomplish intellectual challenges that attain your own standards. It is the zest of life.

Joan Simons
High School
Biology

Both as teacher and individual, I find critical thinking skills essential elements of a full and enjoyable life. With the ability to think critically, one can both appreciate and cope with all aspects of life and learning. When dealing with problems, from the most mundane to the most complex, the ability to think critically eliminates confusion, dispels irrational emotion, and enables one to arrive at an appropriate conclusion. At the same time, as we ponder the beauty and creativity of our environment, we are free to "wonder" and enjoy the complexity around us, rather than be perplexed or intimidated by it, because we have the mental capability to understand it. To live is to be ever curious, ever learning, ever investigating. Critical thinking enables us to do this more fully and pleasurably.

Mary Lou Holoman
High School
Language Arts

A critical thinker never loses the joy of learning, never experiences the sadness of not caring or not wondering about the world. The essence of the truly educated person is that of being able to question, inquire, doubt, conclude, innovate. And beyond that, to spread that enthusiasm to those around him, obscuring the lines that divide teacher and student, enabling them to travel together, each learning from the other.

Jane Davis-Seaver
Grade 3

Critical thinking is a means of focusing energy to learn. The learning may be academic (proscribed by an institutional curriculum or self-directed) or non-academic (determined by emotional need). It provides a systematic organization for gathering information, analyzing that information, and evaluating it to reach reasonable, acceptable conclusions for yourself.

Blair Stetson
Elementary
Academically Gifted

Critical thinking is the ability to reason in a clear and unbiased way. It is necessary to consider concepts or problems from another's point of view and under varying circumstances in order to make reasoned judgments. Awareness of one's own reasoning processes enables one to become a more fairminded and objective thinker.

Karen Marks
Elementary
Academically Gifted

Critical thinking is questioning, analyzing, and making thoughtful judgments about questions, ideas, issues or concepts. It refines thoughts to more specific or definite meanings. The critical thinker must be an active listener who does not simply accept what he/she hears or reads on face value without questioning, but looks for deeper meaning. Critical thinking also involves evaluating the ideas explored or problems addressed and better prepares a student to be able to think about the world around him or her.

Becky Hampton
Grade 6

Critical thinking has given me a broader means of evaluating my daily lesson plans. It has helped me better understand the thinking principles of each student I teach. It has also enabled me to practice strategies in lesson planning and to become a more effective classroom teacher.

Pearl Norris Booker
Grade 2

Critical thinking provides me the opportunity to broaden the thinking process of my students. It can be used to have the students to reason and to think about different ideas of a problem or a given situation.

Portia Staton
Grade 3

Critical thinking is a process that takes all the ideas, questions and problems that we are faced with each day and enables us to come up with solutions. It is the process by which we are able to search for evidence that support already-existing answers, or better yet, to come up with new solutions to problems. Through critical thinking, one begins to realize that many times there is more than one solution whereupon decisions can be made. To me, critical thinking has helped and will continue to help me understand myself and the world around me.

Debbie Wall
Grade 4

Critical thinking is a skill that involves the expansion of thoughts and the art of questioning. This skill must be developed over a period of time. It is a way of organizing your thoughts in a logical sequence. Knowledge is gained through this process.

Carolyn Smith
Grade 5

Critical thinking is questioning, analyzing and evaluating oral or written ideas. A critical thinker is disciplined, self-directed, and rational in problem solving. Reaching conclusions of your own rather than accepting everything as it is presented, is internalizing critical thinking.

Denise Clark
Grade 2

To think critically, one must analyze and probe concepts or ideas through reasoning. It makes one an *active* reasoner, not a *passive* accepter of ideas (or facts). It turns one into a doer, an evaluater, or re-evaluater. Critical thinking occurs everywhere, is applicable everywhere and while it can be tedious, need not be, because as one thinks critically, new ideas are formed, conclusions are drawn, new knowledge is acquired.

Janell Prester
Grade 3

To think through and analyze a concept or idea. You are able to back up your reasoning and think through an idea in a manner which allows an over-all focus. If a person is a critical thinker, a yes-no answer is too brief. An answer to a problem or idea must have an explanation and reasoning backing it.

Donna Phillips
Grade 4

Critical thinking is a tool that teachers can use to offer a new dimension of education to their students: that of thinking about, questioning and exploring the concepts in the curriculum. When critical thinking is an integral part of the teaching-learning process, children learn to apply thinking skills throughout the curriculum as well as in their daily lives. Socratic dialogue fosters critical thinking and motivates the teacher and learner to share and analyze experiences and knowledge. Critical thinking involves the child in the learning process and makes education more meaningful to the individual, thus facilitating learning.

Andrea Allen
Grade 1

The most important part of critical thinking, to me, is *discovery*. We discover a deeper level of thinking. We discover the reasons for ideas instead of just accepting ideas. We are motivated by action, interaction, and involvement. We discover we have the ability to expand our thoughts to include all aspects and perspectives of our beliefs.

Mandy Ryan
Grade 5

Critical thinking, to me, is the process of analyzing new and old information to arrive at solutions. It's the process of learning to question information that you may have taken for granted. It's being independent. Critical thinking is letting people think for themselves and make judgments for themselves.

Leigh Ledet
Grade 4

Critical thinking is the process of taking the knowledge you have gained through past experience or education and re-evaluating conclusions on a certain situation or problem. Because students must evaluate the reasons for their beliefs, they become actively involved in learning through the teacher's use of Socratic questioning. Allowing students to clarify their reasons through the writing process further stimulates the students to become critical thinkers. The ultimate goal for students to understand in using critical thinking is to become active thinkers for themselves.

> Robin Thompson
> Middle School
> Language Arts

Critical thinking, to me, is to be open-ended in my thoughts. It is like opening a door which leads to many other doors through which ideas may evolve, move about, change, and come to rest. It is like a breath of freshness in which one can gain new insight over long-established opinions. It stimulates and generates endless new possibilities.

> Eutha M. Godfrey
> Grades 2-3

Critical thinking is thinking that demonstrates an extension of an idea or concern beyond the obvious. A critical thinker's values are significant to his learning.

> Frances Jackson
> Grade 2

To me, critical thinking means independence. It gives me a tool which lets me explore my own mind extending beyond basic recall to a higher level of reasoning. I then feel more in touch with myself and my own inner feelings. This results in my becoming a better decision-maker.

> Jean Edwards
> Grade 5

Critical thinking is the process of working your mind through different channels. It is the process of thinking logically. Critical thinking is analyzing your thoughts through questions. It is the process of seeing that your ideas and concepts may not be the same as another's. It is opening your mind to those who have different views and looking at their views.

> Cathy L. Smith
> Grade 3

Critical thinking is to question in-depth at every possible angle or point of view, to look at someone else's point of view without making hasty judgments. Critical thinking is to logically and fairly re-orient your own personal point of view, if necessary. To think critically, you are self-directed in your thinking process, as well as disciplined.

> Mary Duke
> Grade 1

Critical thinking is the vehicle by which I encourage students to become active participants in the learning process. I allow more time for and become more aware of the need for students to express ideas verbally and in written form to clarify ideas in their own minds. I recognize the importance of developing skills for analyzing and evaluating. Ultimately, once students become comfortable using critical thinking skills, they assume greater responsibility for their learning.

> Dora McGill
> Grade 6

Critical thinking is clear, precise thinking. I believe that all human actions and expressions involve in some way, thinking. For example, I believe that feelings, emotions and intuitions are much the results of earlier thought (reactions) to stimuli. I think that this, in one way, explains the variations of emotional responses in some people to similar stimuli. Thus, I believe that critical thinking not only has the potential to clarify new and former conscious thoughts but also to effect/change likely (future) emotive and intuitive reactions/responses.

More concrete and less theoretical outcomes of critical thinking may be more relevant to me as an educator. Better questioning skills on the part of the students and the teacher is an obvious outcome. There seem to be several positive outcomes of better questioning: more opportunity for in-depth understanding of content, a natural (built-in) process for accessing the effectiveness of lessons, and more opportunity for student participation, self-assessment, and direction are three apparent outcomes. There are, of course, many other outcomes of developing better questioning skills, and from the other skills of critical thinking.

I simply believe that critical thinking improves the overall integrity of the individual and the collective group, class, school, community, etc.

> Richard Tuck
> High School
> Art

I perceive critical thinking in teaching as a tool for my learning. As I attempt to develop the critical thinker, I will become more aware of the students' thoughts, values, and needs. I must learn from what students offer, and develop acceptance and sensitivity to the individual. The knowledge I gain from the student will determine what I utilize as strategies or principles of critical thinking.

> Loretta Jennings
> Grade 1

Critical thinking is the ability to look at a problem or issue with a spirit of open-mindedness and to take that problem and analyze or evaluate it based on the facts or good "educated" hypotheses. Critical thinking is being flexible enough to suspend one's bias towards an issue in order to study all sides to formulate an opinion or evaluation.

> Mark Moore
> Grade 4

Critical thinking to me involves mental conversations and dialogues with myself. I try first to establish the facts. Then I try to search for criteria to examine my "facts." The next question is whether or not there are distortions and irrelevancies. I have to examine whether I have a personal bias which has led me to select only certain facts and leave others out.

I then try to mentally list facts and arguments on both sides of a question and, finally, draw logical questions and conclusions.

> Barbara Neller
> Middle School
> Social Studies

Critical thinking is a systematic, logical approach to life in which an individual, using this method, truly learns and understands a concept rather than imitates or mimics. Knowledge and intellectual growth are achieved by a variety of strategies which include examining a variety of viewpoints, making assumptions based on viable evidence and forming well thought out conclusions.

> Jane S. Thorne
> High School
> Math

Critical thinking allows students to become active participants in their learning. Socratic dialogue stimulates communication between teacher and students, thus creating an atmosphere where everyone is encouraged to become risk-takers. A teacher needs to become a model of critical thinking for the students. Through this interaction, content can be analyzed, synthesized, and evaluated with thinking.

Carol Thanos
Grade 6

Critical thinking is the complex process of exploring an issue, concept, term or experience which requires verbal as well as non-verbal involvement from the participant. It involves listing ideas related to the subject, so that the person involved could objectively examine the relationship of the ideas thought of. It demands the person involved in the process to investigate the certain issue, concept, or process from varied vantage points, in order that intuitions, assumptions, and conclusions are presented with reasoned opinions or experienced evidences. Critical thinking is a task that involves the participant's in-depth assessment of his or her body of knowledge, experience and emotions on the subject in question.

Ariel Collins
High School
Language Arts

Critical thinking is thinking that is clear, fairminded, and directed. It is not sloppy or self-serving thinking, but deep and probing thought aimed at finding the truth. It is skillful thinking aimed at genuine understanding, not superficial head-shaking. It is *the* tool used by and descriptive of an educated person whose mantra would be "veritas."

Helen Cook
Middle School
Science

Critical thinking is a process of questioning and seeking truth and clarity. It is a continual endeavor as one is constantly exposed to new knowledge which must be reconciled with prior conclusions. As one's body of knowledge grows, it is all the more important to be able to critically consider and determine *what is truth.*

Critical thinking demands certain prerequisites: open-mindedness, willingness to withhold snap judgments, commitment to explore new ideas. The development of such qualities empowers me to participate in the various facets of critical thinking, e.g., clarifying ideas, engaging in Socratic discussions. These skills are not nearly so difficult as achieving the mindset which must precede them. Only a *commitment* to question and persevere and honestly pursue truth will supply the impetus necessary to delve beneath the surface of issues and concepts. Yet this predisposition is difficult to achieve, because it necessitates taking risks, making mistakes, being wrong and being corrected — activities very threatening to our safe ego boundaries.

Only in transcending these ego boundaries does growth occur and genuine learning transpire. Critical thinking is comprised of a sense of wonderment, daring and determination. It is undergirded by a value of truth and personal growth. It is the continual learning process of the individual.

Deborah Norton
High School
Social Studies

The definition of critical thinking that I now hold is one that explains some things that I have felt for some time. I am convinced that everything that I know, that is a part of my education, I have figured out or found for myself. I have had close to twenty years of formal, didactic education, but I could tell you very little about anything that was presented to me in lecture through all those classes, except perhaps some trivia. In college, I did my real learning through the writing that I did, either from research or from contemplation. I have felt that this was true, but a lot of my own teaching has continued to be didactic and students have learned to be very accepting and non-questioning and to *expect* to be told what the right answer is, what someone else has decided the right answer is. I hope that I can change that now. I now feel that it is imperative that my students learn to be critical thinkers, and I hope that I can model that belief and, through all my activities in class, lead them in that direction. We all need to be open-minded, to realize that there are often many sides to a problem, many points of view and that there are strategies and techniques for analyzing, making decisions, and making learning our own. I want to be, and I want my students to be, questioning, open-minded, fairminded, synthesizing individuals — in other words, critical thinkers.

Liza Burton
High School
Language Arts

Regarding a Definition of Critical Thinking

Many people who feel that they don't know what critical thinking is or means request a definition. When they realize there is no *one* definition of critical thinking given by all theorists, many people feel frustrated and confused. "Even the experts can't agree about what they're talking about. How can I teach it if *I* don't know what it is, and no one else can tell me?" What such a reaction misses, however, is that although theorists provide a variety of definitions, they do not necessarily reject each others' definitions. They feel that their particular definition most usefully conveys the basic concept, highlighting what they take to be its most crucial aspects, but do not necessarily hold that other definitions are "wrong" or lacking in usefulness. Novices, on the other hand, typically get caught up in the wording of definitions and do not probe into them to see to what extent their meanings are in fact compatible. The various proposed definitions, when examined, are in fact much more similar than they are different.

Furthermore, because of the complexity of critical thinking, its relationship to an unlimited number of behaviors in an unlimited number of situations, its conceptual interdependence with other concepts such as the critical person, the reasonable person, the critical society, a critical theory of knowledge, learning, literacy, and rationality, not to speak of the opposites of these concepts — it is important not to put too much weight on any one particular definition of critical thinking. A variety of useful definitions have indeed been formulated by distinguished theoreticians, and we should value these diverse formulations as helping to make important features of critical thought more apparent.

Harvey Siegel, for example, has defined critical thinking as "thinking appropriately moved by reasons." This definition highlights the contrast between the mind's tendency to be shaped in its thoughts and beliefs by phenomena other than reasons: desires, fears, social rewards and punishments, etc. It points up the connection between critical thinking and the classic philosophical ideal of rationality. Yet, clearly, the ideal of rationality is itself open to multiple explications. Similar points can be made about Robert Ennis' and Matthew Lipman's definitions.

Robert Ennis defines critical thinking as "rational reflective thinking concerned with what to do or believe." This definition usefully calls attention to the wide role that critical thinking plays in everyday life, for since all behavior is based on what we believe, all human action is based upon what we in some sense *decide* to do. However, like Siegel's definition, it assumes that the reader has a clear concept of rationality and of the conditions under which a decision can be said to be a "reflective" one. There is also a possible ambiguity in Ennis' use of 'reflective.' As a person internalizes critical standards — sensitivity to reasons, evidence, relevance, consistency, and so forth — the application of these standards to action becomes more automatic, less a matter of conscious effort and, hence, less a matter of overt "reflection," assuming that Ennis means to imply by 'reflection' a special consciousness or deliberateness.

Matthew Lipman defines critical thinking as "skillful, responsible thinking that is conducive to judgment because it relies on criteria, is self-correcting, and is sensitive to context." This definition is useful insofar as one has a clear sense of the difference between responsible and irresponsible thinking, as well as what to encompass in the appropriate self-correction of thought, the appropriate use of criteria, and appropriate sensitivity to context. Of course, it would not be difficult to find instances of thinking that were self-correcting, used criteria, and responded to context *in one sense* and nevertheless were *uncritical* in some other sense. Clearly, one's particular criteria might be uncritically chosen, for example, or the manner of responding to context might be critically deficient in a variety of ways.

I make these points not to underestimate the usefulness of these definitions but to point out limitations in the process of definition itself when dealing with a complex concept such as critical thinking. Rather than to work solely with one definition of critical thinking, it is more desirable to retain a host of definitions, and this for two reasons: 1) in order to maintain insight into the various dimensions of critical thinking that alternative definitions highlight, and 2) to help oneself escape the limitations of any given definition. In this spirit, I will present a number of definitions which I have formulated of the cluster of concepts whose relationship to each other is fundamental to critical thinking. Before reading these definitions, you might review the array of teachers' formulations in the section "What Critical Thinking Means to Me." You will find that virtually all the teachers' definitions are compatible with each other, even though they are all formulated individualistically.

Critical thinking is disciplined, self-directed thinking which exemplifies the perfections of thinking appropriate to a particular mode or domain of thinking. It comes in two forms. If the thinking is disciplined to serve the interests of a particular individual or group, to the exclusion of other relevant persons and groups, I call it *sophistic* or *weak sense* critical thinking. If the thinking is disciplined to take into account the interests of diverse persons or groups, I call it *fairminded* or *strong sense* critical thinking.

In thinking critically, we use our command of *the elements of thinking* to adjust our thinking successfully to the logical demands of a type or *mode of thinking*. As we come to habitually think critically in the strong sense, we develop special *traits of mind* : intellectual humility, intellectual courage, intellectual perseverance, intellectual integrity, and intellectual faith in reason. A sophistic or weak sense critical thinker develops these traits only in a restricted way, in accordance with egocentric and sociocentric commitments.

It is important not only to emphasize the dimension of skills in critical thinking, but also to explicitly mark out the very real possibility of a one-sided use of the skills associated with critical thought. Indeed, the historical tendency for skills of thought to be systematically used in defense of the vested interests of dominant social groups and the parallel tendency of all social groups to develop one-sided thinking in support of their own interests, mandates marking this tendency with explicit concepts. It should be clearly recognized that one-sided critical thinking is much more common in the world of affairs than fairminded critical thought.

278

Critical Thinking is:

a) skilled thinking which meets epistemological demands irrespective of the vested interests or ideological commitments of the thinker;

b) skilled thinking characterized by empathy into diverse opposing points of view and devotion to truth as against self-interest;

c) skilled thinking that is consistent in the application of intellectual standards, holding oneself to the same rigorous standards of evidence and proof to which one hold's one's antagonists;

d) skilled thinking that demonstrates the commitment to entertain all viewpoints sympathetically and to assess them with the same intellectual standards, without reference to one's own feelings or vested interests, or the feelings or vested interests of one's friends, community or nation;

e) the art of thinking about your thinking while your're thinking so as to make your thinking more clear, precise, accurate, relevant, consistent, and fair;

f) the art of constructive skepticism;

g) the art of identifying and removing bias, prejudice, and one-sidedness of thought;

h) the art of self-directed, in-depth, rational learning;

i) thinking that rationally certifies what we know and makes clear wherein we are ignorant;

j) the art of thinking for one's self with clarity, accuracy, insight, commitment, and fairness.

And this is by no means all, for sometimes it is important to know whether a question is being raised against the background of a given social system, a given socio-logic. Sometimes, in other words, we are thinking as Americans or as Iranians, or Russians. When we think like the other members of our social group, it is often to our advantage to believe what they believe even when it is *false.* I have alluded to this variable before in terms of the use within social systems of "functional falsehoods." What is justified as an answer to a question, given one social system as the defining context, may very well be different within the logic of another social system. We need to know, therefore, whether we seek to reason within the logic of a given social system or, on the other hand, are asking the question in a broader way. A question may be answerable within one system and not within another, or not in the same sense, or in the same sense but with a different answer. We sometimes forget this complexity when talking about critical thinking.

Going still further, it may be important for a critical thinker to recognize, in asking a question, whether we are framing it within the logic of a technical or natural language. The question, 'What is fear?' asked with the technical language of physiology and biology in mind, may well be a different question than that same interrogative sentence asked in ordinary English, a *natural* language. This is yet another dimension to critical thinking.

Finally, we often need to know, when reasoning about a question, whether that question is most appropriately treated by an established procedure (monological issues), or whether it is plausible for people to approach it from the perspective of diverse points of view (multilogical issues). If there is one dominant theory in a field or an established procedure or algorithm for settling a question, the rational thing to do would be to use that theory, procedure, or algorithm. Many of the routine problems of everyday life as well as many of the standard problems in highly technical or scientific disciplines are of this sort. However, it is crucial for students to learn how to identify those higher order problems for which there are multiple theories, frames of reference, or competing ideologies as the instrumentality for settling the issue, and hence cannot legitimately be approached monologically. Instruction rarely addresses these multilogical issues, even though most of the pressing problems of everyday social, political, and personal life are of this order. Moreover, there is good reason to foster a multilogical approach even to monological issues when students initially approach them. Students learn better when they struggle to understand things on their own terms, so even when we can immediately show them the "best" way to proceed, it is often better to let them argue about alternative ways first.

The Perfections and Imperfections of Thought

clarity	vs	unclarity
precision	vs	imprecision
specificity	vs	vagueness
accuracy	vs	inaccuracy
relevance	vs	irrelevance
consistency	vs	inconsistency
logical	vs	illogical
depth	vs	superficiality
completeness	vs	incompleteness
significance	vs	triviality
fairness	vs	bias or one-sidedness
adequacy (for purpose)	vs	inadequacy

Each of the above are general canons for thought. To develop one's mind and to discipline one's thinking to come up to these standards requires extensive practice and long-term cultivation. Of course, coming up to these standards is typically a relative matter and often has to be adjusted to a particular domain of thought. Being *precise* while doing mathematics is not the same thing as being precise while writing a poem or describing an experience. Furthermore, there is one perfection of thought that may come to be periodically incompatible with the others, and that is adequacy to the purpose. Because the social world is often irrational and unjust, because people are often manipulated to act against their interests, because skilled thought is often used in the service of vested interest, thought adequate to these purposes may require skilled violation of the common standards for good thinking. Skilled propaganda, skilled political debate, skilled defense of a group's interests, skilled deception of one's enemy may require the violation or selective application of any of the above standards. The perfecting of one's thought as an instrument for success in a world based on power and advantage is a different matter from the perfecting of one's thought for the apprehension and defense of fairminded truth. To develop one's critical thinking skills merely to the level of adequacy for success is to develop those skills in a lower or *weaker* sense. It is important to underscore the commonality of this weaker sense of critical thinking for it is dominant in the everyday world. Virtually all social groups disapprove of members who make the case for their competitors or enemies however justified that case may be. Skillful thinking is commonly a tool in the struggle for power and advantage, not an angelic force that transcends this struggle. It is only as the struggle becomes mutually destructive and it comes to be the advantage of all to go beyond the one-sidedness of each that a social ground is laid for fairmindedness of thought. There is no society yet in existence that, in a general way, cultivates fairness of thought in its citizens.

It is certainly of the nature of the human mind to think — spontaneously, continuously, and pervasively — but it is not of the nature of the human mind to think critically about the standards and principles which guide its spontaneous thought. It has no built-in drive to question, for example, its innate tendency to believe what it wants to believe, what makes it comfortable, what is simple rather than complex, what is commonly believed, what is socially rewarded, etc. The human mind is ordinarily at peace with itself as it internalizes and creates biases, prejudices, falsehoods, half-truths, and distortions. Compartmentalized contradictions do not, by their very nature, disturb the mind of those who take them in and selectively use them. The human mind spontaneously experiences itself as in tune with reality, as directly observing and faithfully recording it. It takes a special intervening process to produce the kind of self-criticalness that enables the mind to effectively question its own constructions. The mind spontaneously but uncritically invests itself with epistemological authority with an even greater ease than the ease with which it accepts authority figures in the world into which it is socialized. The process of learning to think critically is therefore an extraordinary process that cultivates capacities merely potential in human thought and develops them at the expense of capacities spontaneously activated from within and reinforced by normal socialization. It is not normal and inevitable nor even common for a mind to discipline itself within a rational perspective and direct itself toward rational rather than egocentric beliefs, practices, and values. Yet it is increasingly possible to describe the precise conditions under which critical minds can be cultivated. The nature of critical thought in contrast to uncritical thought is becoming increasingly apparent.

We should recognize therefore that the process of encouraging critical thinking is a slow, evolutionary one — one that proceeds on many fronts simultaneously. We should recognize that built into our students' minds will be many egocentric and sociocentric tendencies. They will need time and encouragement to come to terms with these. A definition of critical thinking will never be our fundamental need, but rather a sensitivity to the many ways we can help students to make their thinking more clear, accurate, consistent, relevant and fair.

All the various strategies explained in the handbook are couched in terms of behaviors. The principles express and describe a variety of behaviors of the 'ideal' critical thinker; they become applications to lessons when teachers canvass their lesson plans to find appropriate places where those behaviors can be fostered. The practice we recommend helps guard against teachers using these strategies as recipes or formulas, since in each case good judgment is required in the application process.

Some Vocabulary and Distinctions

Critical Thinking: refers to

   a. a body of intellectual skills and abilities which (when used in keeping with the dispositions and values below) enable one rationally to decide what to believe or do.

   b. a body of dispositions

   c. a set of values: truth, fairmindedness, open-mindedness, empathy, autonomy, rationality, self-criticism

Uncritical Person: refers to one who has not learned the intellectual skills above (naive, conformist, easily manipulated, dogmatic, closed-minded, narrow-minded).

Critical Person: refers to any person who, in a weak or strong sense, uses the intellectual skills above. (A critical person may or may not significantly embody the dispositions or be committed to the values of critical thinking. Some critical persons use the intellectual skills to justify or rationalize whatever beliefs they uncritically internalize and do not hold themselves or those with whom they ego-identify to the same intellectual standards to which they hold those they disagree with or disapprove of.)

Weak Sense Critical Thinker: refers to

   a. one who does not hold himself or those with whom he ego-identifies to the same intellectual standards to which he holds "opponents"

   b. one who has not learned how to reason empathically within points of view or frames of reference with which he disagrees

   c. one who tends to think monologically

   d. one who does not genuinely accept, though he may verbally espouse, the values of critical thinking

   e. one who uses the intellectual skills of critical thinking selectively and self-deceptively to foster and serve his vested interests (at the expense of truth)

Strong Sense Critical Thinker: refers to

    a. one who holds himself and those he agrees with to the same intellectual standards to which he holds those with whom he disagrees.

    b. one who thinks empathically within points of view or frames of reference with which he disagrees (one who is able to see some truth and insight within opponents' points of view as well as weaknesses within his own).

    c. one who is able to think multi-logically and dialogically.

    d. one who genuinely strives to live in accordance with the values of critical thinking (hence one who can see occasions in which he or she has failed so to live).

    e. one who uses the intellectual skills and abilities of critical thinking to go beyond those beliefs which serve his or her vested interests and to detect self-deceptive reasoning.

Critical Society: refers to the notion of a society which rewards adherence to the values of critical thinking and hence does not use indoctrination and inculcation as basic modes of learning (rewards reflective questioning, intellectual independence, and reasoned dissent).

Monological Thinking: refers to thinking that is conducted exclusively within one point of view or frame of reference.

Monological Problems: refers to problems that can be rationally solved by reasoning exclusively within one point of view or frame of reference. (Many technical problems can be solved by monological thinking).

Multi-logical Thinking: refers to thinking that goes beyond one frame of reference or point of view.

Multi-logical Problems: refers to problems which to be rationally solved require that one entertain and reason empathically within more than one point of view or frame of reference.

Dialogical Thinking: refers to thinking that involves a dialogue or extended exchange between different points of view or frames of reference.

Dialectical Thinking: refers to dialogical thinking conducted in order to test the strengths and weaknesses of opposing points of view. (Court trials and debates are dialectical in nature).

Dialogical Instruction: refers to instruction that fosters dialogical or dialectic thinking.

Socratic Questioning: refers to a mode of questioning that deeply probes the meaning, justification, or logical strength of a claim, position, or line of reasoning. Socratic questioning can be carried out in a variety of ways and adapted to many levels of ability and understanding.

Reciprocity: refers to the act of entering empathically into the point of view or line of reasoning of others; learning to think as others do and by that means to sympathetically assess that thinking. (Requires creative imagination as well as intellectual skill and a commitment to fair-mindedness.)

Additional Vocabulary

evidence: The data on which a judgment or conclusion might be based, or by which proof or probability may be established.

premise: A proposition upon which an argument is based or from which a conclusion is drawn; logic -- one of the first two propositions of a syllogism, from which the conclusion is drawn.

assumption: A statement accepted or supposed as true without proof or demonstration; unstated premise.

conclusion: A judgment or decision reached after deliberation.

inference: A conclusion based on something known or assumed; derived by reasoning.

reasoning: The mental processes of one who reasons; especially the drawing of conclusions or inferences from observations, facts or *hypotheses*. The evidence or arguments used in this procedure.

truth: Conformity to knowledge, fact, actuality, or logic: a statement proven to be or accepted as true, not false or erroneous.

fallacious: Containing or based on a fallacy; deceptive in appearance or meaning; misleading; delusive.

prove: To establish the truth or validity of something by presentation of argument or evidence; to determine the quality of by testing.

implication: A claim which follows from other stated claims; an indication which is not said openly or directly; hint; what is hinted or suggested by what is said or done.

egocentric: A tendency to view everything else in relationship to oneself. One's desires, values and beliefs (seeming to be self-evidently correct or superior to those of others) are often uncritically used as the norm of all judgment and experience.

ethnocentric: A tendency to view one's own race (culture) as central, based on the attitude that one's own group is superior.

sociocentric: When a group or society sees itself as superior and thus considers its way of seeing the world as correct; there is a tendency to presuppose this superiority in all of its thinking and thus to serve as an impediment to open-mindedness.

Resources for Teaching Critical Thinking

Videotape Library

Videotapes are one of the most important developing resources for critical thinking in-service education. They can be used in a variety of ways: 1) as discussion starters, 2) as sources of information on the nature of critical thinking, 3) as models of critical thinking, and 4) as models for classroom instruction. All of the following videotapes have been developed as low-cost resources. No attempt has been made to achieve broadcast quality. An order form follows the tape descriptions.

1 Critical Thinking in Science

Professor Richard Paul, Chemistry Professor Douglas Martin, and Sonoma State University student Eamon Hickey discuss ways in which critical thinking may be applied in science education. The following issues are raised: "To what extent is there a problem with science education being an exercise in rote memorization and recall? Is there a conflict between preparing science students to become critical thinkers and preparing them for specialized scientific work? To what extent is science being taught monologically? Does monological instruction alienate students from the overall goal of becoming educated thinkers?" This tape is an excellent discussion-starter for in-service use. (50 minutes)

2 Critical Thinking in History

In this videotape, Professor Richard Paul is joined by History Professor Robert Brown and Sonoma State University student Eamon Hickey to discuss the relation of critical thinking to the interpretation, understanding, and construction of history. The following issues are discussed: "What is the place of value judgments in history? To what extent is history written from a point of view or frame of reference? Can students come to understand history from a critical vantage point? How would history be taught if this were the goal? To what extent should history be used to inculcate patriotism? What is it to learn how to think historically? Have teachers been adequately prepared to teach history from a critical vantage point? What can be done to facilitate historical thinking rather than memorization of 'facts'?" (50 minutes)

3 Dialogical Practice I

One of the most important skills of critical thinking is the ability to enter into and reason within opposing viewpoints. In this videotape, Sonoma State University students Stacy Goldring and Jean Hume practice dialogical reasoning, using the Israeli-Arab conflict as the subject. (50 minutes)

4 Dialogical Practice II

In this videotape, Sonoma State University students Hub Lampert and Dave Allender practice dialogical reasoning, using the issue of abortion as the subject. (29 minutes)

(Both of these dialogical practice tapes are excellent illustrations of what it is for students to integrate a host of critical thinking skills and dispositions into their spontaneous thinking.)

5 Critical Thinking: The State of the Field

In this welcoming address to the Third International Conference on Critical Thinking and Educational Reform, Professor Richard Paul addresses the following issues: "What fundamental changes are necessary to give students the incentive to develop critical thinking skills? How does the very nature of belief pose difficulty for critical thinking? How does traditional intra-disciplinary education provide an obstacle to independence of thought? How is critical thinking fundamental to all forms of reference, and how can we use it to think across and beyond disciplinary boundaries? How is the field of critical thinking developing so as to cut across subject matter divisions? What are the social and institutional barriers to the development of critical thinking as a field and as an educational reality?" (65 minutes)

6 Socratic Questioning In Large Group Discussion (4ᵗʰ Grade)

Professor Richard Paul leads a 4ᵗʰ Grade class discussion, using Socratic questions. Issues such as the following are discussed: "What is your mind? Does it *do* anything? Where does your personality come from? Is thinking like an American kid different from thinking like an Eskimo kid? Do you choose to be the kind of person you are going to be? Can you be a good person and people think you're bad? How do you find out what's inside a person?" (60 minutes)

7 Socratic Questioning in Large Group Discussion (6ᵗʰ Grade)

Professor Richard Paul leads a 6ᵗʰ Grade class discussion, using Socratic questions. Issues such as the following are discussed: "Who does the 'our' in the textbook title *Our World* refer to? Are people easy or hard to understand? Are all members of a group alike? Do some groups think they are better than other groups? Are there any groups of people that you think are bad? If you had to list the qualities of most Americans, what would they be? If you had to list the qualities of Germans, what would they be? Italians? Russians? Now imagine all of you are Russian boys and girls: how would you describe Americans?" The students' stereotypes and biases are probed. When contradictions begin to emerge, the students struggle to reconcile them or go beyond them. (70 minutes)

8 Socratic Questioning in Large Group Discussions (7ᵗʰ and 8ᵗʰ Grades)

Professor Richard Paul writes a definition of critical thinking on the board — "Critical thinking is seeing through the surface of things, events, and people to the deeper realities" — and then leads the class to probe the definition by Socratic questioning: "Can anyone give an example of a person you met that you thought was one way whom you later came to think was very different? Have you ever seen a toy advertised on TV that you later saw was very different from the way it appeared on TV? Do people ever try to make things look different from the way they are? Is it common or not common for people to try to trick other people? How can we check to see if people or things are really the way they appear to be? Do we always know what we really want? What we are really like? Are all people around the world basically alike or basically different? How could we check? How could we find out if we are right or wrong?" (65 minutes)

17 Coaching Teachers Who Teach Critical Thinking — John Barell, David Perkins

If we wish students to engage in critical thinking in the 'strong sense,' how do we nurture this intended outcome through teacher-supervisor-coach interactions? Assuming experienced teachers are aware of the nature of critical thinking and find it difficult to engage students in this process, how do we help them become more flexible, empathic analysts and problem solvers? A model coaching process will be demonstrated and related to research on staff development, teacher growth, metacognition and achievement motivation. (90 minutes)

20 Effective Design for Critical Thinking Inservice — Chuck Blondino, Ken Bumgarner

A team approach has been used effectively in the State of Washington to institute and improve the teaching of critical thinking in elementary, secondary, and higher education. Central to this team is effective networking that exists between and among the educational service districts (ESDS) and the curriculum and instruction leadership of the state office. Employee and curriculum organizations as well as parent, citizen and business associations have joined in this team effort focused on the teaching of thinking skills at all levels. Organizing and networking techniques employed are discussed along with approaches taken to garner support of the educational groups, citizen organizations, and outside enterprises. (90 minutes)

22 Bridging the Gap Between Teachers' Verbal Allegiance to Critical Thinking and their Actual Behavior — M. Neil Browne, Stuart Keeley

Faculty and administrators regularly rank critical thinking as a preeminent educational objective. They claim it is the core of what teachers should be doing. Unfortunately, their talk is rarely supported by their teaching behavior. An initial obstacle to transforming verbal devotion to critical thinking into classroom performance is the mistaken belief that the discontinuity between prescription and practice is illusory. Professors Browne and Keeley summarize research done by themselves and others concerning the extent of critical thinking activity in secondary and post-secondary classrooms, and discuss strategies that offer promise for actually integrating critical thinking into the classroom. Especially important is the need to addresss the dominance of the coverage model' in shaping teaching practice. The presenters include suggestions for dialogic conversation with those who are motivated by the 'coverage model.' (90 minutes)

23 Teaching Critical Thinking Across the Curriculum — John Chaffee

Professor Chaffee explores an established interdisciplinary program which teaches and reinforces fundamental thinking skills and critical attitudes across the curriculum. The program is centered around *Critical Thought Skills*, a course specifically designed to improve the thinking, language, and symbolic abilities of entering college students. The course has been integrated into the curriculum through an NEH funded project of faculty training and curriculum re-design. In additition to reviewing the structure, theoretical perspective and evaluative results of the program, special attention is given to exploring practical approaches for developing thinking abilities. (90 minutes)

24 Critical Thinking and the History-Social Sciences Curriculum, Grades 9-12 — Ira Clark, Jerry Cummings

Using the Model Curriculum Standards for Grades 9-12, History-Social Science, the presenters and audience discuss and develop clasroom activities and strategies for getting students to enlarge their views through critical thinking skills. (90 minutes)

25 Language Arts and Critical Thinking for Remedial and Bilingual Students — Connie DeCapite

This workshop focuses on two specific components. Initially, Ms. DeCapite discusses the benefits of using critical thinking skills to help low-achieving or ESL students develop language, reading, and writing proficiency. The second part of the workshop focuses on how to develop and implement a language arts program consisting of activities utilizing critical thinking strategies and interdisciplinary materials. (90 minutes)

26 A Conception of Critical Thinking — Robert H. Ennis

On the assumption that a liberally educated person should be able to think critically in handling the civic and personal problems of daily life, as well as those of the standard subjects as taught in school, Robert Ennis offers a conception of critical thinking that bridges all of these concerns. Starting with the idea that thinking critically is reflectively and reasonably going about deciding what to believe or do, he suggests a number of dispositions and abilites that might well constitute a critical thinking set of goals for the school, K-U. (90 minutes)

27 How To Write Critical Thinking Test Questions — Robert H. Ennis
Dr. Ennis offers suggestions on how to frame questions that test critical thinking skills. (90 minutes)

30 Philosophy For Children — Thomas Jackson
Professor Jackson presents a brief introduction to the Philosophy for Children program followed by a 'hands-on' demonstration of how the program actually works. Participants then read from a section of the novel, *Pixie*, raise questions from the reading, group these questions, and work a follow-up exercise together. (90 minutes)

31 Critical Thinking in Math and Science — Douglas Martin, Richard Paul
A discussion of the sense in which routine and non-routine mathematical and scientific thinking presuppose critical thinking. Consideration is given not only to the 'ultimate' nature of such thinking, but to the forms that thinking takes (or ought to take) as students approach it at various levels of 'ignorance' and incomplete understanding. (90 minutes)

32 Projects for Integrating Critical Thinking — Ogden Morse, Geoffrey Scheurman
The projects discussed help enable teachers to foster the deliberate teaching and integration of thinking skills with the presentation of normal content material. The projects offer several avenues to aid teachers in developing units of study and integrating them into specific subject areas. Mr. Scheurman discusses the Wyoming Critical Thinking Project. Mr. Morse discusses a model he developed for transferring critical thinking theory into practical application in the classroom. (90 minutes)

33 Varieties of Critical Thinking Tests: Their Design and Use — Stephen Norris
Critical thinking tests can serve different purposes. They might be used to examine, for example, critical thinking skills or critical thinking dispositions, or to examine either several aspects of critical thinking or only a few aspects. In addition, the information provided by a critical thinking test might be used to make decisions about individual students, to assess the critical thinking curricula, to evaluate teachers, or to compare the quality of schools.

Dr. Norris argues that not all types of critical thinking tests can serve equally well all of the purposes for which such tests might be used. A systematic matching of type of test to the intended use can help make currently available critical thinking tests more effective. The bottom line in all cases, no matter what type of test is used and no matter what the purposes for using it, is that the reasons be known for students' responses to the tasks on the tests. (90 minutes)

34 Teaching Critical Thinking in the Strong Sense in Elementary, Secondary, and Higher Education — Richard Paul
In his opening address to the Fourth International Conference on Critical Thinking and Educational Reform, Richard Paul argues for the importance of teaching critical thinking at all levels in such a way as to foster the critical spirit and the application of that spirit to the foundations of our own beliefs and actions. He argues that it is inadequate to conceive of critical thinking simply as a body of discrete academic skills. The synthesis of these skills and their orchestration into a variety of forms of deep criticism is accentuated. He comments on the application of strong sense critical thinking to personal and social life as well as to academic subject domains. In this perspective, the strong sense critical thinker is conceived of as having special abilities and a special commitment to becoming an integrated and moral person. (60 minutes)

35 Workshop on the Art of Teaching Critical Thinking in the Strong Sense — Richard Paul
In this workshop, emphasis is placed on strategies which enhance strong sense critical thinking abilities and skills. First, the distinction between weak and strong sense critical thinking is explained. Then, exercises are used to explain and demonstrate how one can use the

macro-abilities of critical thinking (Socratic quesitoning, reciprocity, and dialogical reasoning) to orchestrate micro-skills in achieving 'strong sense' objectives. (90 minutes)

36 Critical Thinking's Original Sin: Round Two — David Perkins, Richard Paul

At the Third International Conference on Critical Thinking and Educational Reform, Richard Paul and David Perkins debated the psychological sources of closed-mindedness and superficial thinking. Paul contended that deep motivational factors such as egocentricity are the culprit. Perkins contended that powerful cognitive factors such as the avoidance of cognitive load lead to one-sidedness and oversimplification. Here, the two review, broaden, and deepen the debate. To demonstrate the spirit of fair thinking, however, each argues the other's side. (90 minutes)

37 Knowledge as Design in the Classroom — David Perkins

This workshop introduces participants to the basic strategies of "knowledge as design," a systematic approach to integrating the teaching of critical and creative thinking into subject-matter instruction. The key notion is that any piece of knowledge or product of mind — Newton's laws, the Bill of Rights, a sonnet by Shakespeare — can be viewed as a design, a structure adapted to a purpose. By examining the purpose of Newton's laws, the Bill of Rights, or a sonnet, analyzing structure, and assessing how and how well the structure serves the purpose, students can achieve genuine insight into such products and into the way knowledge works in general. By redesigning existing designs (for example, make up your own Bill of Rights) and devising new ones, students can learn the art of inventive thinking. (90 minutes)

38 The Possibility of Invention — David Perkins

"How can something come out of nothing?" is a fundamental question not only for physicists pondering the origins of the universe but for psychologists, philosophers, and educators pondering the nature of creative thinking. How can a person invent something genuinely new, or is it so that nothing we invent is really new? This presentation explores the basic 'logic' of invention, arguing that there are fundamental patterns of information processing that can be found in human thought, and some of them even in computers and biological evolution. (90 minutes)

39 The Role of Thinking in Reading Comprehension — Linda M. Phillips

Dr. Phillips discusses the intimate relation between critical thinking and reading comprehension, using case studies to illustrate how the same passage of text is interpreted differently by a critical reader and an uncritical reader. Thinking should not be separated from reading, she concludes, and reading well is thinking well. (90 minutes)

41 Teaching Thinking Strategies Across the Curriculum: The Higher Order Thinking (H O T) Project: Elementary Level — Edys Quellmalz

Dr. Quellmalz describes the Higher Order Thinking (H. O. T.) Projects currently underway in San Mateo County, Sacramento County and the San Juan Unified School District. The projects involve teachers in a collaborative effort to develop and monitor students' higher order thinking skills in school subjects. In the instructional component, teachers examine textbooks and other classroom resources in order to design activities that will involve students in sustained reasoning about significant concepts and problems typically encountered in academic and practical situations. Following an overview of the projects, teachers describe lessons developed and discuss samples of student work. (90 minutes)

43 Why Not Debate? Strong Sense Critical Thinking Assignments — Dianne Romain

After defining strong sense critical thinking values such as fairmindedness, truth, and autonomy, Dr. Romain argues that student debates tend to emphasize some of these values. She presents a dialogue paper assignment, small group projects, and guidelines for class discussion that encourage strong sense critical thinking values. (90 minutes)

44 Introducing Affective Awareness — Vivian Rosenberg

This presentation is based on the assumption that Critical Thinking in the 'strong' sense is more than simply constructing, criticizing and assessing arguments. It involves: 1) understanding how our minds work 2) developing insight into different ways of thinking about problems and ideas and 3) developing strategies to analyze different kinds of problems and ideas. To illustrate how affective awareness can be taught in the classroom, Professor Rosenberg describes a program in which students are directed *consciously and systematically* to focus on feelings — to identify how they feel as they deal with ideas and problems, and to understand how others feel. She concludes that affective awareness is a teachable skill, and that it can — and should — be taught and practiced in critical thinking courses. (90 minutes)

46 A Holistic Approach to Thinking Instruction — Vincent Ryan Ruggiero

Because the development of thinking instruction has taken place in two separate disciplines (philosophy and psychology), it has produced two models of the thinking process — a critical model and a creative model. Unfortunately, neither model is by itself adequate for problem-solving and issue-analysis, which demand both the production and evaluation of ideas. This workshop presents a holistic approach to thinking instruction that combines creative and critical thinking and demonstrates how that approach applies to problems and issues across the curriculum. (90 minutes)

51 Solving Problems in Writing — Joseph Williams

Real life problem solving differs from laboratory problem solving in several ways: real life problems are not easily identified or defined; they have no one right solution nor is there a standard way to solve the problem. There is no way to determine easily the goodness of the solution because the problem is so deeply embedded in a wider context of problems. Teachers who ask students to solve problems in writing often fail to understand that some students think that they are being asked to solve a laboratory-like problem when the instructor is looking for evidence that they appreciate that a problem is ambiguous, complex and open-ended. Or vice-versa.

This workshop addresses the ways to think through the context of a writing problem, ways to anticipate a student's simply following a "set of rules" for solving a writing problem, and ways to demonstrate those rhetorical conventions that most of us take to be the signs of thoughtful problem solving — of good critical thinking. (90 minutes)

Mini Critical Thinking Course

At the Fourth International Conference on Critical Thinking and Educational Reform, several authors of critical thinking texts and other experienced critical thinking instructors were asked to speak on particular aspects of critical thinking. The series of lectures, presented as a mini-course in critical thinking, is now available in video format.

52 Using Arguments to Decide What to Believe — J. Anthony Blair

Faced with contentious claims, there is a tendency to respond with immediate reaction, and also to consider only a few of the pros and cons. Moreover, the reflection that goes into such an examination when it does occur is seldom thorough or tenacious. What seems needed are some easily-understood and readily-applied methods that will extend and deepen the critical examination of contentious claims. The method suggested by Dr. Blair is a systematic collection and examination of (1) the pros and cons of a contentious opinion or claim, (2) the merits of those pros and cons, (3) the overall strengths and weaknesses of the best case for the claim. Dr. Blair describes the theory of the method, then participants are given a chance to apply it and see how it works in practice. (90 minutes)

53 Critical and Creative Problem-Solving — John Chaffee

Solving problems effectively involves an integrated set of critical and creative thinking abilities. This workshop introduces a versatile problem-solving approach which is useful for analyzing complex problems in a creative and organized fashion. Participants work through a sequence of problems, individually and in small groups, and are given the opportunity to discuss and critically reflect on the learning process. In addition, participants explore ways of incorporating problem-solving approaches into the courses that they teach. (90 minutes)

54 Learning About Good Arguments Through the Fallacies — Edward Damer

This session is devoted to the treatment of a selected number of informal fallacies. Since a fallacy is defined as a violation of one of the three criteria of a good argument, the emphasis is upon the ways in which an understanding of the fallacies can help one to develop abilities to construct good arguments and to detect bad ones. (90 minutes)

57 Information and the Mass Media — Ralph Johnson

Professor Johnson makes the following assumption: That in order to be a critical thinker, one must have the following things: first, certain intellectual and logical skills and the propensity to use them appropriately; second, a basis of knowledge and information; third, vigilance against ego- and ethno-centric bias. Professor Johnson concentrates on the second of the above-mentioned items, specifically on how the critical thinker deals with information and the mass media. The idea would be to give the students a crash course in how the critical thinker uses the mass media in such a way as to benefit from their strengths, while avoiding being seduced into thinking we know more than we do. He outlines the elements that go into being a RACON: a reflective and aggressive consumer of the news. (90 minutes)

58 Practical Reasoning — Carol LaBar, Ian Wright

Critical thinking includes reasoning about what ought to be done, as well as what to believe. This sort of reasoning, sometimes called practical reasoning, involves two logically different kinds of reasons: 1) motivating reasons in the form of value standards which the agent accepts, and 2) beliefs about the degree to which the actions under consideration will fulfill the value standard. These two different kinds of reasons lead to a conclusion about what ought to be done; that is a practical judgment. This session focuses on the practical syllogism and the use of principle 'tests' as a way of assessing the value standard. (90 minutes)

59 The Nature of Critical Thinking Through Socratic Interrogation — Richard Paul

Professor Paul interrogates the audience Socratically in order to elicit collective insights into the nature of critical thinking. This parallels the first couple of sessions of his introductory course in critical thinking in which Professor Paul uses a similar strategy for getting his students to begin to come to terms with some of the basic issues. (90 minues)

60 Dispositions: The Neglected Aspect of Critical Thinking — Vincent Ruggiero

All the understanding of creative and critical thinking and all the skill in applying that understanding to problems and issues will profit students little if they lack the *motivation* to think well. This fact has led a growing number of authorities on thinking instruction to urge that classroom instructors give special attention to the *dispositions* that underlie effective thinking. This workshop identifies these dispositions and suggests ways for instructors to assist students in developing them. It also examines the obstacles to such development and ways in which they can be overcome. (90 minutes)

61 Epistemological Underpinnings of Critical Thinking — Harvey Siegel

To be a critical thinker is to base one's beliefs, opinions and actions on relevant reasons. The notions of 'reason' and 'rationality' are, however, philosophically problematic. Just what is a reason? How do we know that some consideration constitutes a reason for doing or believing something? How do we evaluate the strength or merit of reasons? What is it for a belief or action to be *justified*? What is the relationship between justification and *truth*? Dr. Siegel examines these epistemological questions, and explores their relevance for critical thinking. (90 minutes)

63 Designing Faculty Development Programs for Integrating Critical Thinking Across the Curriculum — M. Neil Browne

Many teachers who desire to encourage critical thinking have no formal training in either critical thinking or pedagogical techniques that might stimulate such thinking. Administrators often respond with some form of weakness. What works? What kinds of pitfalls do faculty development programs typically encounter? What can be done to encourage long-term effects of faculty development?

Professor Browne's presentation is a dialogue between someone planning a faculty development program and a potential participant in the program. The content of the dialogue reflects both the author's research on effective faculty development, as well as his own experience as a facilitator at numerous faculty development workshops. (90 minutes)

64 What Human Beings Do When They Behave Intelligently and How They Can Become More So — Art Costa

Studies of efficient thinkers by Feuerstein, Sternberg, Glatthorn and Baron, and others have yielded some rather consistent characteristics of effective human performance. Studies of home, school, and classroom conditions, and the significance of mediative behaviors of parents and teachers are increasing our understanding of how to enhance the acquisition and performance of intelligent behavior. In this session, twelve qualities of human intelligent behavior are cited; indicators of their presence and increased performance in the classroom are identified; and school, home, and classroom conditions that promote their development are presented. (90 minutes)

66 Critical Thinking Staff Development: Developing Faculty Critical Thinking and Critical Teaching Skills — Richard Paul

The problem of long term staff development is a central problem in any attempt to bring critical thinking into the curriculum. Whatever else, we want critical thinking to be infused into all subject matter instruction. But we cannot do this unless, and to the extent that, faculty become comfortable articulating and utilizing critical thinking skills and dispositions. The standard mindset to instruction is an impediment. In this session, Professor Paul presents a general model for staff development and discusses ways of adapting it to different educational levels: elementary, secondary, and university. (90 minutes)

67 Lesson Plan Remodelling: A Strategy for Critical Thinking Staff Development — Richard Paul

The basic idea behind lesson plan remodelling as a strategy for staff development in critical thinking is simple. To remodel lesson plans is to develop a critique of one or more lessons and formulate one or more new lessons based on that critical process. A staff development leader with a reasonable number of exemplary remodels with accompanying explanatory principles can develop a series of staff development sessions that enable teachers to begin to develop new teaching skills as a result of their experience in lesson remodelling. In this session, Dr. Paul illustrates this mode of staff development using the Center's *Critical Thinking Handbook: K-3, A Guide For Remodelling Lesson Plans in Language Arts, Social Studies, and Science*. (40 minutes)

68 Teaching Critical Thinking: Skill, Commitment and the Critical Spirit, Kindergarten through Graduate School — Richard Paul

In his opening address to the 5ᵗʰ International Conference on Critical Thinking and Educational Reform, Professor Paul explains the significant opportunities that critical thinking instruction provides as well as the obstacles it faces. He begins by tracing his own intellectual development in terms of critical thinking. He then illustrates the application of critical thinking to productive, synthetic, and meaningful learning in general. He explains how and why critical thinking represents not only a set of skills but also a set of commitments and mental traits. He discusses the significance, for example, of intellectual courage, intellectual humility, and fairmindedness, which he argues we as educators often don't foster.

Professor Paul uses a variety of everyday examples to make clear how critical thinking cuts across the curriculum and is significant at every grade level. He underscores the growing consensus in the field as to the meaning and nature of critical thinking as well as the wide variety of dimensions of it that need further exploration. (50 minutes)

69 Supervision for Critical Self-Reflection upon Teaching — Richard Paul, David Perkins

How do we help teachers engage in critical thinking in the strong sense and develop those dispositions, such as intellectual humility and openness to diversity, that are fundamental to critical inquiry? In this session, Professors Paul and Perkins model a teaching episode followed by a post observation conference. The purpose of the conference is to exemplify processes designed to help adults become more analytic and reflective about their own performance. This process is related to the research on staff development, adult growth, metacognition and achievement motivation. (90 minutes)

70 Culture and Critical Thinking: The Danger of Group- or Culture-bound Thought — Richard Paul, Carol Tavris

One danger for thought is social or cultural blindness. In this case our critical thinking results in misjudgments of others. Another, but opposite, danger is the refusal to make any judgments about any culture but our own. In this session, Richard Paul and Carol Tavris discuss the nature and significance for education of these deepseated problems. The issue is, in other words, how can we so structure instruction so that students learn how to recognize and overcome their group-bound and culture-bound thinking? (90 minutes)

71 What Makes Science Concepts Hard to Understand? — David Perkins

The learning of science with genuine understanding has emerged as a pressing educational problem not only in pre-university education but even at the university level. Science "misconceptions" prove prevalent in students even after a year or two of physics or chemistry. In this session, Professor Perkins explores through examples some of the factors that lead to deeply rooted misunderstandings of scientific concepts and examines some of the educational strategies that might serve to help students toward real comprehension. (90 minutes)

72 What the Mind is Made Of — David Perkins

The mind can be conceived and modeled in innumerable ways. Two contemporary views of the nature of mind strike a particularly provocative contrast. Alan Newell, in his SOAR model, proposes that the mind is a "production system," a computer-like mechanism that operates by checking for what the situation of the moment is and then "firing" an action that responds more or less appropriately to the situation. In seemingly stark contrast, Marvin Minsky, in his "society of mind" model, proposes that the mind is composed of a loose society of semi-autonomous subminds — "agencies" that have very specialized jobs. In this session, Professor Perkins ponders whether the question, "What is the mind made of?" even makes sense, and what kind of sense it might make. (90 minutes)

75 The Administrator's Role in Thinking Instruction — Vincent R. Ruggiero

In this session, Professor Ruggiero advances the idea that administrators have an important role to play in the thinking movement, a role upon which the ultimate success of the movement could well depend. He examines the nature of this role, identifies numerous ways in which administrators can promote and facilitate thinking instruction in their schools or colleges, and discusses the benefits such initiatives will bring to administrators themselves and to their institutions. (90 minutes)

76 What is the Appropriate Role of Critical Thinking in Pre-Service Education? — Richard Paul, Robert Swartz

In this session, Dr. Swartz and Dr. Paul examine the following: if public school teachers are to foster critical thinking in all of their teaching, how should pre-service education be designed to accomplish this end? What are some of the obstacles and dilemmas to be faced in moving in this direction? (90 minutes)

77 Thinking Critically about Emotion — and the Role of Emotion in Critical Thinking — Carol Tavris

Historically, philosophers and psychologists have divided emotion and cognition into two camps: the "bestial" and the "human," the irrational and the rational, the bad and the good. One implication of this perspective has been that emotion is death to critical thinking; that human beings would be able to think logically and solve their problems if only they didn't have those nasty old mammalian emotions in the way. In her presentation, Dr. Tavris discusses how new research is breaking down old dichotomies: for example, the role of cognition in generating emotion; the role of emotional arousal in influencing thought; and ways in which cognition can be "irrational" and emotion "rational." (90 minutes)

81 What Are State Departments of Education Doing About Critical Thinking? — Ken Bumgarner, Fran Claggett, William Geffrey, Mark Weinstein

This panel explores the general approaches being used to facilitate the infusion of critical thinking into the curriculum in three vanguard states: Washington, California and New York. (90 minutes)

84 State Wide Critical Thinking Testing in California: What Has It and What Has It Not Accomplished? — Robert Ennis, Jan Talbot, Perry Weddle

The nature and impact of mandated statewide critical thinking testing in California is considered by the panel. (90 minutes)

90 Integrating Teaching for Thinking into Mainstream Classroom Instruction — Robert Swartz and Jane Rowe

Robert Swartz and Jane Rowe of the Critical and Creative Thinking Program at the University of Massachusetts, Boston demonstrate and discuss lessons and techniques that infuse a focus on critical thinking into classroom instruction by restructuring traditional content. The concept of critical thinking that is utilized is discussed as well as issues about the structure of instructional programs in schools and school systems that can foster this kind of integration. (90 minutes)

91 Infusing Critical Thinking into Subject Matter Instruction: The Problem of Restructuring Instruction — Richard Paul

Putting the critical thinking movement into a historical perspective, Richard Paul gives his assessment of what is most essential: the need to transform instruction in all academic subjects. He argues for the following changes: *(a)* from a content-dense to a content-deep curriculum, *(b)* from a data-oriented to issue-oriented content, *(c)* from teacher-centered to student-centered instruction, *(d)* from recitation-centered or lecture-centered to activity-centered learning, *(e)* from thought-discouraging to thought-provoking assignments, *(f)* from lock-step to flexibility-paced instruction, and *(g)* from a didactic to a critical concept of education. This requires school-wide or college-wide articulations of a philosophy of education that makes clear how the basic critical thinking objectives are harmonized with each other and infused in a coherent and concrete way into all subject matter instruction. (90 minutes)

92 Designing an Elementary or Middle School Inservice Program for Infusing Critical Thinking into Subject Matter Instruction — Richard Paul

Richard Paul provides a general model for designing an inservice program for elementary or middle schools. After sketching out a brief overview of the problem, discussion follows. Practical, long-range strategies for a progressively deeper integration of critical thinking into subject matter instruction is emphasized. (90 minutes)

94 Facilitating Critical and Creative Thinking Dispositions in Children — Alma M. Swartz

While many in the field of critical and creative thinking acknowledge the importance of the need to teach for critical and creative thinking *dispositions*, the stress has been on the discrete critical and creative thinking *skills*. Based on the assumption that teaching for critical and creative thinking attitudes and dispositions, such as openmindedness, or the tendency to seek reasons, is a necessary precondition to the acquisition and transfer of the discrete skills, Alma Swartz explores the idea of *primary* critical and creative thinking dispositions which underly and impel critical and creative thought.

The primary dispositions are categorized and explored as these interact with critical and creative thinking skills. A discussion of the ways in which cultural bias, as expressed in our schools, often runs counter to the child's natural inclination toward critical and creative thought is provided, with suggestions for the encouragement and facilitation of the dispositions as a means of ensuring the attainment of critical and creative thinking skills in the classroom. (90 minutes)

95 The Pre-Service Preparation of Teachers for Critical Thinking: The Montclair State College Model — Nicholas Michelli, Wendy Oxman, Mark Weinstein, John Barell

This session is a presentation and discussion of the model adopted at Montclair State College for infusing the teaching of critical thinking into the undergraduate pre-service teacher education program. Building upon a tradition of work in the field of critical thinking at Montclair State College, including the Institute for the Advancement of Philosophy for Children and Project THIS-TLE: Thinking Skills in Teaching and Learning, faculty have worked to revise the undergraduate program in light of proposed national standards for the preparation of teachers and recommendations of such groups as the Carnegie Forum on Education and the Economy. Key features of the program, including: the training of public school personnel to work with prospective teachers, the development and implementation of a new course within the undergraduate teacher education sequence on teaching for critical thinking, and revisions of all elements of the undergraduate teacher education curriculum are designed to foster and support teaching for critical thinking. A definition of critical thinking, goals for the program, and a philosophy for the program is shared with participants and discussed. (90 minutes)

97 Critical Thinking Staff Development — Charlie Blatz, Ken Bumgarner, Matthew Lipman, John Barell, Mark Weinstein, Nicholas Michelli

This panel surveys both short-term development projects, such as awareness workshops, and long-term projects, such as district-wide planning, assessment, and budgetary support, K-12. (90 minutes)

103 Think and Think Again! — Jan Talbot

Jan Talbot presents exciting materials and innovative strategies for strong sense critical thinking that teachers have found to be most effective in K-12 classrooms in Sacramento

County's seventeen school districts and in districts throughout the state. The materials are aligned with California's new Frameworks for math, science, language arts, and history-social science. Student work and new ways of assessing the effectiveness of student efforts to think critically are also presented. (90 minutes)

105 Preparing Teachers for Critical Thinking: A National Perspective — David Martin, Nicholas Michelli, David Imig

If we are to be successful in infusing the teaching of critical thinking into our schools, we must prepare new teachers to be sensitive to critical thinking and skilled in its implementation across the disciplines at the elementary level and within their disciplines at the secondary level. This need is especially critical if the projections that 50% of the work force of teachers will change within the next five to ten years are accurate. In addition to attending to the needs of new teachers, we must continue to assist in the professional development of practicing teachers as well. Efforts to develop national standards for the preparation of teachers who are capable of teaching for critical thinking are described and discussed. Model programs for the pre-service and in-service preparation of teachers are also discussed. (90 minutes)

106 A Critical Connection — George Hanford

There is a critical connection between what the Scholastic Aptitude Test measures and what critical thinking is all about. Those who call either for the abolition of our major modifications in the SAT or for a substantial decrease in its use overlook that important connection between the assessment of verbal and mathematical reasoning and the infusion of critical thinking into subject matter instruction. Is the connection, as suggested, critical? Is it understood? Does it need clarification? What will happen to SAT scores if the infusion succeeds? (90 minutes)

107 Teaching Critical Thinking Across the Curriculum: an Approach Through Specific Courses — Gerald Nosich

Initiating a program in critical thinking across the curriculum requires doing two tasks that often seem opposed. First, you need to induce a unified idea of critical thinking (skills, attitudes, values) in both teachers and students, so that what is learned in one course can be seen to be transferable to other, different courses and situations. Second, if you're teaching a course in the social sciences, you want the critical thinking skills to be integrated with the needs of teaching social sciences, and so you need methods and examples geared specifically to that discipline. Gerald Nosich covers both tasks but, instead of concentrating on what all critical thinking has in common, he concentrates on individual courses in Social Sciences (History, Psychology, Sociology), Humanities (English Literature, Fine Arts, Music), Natural Sciences, and Physical Education. In each case, Professor Nosich offers some specific and practical methods for teaching critical thinking in that particular discipline. (90 minutes)

108 The American High School: What Needs to Be Done to Prepare Students for College — George Hanford, Richard Paul

George Hanford and Richard Paul informally discuss what high schools need to do to prepare students for college. (90 minutes)

110 Social Constraints on Critical Thinking and Educational Reforms: An International Perspective — Marek Zelazkiewicz

There is no society without constraints on critical thinking. Ethnocentrism, areas of "taboo," unnoticable blank spots, unrevealed routine thinking, etc., can differ in various societies but do exist in each one. There is no social system without limitations on educational reforms. Conservative social groups, dependence of schools on other institutions, limited resources, complexity of the changes, the time factor, etc., can bury even the best reform. Marek Zelazkiewicz demonstrates how experiences from the Soviet Union, Poland and other countries can help to identify social obstacles for successful educational change and what can be done to avoid these obstacles. (90 minutes)

111 Critical Thinking Across the Disciplines: An Ecological Approach — Mark Weinstein, Wendy Oxman

The relevance of critical thinking requires its broad application. A natural adjunct to a specialized course in critical thinking is its infusion in courses in various academic disciplines. An ecological approach affords a model for infusion. the goal is to empower students to understand the principles and values implicit in the subjects they take and to expose the presuppositions that structure the educational milieu in which they function. (90 minutes)

114 Why Is It Imperative to Distinguish Weak Sense from Strong Sense Critical Thinking? A Challenge to All Comers — Richard Paul

Various reasons have been advanced for abandoning the distinction between weak sense and strong sense critical thinking. Richard Paul responds to these concerns and explains why the distinction is essential to the field. (90 minutes)

115 Mini-Critical Thinking Course: Assignments that Stimulate Critical Thinking — M. Neil Browne, Stuart Keeley

Most of the time spent practicing critical thinking is focused on out-of-class assignments. To be effective, those assignments must be consistent with a coherent method of critical thinking. This workshop uses the model of critical thinking, presented in *Asking the Right Questions*, as a basis for organizing assignments to develop specific critical thinking skills and attitudes. Numerous assignments that can be used in any classroom are illustrated. Participants share critical thinking assignments that they have found to be effective. (90 minutes)

116 Critical Thinking and Literature — Stephen Marx, Jonah Raskin, Donald Lazere

This panel surveys means of emphasizing critical thinking in high school and college literature courses. (90 minutes)

117 On the Nature of Critical Thinking — Richard Paul, Connie Missimer, Robert Ennis, Gerald Nosich

This panel discusses definitions of critical thinking and their applications to classroom practice at all levels, K-U. (90 minutes)

118 Designing Staff Development that Models Thinking Skills — Ken Bumgarner

This presentation features a practical and workable design for staff development in thinking skills that can be adapted to any level—school, district, regional or state. Based on information processing theory, the components of effective staff development design suggested by Joyce and Showers, Knowles and others are coupled with techniques for managing change effectively. The design involves participants in immediate active processing and moves them to an application level with commitment to implement, using an adaptation of Fogarty's "Thinking Log." The techniques designed for workshop presentation are equally adaptable for classroom teaching. Actual conferences employing the design are described. (90 minutes)

119 Mini-Critical Thinking Course: Critical Thinking and Advertising — Ralph Johnson

Why should a mini-course on critical thinking bother with advertising? First, advertising is an important part of the cultural and information environment and, hence, cannot be ignored. Second, advertising is one of the most powerful communications, persuaders, and shapers of values and attitudes that has ever existed. Third, advertising often presents itself as argumentation and reasoning but, in fact, rarely works at that level. The logic of advertising is not the logic of argumentation. Students need to learn how to analyze advertisements and what to watch for, and this does not mean combining ads for fallacies, as some have suggested. Finally, there is a fair amount of mythology and self-deception in consumer attitudes about and responses to advertising. The premise of the mini-course, then, is that advertising is a territory rich in materials for the student of critical thinking. The instructor demonstrates why and brings with him numerous examples. (90 minutes)

120 Remodeling Lesson Plans in Middle School and High School to Infuse Critical Thinking — Richard Paul

To remodel lesson plans is to develop a critique of one or more lessons and formulate one or more new lessons based on that critical process. This process allows teachers to take existing material and restructure it to incorporate critical thinking strategies. In this presentation, Richard Paul maximizes participant involvement in analyzing, assessing, and constructing remodelled lesson plans. (90 minutes)

122 The Montclair State College Institute for Critical Thinking's Approach to Critical Thinking Across the Curriculum — Nicholas Michelli, Wendy Oxman, John Barell, Mark Weinstein

The Institute for Critical Thinking has been established at Montclair State College, to support and enrich faculty development efforts toward critical thinking as an educational goal. The primary purpose of the Institute is to serve as a catalyst in the development of educational excellence across the curriculum at the college level. A collaborative, multi-disciplinary approach has been initiated, with attention to the study of both the theoretical aspects of critical thinking across the disciplines and their implications for teaching and learning at the college level. In addition, the Institute has assumed a leadership role in helping other colleges and schools to incorporate thinking skills into their curricula.

As a state-funded project designed to promote educational reform at a multipurpose state college, as a faculty development project involving interdepartmental collegial collaboration, and as a project with inter-institutional responsibilities, the Institute for Critical Thinking serves as a model for understanding the effects of selected change efforts within similar institutional settings. (90 minutes)

125 Empowering Teachers and Students Toward Critical Thinking: K-12 — John Barell

This session introduces participants to a program that focuses upon empowering students, teachers and administrators with strategies for improving performance, achievement, and the quality of life in schools. Based upon research on staff development, the nature of thinking, and strategic planning for success, this program fosters more self-direction and independent thinking through goal-setting, infusion of problem solving/critical inquiry throughout the curriculum, and written reflection upon our own thinking processes. Participants will practice these programmatic elements. (90 minutes)

127 Teaching Critical Thinking in the Strong Sense: The Practitioner's Perspective — Noreen Miller, Ross Hunt, Karen Jensen, Chris Vetrano

In this panel, teachers share classroom ideas they have successfully implemented for teaching strong-sense critical thinking in grades K-12. (90 minutes)

128 Cultural Literacy and Critical Thinking: Where E.D. Hirsch Is Right, Where He Is Wrong, and What Is Likely to Come of His Influence — Richard Paul

E.D. Hirsch's recent best seller, *Cultural Literacy*, has sent educators scurrying around, making enormous lists of names, events, and facts to which students are to be exposed on the theory that even a superficial recognition of these is essential to reading what is in print. On this view, the fundamental reason why students are poor readers is that they lack the background information presupposed in what they read. Richard Paul spells out where Hirsch's analysis is misleading and apt to reinforce more "trivial pursuit" in the classroom. (90 minutes)

133 Critical Thinking Testing: Recent Developments — Robert Ennis, Stephen Norris, George Hanford

A panel of experts in critical thinking testing discuss positive developments toward testing for strong-sense critical thinking. (90 minutes)

Order Form

(Xerox This Form to Order)

Rates: **Purchase —** $38.00/each, 4-9 tapes $30.00/each
10 or more $25.00/each

Rental — $25.00/each

Postage and Handling — $2.00 for first tape, add $.50 for each additional tape

California Residents add 6% sales tax

Make check or Purchase Order Payable To: SSU Academic Foundation (U.S. dollars only please; no stamps or foreign monies)

Please Mail Order Form and Payment To: Center for Critical Thinking & Moral Critique, Sonoma State University, Rohnert Park, CA 94928 USA

Tape #	Title

NAME: _____

ADDRESS: _____

_____

_____

_____

RENTAL _____ PURCHASE _____ TOTAL ENCLOSED _____

Note: Please do not give Post Office Boxes. UPS will not deliver to them.

Audiotape Library

1   Richard Paul **Teaching Critical Thinking in the Strong Sense in Elementary, Secondary, and Higher Education**

2   Stephen Norris **Varieties of Critical Thinking Tests: Their Design and Use**

8   Gus Bagakis **The Myth of the Passive Student**

10   Dianne Romain **Faculty Development in Critical Thinking**

12   Vincent Ryan Ruggiero **A Holistic Approach to Thinking Instruction**

13   Joseph Williams **Solving Problems in Writing**

14   Ralph Johnson **Mini Critical Thinking Course: Information and the Mass Media**

16   Gerald Nosich **On Teaching Critical Thinking**

17   Edward Damer **Can a Creationist Be a Critical Thinker?**

18   Debbie Walsh **The AFT Critical Thinking Project: The Hammond, IN Pilot**

20   Edys Quellmalz **Teaching Thinking Strategies Across the Curriculum — The Higher Order Thinking (H O T Project: Secondary Level**

22   David Hyerle **Design for Thinking: Making Sense in the Classroom**

23   Richard Paul **Workshop on the Art of Teaching Critical Thinking in the Strong Sense**

24   Edys Quellmalz **Teaching Thinking Strategies Across the Curriculum — The Higher Order Thinking (H O T) Project: Elementary Level**

28   M. Neil Browne, Stuart Keeley **Classroom Assignments that Encourage Critical Thinking**

29   Jack Lochhead **Teaching Kids to Argue: Inciting Riot in the Classroom**

30   Elinor McKinney **Models for Teaching Higher Order Thinking: Introduction**

33   Vivian Rosenberg **Introducing Affective Awareness as a Critical Thinking Skill**

34   Robert H. Ennis **A Conception of Critical Thinking**

35   Richard Paul **Mini Critical Thinking Course: The Nature of Critical Thinking Through Socratic Interrogation**

36   Connie DeCapite **Language Arts and Critical Thinking for Remedial and Bilingual Students**

37   Ralph Johnson **Getting Clear About Vagueness**

41   Dianne Romain **Strong Sense Critical Thinking in Junior High School Social Studies**

43   David Perkins **Knowledge as Design in the Classroom**

45   Vincent Ryan Ruggiero **Mini Critical Thinking Course: Dispositions: The Neglected Aspect of Thinking Instruction**

46   Chuck Blondino, Ken Bumgarner **Effective Design for Critical Thinking Inservice**

50   Perry Weddle **How to Appeal to Authority**

51   Debbie Walsh **Integrating Critical Thinking Skills into the K-12 Curriculum**

307

Order Form

(Xerox This Form to Order)

Rates: **Purchase —** $7.50 per tape

        Postage and Handling — $1.50 for first tape, add $.25 for each additional tape

        California Residents add 6% sales tax

Make check or Purchase Order Payable To: SSU Academic Foundation (U.S. dollars only please; no stamps or foreign monies)

Please Mail Order Form and Payment To: Center for Critical Thinking & Moral Critique, Sonoma State University, Rohnert Park, CA 94928 USA

Tape #	Title

NAME: _____

ADDRESS: _____

_____

_____

_____

TOTAL # TAPES ORDERED _____ TOTAL ENCLOSED _____

Note: Please do not give Post Office Boxes. UPS will not deliver to them.

Annual Conference on Critical Thinking

Every year in the first week of August, the Center hosts the oldest and largest critical thinking conference. In 1988, the conference had over 100 presenters, nearly 300 sessions, and over 1,000 registrants. The conference is designed to meet the needs and concerns of the widest variety of educational levels. Practitioners, administrators, professors, and theoreticians regularly attend the conference. Many registrants have responsibilities for curriculum design and inservice or particular subject matter concerns: math, science, language arts, social studies, humanities, fine arts, ... Others are principally concerned with assessment issues, or remediation, or preservice education. Still others want information about the relation of critical thinking to citizenship, to vocational or professional education, or to personal development, while others are eager to explore the relation of critical thinking to the classic ideals of the liberally educated person and the free society or to world-wide social, economic, and moral issues. The conference discussions and dialogues that result from bringing together such a large number of committed critical thinkers with such a broad background of concerns are not only truly exciting but also rich in practical pay-offs.

Please send me more information on the Center's annual conferences on Critical Thinking:

NAME: _____

ADDRESS: _____

_____

_____

SPECIAL INTERESTS (GRADE LEVELS, SUBJECT, ETC.)

_____

_____

Newly Released
for Staff Development

Lesson Plan Remodelling Videotape

VHS 40 minutes

to accompany the
Critical Thinking Handbooks

Write or call
The Center
for Critical Thinking
(707) 664-2940
Sonoma State University
Rohnert Park, CA 94928

Help Us "Remodel" this Handbook

In the spirit of good critical thinking, we want your assessment of this handbook and ideas for its improvement. Your ideas might be rewarded with a scholarship to the next International Conference on Critical Thinking!

Evaluation:

Here's what I found most useful about the handbook:

_____

_____

_____

_____

This is what I think is in need of change:

_____

_____

_____

_____

Here are my ideas for improving the handbook:

_____

_____

_____

_____

Send evaluation to: Center For Critical Thinking; Sonoma State University; Rohnert Park, CA 94928.

Information About the Center for Critical Thinking and Moral Critique

Sonoma State University

The Center conducts advanced research, inservice education programs, professional conferences, and disseminates information on critical thinking and moral critique. It is premised on the democratic ideal as a principle of social organization, that is, that it is possible

> so to structure the arrangements of society as to rest them ultimately upon the freely-given consent of its members. Such an aim requires the institutionalization of reasoned procedures for the critical and public review of policy; it demands that judgments of policy be viewed not as the fixed privilege of any class or elite but as the common task of all, and it requires the supplanting of arbitrary and violent alteration of policy with institutionally channeled change ordered by reasoned persuasion and informed consent.*

It conducts its research through an international network of fellows and associates, as follows:

Honorary Fellows

Max Black, Professor of Philosophy, Cornell University, Ithaca, NY

Robert Ennis, Director, Illinois Thinking Project, University of Illinois, Champaign, IL

Edward M. Glaser, Psychologist, Founder, Watson-Glaser Critical Thinking Appraisal, Los Angeles, CA

Mathew Lipman, Professor of Philosophy, Founder and Director, Institute for the Advancement of Philosophy for Children, Montclair, NJ

Israel Scheffler, Thomas Professor of Education and Philosophy, Harvard University, Cambridge, MA

Michael Scriven, Professor of Philosophy, University of Western Australia, Nedlands, Australia

Research Associates

J. Anthony Blair, Professor of Philosophy, University of Windsor, Ontario, Canada

Carl Jensen, Associate Professor of Communications Studies, Sonoma State University, Rohnert Park, CA

Ralph Johnson, Professor of Philosophy, University of Windsor, Ontario, Canada

Don Lazere, Professor of English, California Polytechnic State University, San Luis Obispo, CA

Perry Weddle, Professor of Philosophy, California State University, Sacramento, CA

Ian Wright, Professor of Education, University of British Columbia, British Columbia, Canada

Joel Rudinow, Assistant Professor of Philosophy, Sonoma State University, Rohnert Park, CA

Teaching Associates

Carl Jensen, Center Research Associate

Don Lazere, Center Research Associate

Richard Paul, Director

Dianne Romain, Assistant Professor of Philosophy, Sonoma State University

Douglas Martin, Associate Professor of Chemistry, Sonoma State University

Joel Rudinow, Center Research Associate

*Israel Scheffler, *Reason and Teaching* 1973, (Bobbs-Merril Co, Inc.) page 137.

Research Assistants

A.J.A. Binker, Sonoma State University

Ken Adamson, Sonoma State University

Director

Richard W. Paul, Center for Critical Thinking and Moral Critique and Professor of Philosophy, Sonoma State University

The work of the Center includes an annual international Conference on Critical Thinking and Education; Master's Degree in Education with emphasis in Critical Thinking; Supplementary Authorization Program in the teaching of critical thinking (under the Single Subject Waiver Credential Program of the State of California); inservice programs in the teaching of critical thinking; Research Intern program (for graduate students in the field of critical thinking and moral critique); a resource center for the distribution of tests, documents, position papers; and research in the field of critical thinking and moral critique and in the reform of education based upon the teaching of reasoning and critical thinking skills across the curriculum. Other recent contributors include the historian Henry Steele Commager and George H. Hanford, President of the College Board.

Center for Critical Thinking and Moral Critique
Sonoma State University
Rohnert Park, CA 94928

Our Science Consultant

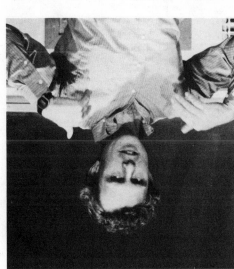

Douglas R. Martin is a Professor of both Chemistry and Education at Sonoma State University, Rohnert Park, California. After receiving his Ph.D. in Physical Chemistry from the University of California at Berkeley, he taught biology, chemistry, and physics at the high school level for five years. During this time, his theoretical and practical interests in reasoning development, particularly in the work of Jean Piaget, led to publications in journals like *The Physics Teacher* and the *Journal of Chemical Education*. He subsequently taught in the sciences and in philosophy of science at the university level.

Professor Martin is actively involved with science education in several ways. He has directed two National Science Foundation-funded projects and has been involved with several others. These projects have been concerned with issues ranging from curriculum development to inservice teacher education and from the elementary grades to high school. Professor Martin's research interests focus on students' naive understanding of basic science concepts and how this naive understanding influences their ability to understand concepts and relationships more accurately. He is also concerned with understanding how the goals of the critical thinking movement are best expressed in science education.

His publications include:

1. "A Primer on Elementary Science," monograph published in curricular materials developed for Project MAST, an elementary science curriculum project supported by the National Science Foundation. 1988.
2. "Encouraging Critical Thought: Alternative Problem Forms," *The Physics Teacher*, 26,5, 1988.
3. "Teacher Helping Teachers in Science," *Teacher Education Quarterly*, Summer, 1987.
4. "Critical Thinking in Science Through the Construction of Meaning," accepted for publication in the *Proceedings of the Fourth International Conference on Critical Thinking and Moral Critique*. Sonoma State University, 1986.
5. "Status of the Copernican Theory Before Galileo, Kepler, and Newton," *American Journal of Physics*, 52, 982, 1984.
6. "How Far Can You See? An Activity Involving Approximate Reasoning," *The Physics Teacher* 20, 318, 1982.
7. "A Piagetian Approach to Physics Teaching," *The Physics Teacher* 18, 34, 1980.
8. "A Group-Administered Reasoning Test for Classroom Use," *Journal of Chemical Education* 56, 179, 1979.